T0137091

Conceptual Modeling Perspectives

Jordi Cabot · Cristina Gómez · Oscar Pastor
Maria Ribera Sancho · Ernest Teniente
Editors

Conceptual Modeling Perspectives

Editors
Jordi Cabot
ICREA
Universitat Oberta de Catalunya
Barcelona
Spain

Cristina Gómez
Department of Service and Information
System Engineering
Universitat Politècnica de Catalunya
Barcelona
Spain

Oscar Pastor
PROS Research Center
Universitat Politècnica de València
Valencia
Spain

Maria Ribera Sancho
Department of Service and Information
System Engeneering
Universitat Politècnica de Catalunya
Barcelona Supercomputing Center
Barcelona
Spain

Ernest Teniente
Department of Service and Information
System Engineering
Universitat Politècnica de Catalunya
Barcelona
Spain

ISBN 978-3-319-88404-2 ISBN 978-3-319-67271-7 (eBook)
https://doi.org/10.1007/978-3-319-67271-7

© Springer International Publishing AG 2017
Softcover reprint of the hardcover 1st edition 2017
This work is subject to copyright. All rights are reserved by the Publisher, whether the whole or part of the material is concerned, specifically the rights of translation, reprinting, reuse of illustrations, recitation, broadcasting, reproduction on microfilms or in any other physical way, and transmission or information storage and retrieval, electronic adaptation, computer software, or by similar or dissimilar methodology now known or hereafter developed.
The use of general descriptive names, registered names, trademarks, service marks, etc. in this publication does not imply, even in the absence of a specific statement, that such names are exempt from the relevant protective laws and regulations and therefore free for general use.
The publisher, the authors and the editors are safe to assume that the advice and information in this book are believed to be true and accurate at the date of publication. Neither the publisher nor the authors or the editors give a warranty, express or implied, with respect to the material contained herein or for any errors or omissions that may have been made. The publisher remains neutral with regard to jurisdictional claims in published maps and institutional affiliations.

Printed on acid-free paper

This Springer imprint is published by Springer Nature
The registered company is Springer International Publishing AG
The registered company address is: Gewerbestrasse 11, 6330 Cham, Switzerland

Preface

When we decided to lead the design of this book for Prof. Antoni Olivé, we did not guess that writing a Preface for our Professor first, our forever Friend later, would be such a hard job. The reality is that summarizing in a few words our respect and admiration for him is probably the most complicated Conceptual Modeling activity that we have ever faced! But we can try to do it, honoring the conceptual modeling passion that we have inherited from him. Always with Conceptual Modeling in mind, there are a few conceptual patterns that he has shown us with the most efficient strategy: his example. He has shown us the value of understanding carefully others' opinions. He has shown us how important is to listen to, before deciding what to do. He has shown us that a brilliant research is modest. He has shown us how a real leader is the one recognized as such by all his pupils, as we -the Editors-all are. He has shown us how the best honor we can grant him is be grateful for the most valuable gift that he has provided to us: the conceptual model of his life as an example to be followed.

With this book we all want to honor Prof. Antoni Olivé. It is a simple but honest recognition to his enormous contribution to the Conceptual Modeling discipline. We were happy to see that finding a set of highly relevant colleagues ready to contribute to it, was the easiest task for us! Everybody was eager to participate. Everybody recognizes Antoni's essential role in the community. Everybody has made a big effort to be present in the book. We appreciated this effort. Thank you everybody for it! The set of selected chapters provides a complete and extremely attractive view of what Conceptual Modeling is, and what perspectives are opened to make it more and more relevant in our society.

We are sure that much more colleagues would have been happy to participate. Sorry for those that could not be in the book: edition constraints made it not possible! We know that in any case we all share our immense gratitude and recognition to his person. We are lucky to have had the chance of enjoying science and life with you. We are ready to still enjoy your figure, Friend and Professor Antoni Olivé for many more years. As a starting point for this exciting future, we hope that this book -written in your honor- will be seen as a source of inspiration for everybody to continue working for making true the never-ended dream that you have transmitted to us: to create a strong, fruitful and creative community of conceptual modelers.

Entre Barcelona i València,
Juliol 2017

Jordi Cabot
Cristina Gómez
Óscar Pastor
Maria-Ribera Sancho
Ernest Teniente

Contents

Chapter 1
A Tribute to Antoni Olivé on the Occasion of His Retirement

Janis Bubenko, Colette Rolland and Arne Sølvberg

Abstract We share a common professional history with Antoni for around 40 years. From that perspective, we give a short overview of the research problems that we encountered and how we tried to contribute in finding solutions on data processing, human computer interaction and modeling languages and tools

As friends of Antoni and also contributors to the field of conceptual modeling, the three of us are happy to have been invited to contribute to this book which is honoring Antoni Olivé's contributions to the field.

All three of us have been retired for several years, ranging from 15 years to just a few. Our professional positions as university professors have been taken over by our former doctoral students. Our previous students are doing splendid work in research as well as in education and technical development, some of them in academia and many of them in industry and public organizations. We cannot today give research contributions which match those of our students. So we will not contribute to this book with new research. We will rather look back and give a short overview of the problems that we encountered, and where our research community tried to contribute in finding solutions.

The three of us share a common professional history with Antoni dating back to the mid-seventies, for around 40 years. The most striking feature during these years has been the fantastic increase in computational capacity and in telecommunication

Janis Bubenko
Stockholm University, Sweden, e-mail: janis@dsv.su.se

Colette Rolland
Université Paris 1, France, e-mail: Colette.Rolland@univ-paris1.fr

Arne Sølvberg
NTNU, Norway, e-mail: arne.solvberg@ntnu.no

© Springer International Publishing AG 2017
J. Cabot et al. (eds.), *Conceptual Modeling Perspectives*,
https://doi.org/10.1007/978-3-319-67271-7_1

capacity. There has been a steady 10-fold increase in computer capacity per dollar every 5 years. This amounts to 100-fold increase every 10 years, and 1000-fold every 15 years. Over the 40 years that we have been professionally active the increase in computational capacity per money unit has been an incredible 100 million.

This has led to major equipment changes every 10-15 years, starting with the batch-processing central computers being replaced by time-shared computers around 1979, and desktop personal computers around 1980, laptop computers around 1990-95, handheld computers 2000-05, into today's smartphones and every-physical-item-having-its own-computer, into a world with computers-everywhere, in to the internet of things

Over the years this has led to important changes in the field, shaping research themes, e.g.,

- change in emphasis from calculation and data processing to information processing
- increasing interaction between humans and computers
- language as communication tool: syntax, semantics, pragmatics → conceptual modeling
- the need for better modeling tools, e.g., information systems engineering

During the 1970's the use of computers expanded quickly. The need for better cooperation between computers and human beings became obvious. This led to an increased interest in methods for building such systems, and an increased interest in building information systems, rather than the more limited data processing systems. The International Federation of Information Processing societies (IFIP) decided to form a Technical Committee on "Information Processing" (TC8). The two first working groups were on the themes "Design and Evaluation of Information Systems" (WG 8.1) and "The Interaction of Information Systems and the Organization" (WG 8.2).

The working groups soon became focal points for arranging international working conferences. Likeminded young researchers found communities of people with common interests. WG8.1 became a focal point for computer science researchers with a common background in mathematics and engineering. The three of us together with Antoni became driving forces in the activities of WG8.1. The close cooperation which was initiated during the IFIP years was carried over to the CAiSE conference series which started in 1990.

In focus of our research interests was how to express the intended properties of planned information systems. Our common backgrounds in mathematics, natural sciences and technology made it a natural objective for us to search for ways to predict the future effects of a planned information system based on its stated properties. The ideal was seen to be able to design an information system in similar ways as engineers designed technological artifacts like bridges and engines. So we sought after approaches to specify software artifacts and human operations in ways that permitted us to calculate emerging properties of the combined system of software operations and human operations. A great encouragement for our work along this line of reasoning was the first paper on formal specifications of an information system which was published by Young and Kent more than sixty years ago. Even if the term "conceptual model" was not used at this time, the basic intention of the abstract specification was to a large extent the same as for developing conceptual models today: to arrive at a precise, abstract, and computing machine independent model of the informational and time characteristics of the data processing problem. The abstract notation should enable the analyst to organize the problem around any piece of hardware. In other words, the purpose of an abstract specification was to use it as an invariant basis for designing different alternative implementations, perhaps even using different hardware components.

Research and practice of abstract modelling of information systems has since the late fifties progressed through many milestones and achievements. In the sixties, pioneering work was carried out by the CODASYL Development committee who in 1962 presented the "Information Algebra". At about the same time BÃűrje Langefors published his elementary message and e-file approach to specification of information systems.

The next decade, the seventies, was characterized by introduction of a large number of new types of, as they were called, "data models". We saw the birth of, for instance, Binary Data Models, Entity Relationship Models, Relational Data Models, Semantic Data Models, and Temporal Deductive Models. At this time, most of the researchers in the modelling field had, essentially, data-base orientation. The first time the term "conceptual schema" was used was probably by the ANSI/X3/SPARC, Study Group on Data Base Management Systems, in 1975 when they formulated the "three schema approach" to data-base management. The conceptual schema was seen as the "essential schema", depicting the content of the database in an implementation, and external representation independent way.

The term conceptual modelling gradually gained general acceptance, perhaps largely due to use of the term conceptual schema in the ISO working group's TC97/SC5/WG5 preliminary report, Concepts and Terminology for the Conceptual Schema edited by J.J. van Griethuysen, et. al. in 1982. At about the same time information system researchers began to use the term "conceptual modelling" for modelling of information systems in an implementation independent way. Usually, this kind of modelling was carried out during the requirements elicitation and specification phase of systems development.

The last two decades of conceptual modelling practice are dominated by two main trends. The first is the spread and use of the object oriented language and approach UML, including its language OCL (Object Constraint Language) for formulating business rules and constraints. The second trend, in our opinion, is the change of mode of modelling towards a way where users and stakeholders are very much more actively involved - participatory modelling. This trend points to the importance of modelling skills and knowledge becoming important not only to system development professionals but also to stakeholders and users.

Antoni Olivé has in his professional working life made an impressive amount of contributions that brings and puts together knowledge of conceptual (and data-) modeling, produced in research during more than half a century.

One of the first important contributions of Antoni to conceptual modeling was the DADES methodology presented at the IFIP WG8.1 conference on 'Comparative Review of Information Systems Design Methodologies' in 1982. The idea of the conference was to select the seven methodologies the most representative of the state-of-art based on a call, which was not only requiring the presentation of the methodology but also imposing a test case to be solved. This event has also been the starting point of our cooperation with Antoni as the three of us were also presenting our own methodologies at the conference.

DADES was one of the selected methodologies and its originality was to promote a deductive approach to design whereas most of the competitors were defending 'operational' ones. The main characteristic of the former is to provide a complete specification of an information system expressing only its logic component whereas the latter define also part of the control component. In deductive approaches like DADES, the specification of the control component is entirely left to the subsequent phases of the information system development. On the contrary a deductive approaches uses deduction rules to relate the information base to external events thus providing an elegant and synthetic conceptual view of what the information system is supposed to do.

Antoni was the first to introduce in information system design a logic-based approach in the line of logic programming which was emerging at that time. He contributed to the understanding of the respective advantages of operational approaches versus deductive approaches (refs) and to the transformation of a deductive conceptual schema to an operational one as well as. It is not possible to detail all of the many contributions of Antoni to conceptual modeling; the focus on this one is due to the fact that it has been the starting point of a long cooperation between us.

Most of Antoni's contributions are manifested in his book "Conceptual Modelling of Information Systems" (Springer, 2007). The book puts in context, research on conceptual modelling presented in more than 200 references. It deals with most essential aspects of conceptual modelling, thoroughly explained and illustrated in detail. Structural as well as behavioural conceptual modelling concepts are explained in detail. Every chapter is concluded with a bibliographical note that gives the research-oriented reader a possibility to further dwell into references to works on that particular topic. Each chapter also gives students a challenge to test their new knowledge acquired by solving a number of problems. A fairly large chapter at the end, describing a case study, illustrates the use of modelling constructs presented earlier. Of practical interest are the frequent translations of modelling concepts introduced to UML and OCL. A chapter on "Metamodelling" and a chapter on "Meta-metamodelling" and Metadata Interchange (XMI), a standard that enables the exchange of data about schemas as well as about schema instances, conclude the book. Metamodeling is also an important mechanism for reasoning about conceptual schema languages of different types and for integrating conceptual models with other kinds of models, such as business and enterprise models.

The book is one of the most informative and comprehensive texts on conceptual modelling published to date. It is very appropriate for students of advanced level university courses in information systems, requirements engineering, or in data base design, as well as for qualified practitioners of the field. In conclusion, we would like to offer Antoni our most sincere appreciation for more than thirty years of co-operation and friendship. It has been great fun to produce research work together and to arrange research events and conferences. We look forward to continued co-operation.

Chapter 2
30 Years of Contributions to Conceptual Modeling

Jordi Cabot, Cristina Gómez, Maria-Ribera Sancho and Ernest Teniente

Abstract This chapter is aimed at summarizing the contribution of Antoni Olivé to the field of conceptual modeling over the last three decades. It starts with his initial proposals around the year 1986 and it finishes with his most recent, not to say current, work on the field. The summary encompasses different topics, beginning with the deductive approach to conceptual modeling and its application to deductive databases, evolving later to object-oriented conceptual schemas and, more recently, to conceptual-schema centric development. All in all, the trajectory covers a wide range of topics, all of them of great importance at the time they were treated, and has meant an important advance of the knowledge in this area during all these years.

2.1 Introduction

Trying to summarize 30 years of research of Antoni Olivé at the Universitat Politècnica de Catalunya in just a few pages is not an easy task. On the one hand, because of his huge contribution to the field, with more than eighty papers (most of them in the most prestigious journals and conferences in the field), fourteen PhD thesis advised and multitude of talks and keynotes. On the other, because it is also a summary of our life. At least of its academic part. We feel, directly or indirectly, disciples of

Jordi Cabot
ICREA, e-mail: jordi.cabot@icrea.cat
Universitat Oberta de Catalunya

Cristina Gómez
Universitat Politècnica de Catalunya,e-mail: cristina@essi.upc.edu

Maria-Ribera Sancho
Universitat Politècnica de Catalunya
Barcelona Supercomputing Center, e-mail: ribera@essi.upc.edu

Ernest Teniente
Universitat Politècnica de Catalunya, e-mail: teniente@essi.upc.edu

© Springer International Publishing AG 2017
J. Cabot et al. (eds.), *Conceptual Modeling Perspectives*,
https://doi.org/10.1007/978-3-319-67271-7_2

Antoni and we owe much of our research to what we have learned from him during all these years. Therefore, since we are so thankful to him, it is very difficult for us to be fully objective although we will do our best to be as fair as possible while summarizing his most important contributions.

Antoni carried out all his research as a Professor at the Universitat Politècnica de Catalunya. During all these years, more than thirty people were members of his research group at one time or another. Therefore, it would be unfair saying or thinking that Antoni did all the contributions alone. In fact, he always believed in the strength of the group, above the specific individuals, and for that reason he always tried to be fair in relation to the contributions of each one of us. Nevertheless, and despite the risk of not being always understood, we will only use his name while describing the different proposals since he has been an important contributor to all of them and because this chapter is a tribute to his career. For this same reason, we have not considered those contributions to conceptual modeling from people in the group not having Antoni as a coauthor.

This chapter is divided into four different sections, each one of them addressing a different period and a different center of interest for research. The first period (1986-1989) was devoted to analyze the deductive approach to conceptual modeling. Then, Antoni moved towards techniques for deductive databases and deductive conceptual models (1989-1999) to make later an important turn and move on to object-oriented conceptual schemas (1999-2007). Finally, the last periode (2007-present) has been dedicated to deepen into conceptual schema-centric development and contributing to a number of related research problems.

2.2 The Deductive Approach to Conceptual Modeling

The beginning of the research of Antoni Olivé in conceptual modeling of information systems goes back to the remote year 1986, i.e. almost 30 years ago. At that time he published a seminal paper comparing the operational and the deductive approaches to conceptual information systems modeling [12].

Intuitively, the main feature of the deductive approach is that the basic part of the Information Base (IB) (i.e. the information explicitly stored) contains only the events that happen in the domain — aka *Universe of Discourse (UoD)*, as named in the paper. All other informations of the IB are deduced by means of derivation rules which allow to define the knowledge about the concepts in the domain from the stored events. Time plays also a major role in this approach because for every information about the UoD is associated with a time point which states the time when the information holds.

As an example, assume that an information system provides with the ability of starting projects by means of an event like: *startProj(proj,end,dept,t)*; where *end* is the expected date to finish the project, *dept* is the department running it and *t* is the time at which the project starts. Then, from this event we could define active projects as follows in the deductive approach:

```
1 activeProj(p,t) ← startProj(p,e,d,t1), t1<=t, ¬cancelled(p,t)
```

i.e. project *p* will be active at time *t* if it was started at a previous time and it has not yet been cancelled.

As a conclusion of this analysis, Antoni claimed that "deductive languages show a number of advantages, which might justify to pursue their development at a level comparable to that of operational languages. Model verification and efficient implementation methods would be the main issues for research (...)". It is worth mentioning that, as we will see in Section 2.3, Antoni was premonitory since a significant amount of research was devoted later to these topics by his first PhD students. Not to mention also that this paper will never be forgotten by his closest collaborators at that time because of the efforts they had to devote to understand and assimilate this deductive approach.

These ideas guided the initial steps of Antoni's research and lasted for almost five years. He did not had properly a research group at that time (at least as they are currently understood) but work in this area gave rise in 1987 to the PhD thesis of Jaume Sistac†, whose main ideas were related to the automatic generation of information system prototypes from a deductive conceptual model [29].

Also in 1987, Antoni published a first proposal about the design and implementation of information systems from deductive conceptual models (DCMs) [13], one of the open areas of research he identified from the beginning. In this paper, he presented a formal method to derive from a DCM a new model, called the *internal events model*, which is much easier to implement. This model was a useful basis from which several design alternatives could be systematically developed and evaluated. Possible uses of the internal events model in data base and transaction design were also outlined.

The last claim of the paper was, again, premonitory: "we also expect that the internal events model (...) can be useful in the field of deductive databases although this has not been elaborated in the paper". Thirty years later, the main notions provided by the internal event rules are still being used and applied to different settings such as handling updates in UML/OCL schema or in Description Logics.

2.3 Techniques for Deductive Conceptual Models

After this initial period, Antoni expanded his research and proposed techniques based on the deductive approach and applied them to three different areas: deductive databases, deductive conceptual models of information systems and, finally, to object-oriented deductive conceptual models.

His research group grew significantly during this period, which lasted approximately from 1989 to 1999, and which gave also as a result the doctoral thesis of six of his PhD students at that time: Ernest Teniente (1992), Toni Urpí (1993), Maria-Ribera Sancho (1994), Dolors Costal (1995), Joan Antoni Pastor (1997) and Carme Quer (1999).

2.3.1 Deductive Databases

The name *deductive*, in the deductive approach to conceptual modeling, came from its similarity to *deductive databases*, where deductive rules play also a major role. Moreover, as we have just seen, the idea of applying the internal events model to deductive databases was already stated when this model was proposed. Therefore, it is not surprising that he also significantly contributed to this field. In particular, addressing the problems of ***change computation*** (and its applications to *integrity checking, materialized view maintenance and condition monitoring*) and ***(consistency preserving) view updating***.

2.3.1.1 Change Computation

A deductive database consists of three finite sets: a set of *facts* that are explicitly stored in the database; a set of *deductive rules*, that allow to define new knowledge in the form of derived predicates from base and other derived predicates; and a set of *integrity constraints*, specified in terms of base or derived predicates and defining conditions that every state of the database should satisfy.

Change computation refers to the general problem of computing the changes induced by an update on the base factes on one or more derived predicates. Efficient change computation is essential in several capabilities of a deductive database, such as integrity constraints checking, view maintenance or condition monitoring. These problems are still relevant and need to be solved in all contexts that use any kind of rules to define intensional information in terms of that explicitly stored.

One of the most cited papers from Antoni was published in this topic in 1992 [36]. This paper proposes a general method for change computation that can be applied in all database capabilities mentioned above. It is based on the use of transition and internal events rules, which explicitly define the insertions, deletions and modifications induced by a database update on the contents of derived predicates. The method computes the changes once the database has been updated, providing more efficient ways of change computation than those of previous research. These ideas were later extended and applied also to active databases in [35].

2.3.1.2 Consistency-Preserving View Updating

Transition and insertion event rules where also applied to deal with the problem of consistency-preserving view updating [30, 31]. View updating is related to the problem of translating a request for updating the contents of a derived predicate in terms of updates of the underlying base facts.

However, some of the obtained translations may not satisfy all the integrity constraints. For this reason, view updating is usually followed by an integrity enforcement process in order to ensure consistency of the data and this is why we call the whole approach consistency-preserving. In particular, [30, 31] follow an integrity maintenance approach aimed at finding repairs, i.e. additional updates of the base facts, for each constraint violation so that the final set of solutions is ensured to satisfy all constraints. In general, there may be several solutions and the user must select one of them. In some cases, no such repair exists, and the view update must be rejected.

As a result, this work resulted in a method that uniformly handles both insert and delete requests and that allows for complex updates, such as mixed multiple updates or modification requests. It also naturally encompasses several additional features like preventing side effects on other views, repairing inconsistent knowledge bases or maintaining transition integrity constraints. All in all, the method extended the functionalities of those previously proposed and its contribution has been extensively recognized by many citations. It is worth mentioning also that the method was proved to be sound and complete, but termination was not guaranteed and efficiency and complexity issues were not considered in the proposal.

2.3.2 Deductive Conceptual Models

Antoni's techniques proposed in this area where mainly concerced with the validation of conceptual schemas and with the (semi)automatic generation of transactions from the specified schema. The main contributions of these techniques are summarized in the following.

2.3.2.1 Reasoning about Deductive Conceptual Models

Reasoning on a schema has always been concerned with determining whether the schema is correct or not (i.e. verification) and whether it satisfies the user needs and requirements (i.e. validation). This is one of the most important and crucial problems in information systems engineering since determining errors at the early stages of information systems development is directly related to improving the quality and the adequacy of the final system.

Antoni's main proposals for validating DCMs by means of reasoning were published in [8]. The proposed method uses SLDNF resolution as proof procedure and plan generation techniques developed in the Artificial Intelligence field to perform reasoning on the schema. Its main capabilities are the following:

- Given an initial and a target state of the IB, together with a sequence of external events, check whether the sequence is able to perform the transition between both states.
- Given an initial and a target state, obtain one or more sequences of external events (plans) able to perform the transition between both states.

This method was not only able to reason about DCMs but it had also the full power of the methods developed so far for the traditional operational approach to conceptual modelling. Moreover, the reasoning capabilities it provided were helpful and helped to improve the validation task of conceptual models of information systems.

2.3.2.2 Validating Conceptual Specifications

Work on validation was also carried out from a wider perspective to propose a method for explaining the behaviour of conceptual models of information systems [22]. This method assumed a conceptual model in terms of information base structure (with base and, optionally, derived information), integrity constraints and transactions. Therefore, the method could be adapted to most existing methodologies.

This method contributed to model validation by providing explanations about the results of model execution. Specifically, it can explain, in several complementary ways, why some facts hold (or do not hold) in the IB; why some facts have been inserted to (or deleted from) the IB when applying a transaction; how some intended effect on the IB can be achieved; and what would have happened if some other inputs were given (hypothetical explanations).

Answers to some of the above questions were given by some existing explanation systems, but properly extended by providing answers to questions about derived facts, to questions about how a fact can be made true or false, and to hypothetical questions. The method grows mainly on results in the field of deductive databases and this was useful to show how the procedures developed in that field for explaining the results of queries, or their failure, and for consistency-preserving updates may be useful for behaviour explanation of conceptual models. In this sense, this work linked the fields of DCMs and deductive databases.

2.3.2.3 Supporting Transaction Design

Grounded on his previous work on deductive databases, Antoni contributed also to deriving transaction specifications from deductive conceptual models of information systems [28]. This work used a logic-based language for the specification of conceptual models and applied logic-based techniques for the automatic generation of a system design from them. The idea was to build a a transaction for each external event that should be handled by the system. Preconditions of this transaction were then determined from the integrity constraints in the schema while the postconditions were drawn from an analysis of its deductive rules.

This work was extended in [24], with the goal of automatically deriving a transaction specification integrating in a uniform manner the updating of base and derived information and the checking and maintenance of integrity constraints within the IB of a DCM. In this way, the obtained transaction specifications may guarantee at definition time that the consistency of the IB is preserved. Therefore, no enforcement has to be performed at run time to ensure it. When there are several possible solutions, the method derives all of them and the designer has to intervene to select the most appropriate one to apply.

It is worth noting that it was not alway possible to derive the transaction specification satisfying a given update because of the well-known undecidability of integrity maintenance and view updating.

2.3.3 *Object-Oriented Deductive Conceptual Models*

Antoni's first attempt to evolve towards object-orientation was proposed in [26], where he provided a combination of the deductive and object-oriented approaches, by which the IB predicates were grouped using the concept of object. Therefore, one of the main goals of this work was to present the main components of an object-oriented deductive approach to conceptual modeling of information systems. This approach did not model object interaction explicitly. However, a method for deriving these interactions was outlined in the paper.

Based on these results, the paper discussed whether explicit object interaction is a desirable feature of conceptual models and it ended up by showing that most difficulties in the modeling of the dynamic aspect with object-oriented methods existing at that time arose because they tried to model explicitly the interaction among objects, which was shown in the paper not to be necessary from a conceptual point of view.

2.4 Object-Oriented Conceptual Schemas: definition and evolution

During the period between 1999 and 2007 Antoni Olivé focused his research on the essential aspects and principles of conceptual modeling, on the formal basis of conceptual schemas and on the evolution of conceptual schemas. The result of this period of intense research was the publication of his book "Conceptual Modeling of Information Systems" [19] in 2007.

His research group continued growing during this period, which gave as a result the doctoral thesis of two of his PhD students: Juan Ramón López (2001) and Cristina Gómez (2003).

2.4.1 *Definition*

At the end of the nineties Antoni Olivé began to deepen in the study of object-oriented conceptual modeling. Conceptual modeling is defined in [19] as the activity to elicit and describe the general knowledge a particular information system needs to know. The main objective of conceptual modeling is to obtain the description of the conceptual schema, formed by the structural schema and the behavioral schema. Antoni's passion and rigor in the study and analysis of conceptual modeling constructs used in conceptual schemas resulted in a considerable number of publications in top international conferences and journals.

2.4.1.1 Entity types.

Entity and relationship types, the most important constructs in structural conceptual schemas, attracted Antoni's attention in several works. An entity type is a concept whose instances at a given time are identifiable individual objects that are considered to exist in the domain at that time [19]. In [5], Antoni reviewed the definition of entity types derived by symbol-generating rules. These types appear frequently in conceptual schemas but most conceptual modeling languages, like the UML and ORM, did not allow their formal definition. He proposed a method for the definition of entity types derived by symbol-generating rules based on the fact that these types can always be expressed as the result of the reification of a derived relationship type.

2.4.1.2 Relationship types.

A relationship type is a concept whose instances at a given time are identifiable individual relationships between objects that are considered to exist in the domain at that time [19]. There exist some relationship types, called generic relationship types, that appear in many structural conceptual schemas and even several times in the same schema that have a particular meaning. Typical examples are IsPartOf or IsMemberOf. Antoni studied generic relationship types in [15] and proposed two alternatives methods for their representation. Moreover, he described the contexts in which one or the other representation is more appropriate, showed their advantatges and the described the adaptation of the methods to the UML.

2.4.1.3 Temporal Aspects of Entity and Relationship Types.

Temporal aspects of structural conceptual schemas were investigated by Antoni in [6] and [14]. In [6] he proposed a standard extension of the UML that allows the designer to define a set of temporal features of entity and relationship types appearing in a conceptual schema. Moreover, he also defined several temporal operations to refer to any past state of the information base that may be used to deal with UML/OCL as if it were a temporal conceptual modeling language. He also presented a method for the transformation of a conceptual schema in this extended language into a conventional one. The temporal view of relationship reification was presented in [14]. Refying a relationship consists in viewing it as an entity [19]. Antoni generalized previous work on reification, and proposed three temporal reification kinds.

He defined the characteristics of the entity types, and of their intrinsic relationship types, produced by each reification kind. The result of his work may be applicable to any temporal conceptual model.

2.4.1.4 Derived Types.

An entity type or relationship type is derived when its instances need not to be explicitly represented in the information base, because the information system may derive (i.e. infer or calculate) them at any time. For each derived type, there is a derivation rule, which is an expression that defines the necessary and sufficient conditions for an entity or relationship to be an instance of a given type [19]. In [16], Antoni proposed three methods for the definition of derivation rules in object-oriented conceptual modeling languages. The first method proposed applies to static rules, and associates each derived element with a defining operation. The specification of this operation is then the definition of the corresponding derivation rule. The second method applies to constant relationship types whose instances can be derived when the instances of one of its participant entity types are created and the third one deals with hybrid types, and defines their partial derivation rules. The three methods are adapted to the UML.

2.4.1.5 Integrity Constraints.

Integrity constraints are conditions that might not be satisfied in some states of the information base or by some events, but it is understood that the information system will include mechanisms to guarantee its satisfaction at any time [19]. A method that eases the definition of integrity constraints in object-oriented conceptual modeling languages was introduced by Olivé in [18]. The method propose to represent constraints by special operations called constraint operations. The formal specification of these operations is the definition of the corresponding constraints. The method allows the specialization of constraints and the definition of exceptions. The main application of the method is for static constraints. However, a variant of it can also be applied for creation-time and deletion-time constraints, two particular classes of temporal constraints. The method can be adapted to any object-oriented language.

2.4.1.6 Taxonomies.

In some cases instances of an entity type must also necessarily be instances of another entity type. This type of relationship between entity types is called IsA relationships. Entity types and their IsA relationships form a network structure called a taxonomy [19]. Antoni's extensive study of taxonomies produced two relevant publications in this area. The first one [9] deal with relationship type refinements, tha is, the specification of additional constraints when some of the participant entities are also instances of other entity types. In this paper, he characterized relationship type refinements in conceptual models with multiple classification, provided a graphical and textual notation for their specification, and gave their formal definition in logical terms. Moreover, he presented a set of necessary conditions to guarantee that a given set of refinements is valid. The second publication [23] analyzes the relationships between derived types and taxonomic constraints to see which taxonomic constraints are entailed by derivation rules and to analyze how taxonomic constraints can be satisfied in presence of derived types.

2.4.1.7 Events.

Antoni also focused his attention on the behavioral conceptual modeling. A method for modeling events as entities was proposed in [21]. The method makes extensive use of language constructs such as constraints, derived types, derivation rules, type specializations and operations, which are present in all complete object-oriented conceptual modeling languages. The method can be adapted to most object-oriented languages, including the UML.

2.4.2 Evolution

Another Antoni's main line of research during this period was the evolution of conceptual schemas. As he argued in [11], changes in the requirements of information systems should be defined and managed at the conceptual schema level, with an automatic propagation down to the logical database schema(s) and application programs. He proposed a framework for the evolution of temporal conceptual schemas of information systems. The framework uses a reflective architecture with two levels: a meta schema and schema, and two loosely coupled information processors, one for each level and it can be used to specify schema changes. The evolution of the partitions modeling construct in conceptual models with multiple specialization and classification, and considering base and derived entity types was analyzed in [10]. He provided a list of possible schema changes and, for each of them, he gave its formal specification.

In the same field, Antoni characterized in [20] the set of valid type configurations, taking into account the constraints defined by specializations and generalizations and considering multiple specialization, generalization and classification, as well as dynamic classification.He also analyzed the problem of determining the valid evolution of the type configuration of entities in the context of IsA hierarchies.

2.5 Conceptual Schema-Centric Development

In his most recent works, Antoni Olivé has expanded his research interests to study the role of conceptual modeling in the broader field of systems and software engineering and the additional challenges conceptual modelers would face in such context, specially regarding the quality and scalability aspects that models should comply to answer real-life industrial problems.

This vision was first outlined in his CAiSE keynote "Conceptual Schema-Centric Development: A Grand Challenge for Information Systems Research" [17]. He named the challenge "conceptual schema-centric development" (CSCD) in order to emphasize that the conceptual schema should be the center of the development of information systems.

Indeed, the goal of automating information systems building was already stated in the sixties but forty years later it is clear that the goal has not been achieved in a satisfactory degree. Antoni revisits this goal by emphasizing the key role conceptual schemas can play in it, now that standard modeling languages and platforms are available. He shows that to develop an information system it is necessary to define its conceptual schema and that, therefore, the CSCD approach does not place an extra burden on developers. In CSCD, conceptual schemas are explicit, executable in the production environment and the basis for the system evolution.

Obviously, this is an ambitious goal that involves solving as well a number of related research problems. Some of them were the focus on his work in the subsequent years as we will see below. This work was done in collaboration with a final generation of PhD students that completed their thesis during this period: Jordi Conesa (2008), Ruth Raventós (2009), Albert Tort (2012), Antonio Villegas (2013) and David Aguilera (2014).

2.5.1 Very large conceptual schemas

One of the major challenges is to be able to specify, understand and transform large conceptual schemas, required to model with enough level detail complex systems.

2.5.1.1 Specification of large schemas

In the past, most conceptual schemas of information systems have been developed essentially from scratch. However, Antoni explored an alternative approach that tries to reuse as much as possible the knowledge included in existing ontologies. Using this approach, conceptual schemas would be developed as refinements of (more general) ontologies. However, when the refined ontology is large, a new problem that arises using this approach is the need of pruning the concepts in that ontology that are superfluous in the final conceptual schema. He developed new automatic method for pruning ontologies [7] that can be adapted to most conceptual modeling languages and ontologies, though his approach takes as example the Cyc ontology.

Recently, he has also shown that the same approach can also be adapted to a more technological problem, which is the modeling of the microdata tagging a website content [33]. Similar in philosophy to the ontology pruning problem, here the goal is to prune schema.org vocabularies to derive the tags relevant for an individual website. Indeed, for large websites, implementing microdata can take a lot of time. In general, it is necessary to perform two main activities: (i) designing what he calls the website schema.org, which is the fragment of schema.org that is relevant to the website and (ii) adding the corresponding microdata tags to the web pages. Antoni's approach consists in using a human-computer task-oriented dialogue, whose purpose is to arrive at that design.

2.5.1.2 Understanding large schemas

Once you have built a very large schema, the next problem is how to effectively visualize and understand it. This problem appears in many information systems development activities in which modelers need to cooperate. While they need to have access to the global schema, most times their main focus and role in the collaboration is to take care of a small piece of the knowledge contained in that schema.

Therefore, Antoni proposed a method for filtering a fragment of the knowledge contained in a large conceptual schema [37]. In his method, once a user focuses on one or more entity types of interest for her task at hand, the method automatically filters the schema in order to obtain a set of entity and relationship types (and other knowledge) relevant to that task, taking into account the interest of each entity type with respect to the focus, computed from the measures of importance and closeness of entity types.

Later this method was extended to cover also the constraint expressions (also called schema rules) in the schema. Understanding such expressions is complex since the types they refer to may be located in very different places in the schema, possibly distant from each other and embedded in an intricate web of irrelevant elements. In [38], he described a method that, given a set of constraint expressions and a large conceptual schema, automatically filters the conceptual schema, obtaining a smaller one that contains the elements of interest for the understanding of the expressions.

Another factor that plays a role in this readability problem is the naming conventions for schema elements. The problem is significant because in general there are many elements that require a name, and the names given have a strong influence on the understandability of that schema. Following the same naming conventions across a large schema clearly helps modelers to identify the type and role of elements they are looking at. In [2], Antoni proposed a guideline for every kind of element to which a conceptual modeler may give a name in UML. The guideline comprises the grammar form of the name and a pattern sentence. A name complies with the guideline if it has that form and the sentence generated from the pattern sentence is grammatically well-formed and semantically meaningful.

2.5.1.3 Transforming large schemas

Many model manipulation operations involve a schema translation that reexpresses the input model in a new language / metamodel. Nowadays, more metamodels are defiend as instances of the OMG's MOF standard but the specification of the mappings and translations remains a difficult and error-prone task.

Antoni proposes a new approach to the schema translation problem. to make an extensive use of object-oriented concepts in the definition of translation mappings, particularly the use of operations (and their refinements) and invariants, both of which are formalized in OCL [27]. Then, these translation mappings can be used to check that two schemas are translations of each other, and to translate one into the other, in both directions. The translation mappings are declaratively defined by means of pre- and postconditions and invariants, and they can be implemented in any suitable language. From an implementation point of view, by taking a MOF-based approach, you have immediately a wide set of tools available, including tools that execute OCL.

2.5.2 Quality in modeling

In the CSCD approach, the final software implementation is (at least partially) derived from the initial conceptual schema. Therefore, the quality of the schema has a direct impact on the quality of the final system. As a result, another major focus of Antoni's work on the CSCD challenge has been devoted to ensure the quality of schemas.

A first step was to come up with a precise definition of quality properties for conceptual schemas. As he reported, in the literature, there are many proposals of quality properties of conceptual schemas, but only a few of them (mainly those related to syntax) have been integrated into the development environments used by professionals and students. A possible explanation of this unfortunate fact may be that the proposals have been defined in disparate ways, which makes it difficult to integrate them into those environments.

As a reaction to this situation, Antoni proposed a list of quality issues, which essentially are conditions that should not happen in a schema, and a unified method for their definition and treatment [1]. In this same work, he also showed that his method could be used to successfully describe most of the quality properties already described in the literature in an homogeneous way, which should facilitate building a catalogue of quality properties to be enforced in integrated development environments (IDEs). This is specially relevant since the support provided by current IDEs wrt the enforcement of quality criteria is still very limited [3] and, clearly, one of the most effective ways of increasing the quality of conceptual schemas in practice is by using an IDE that assists the designers in this matter.

An alternative to enforce quality properties on a conceptual schema is to test if the schema satisfies them. Testing is sometimes regarded as "poor man's verification" but still a very reasonable trade-off when the size or complexity of the schema hampers its verification in a reasonable amount of time. Antoni proposed a list of five kinds of tests that can be applied to conceptual schemas [32]. Two of them require schemas comprising both the structural and the behavioral parts, but he showed that it was possible and useful to test incomplete schema fragments, even if they consist of only a few entity and relationship types, integrity constraints and derivation rules. Tests are specified in CSTL, a language for writing automated tests of executable schemas written in UML/OCL. CSTL includes language primitives for each of the above kinds of tests. CSTL follows the style of the modern xUnit testing frameworks.

When testing, a more ambitious approach is to go from testing an existing model to using the tests to build the model itself, which is known as Test-Driven Development (TDD). TDD is an extreme programming development method in which a software system is developed in short iterations. Antoni proposed the Test-Driven Conceptual Modeling (TDCM) method [34], which is an application of TDD for conceptual modeling, and showed how to develop a conceptual schema using it. In TDCM, a system's conceptual schema is incrementally obtained by performing three kinds of tasks: (1) Write a test the system should pass; (2) Change the schema to pass the test; and (3) Refactor the schema to improve its qualities.

2.6 Conclusions

We have summarized in this chapter thirty years of contributions of Antoni Olivé to conceptual modeling. They began with fostering the deductive approach to conceptual modeling of information systems and by proposing techniques aimed at dealing with some of the most relevant problems in this field. The *internal events rules* were probably the most significant contribution at that time, and they were also successfully applied for handling several problems in deductive databases. This first period of research lasted for almost fifteen years, from 1986 to 1999.

Then, he progressively moved to object-oriented conceptuals schemas, field were he was contributing for about ten years, devoting a lot of efforts to set up the basis of the main components of conceptual schemas and analyzing how to facilitate its evolution over time. The leading landmark of this period was his seminal book *"Conceptual Modeling of Information Systems"*, published by Springer in 2007, which is still a frame of reference at many Universities in the world.

After that, Antoni's research interests moved to analyze the role conceptual modeling should play in software engineering and the challenges that conceptual modelers should face in this context. His outmost contribution from this period is probably his proposal for *conceptual schema-centric development*, emphasizing that the conceptual schema should be the driving force in information systems development.

As a conclusion, we would like to say that it is impossible to review all this huge amount of work just in a few pages, although we expect that we have been able to provide a fair summary of its significance to the conceptual modeling discipline. All of us are indebted to this long journey and we will modestly do our best to further pursue in the direction that Antoni has shown us during all these years.

Acknowledgements As coauthors of Antoni's papers, several people from the Universitat Politècnica de Catalunya have contributed to the field of conceptual modeling, and are still doing it with new, younger, researchers. We are grateful to all of them since they also made this chapter possible. So, we wish to thank David Aguilera, Jordi Conesa, Dolors Costal, Juan Ramón López, Joan Antoni Pastor, Carme Quer, Ruth Raventós, Jaume Sistac†, Albert Tort, Toni Urpí and Antonio Villegas for all the good work they did while being PhD students and collaborators of Antoni.

References

1. Aguilera, D., Gómez, C., Olivé, A.: A method for the definition and treatment of conceptual schema quality issues. In: Atzeni et al. [4], pp. 501–514
2. Aguilera, D., Gómez, C., Olivé, A.: A complete set of guidelines for naming UML conceptual schema elements. Data Knowl. Eng. 88, 60–74 (2013)
3. Aguilera, D., Gómez, C., Olivé, A.: Enforcement of conceptual schema quality issues in current integrated development environments. In: Salinesi, C., Norrie, M.C., Pastor, O. (eds.) Advanced Information Systems Engineering - 25th International Conference, CAiSE 2013, Valencia, Spain, June 17-21, 2013. Proceedings. Lecture Notes in Computer Science, vol. 7908, pp. 626–640. Springer (2013)
4. Atzeni, P., Cheung, D.W., Ram, S. (eds.): Conceptual Modeling - 31st International Conference ER 2012, Florence, Italy, October 15-18, 2012. Proceedings, Lecture Notes in Computer Science, vol. 7532. Springer (2012)
5. Cabot, J., Olivé, A., Teniente, E.: Entity types derived by symbol-generating rules. In: Song, I., Liddle, S.W., Ling, T.W., Scheuermann, P. (eds.) Conceptual Modeling - ER 2003, 22nd International Conference on Conceptual Modeling, Chicago, IL, USA, October 13-16, 2003, Proceedings. Lecture Notes in Computer Science, vol. 2813, pp. 376–389. Springer (2003)
6. Cabot, J., Olivé, A., Teniente, E.: Representing temporal information in UML. In: Stevens, P., Whittle, J., Booch, G. (eds.) UML 2003 - The Unified Modeling Language, Modeling Languages and Applications, 6th International Conference, San Francisco, CA, USA, October 20-24, 2003, Proceedings. Lecture Notes in Computer Science, vol. 2863, pp. 44–59. Springer (2003)
7. Conesa, J., Olivé, A.: A method for pruning ontologies in the development of conceptual schemas of information systems pp. 64–90 (2006)
8. Costal, D., Olivé, A.: A method for reasoning about deductive conceptual models of information systems. In: CAiSE. pp. 612–631 (1992), `https://doi.org/10.1007/BFb0035156`
9. Costal, D., Olivé, A., Teniente, E.: Relationship type refinement in conceptual models with multiple classification. In: Kunii, H.S., Jajodia, S., Sølvberg, A. (eds.) Conceptual Modeling - ER 2001, 20th International Conference on Conceptual Modeling, Yokohama, Japan, November 27-30, 2001, Proceedings. Lecture Notes in Computer Science, vol. 2224, pp. 397–411. Springer (2001)
10. Gómez, C., Olivé, A.: Evolving partitions in conceptual schemas in the UML. In: Pidduck et al. [25], pp. 467–483

11. López, J., Olivé, A.: A framework for the evolution of temporal conceptual schemas of information systems. In: Wangler, B., Bergman, L. (eds.) Advanced Information Systems Engineering, 12th International Conference CAiSE 2000, Stockholm, Sweden, June 5-9, 2000, Proceedings. Lecture Notes in Computer Science, vol. 1789, pp. 369–386. Springer (2000)
12. Olivé, A.: A comparison of the operational and deductive approaches to conceptual information systems modelling. In: IFIP Congress. pp. 91–96 (1986)
13. Olivé, A.: A formal approach to timing analysis and design of information systems. Inf. Syst. 12(1), 1–10 (1987), https://doi.org/10.1016/0306-4379(87)90013-5
14. Olivé, A.: Relationship reification: A temporal view. In: Jarke, M., Oberweis, A. (eds.) Advanced Information Systems Engineering, 11th International Conference CAiSE'99, Heidelberg, Germany, June 14-18, 1999, Proceedings. Lecture Notes in Computer Science, vol. 1626, pp. 396–410. Springer (1999)
15. Olivé, A.: Representation of generic relationship types in conceptual modeling. In: Pidduck et al. [25], pp. 675–691
16. Olivé, A.: Derivation rules in object-oriented conceptual modeling languages. In: Eder, J., Missikoff, M. (eds.) Advanced Information Systems Engineering, 15th International Conference, CAiSE 2003, Klagenfurt, Austria, June 16-18, 2003, Proceedings. Lecture Notes in Computer Science, vol. 2681, pp. 404–420. Springer (2003)
17. Olivé, A.: Conceptual schema-centric development: A grand challenge for information systems research. In: Pastor, O., e Cunha, J.F. (eds.) Advanced Information Systems Engineering, 17th International Conference, CAiSE 2005, Porto, Portugal, June 13-17, 2005, Proceedings. Lecture Notes in Computer Science, vol. 3520, pp. 1–15. Springer (2005)
18. Olivé, A.: A method for the definition of integrity constraints in object-oriented conceptual modeling languages. Data Knowl. Eng. 59(3), 559–575 (2006)
19. Olivé, A.: Conceptual modeling of information systems. Springer (2007)
20. Olivé, A., Costal, D., Sancho, M.: Entity evolution in ISA hierarchies. In: Akoka, J., Bouzeghoub, M., Comyn-Wattiau, I., Métais, E. (eds.) Conceptual Modeling - ER '99, 18th International Conference on Conceptual Modeling, Paris, France, November, 15-18, 1999, Proceedings. Lecture Notes in Computer Science, vol. 1728, pp. 62–80. Springer (1999)
21. Olivé, A., Raventós, R.: Modeling events as entities in object-oriented conceptual modeling languages. Data Knowl. Eng. 58(3), 243–262 (2006)
22. Olivé, A., Sancho, M.: Validating conceptual specifications through model execution. Inf. Syst. 21(2), 167–186 (1996), https://doi.org/10.1016/0306-4379(96)00010-5
23. Olivé, A., Teniente, E.: Derived types and taxonomic constraints in conceptual modeling. Inf. Syst. 27(6), 391–409 (2002)
24. Pastor-Collado, J.A., Olivé, A.: Supporting transaction design in conceptual modelling of information systems. In: International Conference on Advanced Information Systems Engineering. pp. 40–53. Springer (1995)
25. Pidduck, A.B., Mylopoulos, J., Woo, C.C., Özsu, M.T. (eds.): Advanced Information Systems Engineering, 14th International Conference, CAiSE 2002, Toronto, Canada, May 27-31, 2002, Proceedings, Lecture Notes in Computer Science, vol. 2348. Springer (2002)
26. Quer, C., Olivé, A.: Deteriming object interaction in object-oriented deductive conceptual models. Inf. Syst. 19(3), 211–227 (1994), https://doi.org/10.1016/0306-4379(94)90042-6
27. Raventós, R., Olivé, A.: An object-oriented operation-based approach to translation between MOF metaschemas. Data Knowl. Eng. 67(3), 444–462 (2008)
28. Sancho, M.R., Olivé, A.: Deriving transaction specifications from deductive conceptual models of information systems. In: International Conference on Advanced Information Systems Engineering. pp. 311–324. Springer (1994)
29. Sistac, J.: The DADES/GP approach to automatic generation of information system prototypes from a deductive conceptual model. Inf. Syst. 17(3), 195–208 (1992), https://doi.org/10.1016/0306-4379(92)90013-D
30. Teniente, E., Olivé, A.: The events method for view updating in deductive databases. In: Advances in Database Technology - EDBT'92, 3rd International Conference on Extending

Database Technology, Vienna, Austria, March 23-27, 1992, Proceedings. pp. 245–260 (1992), https://doi.org/10.1007/BFb0032435
31. Teniente, E., Olivé, A.: Updating knowledge bases while maintaining their consistency. VLDB J. 4(2), 193–241 (1995), http://www.vldb.org/journal/VLDBJ4/P193.pdf
32. Tort, A., Olivé, A.: An approach to testing conceptual schemas. Data Knowl. Eng. 69(6), 598–618 (2010)
33. Tort, A., Olivé, A.: An approach to website schema.org design. Data Knowl. Eng. 99, 3–16 (2015)
34. Tort, A., Olivé, A., Sancho, M.: An approach to test-driven development of conceptual schemas. Data Knowl. Eng. 70(12), 1088–1111 (2011)
35. Urpí, T., Olivé, A.: Evants and events rules in active databases. IEEE Data Eng. Bull. 15(1-4), 56–59 (1992), http://sites.computer.org/debull/92DEC-CD.pdf
36. Urpí, T., Olivé, A.: A method for change computation in deductive databases. In: 18th International Conference on Very Large Data Bases, August 23-27, 1992, Vancouver, Canada, Proceedings. pp. 225–237 (1992), http://www.vldb.org/conf/1992/P225.PDF
37. Villegas, A., Olivé, A.: A method for filtering large conceptual schemas. Conceptual Modeling–ER 2010 pp. 247–260 (2010)
38. Villegas, A., Olivé, A., Sancho, M.: Understanding constraint expressions in large conceptual schemas by automatic filtering. In: Atzeni et al. [4], pp. 50–63

Chapter 3
Modeling Life: A Conceptual Schema-centric Approach to Understand the Genome

Óscar Pastor López, Ana León Palacio, José Fabián Reyes Román and Juan Carlos Casamayor

Abstract Programs are historically the basic notion in Software Engineering, which represents the final artifact to be executed in a machine. These programs have been created by humans, using a silicon-based code, whose final components use a binary code represented by 0s and 1s. If we look at life as a program with a DNA-based genetic code with a final representation that uses four essential units (A, C, G and T), one challenging question emerges. *Can we establish a correspondence between life – from a genomic perspective – and programs – from a Software Engineering perspective?* This paper assumes a positive answer to this question and shows how genomic can benefit from Information Systems Engineering by applying conceptual modeling to determine those relevant data that life represents in order to manage them accordingly, with special emphasis in the health domain. The main contributions focus on i) a concrete materialization of a Conceptual Schema of the Human Genome, ii) the need of having a method to provide a methodological guidance concerning genome data management, and iii) the importance of assessing data quality for all generated data that are going to be used in critical domains such as health and Precision Medicine.

Óscar Pastor López
PROS Research Center, Universitat Politècnica de València, e-mail: opastor@pros.upv.es

Ana León Palacio
PROS Research Center, Universitat Politècnica de València, e-mail: aleon@pros.upv.es

José Fabián Reyes Román
PROS Research Center, Universitat Politècnica de València, e-mail: jreyes@pros.upv.es
Dept. of Engineering Sciences, Universidad Central del Este (UCE)

Juan Carlos Casamayor
Departamento de Sistemas Informáticos y Computación (DSIC), Universitat Politècnica de València, e-mail: jcarlos@dsic.upv.es

© Springer International Publishing AG 2017

J. Cabot et al. (eds.), *Conceptual Modeling Perspectives*,
https://doi.org/10.1007/978-3-319-67271-7_3

3.1 Introduction

The goal of this paper is to show how Conceptual Modeling provides a sound background to face the challenging problem of understanding the genome. The ideas and results presented here are inspired in the keynote presented by Prof. Antoni Olivé in CAiSE 2005 in Porto, Portugal [1]. He introduced a Conceptual Schema-centric Software Development approach, intended to make true a precise model-driven development solution: in modern *Information Systems Engineering* (ISE), what it should be true is that *"the conceptual model is the code"*, instead of the conventional perspective based on the fact that *"the code is the model"*. Prof. Olivé was also explaining in his work how the term *"conceptual model"* was too frequently misused, substituting the correct term of *"conceptual schema"*, the one to be used when referring to concrete instantiations of a conceptual modeling exercise.

This inspiring keynote was reflecting very well our work in the last decade around building conceptual schema compilers and providing a software process where conceptual modeling and model transformations (*from requirements to code*) conform the strategy to be followed.

But when looking for new challenges where our experience in conceptual modeling could be effectively applied, one particular domain came to our mind: modeling life. How to face the challenge of modeling life by understanding the genome became the problem to be solved. We show in this paper how conceptual modeling can provide the required techniques to manage adequately the huge amount of data that the genome-related working context continuously generate.

The reality is that understanding life as we know it on our planet can probably be considered the biggest challenge of our century. However, how to face the problem of understanding life from an ISE perspective is a complex question. *Can ISE help us to achieve the goal of understanding life?* Answering this question becomes a relevant issue that particularly affects how modern Precision Medicine can reach our society, changing and improving medicine, as we historically know it.

As said before, in our previous work we have been using CM to explain how we, humans, generate programs, that in their final form are constituted by silicon-based binary code. These programs are the written representation of CM that abstractly represent a relevant part of the real work we are interested in. We based our use of a conceptual modeling-based approach in the definition of conceptual modeling proposed by Prof. Olivé in his outstanding book on conceptual modeling [8]. In a few words, we assume from his work that conceptual modeling refers to the activity that elicits and describes the general knowledge that a particular IS needs to know. In this paper this particular information systems is the *"genome"*. Its main objective is to obtain that description, represented in which it is called a CS. Accordingly, a conceptual schema of the genome constitutes a significant result that will be presented later.

We also assume that conceptual schemas are written in languages called conceptual modeling languages. Additionally, in our perspective of a sound software process that covers all the conceptual modeling steps that go from requirements modeling (at the earliest software production process steps) to application code generation (as the final result of such a precisely-defined software process), conceptual modeling is an important part of that requirements engineering task, the first and most important phase in the development of an IS.

What is then the connection between conceptual modeling and life? Why did we move to the fascinating working domain of modeling life by facing the challenging problem of understanding the genome?

We applied an attractive and similar metaphor to achieve our desired clear understanding of life. In this case the programs are living beings whose genetic code includes the instructions that explain life as we perceive it. Instead of having the ISE materialization in the form of a binary executable code, in this case we have what we could call a quaternary executable code, based on four letters (A, C, G, T) that represent the four nucleotides that form the basic components of this *"carbon-based"* executable code (see the lower part of Fig. 3.1).

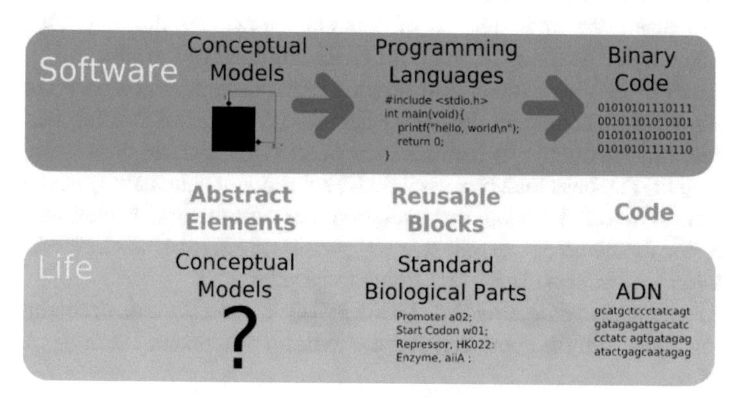

Fig. 3.1 From conceptual models to code: a SE-perspective and a life understanding perspective.

If we want to develop this idea, one immediate question that arises is: What is then the *"programming language of life" that would allow us to understand and manage life as we understand and manage ISE-based programs?* We are perfectly aware of the magnitude of the challenge that arises from this question. But at the same time, we are aware that the race to face this challenge has not only started but is proceeding at full speed.

In this context, *what is the role of conceptual modeling? Why a conceptual schema-centric approach intended to understand the genome?* Let us answer these questions by introducing a bottom-up perspective, instead of the conventional top-down approach that is normally used in ISE.

By top-down we mean that if the *"conceptual schema is the code"*, what we could call conventional ISE must create code from models. We start with the conceptual schema, we convert it into the final application code.

Considering life, we face a different situation. We have now living beings that can be seen as individual *"programs"*. We perceive them as running programs. But in this case, we don't know the models that these programs exactly represent. The problem is similar to trying to understand the meaning of a program just looking at its binary code, just analyzing how it executes. This is what we call a "bottom-up" perspective. Analyzing individuals, collecting data about their genomes, we should be able to infer relevant information, we should be able to identify relevant conceptual patterns. To do it, it is essential to understand the nature of the data to be managed, and to understand its structure, including basic entities and relationships among them.

Considering the complexity of the problem, and although DNA is the basis of all life as we know it on the Earth, we focus here on the human genome, where rapid progress is being made specially in the context of PM (also previously known as *Personalized Medicine*). It is in this context that we want to focus our work, and where we want to report the experience accumulated in the last years in three main areas:

1. How essential it is to have a *Conceptual Schema of the Human Genome* (CSHG) for structuring the huge amount of data and knowledge that day after day are generated in the genomic domain. A CSHG will then be introduced.
2. The need of having a method to provide methodological guidance concerning genome data management, including the crucial phases of i) valid data sources "search and selection"; ii) identification of the valid data in those selected data sources; iii) database load process; and iv) subsequent data management platform oriented to an efficient data interpretation and exploitation. A method so-called SILE (for the name of the four relevant phases of *"Search, Identification, Load, Exploitation / Interpretation"*) is going to be presented.
3. The importance of assessing Data Quality (DQ) when a big data problem is faced, as occurs when all the generated data are to be used in practical settings as critical as PM.

The conceptual thread of our book chapter is going to follow these aspects. What we want to indicate with the selected title of this paper is how important a conceptual schema-centric approach is to draw a parallel between ISE and genomics. By considering live beings a particular kind of programs whose (*genomic*) code is started to be known, a challenging needs emerge precisely: to design the conceptual schemas that must lead to the relevant genome knowledge discovery. In our work we are not simply applying one essential ISE technique (conceptual modeling) to a complex domain (human genomics). We go much further: what we want to show is how conceptual modeling and genomics can share a same picture (as Fig.3.1 represents), and particularly, how genomics can benefit from ISE by applying conceptual modeling to determine those relevant data that life represents in order to manage them accordingly, with especial emphasis in the health domain.

The structure of this chapter follows the presented ideas. A concrete materialization of a CSHG is introduced in section 3.2, explaining our experience in its evolutionary and continuous design. It conforms a solid information system core intended to correctly manage genome data. This is followed in section 3.3 by the presentation of a methodological background the SILE methodology designed to characterize a sound conceptual schema-centric genome data management process. This section ends discussing a final essential issue: what is to be done to assess the quality of the data used in the PM clinical context, guided by the CSHG and based on the use of the SILE method. Finally, our conclusions and intentions for future work close the chapter.

3.2 Conceptual Schema of the Human Genome (CSHG)

It is widely accepted that applying conceptual models [8] facilitates the understanding of complex domains (such as *genomics*). In our case we used this approach to define a model representing the characteristics and behavior of the human genome [12, 16].

Through the application of CM, a wide range of benefits are obtained, which have a positive impact on the creation of Information Systems *-based on clear and precise structures-*. For example, conceptual modeling allows to represent more precisely the relevant concepts of the studied domain. A fundamental task before beginning the process of creating a conceptual schema is the analysis of the problem domain (in our case, *genomics*). Working together with teams specialized in *Software Engineering* (SE) and genomics (i.e., *biologists*, *geneticists*, etc.) allowed us to start designing the representation of the domain, giving as a result a *"Conceptual Schema of the Human Genome (CSHG)"*.

The main objective of this CSHG is to improve the treatment and integration of genomic data in order to enhance and guarantee PM. The CSHG has been adapted according to the new discoveries made in the domain. This evolution is necessary because the genomic domain produces large amounts of information in constant change and growth. For this reason, conceptual modeling has a great advantage in representing this domain because it facilitates the integration of new knowledge in the model and provides a positive support to the knowledge on which PM is based.

Understanding the human genome is a great challenge because it requires the development of (complex) data abstraction tasks. Only in this way we can get the relevant data to be included in the conceptual representation. The first version of the CSHG (v1) was the result of a series of meetings with experts in the domain, this version focuses on the analysis of individual genes, their mutations, and their phenotypic aspects (see details in [12, 10]). Next, the classification of that first version is presented in three main views:

- *Genome view:* responsible for modeling individual human genomes (Fig. 3.2).
- *Gene-Mutation view:* used to model knowledge about genes, their structure and their allelic variants.
- *Transcription view*: intented to model the basic components of the transcription process and the synthesis of proteins (which is what we know as "*gene expression*").

After finishing version 1, we started the task of evaluating the capacity of the model to deal with the actual data manipulated in the bioinformatics domain. At the moment of putting into practice this initial version of the CSHG, it was necessary

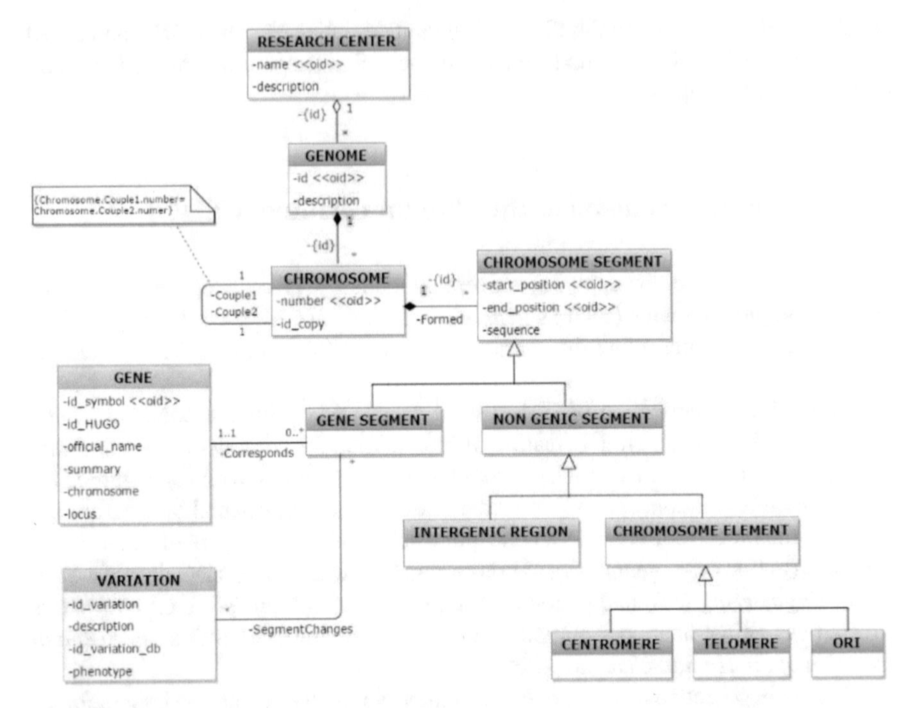

Fig. 3.2 Genome View (v1).

to generate a new version (CSHG v2), which changes its central axis and goes from representing a *"gene-centered"* vision to a vision centered on the concept of *"chromosome"*. This change of vision in the model represents the main difference with respect to previous versions of the model.

In this change of perspective, we identified a series of questions to address:

1. We were not sure about the suitability of mixing a Genome view related to the storage of individual genomes – the so-called Genome view in v1 – with a more theoretical, structural Genomic view related to the Genome configuration and characterization as a whole (the so-called Gene-Mutation and Transcription view).
2. Concerning the core concept of gene, it is not always feasible to describe DNA structure in terms of genes as basic constructs. We concluded that the most suitable structure is suing chromosome elements as the basic building blocks.
3. More relevant concepts were needed, for instance, the concept of SNPs.
4. We detected the need for extending the first version with more significant genome-related information. To go from genotype to phenotype in a complete, sound way, we needed the specification of the pathway description perspective.

The development of these four ideas are explained in detail in the following works [12], [16], and make up the so-called version 2 of the model (CSHG v2). This version of the model is organized into five main parts (called "*views*") (Fig. 3.3):

- *Structural view:* basic elements of the DNA sequence.
- *Transcription view:* components involved in going from DNA to the diversity of RNAs.
- *Variation view:* to characterize changes in the sequence of reference that have functional implications in how the genome expresses.
- *Pathways view:* intended to enrich the conceptual model with information about metabolic pathways to join genome components that participate in pathways with phenotype expressions.
- *Bibliography and data bank view:* to assess the source of any information in order to pinpoint the data source.

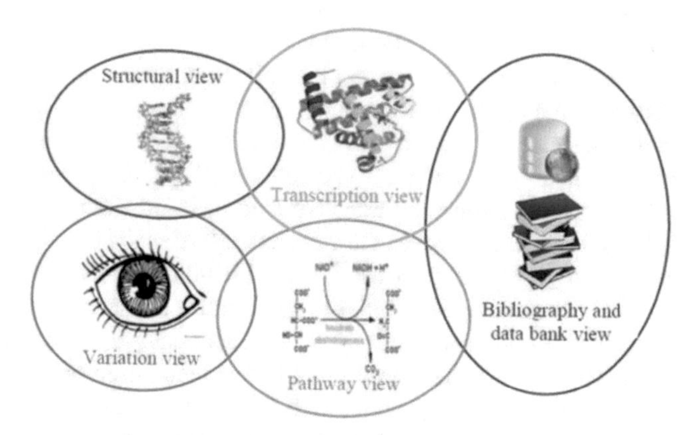

Fig. 3.3 Views of the CSHG version 2.

The CSHG v2 has been the basis for validating the management of genomic data related to diseases of genetic origin (i.e., *breast cancer* [3], *alcohol sensitivity* [13], *neuroblastoma* [4], among others). Currently, the next version of the CSHG (v3) has been developed. This new version aims to integrate all the relevant information on haplotypes [14, 15]. To do it, an extension of the *"variation view"* was done in order to manage the information related to *allelic/genotypic frequencies*, and *populations*. This conceptual schema is definitely intended to be able to generate the required number of versions in order to incorporate the genomic knowledge that continues to emerge in the domain.

The design of the CSHG is essential for the development of a *Genomic Information System* (GeIS) that guarantees the quality of the stored information. This approach facilitates a conceptual modeling perspective to provide a clear and open structure ready to be adapted to new changes, which in practical terms improves the reliability of the information and generates an accurate framework for a genomic diagnosis.

3.3 SILE Methodology and Data Quality

By defining a CM of the genomic domain we assure that data will be gathered under a single and comprehensive information perspective. The right interpretation of data is key to the PM, because it may affect *health decision making, research* and *clinical practice*. For this reason, the IS must be loaded with accurate, structured, relevant and consistent information. But this is not a trivial task. Thousands of biological databases have been developed over the last two decades, and they have widely varying content, resources, infrastructures and quality. The search and identification of relevant genomic information has become a time consuming process, highly dependent on the knowledge and experience of the researcher. Discussions with experts in the field highlighted that there is not any protocol or systematic method to search and identify relevant information. This behaviour leads to problems such as loss of relevant information resources and the collection of non-standardized data. In order to assure that as many relevant data repositories as possible are taken into account, and the data gathered are accurate and have a high quality level, the process must be performed in a systematic way. The addition of specific quality controls on each stage of the process assures an effective load of information in the database that represents the IS, and it improves the value of further analysis and exploitation.

According to this approach, the SILE (Search-Identification-Load-Exploitation) methodology has been developed in order to systematize the search and identification process of genomic information, which is loaded, analyzed and exploited by an IS that is based on the CSHG. Currently, SILE is being used by a group of researchers in an academic context, who search for genomic variations related to a set of diseases with a high social impact such as: *Alzheimer, Neuroblastoma* and *Lung Cancer*. In the next section a brief explanation of the main levels of the SILE Methodology is going to be made. Next, a first approach to the Data Quality Framework (DQF) used to complement the methodology will be presented.

3.3.1 SILE Methodology

The SILE methodology goal is to efficiently populate a *Human Genome Database* (HGDB), corresponding to the CSHG, with sound and high-quality information. But, *where can relevant information be found? Which data is significant to be loaded in the database?* And finally, *is this information of enough quality to offer an advantage to PM over traditional medicine?*

Through a methodology as SILE, as well as a proper quality framework specific for genomic data, those previous questions are precisely answered and quality errors are solved or considerably reduced.

This methodology is a four-level approach where each level provides information used as input to the next one: Search, Identification, Load and Exploitation. Next, a brief description of each level is provided.

3.3.1.1 Search (S)

Scientific sources (e.g. articles, databases) are thoroughly analyzed in order to determine the optimal ones to obtain information from. In the Search level the context of the information which is going to be searched needs to be defined (i.e., *a particular disease*). Once the context is delimited, the search must be focused on the available databases which can provide detailed information about the topic we are interested in.

Due to the huge amount of available repositories in the genomic domain, the use of biological databases catalogues is very useful to perform the search. These catalogues provide a complete list of data sources, grouped by category or topic, as well as a brief description of their content and links to the information home page. The most important ones are the catalogues provided by the *Nucleic Acid Research Journal* (NAR) [17] and the *Human Genome Variation Society* (HGVS)[1].

3.3.1.2 Identification (I)

The first step in the Identification level is to determine which information characterizes the domain of interest, according to the Conceptual Schema which describes it. As an example, Table 3.1 shows the information needed to represent a variation.

Table 3.1 HGDB Variation information

Attribute	Description
DESCRIPTION	Variation description.
DB_VARIATION_ID	Identifier provided by the data source where the information was extracted from.
CLINICALLY_IMPORTANT	Clinical importance of the variation related to a phenotype.
OTHER_IDENTIFIERS	Other possible identifier as for example HGVS expressions.
ASSOCIATED_GENES	Genes affected by the variations.
OMIM	Identifier provided by OMIM [9].
SPECIALIZATION_TYPE	Type of variation
FLANKING_RIGHT	Sequence made by 20 nucleotides on the right of the variation.
FLANKING_LEFT	Sequence made by 20 nucleotides on the left of the variation.
ALN_QUALITY	Alignment quality of the variation inside the gene.
POSITION	Position where the variation is located inside the chromosome.
INS_SEQUENCE	Sequence of inserted nucleotides.
INS_REPETITION	How many times the inserted sequence is repeated.
DEL_BASES	Number of nucleotides deleted.

Once the needed information is clear, the next step is to find out which part of the information is provided by each database selected in the previous level and how it can be extracted.

[1] HGVS Databases catalogue: `http://www.hgvs.org/content/databases-tools`

3.3.1.3 Load (L)

During the load phase the interesting information that as been previously identified will be extracted from each database and, after a transformation process, it will be used to populate the HGDB. To perform this tasks an ETL framework is used:

- The first step is to *"Extract"* (E) the information of interest from the databases, using the mechanisms they provide for such task (reports, FTP sites, APIs, etc.).
- The second step is to determine if the extracted information needs to be *"Transformed"* (T) to fit the format and the rules established by the HGDB and the CSHG.
- The final step is to *"Load"* (L) the information into the HGDB.

3.3.1.4 Exploitation (E)

The exploitation level concerns to extract knowledge from data. The data exploitation system might be able to guide experts through complex scenarios that take into account multiple types of data. In this level, the quality controls applied at the previous levels take an important value since the conclusions obtained in the extraction of knowledge depend on them. The requirements in this level are:

- *Data Discovery:* Users need to explore data by conducting ad-hoc queries with specific information goals in mind.
- *Data Visualization:* Users need ways to represent the data, identify patterns in the data and even more, to explore the most accurate interactive representation associated to those patterns.
- *Data Analysis:* Users need to analyze and understanding the relationships between the data in order to draw conclusions and inferring new relevant information.

In our case, the information stored in the HGDB is analyzed by a proper tool developed specifically for the use of variation data, called *"VarSearch"* [18]. This tool analyses the information obtained from a patient sample and determines if there are variations associated to a certain disease, according to the data stored in the database. Although the automated analysis is useful to determine the potential variation-diseases associations, additional *collaborative* and *interactive* mechanisms to explore and visualize the information are needed. Currently, a research is under-way to determine and integrate such mechanisms into *VarSearch*. The main idea is to enhance the data exploitation by easing the user-data interaction through intuitive user interfaces for non-technical users [5].

In summary, the SILE Methodology provides a framework to systematize the searching process and the population of IS developed to manage data in complex domains. This method helps to structure data collected from different public repositories, and the data-to-knowledge process becomes more efficient and more comprehensive. This methodological guidance is essential to assess an effective and efficient conceptual schema-centric genome data management environment.

3.3.2 Data Quality

Types of genomic databases range from huge data warehouses containing millions of unreviewed raw sequences to high-reviewed databases manually curated by experts in the field. Quality needs to be evaluated because these databases may affect *health decision making, research* and *clinical practice* as we mentioned before. Next, a summary of some common issues which can be found in genomic databases are briefly presented. Afterwards a first approach about the data quality framework that is proposed to be applied together with the methodology, will be explained.

3.3.2.1 Data Quality Issues

Due to its complexity and heterogeneity, genomic databases present issues related to the quality of the information that they store. These issues can be classified according to a set of six basic data quality dimensions proposed by Askham, which can be applied to genomic databases [2]:

- *Accuracy*: Data correspond to real-world values and are correct. Accuracy errors mainly affect genomic data warehouses, where DNA sequences are submitted to the database by researchers and not reviewed by external experts. Common errors are sequence conflicts, misspellings, taxonomical or curation errors.
- *Completeness*: The extent to which data is not missing and all necessary data values are represented. Primary non-curated databases have a low level of completeness while those reviewed and curated by experts are usually fairly complete.
- *Reliability:* The extent to which data is regarded as true and credible. To get proper conclusions from a study in the genomic domain, the information used must be well supported by published research results. Besides, manually curated databases are much more reliable than non-curated or automatically curated ones, due to the expert's efforts to verify the existence and correctness of assertion criteria.
- *Consistency*: Data must be consistent between systems and represented in the same format. Information extracted from one data source is not enough to reach proper and meaningful conclusions. This means that diverse data sources must be checked and integrated. But an obvious problem is faced if each one presents its information in its own format (i.e., flat files, XML, HTML, etc.) and uses specific nomenclature based on its own need (for example to determine the type of the variations). Besides, colloquial designations for genes or mutations are used so broadly that many scientists are probably unaware that they are non-standard [7]. Consistency problems lead to a highly time-consuming process of normalization to represent the information under a single normalized model.

- *Uniqueness*: The database won't have redundant data or duplicate records. The number of entries in genomic databases has grown enormously in the last few decades, but this growth was accompanied by higher redundancy. This has become a noteworthy problem and some strategies have been developed to try to minimize it. For example, UniProtKB has developed an algorithm called Proteome Redundancy Detector [11]. When it was applied to their data warehouse (TrEMBL) for the first time, 46.9 million entries were removed from its database [11].
- *Currency*: This dimension can be defined as the extent to which data is sufficiently up-to-date. Genomic domain evolves quickly and information can get obsolete in a relatively short period of time so, this dimension is one of the most important ones to be assessed.

The issues presented are the most common ones that Bioinformaticians, Geneticists and researchers have to face in their daily work. For more specific information and examples see [6]. To reduce its impact, the SILE methodology is enriched with a DQF, which ensures that the information that is collected will have the quality required by the task to be accomplished.

3.3.2.2 Data Quality Framework

In order to assure the quality of the information to be loaded in the database, a set of quality controls needs to be applied in all the three first levels of the methodology: Search, Identification and Load. In Fig. 3.4, the entire process of the methodology can be shown.

The quality controls are based on the six major data quality dimensions presented in the previous section: accuracy, completeness, uniqueness, consistency, reliability and currency:

- *Search level (S)*: The most important dimension to be checked in this level is currency. Currency problems are closely related to accuracy and completeness issues. Examples of parameters used to assess the currency of the genomic information are i) the assembly used to represent a variation ii) the version of the database and iii) the specific last update of each registry. It is very common the use of external identifiers (IDs) to enrich the information provided by the database. When external IDs are being managed, it must be assured that they are currently valid and the links to the databases are working correctly. Situations where the source that is associated to the identifier changes and the link to the involved information becomes obsolete, must be avoided.
- *Identification level (I)*: The dimension checked in this level is reliability. Once the interesting information it is identified among the databases selected in the previous level, the next step is to identify which data has enough quality to be loaded into de HGDB. The minimum criteria to check the reliability of the information depends on the context where it belongs. For example in the case of variations associated to a certain disease the minimum reliability criteria considered are:

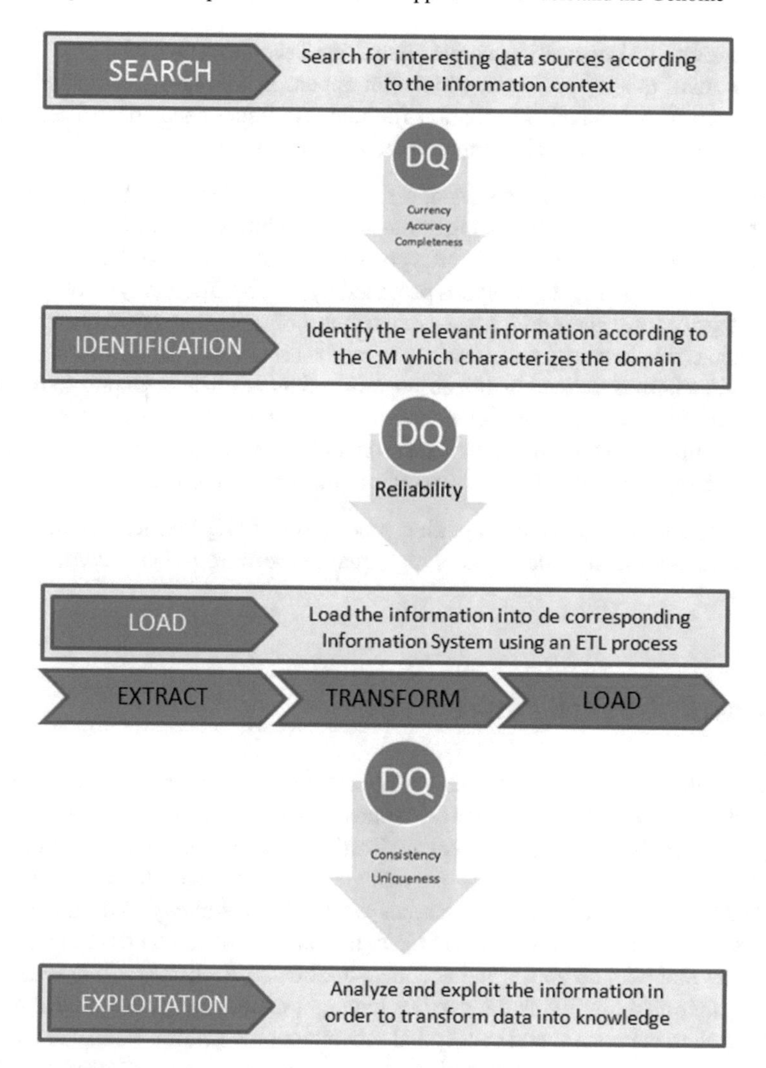

Fig. 3.4 SILE methodology and Data Quality Assessment Process.

1. *The clinical significance* of the variation must be clearly defined.
2. There must be *enough assertion criteria* provided for the relationship between the variation and the phenotype associated to it.

Additional quality criteria can be defined, such as the number of publications supporting the evidence and their impact factor, the number and relevance of authors and research institution, statistic metrics such as *p-value, odds ratio*, etc.

- *Load level (L)*: In this level, the information identified in the data sources is going to be extracted and loaded in the HGDB. During the extraction process, information from different databases is going to be collected and merged. One of the main problems of biological databases is the lack of use of proper standards to represent the information, so the integration becomes a no trivial process. Two of the main quality problems which can appear in this level are related to the existence of redundant information (uniqueness issues) and inconsistencies in the representation of the information (consistency issues):

- Consistency: The set of semantic rules can be determined by i) looking at the allowed values; ii) looking at mandatory values (Primary Keys or not nullable values); iii) looking at the type of value the fields should have (*integers, strings, booleans*, etc) which is provided by the HGDB; and iv) looking at the integrity constraints which involve attributes of more than one table (speaking from a relational point of view) or more than one group of attributes.
- Uniqueness is defined as the absence of redundant data or duplicate records. When information from different databases is merged, it is important to identify and remove all redundant records and to assure that the information of those representing the same variation is similar and correct.

With the addition of a corresponding precise set of DQ Metrics, the methodology assures that the information is of high quality (*current, reliable, consistent* and *accurate*).

3.4 Conclusions and Future Work

Precision Medicine is going to change the way in which we have historically understood medicine. The new practical context associated with it requires a sound working environment, and the correct application of the adequate Information Software Engineering (ISE) practices. We assume that Conceptual Modeling together with Data Quality Assessment techniques are the basic strategy to design and develop the required sound and efficient Genomic Information Systems (GeIS), which will assure that both diagnosis and adequate treatment selection are fully reliable.

The paper also highlights the need of having a methodological background designed to characterize a sound conceptual schema-centric genome data management process. Following this need, the SILE methodology has been proposed as a concrete solution.

Future research work will focus on the development, improvement and assessment of all these statements, in order to face the challenge of understanding life from an Information Software Engineering (ISE) perspective, inspired by the Conceptual Schema-centric approach introduced by Prof. Olivé in this research career.

Acknowledgements The authors are grateful to the members of the PROS Center Genome group for fruitful discussions. This work has been supported by the Ministry of Higher Education, Science and Technology (MESCyT) of the Dominican Republic and also has the support of Generalitat Valenciana through project IDEO (PROMETEOII/2014/039), the Research and Development Aid Program (PAID-01-16) of the UPV under FPI Grant 2137. and Spanish Ministry of Science and Innovation through project DataME (ref: TIN2016-80811-P).

References

1. Olivé, A.: Conceptual Schema-Centric Development: A Grand Challenge for Information Systems Research. In: Pastor O., Falcão e Cunha J. (eds) Advanced Information Systems Engineering. CAiSE 2005. Lecture Notes in Computer Science, vol 3520. Springer, Berlin, Heidelberg (2005)
2. Askham, N., Cook, D., Doyle, M., Fereday, H., Gibson, M., Landbeck, U., Lee, R., Maynard, C., Palmer, G., Schwarzenbach, J.: The Six Primary Dimensions for Data Quality Assessment. In: DAMA UK Working Group (2013) Available via White Papers. `http://bit.ly/2qcimnf`
3. Burriel Coll, V., Pastor, O.: Conceptual Schema of Breast Cancer: The background to design an efficient information system to manage data from diagnosis and treatment of breast cancer patients. In IEEE-EMBS International Conference on Biomedical and Health Informatics (BHI), pp. 432–435. IEEE (2014)
4. Burriel Coll, V., Reyes Román, J.F., Heredia Casanoves, A., Iñiguez-Jarrín, C., León Palacio, A.: GeIS based on Conceptual Models for the Risk Assessment of Neuroblastoma. In IEEE Eleventh International Conference on Research Challenges in Information Science (RCIS), pp. 1–2 (2017)
5. Iñiguez, C.: A conceptual modelling-based approach to generate data value through the end-user interactions: A case study in the genomics domain. PoEM Doctoral Consortium, pp. 14-21 (2016)
6. León, A., Reyes, J.F., Burriel, V., Valverde, F.: Data Quality problems when integrating genomic information. In 3rd. Workshop Quality of Models and Models of Quality (QMMQ 2016) in conjunction with the 35th International Conference on Conceptual Modeling (ER2016). Springer International Publishing pp. 173-182 (2016)
7. Ogino, S., Gulley, M.L., den Dunnen, J.T., Wilson, R.B., and the Association for Molecular Pathology Training and Education Committee: Standard Mutation Nomenclature in Molecular Diagnostics: Practical and Educational Challenges. The Journal of molecular diagnostics (2016) doi:10.2353/jmoldx.2007.060081.
8. Olivé, A.: Conceptual modeling of information systems. Springer-Verlag Berlin Heidelberg pp. 1-445 (2007)
9. Online Mendelian Inheritance in Man Homepage. Available via OMIM. `https://www.omim.org/`
10. Pastor, O., Reyes Román, J.F., Valverde, F.: Conceptual Schema of the Human Genome (CSHG). Universitat Politècnica de València (2016) Available via RiuNet. `http://hdl.handle.net/10251/67297`
11. Reducing proteome redundancy (2016) Available via UniProt. `http://www.uniprot.org/help/proteome_redundancy`
12. Reyes Román, J.F., Pastor, O., Casamayor J.C., Valverde F.: Applying Conceptual Modeling to Better Understand the Human Genome. In The 35th International Conference on Conceptual Modeling, Springer International Publishing, pp. 1-9 (2016)
13. Reyes Román, J.F., Pastor, O. Use of GeIS for Early Diagnosis of Alcohol Sensitivity. In Proceedings of the 9th International Joint Conference on Biomedical Engineering Systems and Technologies (BIOSTEC 2016), pp. 284–289 (2016)
14. Reyes Román, J.F., Pastor, O., Valverde, F., Roldán, D.: Including haplotypes treatment in a Genomic Information Systems Management. In Ibero-American Conference on Software Engineering, pp. 11–24 (2016)
15. Reyes Román, J.F., Pastor, O., Valverde, F., Roldán, D.: How to deal with Haplotype data?: An Extension to the Conceptual Schema of the Human Genome. Universitat Politècnica de València (2016). Available via RiuNet. `https://riunet.upv.es/handle/10251/82704`
16. Reyes Román, J.F., León Palacio, A., Pastor López, O.: Software Engineering and Genomics: The Two Sides of the Same Coin?. In Proceedings of the 12th International Conference on Evaluation of Novel Approaches to Software Engineering (ENASE 2017), pp. 301–307 (2017)

17. The 24th annual Nucleic Acids Research database issue. Available via Oxford Academic. `http://www.oxfordjournals.org/our_journals/nar/database/c/`
18. Reyes Román, J.F., Iñiguez-Jarrín, C., Pastor López, O.: GenesLove.Me: A Model-basedWeb-application for Direct-to-consumer Genetic Tests. In Proceedings of the 12th International Conference on Evaluation of Novel Approaches to Software Engineering (ENASE 2017), pp. 133–143 (2017)

Chapter 4
Strategic Reading & Conceptual Modeling*

Oscar Díaz

Abstract "Strategic reading" is a term coined to conceive reading as a process of constructing meaning by interacting with text. While reading, individuals use their prior knowledge along with clues from the text to construct meaning, and place the new knowledge within this frame. Strategic reading is then a pivotal ability for conceptual modelers, more so if domain knowledge needs to be acquired mainly from the literature as it is the case for research projects. But this might turn problematic. In Quora and other PhD forums, students moan about their frustrating reading and literature review experiences. Traditionally, students are encouraged to annotate while reading. Digital annotations are expected to be useful for supporting comprehension and interpretation. Our belief is that strategic reading (and hence, conceptual modeling) can be more effective if annotation is conducted in direct relationship to a main research activity: root-cause analysis (RCA). RCA can provide the questions whose answers should be sought in the literature. Unfortunately, this process is not supported by current tools. When reading papers, researchers might not be all aware of the issues being raised during RCA. And the other way around, when it comes to RCA, evidences found in the literature might not be promptly accessible. This paper reports on research to develop a technical solution to this problem: a plug-in for Google Chrome that provides seamless integration between a RCA platform (i.e. MindMeister) and a reading platforms (i.e. Mendeley). The aim: improving RCA awareness while reading so that annotations can be traced back to the RCA issues.

Key words: Strategic Reading, Root-Cause Analysis, Annotating, Mind Mapping

Oscar Díaz
University of the Basque Country (UPV/EHU)
ONEKIN - Facultad de Informática - San Sebastián, Spain, e-mail: oscar.diaz@ehu.eus

* This work is being jointly developed by Jeremías P. Contel from the University of the Basque Contry (Spain), and John Venable from Curtin Universtity, Perth (Australia).

© Springer International Publishing AG 2017

J. Cabot et al. (eds.), *Conceptual Modeling Perspectives*,
https://doi.org/10.1007/978-3-319-67271-7_4

4.1 Introduction

Some years ago, I was working on Active Databases. At this time, my interests were on formalizing database triggers and their execution model to help debugging large trigger sets. We resorted to the Event Calculus, and here, Antoni's work was most influential. Specifically, our work was strongly inspired by his paper "Validating conceptual specifications through model execution"[8]. This could have been a possible subject for this chapter. However, I would like to acknowledge here another side of Antoni's efforts: his dedication to teaching. I had the chance of chatting with Antoni in numerous occasions, and both teaching and students were a common subject. His book on Conceptual Modeling illustrates this concern . Here, I would like to report a recent work which was inspired by one of these chats with Antoni.

It was in Stockholm at CAiSE 2015. After the reception at the City Hall, and wandering along the nice canals that hug this magnificent building, Antoni observed how his students struggle with reading the literature, and particularly, the tendency of students to focus too early on the details of their PhD projects without keeping an eye on related research. This passing comment resonated one year later when I met Prof. John Venable. John has been working on Design Science Research (DSR) for more than fifteen years. DSR highlights the importance of root-cause analysis (RCA) not only at the start of the project but throughout, and how this analysis should be based on data either directly obtained or provided by the literature. The latter reminds me of Antoni's concerns about students focusing too early on their projects without keeping a wider radar at related literature. And then the bulb lighted up: if a pivotal skill for researchers is that of asking the right questions then, we can conjecture that RCA could be the means to find these questions. This paper reports on how this idea was developed[1]

DSR requires a profound understanding of the problem to be solved, the consequences to be alleviated, and the causes to be prevented. This in turn usually implies extracting evidence from the literature that warrants the project's RCA. Reading then, becomes the process of extracting evidence from the literature that sustains the project's RCA. We then conceive of RCA and reading as two inter-related processes which re-adjust and feed off each other: RCA progresses as new insights are obtained from the literature while the literature is scrutinized along the concerns that arise during RCA.

Unfortunately, this interplay lacks appropriate support in current reading tools (e.g. Acrobat Reader, Mendeley) or reference managers (e.g. Mendeley, NVivo, or End-Note). What is needed is a way to bridge the gap between conceptualizing tools – where ideas are shaped and framed – and reading tools – where ideas are sustained and opposed. We believe the challenge is not on creating brand new tools, but on coupling existing tools with minimal interference with existing practices. What is needed is for tools to keep their autonomy, but interact with a double aim:

1. to guide reading (where reading purposes are to be sought in RCA), and

[1] This is an excerpt from a paper presented at DESRIST 2017 [1].

2. to draw on and document supporting evidence for RCA issues (where evidences are obtained during reading).

These two flows are in overlapping motion: RCA concerns guide the reading while the reading comes up with new insights that confirm or refute the RCA issues. This work then addresses the following research question:

> *How can we provide seamless integration between RCA tools and reading tools to improve strategic reading for novice DSR researchers?*

To ground this research in concrete examples, we resort to MindMeister (as the RCA tool) and Mendeley (as the reference manager), being the challenge the one of coupling these tools for the sake of strategic reading (Section 4.3). DSR is defined as "research that invents a new purposeful artifact" [15]. In this case, the artifact is a Chrome plug-in, *DScaffolding*, which bridges the gap between MindMeister and Mendeley (Section 4.4). During reading in Mendeley, *DScaffolding* makes practitioners aware of the evidences being looked for. During RCA in MindMeister, *DScaffolding* makes researchers aware of the evidences that sustain/refute the causes/consequences elaborated during the RCA. *DScaffolding* is publicly available for download at the Chrome's Web Store. Next section elaborates on how Antoni's insight is not just a locale practice but a general concern.

4.2 Student Reading Experience

One of the most important skills for researchers to acquire is that of asking the right questions when accessing the literature. The answers you get much depend on the questions you ask. This skill is specially important for PhD students who struggle with an increasing number of papers[2] and stringent PhD deadlines. Based on Mendeley data, PhD students were the main readers of articles in 2008 for all articles [6]. This puts PhD students at the forefront of scientific literature consumption, even ahead of their supervisors! However, it is not rare to come across in Quora or other PhD forums with students moaning about their frustrating reading experiences[3]. Causes can be multifold: lack of time (increasing reading loads), lack of motivation (no prompt feedback from supervisors, reading considered an ancillary activity as opposed to programming where the real meat is) or lack of knowledge (no clear what to look for). If we focus on the latter, forums give some advices:

- "Before you start reading, have a clear idea of what information you are looking for in these papers. This by itself is about 60% of psyching yourself up for reading papers" [12]

[2] A UK study reported an average 39 scholarly readings per month, comprising 22 articles, seven books, and ten other publications \cite{Tenopir2012}, amounting to an estimated 448 hours per year spent reading (equivalent to 56 8-hour days).

[3] As a case in point, refer to `https://www.quora.com/Do-researchers-scientists-find-reading-scientific-papers-exciting` with 17 followers.

- "Make notes of how the research in the paper you're reading connects with your own" [11]
- "Reading a scientific paper should not be done in a linear way (from beginning to end); instead, it should be done strategically and with a critical mindset, questioning your understanding and the findings" [13].
- "As you read, look for the author's main points. Generate questions before, during, and after reading. Draw inferences based on your own experiences and knowledge. And to really improve understanding and recall, take notes as you read" [10].
- "If you want to make it a productive exercise, you need to have a clear idea of which kind of information you need to get in the first place, and then focus on that aspect." [9]
- "At the beginning, new academic readers find it slow because they have no frame of reference for what they are reading. But there are ways to use reading as a system of creating a mental library, and after a few years, it becomes easy to slot papers onto your mental shelves. Then you can quickly skim a paper to know its contribution." [9]

The underpinning assumption seems to be the existence of a "frame of reference". This frame serves to guide the reading, helping in having "a clear idea of which kind of information you need to get in the first place". Purposeful reading is then a distinctive feature of scientific reading as opposed to let's say, playful reading where the aim is to not to know the outcome but instead, to enjoy the poetic narrative and thrilling plot. To get the best of scientific reading, a frame of reference needs to be present.

This work addresses the case for Design Science Research (DSR), a popular approach in Information System [3]. The first question is then how will a "DSR's frame of reference" looks like. This paper's main assumption is that most of the readings during DS projects have (at least) five main foci, namely,

- finding evidence for the importance of the problem,
- ascertaining causal relationships in the problem,
- becoming acquainted with works addressing similar problems,
- becoming acquainted with work that can serve as a kernel theory or other inspiration,
- becoming acquainted with work relevant to research (method) design for the DSR project.

RCA relates to the first two of these. We can then state the problem as

PhD students not bearing "the RCA frame" in mind when reading

This might have a manyfold impact:

- Important facts might be overlooked when reading. This in turn, might involve a loss of opportunity for DSR projects. If not properly documented in the RCA, read-ing insights might be forgotten by the time they could impact the project's design, leading to overconfident problem analysis.

- Unfocused reading might result in boredom, lack of engagement and research effort discontinuity among PhD students,
- Literature references might not be traced back to their RCA rationales. This might cause poor reference recoverability when it comes to writing the paper, and hence, forcing re-reads

So far, we can only hypothesize those consequences. Some studies exist on the impact of reading comprehension [2, 4, 14] but this is for settings other that scientific reading. We are unaware of any study that looks into those symptoms for PhD students. That said, the frequent recurrence of this issue in the so-called grey literature (e.g. Q&A forums), provides substantial evidence of the existence of this problem. As a case in point, refer to this Quora entry [11] with 774 followers.

If the consequences are important enough to vindicate a deeper study then, next step is to delve into the causes: *why PhD students do not bear the "the RCA frame" in mind when reading*? We conjecture the following causes:

- No RCA frame available. Students might overlook the importance of RCA in DS projects. In some cases, RCA is hardly sketched, and only verbalized at the time of writing. This may already be too late to surface weak causal links or dubious if not, banal consequences that may hardly sustain the importance of the work. The importance of early RCA can not be stressed enough. This work underlines its role as a reading guideline.
- A RCA frame is available but not easy accessible. Students might have done their homework but they fail to have a presence of the RCA issues when reading. This might be due to reading and RCA being conducted through different tools. So far, the coupling falls on the shoulders of the students through the use of book-notes and copying & pasting between the tools.

This work tackles the second cause. It is not uncommon for researchers to struggle with switching back and forth between e.g. Endnote and Word, to add notes. These approaches tend to be highly manual and error prone, even if conducted through state-of-the-art reference managers. In the end, keeping track of readings represents a considerable burden for students. We then refine the research question as follows:

How can we bridge reading tools and RCA tools to ensure the presence of both RCA concerns when reading, and of reading evidences when conducting RCA?

Next sections elaborates on this question, illustrating the case for MindMeister (as the RCA tool) and Mendeley (as the reference manager). For details about how this example is factored out into general meta-requirements refer to [1].

4.3 Coupling MindMeister & Mendeley

Students should be able to freely move between RCA and reading. The interplay between these two activities should be reflected in a tighter integration so that reading is guided by issues risen during RCA, and RCA is further elaborated as ad-

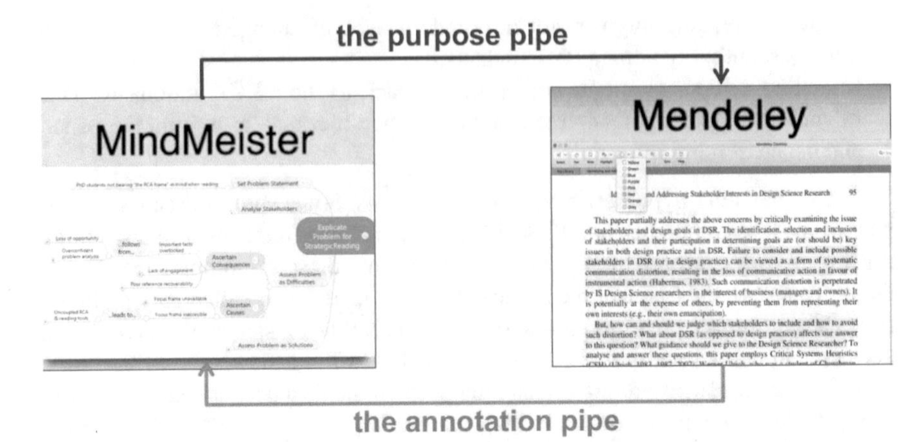

Fig. 4.1 Coupling through pipes: the purpose pipe & the annotation pipe.

ditional insights are gained from the literature. Figure 4.1 reflects this vision. The RCA-reading coupling is achieved through two pipes. During reading, practitioners should be aware of the evidences being looked for ("the purpose pipe"). During RCA, practitioners should be aware of the evidences that sustain/refute the causes/-consequences in the RCA ("the annotation pipe"). This section introduces how has this been achieved for MindMeister and Mendeley using ***DScaffolding***, a Chrome plug-in. This plug-in is available at the Chrome's Web Store:

`https://chrome.google.com/webstore/detail/hkgmnnjalpmapogadekngkgbbgdjlnne`

Videos are provided for:

- installation: `https://youtu.be/hl6pnJGbVXY`
- the Strategic Reading Process: `https://youtu.be/jHP1MiqjVBM`

Next, we provide an outline.

4.3.1 The RCA tool: MindMeister

MindMeister is a web-based collaborative mind mapping application, which allows its users to visualize their thoughts in terms of mind maps [18]. A mind map is a diagram used to visually organize information. This can be pre-set in terms of a map template, i.e. a set of labelled nodes which can be later expanded by the user by adding new child nodes. This provides a guide to gather information, especially interesting when this information is abundant and multi-sourced. This ductility together with the popularity mind maps enjoy, make mind mapping an interesting approach when it comes to explicating the problem i.e. "to formulate the initial problem precisely, justify its importance, investigate its underlying causes, provide evidences and acknowledge related work" [3].

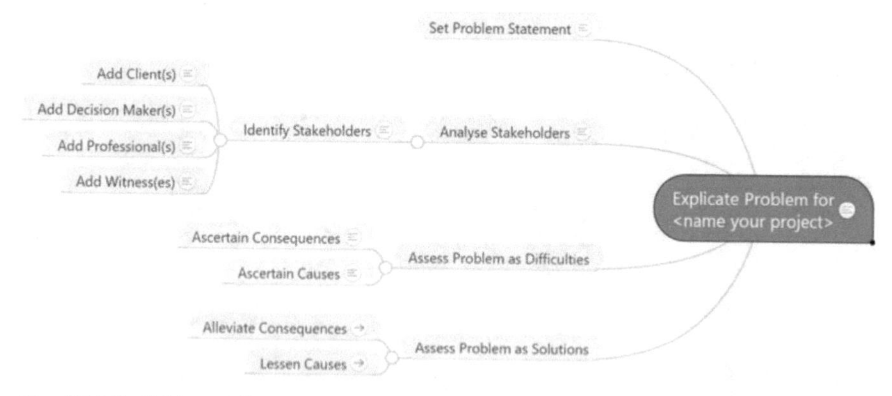

Fig. 4.2 MindMeister. The RCA template.

Figure 4.2 depicts the *ExplicateProblem* template at the onset. The template provides a head-start as for the information to be collected. Specifically, we resort to Coloured Cognitive Maps (CCM) [16]. The template supports the two types of CCM:

- the "Problem as Difficulties" node, which focuses on the problem, what is undesirable about it (i.e. consequences), and what causes the problem and allows it to persist, and,
- the "Problem as Solutions" node, which focuses on the solution of the problem, what benefits would accrue from solving the problem or what causes of the problem might be reduced or eliminated to solve the problem.

Details are outside the scope of this chapter. For further information refer to [16].

4.3.2 The reading tool: Mendeley

Mendeley is an Elsevier-owned desktop and a Web program helping to manage and share research papers [17]. Papers can be arranged into folders, and tagged for easy retrieval. Figure 4.3 shows the content of the *StrategicReading* folder, and particularly, the metadata for the selected paper. Mendeley includes a PDF viewer with sticky notes, text highlighting and full-screen reading. Quote annotation is achieved through highlighting where different colours are available.

4.3.3 The coupling

Broadly, coupling MindMeister and Mendeley involves three main challenges:

- the ability to indicate what issues risen during RCA in MindMeister need supporting literature evidence (hereafter referred to as "reading concerns"),

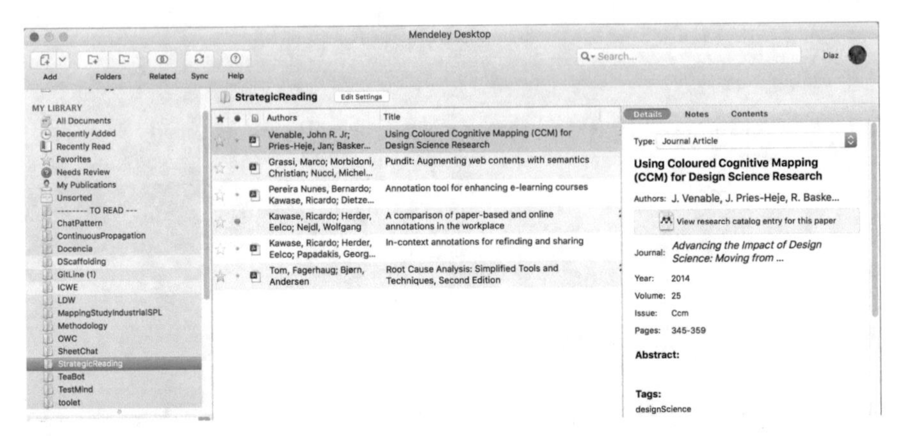

Fig. 4.3 Mendeley. Papers are organized along folders (e.g. *StrategicReading*).

- a way to keep the presence of reading concerns while reading in Mendeley,
- the ability to access quotes from Mendeley while ellaborating RCA in MindMeister, so that students can assess the extent causes/consequences are backed up by quotes.

Next section illustrates how is this fleshed out by *DScaffolding*.

4.4 DScaffolding at work

Broadly, three mains tasks interplay during RCA-based strategic reading, namely, "conducting RCA", "setting RCA issues" and "reading". The first two are conducted in MindMeister while reading takes place in Mendeley. This section illustrates these steps for the problem: *"PhD students not bearing the RCA frame in mind when reading"*, i.e. our very problem!

4.4.1 Conducting RCA

To provide a head-start, MindMeister is being extended with the "Explicate Problem" template (see Figure 4.2). Students need to add the corresponding children nodes. Figure 4.4 instantiates the RCA template for the problem *"PhD students not bearing the RCA frame in mind when reading"*. We stick to MindMeister gestures for node management, so no new interaction needs to be learnt.

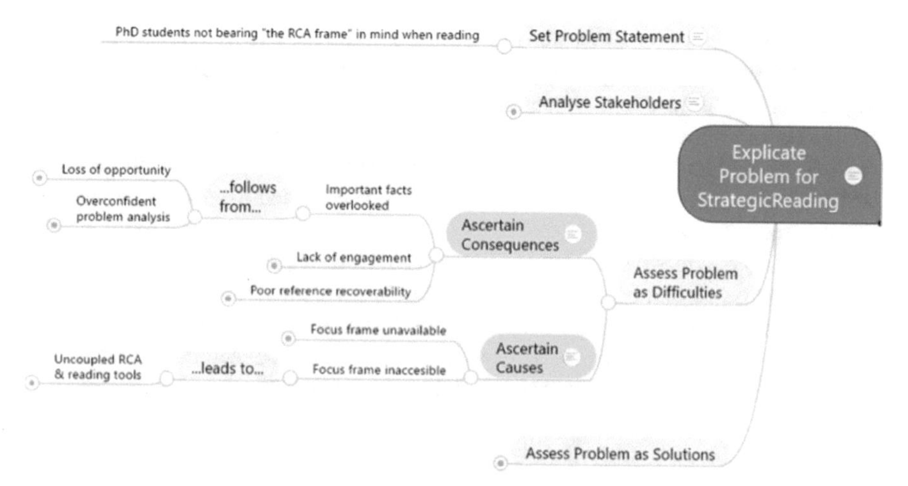

Fig. 4.4 MindMeister. *ExplicateProblem* template instantiated for the problem *"PhD students not bearing the RCA frame in mind when reading"*.

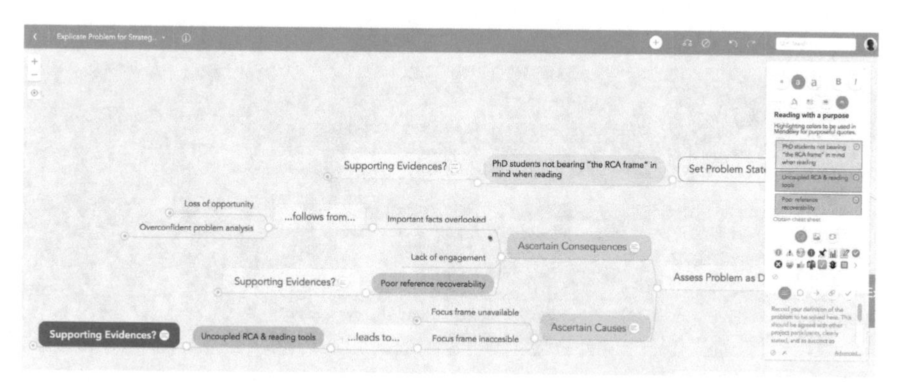

Fig. 4.5 MindMeister. Setting reading concerns by adding *"Supporting Evidences?"* nodes. The panel at the right keeps track of the current reading concerns.

4.4.2 Setting RCA issues

During RCA, students might wonder: what proof do I have that this cause exists?, what proof do I have that this cause actually contributed to the problem I am looking at?, are they merely asserting causation?, is anything else needed, along with this cause, for the stated effect to occur? is it self-sufficient? Frequently, the answers to these questions should be sought in the literature. However, questions might be too numerous to be addressed simultaneously. Hence, users might decide to focus on some aspects while postponing others. Current foci are termed "reading purposes" as far as they refer to causes/consequences than need to be backed up by the literature.

Back to *DScaffolding*, RCA nodes are turned into "reading purposes" by adding a child with the label ***"Supporting Evidences?"*** Introducing such node turns the father into a "reading purpose". This is indicated by decorating the father node with one of up to eight of the different background colours used in Mendeley (see later). Figure 4.5 illustrates the case for the running example. The user sets three reading concerns: the problem statement (in green), *"Poor reference recoverability"* (in pink), and *"Uncoupled RCA and reading tools"* (in purple). This means that students should look for quotes that somehow sustain these issues during their current readings. The current reading concerns can be obtained from the MindMeister panel. Reading concerns can be modified at any time as evidences are found or new insights advice to move the focus to another cause/consequence. To turn a node into a reading concern just extend it with the ***"Supporting Evidences?"*** child. To stop a node from being a reading concern, go to the MindMeister panel and delete it. The corresponding *"Supporting Evidences?"* node is not deleted but its associated cause/consequence is no longer track in Mendeley (see next).

4.4.3 Strategic Reading

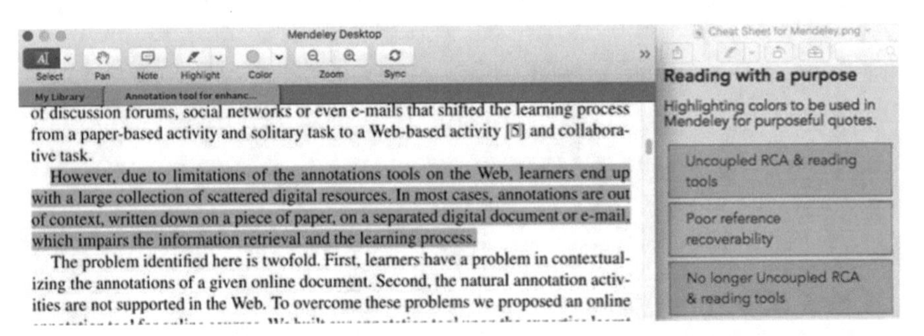

Fig. 4.6 Mendeley. Cheat-sheet used for RCA awareness (left side). The cheat-sheet is obtained as a screenshot through MindMeister panel.

Strategic reading implies an aim. Here, the aim is looking for evidences for the current reading concerns. Here, we resort to annotation to denote the existence of evidences. Digital annotations are expected to be useful for supporting comprehension and interpretation [5, 7]. Here, strategic reading is realized as annotation highlighting.

Mendeley provides eight different colours for annotation highlighting. Yellow is left for "structural" highlighting (i.e. attributing different levels of importance). The remaining seven are mapped to RCA-based reading concerns. Specifically, By using the very same colors in Mendeley and MindMeister, a mapping is set between Mendeley highlights and reading concerns in MindMeister. A cheat sheet about what these colours stand for can be obtained from MindMeister[4]. Researchers can

[4] A request is being posted to Mendeley to permit color legends to be configurable. This will permit *DScaffolding* to set legends based on RCA issues, avoiding to resort to the burdersome cheat-sheet.

then place this cheat-sheet by their Mendeley desktop application. Figure 4.6 provides an example. While reading a paper, a paragraph might well sustain one of the concerns risen during RCA: *"RCA & reading tool coupling"*. Since this issue is associated with the velvet color, this is the color used for highlighting. In this rudimentary way, students will keep a presence of what they are looking for.

4.4.4 Back to conducting RCA

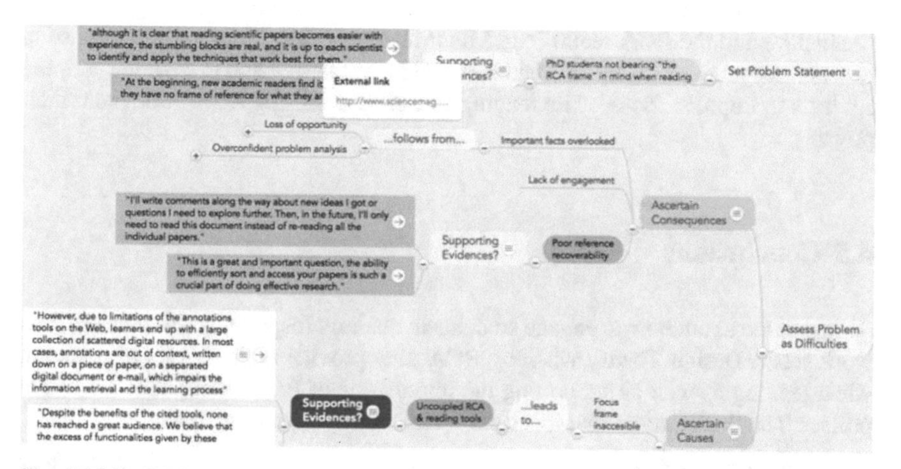

Fig. 4.7 MindMeister. Quotes are automatically brought at the RCA map and hung below their related issues.

At any time, students can go back to their RCA maps. *DScaffolding* tracks annotations made in papers held in Mendeley folders, to enrich the **namesake** MindMeister map. That is, students can keep different RCA maps and different Mendeley folders. The mapping between maps and folders is set based on sharing the same name.

On uploading a MindMeister map, *DScaffolding* checks out whether any new quote is being found since it was last sync with the user's Mendeley account. If so, *DScaffolding* automatically enriches the map with the new quotes. Specifically, quote nodes hang from the nodes to which they provide an evidence for. Figure 4.7 illustrates our sample map at a later stage where some new quotes have been found.

Node properties include: a label, an attached comment and a background colour. For nodes created automatically out of quotes, these properties behave as follows:

- the label holds the text being highlighted in the annotated resource,
- the comment keeps a link to the resource URL (if available). Researchers can click on the link icon to move straight to the manuscript in Mendeley, and in so doing, looking at the quote in context,

- the background colour reflects the nature of the source: "white" for annotations coming from journals and conferences, and "grey" if coming from the grey literature (not discussed here).

In addition, quotes inherit the reputation of their sources. Annotations coming for reputable sources add a "star" icon to their labels. So far, the reputation is set by users. For instance, Mendeley allows users to tick a "star" to mark sources as favourites. Although "favourite" is quite an elusive notion (no clear rationale for ticking this off), *DScaffolding* interprets the star as a sign of the source's reputation and soundness. This reputation travels together with the reference.

To conclude, this work considers reading and RCA as two inter-related processes. If this is so, practitioners should be helped in moving between the reading realm (e.g. Mendeley) and the RCA realm (e.g. MindMeister). *DScaffolding* aims at assisting in seamlessly moving between Mendeley and MindMeister, and in so doing, helping students to improve focus while reading as well as fostering RCA throughout their projects.

4.5 Conclusions

Antoni cared about how to engage students in reading. Inspired by this concern, this work sets a Design Theory whereby RCA may provide main drivers of attention when reading as well as supporting the importance of RCA throughout the whole project. The theory states that this can be achieved by sustaining both

- "RCA awareness" while reading (i.e. the purpose pipe that channels RCA issues to reading platforms), and
- "literature awareness" while conducting RCA (i.e. the annotation pipe that channels literature quotes towards RCA platforms).

We built *DScaffolding* to assess the extent to which this theory holds. First evaluations indicate that not only reading but also RCA might benefit from a tight coupling between these two processes (refer to [1] for further insights). We do hope Antoni like the approach!

References

1. Díaz, O., Contell, J.P., Venable, J.R.: Strategic reading in design science: Let root-cause analysis guide your readings. In: Designing the Digital Transformation - 12th International Conference, DESRIST 2017, Karlsruhe, Germany, May 30 - June 1, 2017, Proceedings. pp. 231–246 (2017), `https://doi.org/10.1007/978-3-319-59144-5_14`
2. Israel, S.E., Duffy, G.G.: Handbook of research on reading comprehension. Routledge (2014)
3. Johannesson, P., Perjons, E.: An introduction to design science. Springer (2014)
4. Margolin, S.J., Driscoll, C., Toland, M.J., Kegler, J.L.: E-readers, computer screens, or paper: Does reading comprehension change across media platforms? Applied Cognitive Psychology 27(4), 512–519 (2013)

5. Marshall, C.C.: Toward an ecology of hypertext annotation. In: Proceedings of the ninth ACM conference on Hypertext and hypermedia: links, objects, time and space—structure in hypermedia systems: links, objects, time and space—structure in hypermedia systems. pp. 40–49. ACM (1998)
6. Mohammadi, E., Thelwall, M., Haustein, S., LariviÃÍre, V.: Who reads research articles? an altmetrics analysis of mendeley user categories. Journal of the Association for Information Science and Technology 66(9), 1832–1846 (2015), http://dx.doi.org/10.1002/asi.23286
7. O'hara, K., Sellen, A.: A comparison of reading paper and on-line documents. In: Proceedings of the ACM SIGCHI Conference on Human factors in computing systems. pp. 335–342. ACM (1997)
8. Olivé, A., Sancho, M.R.: Validating conceptual specifications through model execution. Information Systems 21(2), 167–186 (1996)
9. Pain, E.: How to (seriously) read a scientific paper, http://www.sciencemag.org/careers/2016/03/how-seriously-read-scientific-paper. Accessed 6 Feb 2017
10. Purugganan, M., Hewitt, J.: How to read a scientific article, http://www.owlnet.rice.edu/ cainproj/courses/HowToReadSciArticle.pdf. Accessed 6 Feb 2017
11. Quora: How do you keep your notes while reading scientific papers?, https://www.quora.com/PhD-students-How-do-you-keep-your-notes-while-reading-scientific-papers. Accessed 6 Feb 2017
12. Quora: I am a robotics phd student and i have a hard time reading research papers. i am very slow at it and find the task kind of boring. is there any way i can make paper reading fun and become faster at it?, https://www.quora.com/Iam-a-robotics-PhD-student-and-I-have-a-hard-time-reading-research-papers-Iam-very-slow-at-it-and-find-the-task-kind-of-boring-Is-there-any-way-I-can-makepaper-reading-fun-and-become-faster-at-it. Accessed 6 Feb 2017
13. Rodriguez, N.: Infographic: How to read a scientific paper, https://www.elsevier.com/connect/infographic-how-to-read-a-scientific-paper. Accessed 6 Feb 2017
14. Stern, P., Shalev, L.: The role of sustained attention and display medium in reading comprehension among adolescents with adhd and without it. Research in developmental disabilities 34(1), 431–439 (2013)
15. Venable, J., Baskerville, R.: Eating our own cooking: Toward a more rigorous design science of research methods. Electronic Journal of Business Research Methods 10(2), 141 – 153 (2012), http://search.ebscohost.com/login.aspx?direct=true{&}db=bsx{&}AN=87404098{&}lang=es{&}site=eds-live
16. Venable, J.R.: Using coloured cognitive mapping (ccm) for design science research. In: International Conference on Design Science Research in Information Systems. pp. 345–359. Springer (2014)
17. Wikipedia: Mendeley, https://en.wikipedia.org/wiki/Mendeley. Accessed 6 Feb 2017
18. Wikipedia: Mindmeister, https://en.wikipedia.org/wiki/MindMeister. Accessed 6 Feb 2017

Chapter 5
Conceptual Modeling for Indicator Selection

Alejandro Maté, Juan Trujillo and John Mylopoulos

Abstract Indicator-based management enables decision makers to make decisions based on quantitative measures. This approach has been successfully applied in multiple domains beyond traditional business-related ones, including Education, Healthcare, and Smart Cities, among others. Yet, it remains a difficult and error-prone task to find suitable Key Performance Indicators (KPIs) that are aligned with business goals. Indeed, there is a general lack of adequate conceptualizations and formal models of indicators, that captures the subtle yet important differences between performance and result indicators. Moreover, there is a lack of approaches interleaving business modeling techniques with data analysis in an iterative process. In order to tackle these deficiencies, we propose a methodology for eliciting, selecting and assessing explicitly KPIs and Key Result Indicators (KRIs). Our methodology is comprised of (i) a novel modeling language that exploits the essential elements of indicators, covering KPIs, KRIs and measures, ii) a data mining-based analysis technique for providing domain experts with data-driven information about the elements in their model and their relationships, thereby enabling them to validate the KPIs selected, and iii) an iterative process that guides the discovery and definition of indicators. Finally, we apply our approach to a water management case study to show its benefits.

Key words: Conceptual Modeling, Strategic goals, KPIs, KRIs, Analysis

---

Alejandro Maté
Lucentia Research Group, Department of Software and Computing Systems, University of Alicante, Spain, e-mail: `amate@dlsi.ua.es`

Juan Trujillo
Lucentia Research Group, Department of Software and Computing Systems, University of Alicante, Spain, e-mail: `jtrujillo@dlsi.ua.es`

John Mylopoulos
Department of Computer Science, University of Trento, Italy, e-mail: `jm@cs.toronto.edu`

© Springer International Publishing AG 2017
J. Cabot et al. (eds.), *Conceptual Modeling Perspectives*,
https://doi.org/10.1007/978-3-319-67271-7_5

5.1 Introduction

Key Performance Indicators (KPIs) constitute a popular and useful tool for monitoring the performance of an enterprise [19]. KPIs translate ambiguous enterprise goals, such as "Increase revenue", into measurable ones with concrete thresholds, such as "Revenue increased by 5%", which can be objectively assessed in order to obtain a clear picture of the current status of an enterprise. Due to their popularity and usefulness, there have been efforts to apply them to multiple other areas besides enterprises, including Education [12], Healthcare [2], or Smart Cities [11]. However, whenever KPIs are defined to monitor objectives and strategic goals in any area the same question arises "is this an adequate KPI?" Answering this question is far from trivial.

First, the selection of a wrong KPI can have a severely detrimental effect for an organization. A wrong KPI wastes resources in the wrong place and those responsible for its improvement develop a resilience over time to change the KPI they are focusing on [23]. Second, even though domain experts do know their business, once we start moving from measures related to results (e.g. number of products sold) to measures related to actual performance it is no longer clear which are the KPIs that the enterprise should focus on, their priorities and even more, their interrelationships and influences [1]. This is aggravated by the fact that value thresholds that should be established for each KPI are also unknown. Third, although organizations within the same industry sector typically share a common set of candidate KPIs [5], each of them actually operates in a slightly different fashion and different priorities, leading to subtle yet significant differences in the KPIs they use.

With these problems in mind, we argue that the difficulty of selecting adequate KPIs has been accentuated by several factors. First, there is a common error in strategic modeling literature, all indicators are treated as KPIs disregarding whether they refer to actual performance (KPIs) or measured results (Key Result Indicators - KRIs) [13, 14, 7, 25, 16]. The distinction between the concepts of KPI and KRI [19] is crucial to enable the process of finding an adequate KPIs to focus on for an enterprise objective, and will be further discussed in the related work and in the description of our modeling language. Second, while management literature considers the distinction between KPIs and KRIs, it does not provide formal models such as ones proposed within strategic modeling literature, that support formal analysis and exploration [7]. As a consequence, domain experts cannot understand their choices and implications when discovering, selecting, and discarding potential KPIs. Third, none of the previous approaches considers data analysis as an important piece of the puzzle, and the few analytic approaches that have been proposed so far [20, 15] do not provide a modeling language that allows domain experts to participate with their knowledge, iteratively building a desired KPI model. Yet here is the key: eliciting the correct KPIs requires data analysis in order to propose and analyze the suitability of candidate indicators. Moreover, the participation of domain experts is fundamental in order to both prune the search space and validate the resulting alignment between indicator maps and business strategy.

Therefore, in this paper we present a methodology for eliciting, assessing, and selecting KPIs and KRIs. The main objective of our methodology, is to establish a baseline for improving indicator elicitation and selection, and it is comprised of the following contributions:

1. A modeling language that extends the expressivity of traditional models by including KPIs, KRIs, and measures as first class citizens.
2. A data mining approach to analyze the relationship between indicators by exploiting the conceptual model created by the domain experts.
3. A three step iterative process that covers the definition of the indicator map, as well as its refinement and assessment through data analysis, thereby connecting objectives to data through data mining.

The rest of the paper is structured as follows. Section 5.2 describes related work, covering both management as well as strategic modeling literature. Section 5.3 presents the proposed methodology and the modeling language, including details of the analysis process for mining indicator relationships. Section 5.4 describes a case study based on water management for the validation of the proposal. Section 5.5 discusses the limitations of the proposed methodology, and lists the future lines of research related to each of them, which are further discussed in Section 5.6 where conclusions and directions for future work are presented.

5.2 Related Work

There is a broad literature on performance indicators due to their attractiveness as a monitoring tool. The two bodies of knowledge that have traditionally focused most on KPIs are strategic modeling and management. Due to the large amount of works on each area, we summarize the main points related to performance indicators within each discipline:

On the one hand, conceptual modeling [18, 17, 17], and more specifically strategic modeling [13, 14, 7] aims to enable formal analysis for businesses in order to aid in making better, more informed strategic decisions. Strategic modeling proposals are very useful for domain experts to explore and analyze their business since they provide a unified view of the most important strategic elements. The attractiveness of KPIs for strategic modeling comes from their capability to connect business objectives to data. This way, KPIs translate otherwise subjective or ambiguous goals into objective satisfaction values and provide more detailed information about the nature of the relationships between objectives than simple contributions (such as in [7]). Therefore, KPIs help strategic modeling proposals to analyze the suitability of a business strategy within a given context, and propagating satisfaction values in order to find potential problems and lacking areas [25, 14]. Most of the work in strategic modeling related to KPIs has been towards their definition, conceptualization, and usage in analysis in different languages, including i* [21], the Business Intelligence

Model [13, 7, 25], or the Business Motivation Model [16][1]. Within these works, KPIs are treated as a quantification, with no distinction between performance and result indicators. That is because strategic modeling provides the tools for defining and representing indicators, but their selection rests entirely on the shoulders of the domain expert or the business strategy modeler.

On the other hand, management literature [4, 24, 19, 10] aims to improve business management by providing tools to identify problems within organizations and guide their efforts towards successful business operations. The attractiveness of KPIs for management comes from their ability to both represent areas of focus for the organization and to detect problems within the business. They are a simple yet powerful tool that can be easily implemented into Scorecards and Dashboards [8]. The lack of formal models available in this area, and their focus on providing concrete solutions for business problems, that can be directly implemented, has led management literature to put more importance on the selection and nature of indicators. As such, management literature includes numerous research works on the use of predefined set of indicators and their effectiveness in different organizations [4, 24], as well as the differentiation between *lag* (an indicator which provides information when the objective has already been fulfilled or failed) versus *lead* (an indicator which provides information before the objective has been fulfilled and is not always accurate) indicators [10]. More recently this differentiation has moved towards the concepts of Performance Indicator and Result Indicator [19]. The main drawback is that this knowledge has not been mapped into formal models which can be used for analysis. Not even traditional management tool models such as Scorecards, dashboards, or Strategy Maps [9], which served as base for strategic modeling proposals such as [7], have been updated to carry implicitly this knowledge, which is only carried (if) by managers and domain experts themselves.

Aside from these disciplines it is worth mentioning the existence of data analysis approaches [20, 15]. These approaches aim to partially cover the knowledge gap between the domain expert and the reality by taking indicator formulae as input and analyzing the data behavior in order to elicit potentially unknown relationships and effects between indicators. Most of these approaches are strongly data driven, with a clear input and output to a process where domain experts have limited or no interaction at all depending on the approach. They are effective but not flexible, which limits their application when there is not enough knowledge for running them (e.g. we are in the initial stages where we have measures but we do not have indicators defined) or there are additional factors which should be taken into account (e.g. the context is affecting our results, such as when there is a recession; we have knowledge about it, but there is no data available).

As we can see, there has been a lot of interest from both research and industry on the topic of performance indicators. However, the lack of adequate tools combined with the extreme nature of current solutions, ranging from relying entirely on domain experts to not even considering them, has maintained indicator selection as one of the key problems in strategic management. Even more, the lack of connec-

[1] Note that while BMM does provide a model it does not include a graphical representation or a formal semantics.

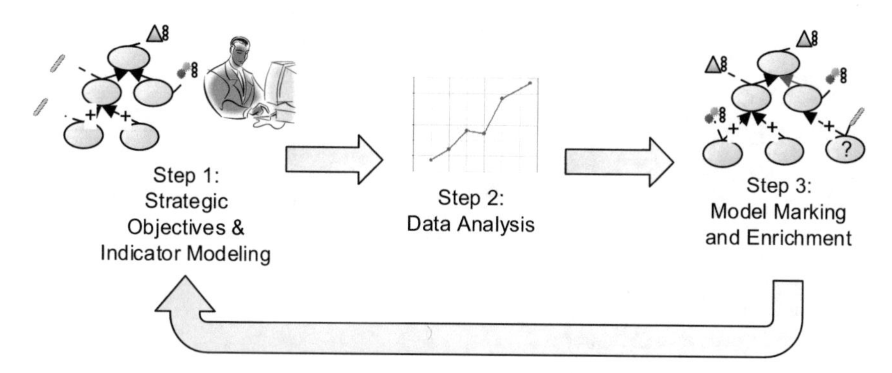

Fig. 5.1 3-step iterative process for Result and Performance Indicator elicitation and selection

tion between the KPIs and KRIs specification and modeling, and the data analysis to populate them, leads experts to question whether effort is being focused in the right direction until the final results have been achieved. By then, answering the question whether the set of performance indicators used was adequate or not is no longer relevant, as results cannot be changed.

5.3 A Methodology for Eliciting and Selecting Business Indicators

Selecting adequate indicators for business objectives requires exploring the business strategy together with domain experts, while providing data-driven insights whenever confirmation or additional information is required. Therefore, the ideal solution is an iterative methodology that alternates conceptual modeling with data analysis for enriching the strategic model obtained. Our proposal for this methodology is depicted in Figure 5.1, where our 3-step iterative process is shown.

In the first step, domain experts construct a strategic model in collaboration with the analyst. The aim of this initial model is twofold: i) establishing the main business objectives pursued, which can be clearly related to a set of result indicators or performance indicators, and ii) exploring other existing indicators, measures and objectives. Next, in the second step, the set of indicators and measures is passed as input for the data analysis. The goals of this analysis are to analyze potential or hidden relationships between indicators and to establish performance levels for measures, which do not yet have any thresholds assigned. Finally, in the third step, the findings from the data analysis are mapped back into the strategic model, and a new cycle starts until a stable strategic model is obtained (i.e. the model does not suffer a variation with respect to the previous iteration) or domain experts are satisfied with the current model.

In the following, we describe in more detail each step and its components.

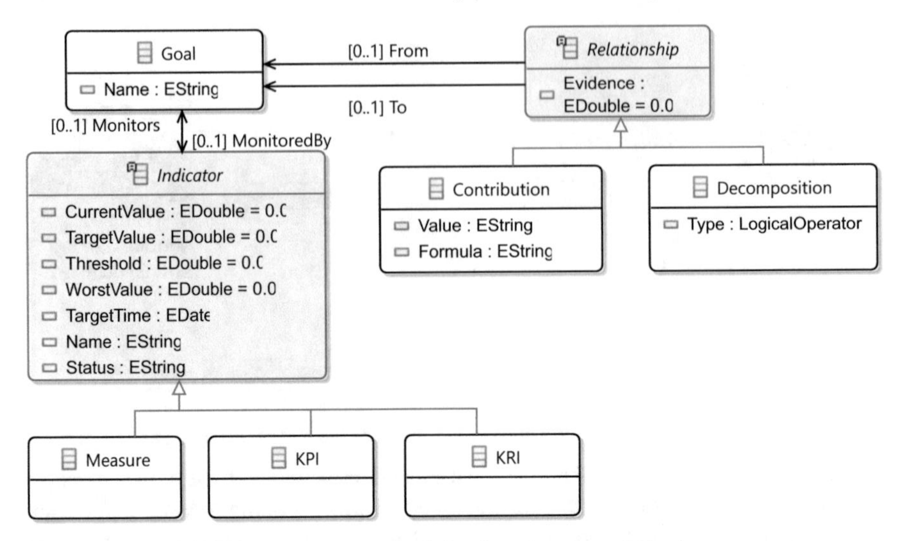

Fig. 5.2 Metamodel with the concepts and relationships for our modeling language

5.3.1 Business Modeling and Indicator Metamodel

Business strategy modeling can be a very complex task. Existing modeling languages [21, 7, 16] include a large set of concepts that are required for analyzing different aspects of the business strategy, such as dependencies across organizations, external influences, or the business mission and vision. However, these are unnecessary for the task at hand and, additionally, do not provide the expressiveness required for the indicator analysis. In order to keep the analysis simple, we propose a reduced metamodel that includes only the the concepts required for applying our methodology, and can be integrated as an extension for any of the existing modeling languages. Our metamodel is shown in Figure 5.2.

In this Figure we can see the following concepts:

1. **Goals** are desired state of affairs. They represent business objectives, such as "Increase sales" and are the basic blocks of the strategic model with no distinction of whether they are strategic, operational or tactical. They are included in pretty much every strategic modeling language [21, 7, 16].
2. **Relationships** allow domain experts and analysts to express the expected relationships between goals and, therefore, between their associated indicators. They can be either contributions (with positive or negative effect) or decomposition. For example, "Increase revenue" can be decomposed into "Increase profit" and "Decrease costs". The expressivity of relationships varies in full fledged strategic modeling languages. In our language, relationships have the evidence property, which captures the results from the analysis step showing whether the relationship is supported by the data or not.
3. **Indicators** measure the satisfaction of goals. They translate business objectives into measures that can be monitored, such as "Increment in sales by 5%". In order to make indicators from our model compatible with existing proposals [21, 7] all

indicators can have a formula, a current value, a target value, a threshold, a worst value, and a target time. Furthermore they also have a status, which provides information on the status of the indicator with respect to the data available. They are further specialized into three types required for our methodology, which are not found in current modeling languages:

a. **Measures** are the simplest form of indicators. They represent known formulas for measuring business activities with no known targets or thresholds. Given that measures only provide a current value and do not include any criteria, they cannot be used to make any statements with regards to goal satisfaction. For example, given the "Total sales" measure we cannot argue whether the associated objective has been fulfilled or not. Their utility comes from their exploration as potential KPI and KRI candidates.
b. **Key Result Indicators** are indicators which directly correlate with the satisfaction of a goal. For example, "Increment in sales by 5 %" is a KRI, since it provides information about the results of the business objective "Increase sales". Every KRI must have clear defined thresholds and values, and its usefulness comes from the capability to determine the exact status of the associated business objective. However, compared to KPIs, i) KRIs always provide information at the same point in time when the associated objective should be fulfilled, thus they can only be used for making decisions via forecasting, and ii) organizations cannot effect KRIs directly, because they always represent results of the business activity. Following our examples, an organization cannot increase sales directly, they have to effect them through promotions, opening new channels, etc.
c. **Key Performance Indicators** are indicators that measure the performance of key activities and initiatives that affect the objectives measured by KRIs. As KRIs, KPIs have clear defined thresholds, but they may or may not have a target time since they can monitor continuous tasks. For example, "Average response time under 3 days" is a continuous task. KPIs are important for the company due to the ability to effect them directly and, in turn, their associated KRIs. Therefore, if KRIs change, it is likely the set of KPIs to monitor also changes. Finally, compared to KRIs, KPIs provide information ahead of time about the satisfaction of KRIs. Intuitively, if we perform well, we will obtain good results. However, this information is not accurate, as KPIs only measure a subset of the factors influencing a KRI.

With this metamodel, we can construct strategic models focused on indicators in collaboration with domain experts. The process for building the initial strategic model is approached in a top-bottom fashion as follows. First, the main objectives pursued by the organization are listed as top level goals. For each of these top level goals assign a candidate KRI (if known) or a measure that quantifies it. Next, using the information provided by the main objectives established and the KRIs and measures, we start refining the goals. Goals that are very coarse grained can be decomposed into simpler goals. For example, "Increase revenue" can be further decomposed into "Increase profit" and "Decrease costs". It is important to note that goals obtained by decomposition will still share the same type of indicator associated, as we will not move from results to activities through decomposition. Once we have simpler goals, we can ask how/what are we doing (or plan to do) in order to achieve them, and what effect these actions have any of the current goals in our strategic model. The lower level goals obtained will be candidates to be monitored through KPIs. If any candidate KPIs or measures are known (for example extracted from management predefined lists), they are assigned to these goals. As previously, if these goals are too coarse grained for assigning them KPIs, they can be further decomposed into simple goals. Finally, any candidate KRI, KPI, or measure not related to any goal is listed and included into the model with no relationship to the rest of elements.

After the strategic modeling step, we will have obtained a candidate strategic model, that will have varying degrees of completion depending on the knowledge available about the business and its measurement. The indicators in the model will then be passed as input to the second step in our process, the data analysis, in order to test their suitability according to existing data.

5.3.2 Analysis

Indicators included in the strategic model represent specific formulas that allow us to obtain data about their behavior over time. However, quality data is often scarce, and can be present in different formats. Therefore, we have defined a multi-step analysis process that accounts for several challenges that can be found during data analysis. An overview of the process can be seen in Figure 5.3. Due to space constrains we only mention briefly the key aspects of the analysis.

During the preprocessing step we determine the availability and characteristics of the data. We also discard indicators that are entirely flat or with largely missing values (see [6] for a deeper discussion on sample sizes) through quick data profiling, since they cannot be used for the analysis. Furthermore, we determine whether we

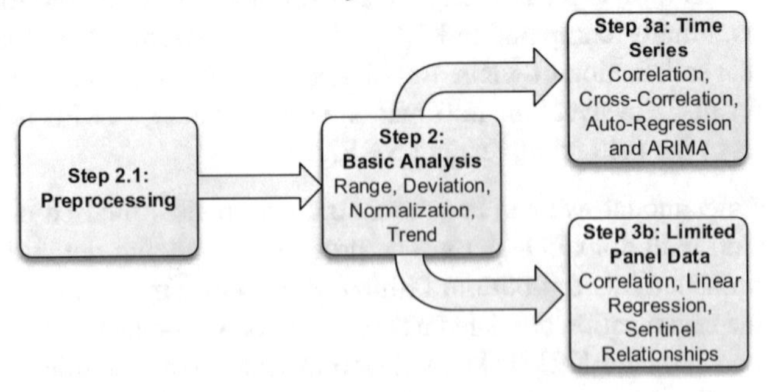

Fig. 5.3 Overview of the analysis process

are working with pure time series or panel data[2]. Afterwards, during the basic analysis step, we analyze each measure to identify measures large deviations. This is specially relevant if working with panel data, since discrepancies between instances will require either separate analysis or normalization in order to make their behavior comparable. Finally, in the statistical analysis step we proceed as follows:

If we have enough time data, then we start our time series by analyzing the correlation between indicators, in order to obtain candidate relationships within the data. These relationships are further analyzed though cross-correlation to estimate the time difference between the behavior of one variable and its effect on the other. Finally, we fit an ARIMA [3] model to estimate the confidence and direction of the relationship identified.

If there is not enough time data and instead we rely on large number of instances with few time points, then we require simpler models. As previously, we start by analyzing the correlation between indicators. Then, we generate multiple linear regressions (one per region) in order to compare the behavior of indicators across regions and confirm the existence and direction of the relationship. Finally, we estimate the confidence of the relationship using simple sentinel-like rules [15]. These rules are calculated by using the difference in values across time for each indicator and comparing if a positive (negative) value for the predicting indicator results in a positive (negative) value for the affected indicator. Occurrences of the same type (direct/inverse relationship) are added, while opposites subtract from each other.

The information obtained during the analysis is used to update the model in order to feed the next iteration of the process.

5.3.3 Model Update

Updating the model allows users and analysts to (i) compare how their expectations match the data, and (ii) gain new insights from newly discovered relationships, leading to the definition of new goals or the assignment of indicators to existing objectives. According to the results of the analysis, the model is updated as follows.

First, relationships which for which there is data available but have not been supported by the data are marked in red. Relationships supported are updated with the correlation and confidence coefficients. New contribution relationships are added between goals whose indicator have a correlation with a confidence rate higher than the threshold defined during model update. If indicators do not currently have any associated goal, a new goal is created with "?" as its description. Second, measures unrelated, related by a decomposition relationship to another measure or result indicator, or that present a cross-correlation with 0 time difference and a defined trend, are transformed into KRIs. Measures related by contribution relationships to another indicator with a time difference less than 0 or no trend are transformed into KPIs.

[2] Bi-dimensional data, most often referring to time and geographical or product dimensions, but not necessarily restricted to. We will use regions as an example.

For these new indicators, if the indicator presents a trend (e.g. sales), then the target value is tentatively set to its value in the last period read (e.g. last year) plus the average of the trend. The threshold for failure will be set to its value in the last period minus the standard deviation, and the worst value mark to its last period minus twice the standard deviation. If the indicator does not present a trend then the target value is tentatively set to its value in the last period read, while the threshold and worst values are calculated as before.

With this information, the domain experts and the analysts can begin the next iteration of the process, by defining composite measures and re-designing the strategic model using the newly obtained insights.

5.4 Case Study: Performance Indicators for Water Supply Management

Water supply management companies focus on ensuring water supply to multiple zones. It is a complex activity that involves multiple elements and processes. On the one hand, water provided requires an adequate quality for its target, whether urban zones or farms, and cuts in service must be kept to a minimum. On the other hand, the water supply network incurs into loses, and must be renovated once critical points are reached. However, finding the specific parts of the network that require renovation is a challenging task, and thus entire blocks of the network have to be renovated, which is costly. In order to aid in this task, a number of measures are gathered by the water supply management company in our study. Unfortunately, none of these measures has associated any criteria to make decisions regarding the water supply network. Therefore, in the following we apply our methodology in order to help the company explore their objectives and metrics and improve both their performance monitoring as well as decision making. The application of our methodology has been done using Pentaho Data Integration for automating data transformation and RStudio for data analysis scripts respectively[3].

We started with a simple indicator model depicting the high level goals pursued and including the whole list of measures (cropped due to space constraints, and mostly anonymized due to privacy reasons). The highest level goal is to provide an efficient water supply, which does not have any known measure associated. In order to track this high level objective, it is further decomposed into minimizing water lost and improve network efficiency. In order to minimize water lost, intuitively the company wishes to minimize breakdowns and leaks, which are avoided by maintaining the supply network and renovating it when needed. However, renovating the supply network involves a costly process, and thus harms the reduction of maintenance costs. With regards to improving network efficiency, Measure 9 is proposed, which is related to the population density and cannot be directly effected

[3] Pentaho Data Integration and R-Studio are freely available here: `http://community.pentaho.com/projects/data-integration/` and here: `https://www.rstudio.com/`

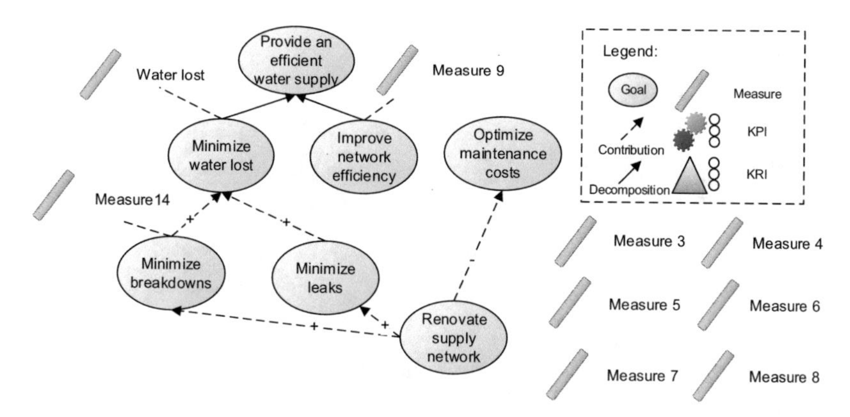

Fig. 5.4 Subset of the initial model for our case study

by the company. Therefore, no further goals are related to this objective, which acts merely as a monitoring tool.

For the first iteration of the analysis we start with 21 measures, which contain yearly readings for the period of 2008 to 2014 (6 data points) for 574 instances of the data. We start the preprocessing by extending the set of measures, calculating water lost (not directly available), from water supplied and water registered. Furthermore, due to the presence of missing values across different measures, we remove Measure 15, which presents largest number of missing values (382) and limits statistical methods that do not support missing values.

After the preprocessing, we perform the basic analysis. The deviation between zones shows large discrepancies in multiple measures, e.g. zones ranging in the thousands of m^3 of water supplied per year while others in range of millions. Since we do not have enough data points for analyzing separate time series, we normalize the values within regions. Afterwards, we analyze the correlations between measures by removing any missing values in pairwise observations. The correlation analysis shows a total of 12 correlations stronger than our 0.5 threshold, which are further analyzed using linear regression to determine the predicting power of each factor.

The statistical analysis using linear regression does not show significant discrepancies in the behavior across zones for the relationships identified and confirms the relationships between variables except in 2 cases. Finally, we estimate the confidence of each relationship using sentinel rules across all the available zones. With these results, we update our initial model, leading to the indicator model shown in Figure 5.5, where N depicts the indicator has been normalized during the analysis.

As we can see, our analysis has identified a number of potential relationships between result indicators (trend and lag 0 relationships), generating new potential goals that may be hidden and require exploration. Conversely, an initially expected relationship between Measure 14 and water lost is not supported by the data. This indicates that we need to review either the way we are monitoring our goal. i.e. how are we measuring breakdowns, or review the suitability of the relationship, i.e. breakdowns not cause severe water loses?. During the first step of the next iteration

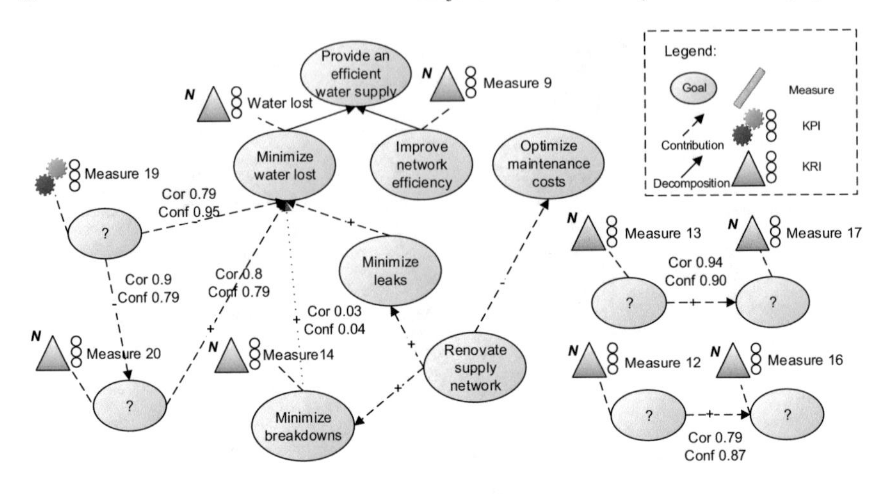

Fig. 5.5 Subset of the indicator model updated with data analysis results

we identified three relationships (Measures 12-16, 13-17, 20-water lost) as not interesting, since the measures involved calculated in a similar fashion, while another three relationships (4-5,7-11,19-20) were marked as of special interest.

5.5 Discussion and Limitations

The methodology presented tackles several problems and challenges that have not been addressed yet in the literature for aiding in the elicitation and selection of business indicators (KPIs and KRIs) for business objectives. As shown in the case study, the combination of strategic models together with data analysis contributes greatly to progress in this search. However, it is important to highlight a series of current limitations of the approach in order to avoid errors in its interpretation and application. First of all, our methodology pinpoints best strong pairwise relationships between measures and indicators. When multiple factors are required to jointly affect a target indicator it is more difficult to identify and estimate the effects of each individual factor. Thus, our methodology relies on the domain experts to take notice of these weak relationships during an iteration and create composite indicators that take into account this interaction for the next iteration. Second, our methodology assumes the existence of data in order to test hypotheses posed by the strategic model. If a company is relatively new or small and has little data available, then it is best to rely solely on strategic analysis techniques [7], since data driven analysis will not be feasible.

5.6 Conclusions and Future Work

We have presented a methodology for the elicitation, assessment and selection of KPIs and KRIs. Our methodology tackles the problem of eliciting and selecting adequate KPIs and KRIs for objectives within a strategic model. To the best of our knowledge, it is the first proposal that explicitly includes the distinction between KPIs, KRIs, and measures within its modeling language and exploits this information in order to drive the analysis. Thanks to this information, our methodology enables domain experts to explore their candidate indicators, as well as their data, helping them to iteratively build an indicator map that reflects their priorities and is aligned with the results pursued. Additionally, the components involved in our methodology, the conceptual model, the process, and the analysis techniques, can be applied in isolation or easily integrated within existing strategic modeling frameworks, such as BIM [7] or BMM [16] to improve their capabilities. Furthermore, we have applied our methodology to a real case study based on the water management sector, where we needed to elicit and select indicators for improving water efficiency. Finally, we have discussed our approach and its current limitations. Our main goal is to establish a baseline methodology for indicator selection, which tackles the existing problems in indicator selection and can be further improved by future works.

In the short term, we plan to focus on improving the data analysis with richer, and more sophisticated algorithms, that can detect more complex relationships between indicators. This will likely contribute to create more detailed models and possibly extend the modeling language, where these complex relationships can be reflected explicitly in order to provide additional insights and ideas for domain experts.

References

1. Angoss: Key Performance Indicators, Six Sigma and Data Mining. White Paper. `http://www.angoss.com/white-papers/key-performance-indicators-six-sigma-data-mining/` (2011)
2. Barone, D., Topaloglou, T., Mylopoulos, J.: Business intelligence modeling in action: a hospital case study. In: Advanced Information Systems Engineering. pp. 502–517. Springer (2012)
3. Box, G.E., Jenkins, G.M., Reinsel, G.C., Ljung, G.M.: Time series analysis: forecasting and control. John Wiley & Sons (2015)
4. Chae, B.: Developing key performance indicators for supply chain: an industry perspective. Supply Chain Management: An International Journal 14(6), 422–428 (2009)
5. Chan, A.P., Chan, A.P.: Key performance indicators for measuring construction success. Benchmarking: an international journal 11(2), 203–221 (2004)
6. Green, S.B.: How many subjects does it take to do a regression analysis. Multivariate behavioral research 26(3), 499–510 (1991)
7. Horkoff, J., Barone, D., Jiang, L., Yu, E., Amyot, D., Borgida, A., Mylopoulos, J.: Strategic business modeling: representation and reasoning. Software & Systems Modeling 13(3), 1015–1041 (2014)
8. Kaplan, R.S., Norton, D.P.: Putting the balanced scorecard to work. Performance measurement, management, and appraisal sourcebook 66, 17511 (1995)

9. Kaplan, R.S., Norton, D.P.: Strategy maps: Converting intangible assets into tangible outcomes. Harvard Business Press (2004)
10. Laursen, G., Thorlund, J.: Business analytics for managers: Taking business intelligence beyond reporting, vol. 40. John Wiley & Sons (2010)
11. Marsal-Llacuna, M.L., Colomer-Llinàs, J., Meléndez-Frigola, J.: Lessons in urban monitoring taken from sustainable and livable cities to better address the smart cities initiative. Technological Forecasting and Social Change 90, 611–622 (2015)
12. Maté, A., De Gregorio, E., Cámara, J., Trujillo, J., Luján-Mora, S.: Improving massive open online courses analysis by applying modelling and text mining: a case study. Expert Systems (2015)
13. Maté, A., Trujillo, J., Mylopoulos, J.: Conceptualizing and Specifying Key Performance Indicators in Business Strategy Models. In: Conceptual Modeling, pp. 282–291. Springer (2012)
14. Maté, A., Zoumpatianos, K., Palpanas, T., Trujillo, J., Mylopoulos, J., Koci, E.: A systematic approach for dynamic targeted monitoring of kpis. In: Proceedings of 24th Annual International Conference on Computer Science and Software Engineering. pp. 192–206. IBM Corp. (2014)
15. Middelfart, M., Pedersen, T.B.: Implementing sentinels in the targit bi suite. In: Data Engineering (ICDE), 2011 IEEE 27th International Conference on. pp. 1187–1198. IEEE (2011)
16. Object Management Group: Business Motivation Model (BMM) 1.3. `http://www.omg.org/spec/BMM/1.3` (2014)
17. Olivé, A.: Conceptual modeling of information systems. Springer (2007), `https://doi.org/10.1007/978-3-540-39390-0`
18. Olivé, A.: A formal method for conceptual fit analysis. Complex Systems Informatics and Modeling Quarterly (5), 14–25 (2015)
19. Parmenter, D.: Key performance indicators: developing, implementing, and using winning KPIs. John Wiley & Sons (2015)
20. Rodriguez, R.R., Saiz, J.J.A., Bas, A.O.: Quantitative relationships between key performance indicators for supporting decision-making processes. Computers in Industry 60(2), 104–113 (2009)
21. Silva Souza, V.E., Mazón, J.N., Garrigós, I., Trujillo, J., Mylopoulos, J.: Monitoring strategic goals in data warehouses with awareness requirements. In: Proceedings of the 27th Annual ACM Symposium on Applied Computing. pp. 1075–1082. ACM (2012)
22. Tort, A., Olivé, A.: An approach to testing conceptual schemas. Data Knowl. Eng. 69(6), 598–618 (2010), `https://doi.org/10.1016/j.datak.2010.02.002`
23. Van Thiel, S., Leeuw, F.L.: The performance paradox in the public sector. Public Performance & Management Review 25(3), 267–281 (2002)
24. Wu, H.Y.: Constructing a strategy map for banking institutions with key performance indicators of the balanced scorecard. Evaluation and Program Planning 35(3), 303–320 (2012)
25. Zoumpatianos, K., Palpanas, T., Mylopoulos, J.: Strategic management for real-time business intelligence. In: Enabling Real-Time Business Intelligence, pp. 118–128. Springer (2012)

Chapter 6
Conceptual Modeling in Accelerating Information Ingest into *Family Tree*

David W. Embley, Stephen W. Liddle, Tanner S. Eastmond, Deryle W. Lonsdale, Joseph P. Price and Scott N. Woodfield

Abstract *Family Tree* is a wiki-like shared repository of interconnected family genealogies. Because information ingested into the tree requires human authorization as verified in source documents, ingest is tedious and time-consuming. To significantly increase ingest efficiency while maintaining human oversight, we propose a pipeline of tools and techniques to transform source document genealogical assertions into verified information in the *Family Tree* data repository. The automation pipeline transforms pages of printed, scanned and OCRed family history books into a GEDCOM X conceptualization that can be ingested into *Family Tree*. All steps of the pipeline are fundamentally grounded in ontological conceptualizations. We report on the pipeline implementation status and give results of initial case studies in semi-automatically ingesting information obtained from family history books into *Family Tree*.

David W. Embley
Brigham Young University, Provo, Utah 84602, USA, e-mail: embley@cs.byu.edu
FamilySearch, Orem, Utah 84097, USA

Stephen W. Liddle
Brigham Young University, Provo, Utah 84602, USA

Tanner S. Eastmond
Brigham Young University, Provo, Utah 84602, USA

Deryle W. Lonsdale
Brigham Young University, Provo, Utah 84602, USA

Joseph P. Price
Brigham Young University, Provo, Utah 84602, USA

Scott N. Woodfield
Brigham Young University, Provo, Utah 84602, USA

© Springer International Publishing AG 2017

J. Cabot et al. (eds.), *Conceptual Modeling Perspectives*,
https://doi.org/10.1007/978-3-319-67271-7_6

6.1 Introduction

FamilySearch [8] maintains a freely accessible collection of records, resources, and services designed to help people learn more about their family history. Its *Family Tree* allows users to collaborate on a single, shared, worldwide family tree. Currently *Family Tree* has information on about a billion people, including their names, birth and death data, and their marriage and parent-child relationships to others in the tree. Users can also attach to each person stories, photos, and images of documents from which the genealogical information is derived.

Users add persons one-by-one to *Family Tree* and update information already in the tree one item at a time. Users are expected to have verified the information they add to the tree, and their contact information is added to all updates they make. They should also document information they add by including source information—ideally images of documents that verify tree updates.

Using principles of automated conceptual-model-based information extraction [3, 5], we are building a system to accelerate ingest of information into *Family Tree*. As source documents, the system we are building targets the collection of several hundred thousand family history books, which are being scanned, OCRed, and placed online by FamilySearch. The collection contains genealogical information about millions of people, many of whom are already in the tree, but many of whom are not. For those already in the tree these books may contain corroborating information, information not yet recorded in *Family Tree*, and in some instances conflicting information that needs to be resolved.

Figure 6.1 shows a paragraph from a page of one of these books, *The Ely Ancestry* [25]. The information of interest to be placed in the tree for Mary Augusta Andruss is highlighted—her birth date, her death date and place, her burial date, her parents, and her spouse along with their marriage date and their children. Figure 6.2 shows the information captured by our system for Mary. The captured data is ready to be automatically ingested into the *Family Tree* along with its source documentation, the text with highlights in Figure 6.1.

We call our system **Fe6** (**F**orm-based **e**nsemble with **6** extraction tools). Figure 6.3 shows the pipeline beginning with a source-document book and ending with the genealogical information from the book being ingested into *Family Tree*. The figure also illustrates the steps in the process:

1. Split the PDF document resulting from scanning a book into individual pages.
2. Apply an ensemble of extraction engines to each page.
3. Merge the extracted data and split it into three filled-in forms—*Person*, *Couple*, and *Family*, focusing respectively on individual, marriage, and parent-child information.
4. Check and correct the automatically filled-in forms.
5. Enhance the checked data by standardizing it and by inferring gender and birth and married names.
6. Transform Fe6's internal conceptualization of the data into *Family Tree*'s internal conceptualization.

THE ELY ANCESTRY. 419

SEVENTH GENERATION.

241213. Mary Eliza Warner, b. 1826, dau. of Samuel Selden Warner and Azubah Tully; m. 1850, Joel M. Gloyd (who was connected with Chief Justice Waite's family).

243311. Abigail Huntington Lathrop (widow), Boonton, N. J., b. 1810, dau. of Mary Ely and Gerard Lathrop; m. 1835, Donald McKenzie, West Indies, who was b. 1812, d. 1839.

(The widow is unable to give the names of her husband's parents.) Their children:

1. Mary Ely, b. 1836, d. 1859.
2. Gerard Lathrop, b. 1838.

243312. William Gerard Lathrop, Boonton, N. J., b. 1812, d. 1882, son of Mary Ely and Gerard Lathrop; m. 1837, Charlotte Brackett Jennings, New York City, who was b. 1818, dau. of Nathan Tilestone Jennings and Maria Miller. Their children:

1. Maria Jennings, b. 1838, d. 1840.
2. William Gerard, b. 1840. } Twins.
3. Donald McKenzie, b. 1840, d. 1843. }
4. Anna Margaretta, b. 1843.
5. Anna Catherine, b. 1845.

243314. Charles Christopher Lathrop, N. Y. City, b. 1817, d. 1865, son of Mary Ely and Gerard Lathrop; m. 1856, Mary Augusta Andruss, 992 Broad St., Newark, N. J., who was b. 1825, dau. of Judge Caleb Halstead Andruss and Emma Sutherland Goble. Mrs. Lathrop died at her home, 992 Broad St., Newark, N. J., Friday morning, Nov. 4, 1898. The funeral services were held at her residence on Monday, Nov. 7, 1898, at half-past two o'clock P. M. Their children:

1. Charles Halstead, b. 1857, d. 1861.
2. William Gerard, b. 1858, d. 1861.
3. Theodore Andruss, b. 1860.
4. Emma Goble, b. 1862.

Miss Emma Goble Lathrop, official historian of the New York Chapter of the Daughters of the American Revolution, is one of the youngest members to hold office, but one whose intelligence and capability qualify her for such distinction. Miss Lathrop is not without experience; in her present home and native city, Newark, N. J., she has filled the positions of secretary and treasurer to the Girls' Friendly Society for nine years, secretary and president of the Woman's Auxiliary of Trinity Church Parish, treasurer of the St. Catherine's Guild of St. Barnabas Hospital, and manager of several of Newark's charitable institutions which her grandparents were instrumental in founding. Miss Lathrop traces her lineage back through many generations of famous progenitors on both sides. Her maternal ancestors were among the early settlers of New Jersey, among them John Ogden, who received patent in 1664 for the purchase of Elizabethtown, and who in 1673 was

Fig. 6.1 Highlighted Data for Mary Augusta Andruss in *The Ely Ancestry*[25].

```
************************************
Person osmx393: Mary Augusta Andruss
*************************************
Name:
      Conclusion Name: Mary Augusta Andruss
      Original Document Text: Mary Augusta Andruss
      Interpreted Document Text: Mary Augusta Andruss
      Married Name: Mary Augusta Andruss Lathrop
      Married Name: Mary Augusta Andruss Lathrop
Gender: Unknown
Facts:
      BirthDate:
           Conclusion: 1825
           Original Document Text: 1825
           Interpreted Document Text: 1825
      BirthPlace:
Marriage Relationships:
      Spouse: osmx334 (Charles Christopher Lathrop)
      MarriageDate:
           Conclusion: 1856
           Original Document Text: 1856
           Interpreted Document Text: 1856
ParentOf Relationships
      osmx260 (Charles Halstead Lathrop)
      osmx319 (William Gerard Lathrop)
      osmx168 (Theodore Andruss Lathrop)
      osmx434 (Emma Goble Lathrop)
ChildOf Relationships:
      osmx290 (Judge Caleb Halstead Andruss)
      osmx427 (Emma Sutherland Goble)
```

Fig. 6.2 Person Information Record.

The remainder of this chapter describes details of the ingest pipeline (Section 6.2), which from beginning to end is fundamentally grounded in conceptual modeling [4, 2, 24, 19, 6, 1, 7]. We therefore particularly highlight the pipeline's connection to conceptual modeling. Next we give the status of our project (Sec-

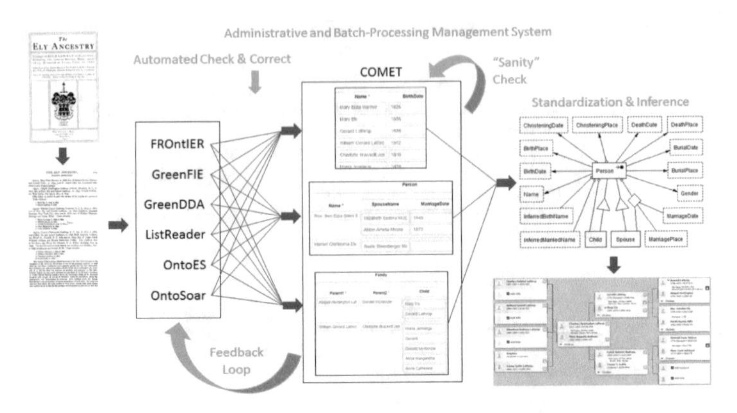

Fig. 6.3 Fe6 Pipeline.

tion 6.3)—meeting FamilySearch's human-oversight requirements (Section 6.3.1), the implementation status of the pipeline (Section 6.3.2), and some preliminary results about our ingest experience (Section 6.3.3). We conclude by discussing potential impact (Section 6.4).

6.2 Fe6 Pipeline

The objective of the Fe6 pipeline is to populate the conceptual-model diagram on the right in Figure 6.3 and then to transform the data in this conceptualization into *Family Tree*. We begin by automatically extracting data into the conceptual model diagrammed in Figure 6.4, which models the target data directly extractable from a text document. The views superimposed on this diagram correspond to Person, Couple, and Family forms, which are automatically filled in so that a user can check and correct the output generated by the tool ensemble. We refer to our conceptual models as ontologies, which emphasizes the philosophical notion of "the nature of being"—the reality of the existence of families and individuals.

6.2.1 Import Book

Given a printed historical book containing genealogical information, it is scanned, OCRed, and rendered as a PDF document. It is then split into pages and for each page we produce five files: (1) a single-page PDF document; (2) a PNG image of the page; (3) a `.txt` file with the OCRed text; (4) an XML document containing bounding-box information for every character, word, and line of the OCRed text in the PNG image; and (5) an HTML web page that renders the PNG image superimposed over hidden OCRed text for use in the user interface that allows for checking and correcting automatically generated extraction results.

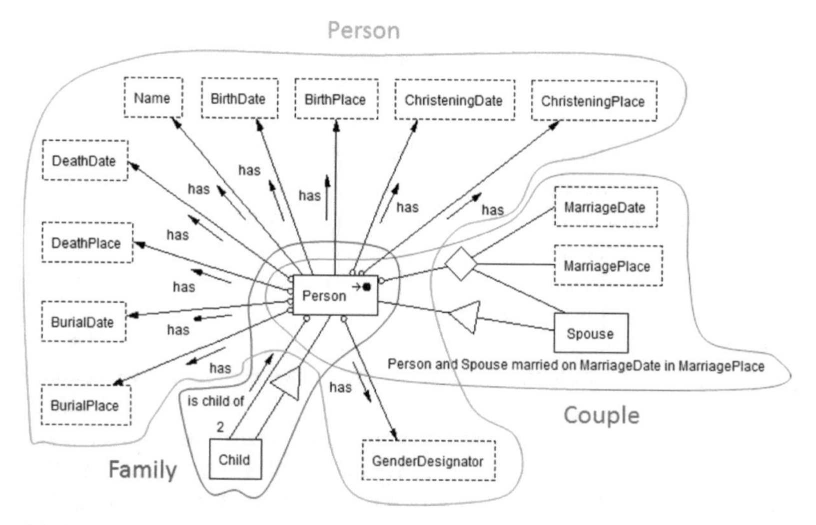

Fig. 6.4 Target Ontology for Extraction Engines.

6.2.2 Run Extraction Tools

Conceptual modeling is the underlying formalism of all six of the Fe6 ensemble's extraction tools. In essence, the tools "read" the text on a page by converting word sequences into conceptual entities and relationships among the entities. Categorically, the extraction tools stem from work in expert systems, natural language processing, and machine learning. Spanning across these categories helps the ensemble work with document types that range from those that are highly structured (e.g. cemetery records that are near table-like in structure) to those that are free running text (e.g. narrative family history stories) and everything in between (e.g. the page in Figure 6.1 from the 830-page Ely book).

FROntIER [21] extends our work on conceptual-model-based data extraction [3]. It extracts and attempts to organize data, reasoning about the extracted information to infer facts not explicitly stated in the underlying text and deduplicating extractions of different references to the same person. FROntIER extraction rules are solidly based on conceptual modeling. Each lexical object set *s* has a collection of regular expression extraction rules that identify instances in running text that belong to an extension of *s*. Nonlexical object sets such as *Person* are instantiated by *ontological commitment*—a relationship between language and an object postulated to exist by that language, so that when a person name is extracted, a *Person* object is instantiated. Relationships between and among entities are instantiated by regular expression recognizers with embedded entity instance recognizers. For example, the rule "*person-name* was born on *date*", where *person-name* and *date* are any of the regular expression recognizers in the collection of recognizers for person names and dates, can instantiate a relationship in the *Person-has-BirthDate* relationship set in Figure 6.4.

OntoES is another extension of [3] based on extracting ontology snippets, which let users specify extraction rules for a collection of object and relationship sets. An ontology snippet is a view over a conceptual model, and each ontology snippet regular expression recognizer identifies and extracts some or all of the objects and relationships for the view in a single execution of the rule. For our application, we tailor these views to our three forms: Person, Couple, and Family. Thus, ontology snippet extractors are an efficient way to fill in the fields of these forms. We note that there is a strong relationship between forms and these ontology snippet views; indeed, for any view we can derive a form and from any collection of related forms we can derive a conceptual model [23].

GreenFIE [12] "watches" users fill in form-records, namely records for our Person, Couple, or Family form, and can generate ontology snippet extraction rules from each of the filled-in records it "sees." It then executes these extraction rules on subsequent pages to prepopulate forms for users to check and continue to fill in for record patterns not yet encountered. GreenFIE is "green" in the true sense of the word, which in this context stands for tools that improve themselves as they are used in real-world work [17].

ListReader [20] discovers record patterns in text. It abstracts the text of an entire book, replacing, for example, words that begin with an uppercase letter like "Mary" by the symbol "[UpLo]" and digit sequences like 1836 by the symbol "[DgDgDgDg]". It then groups text into the patterns it encounters. For example, in Figure 6.1, it groups children with a birth and death date like "1. Mary Ely, b. 1836, d. 1859" whose pattern is "[Dg]. [UpLo] [UpLo], b. [DgDgDgDg], d. [DgDgDgDg]" into one group and children with just a birth date into another group. A user then labels a ListReader-chosen prototypical example by filling in a form—in this Mary Ely example, by putting "Mary Ely" in the Person-form's *Name* field, "1836" in the form's *BirthDate* field, and "1859" in the form's *DeathDate* field. This form filling process establishes a correspondence between the record in the group and a form and thus also the ontology because of the correspondence between form and conceptual model [23]. It also labels every other record in the group. Thus, with one record labeling, all the information for all the records in the group is extracted into the conceptual model—usually hundreds of records in books like *The Ely Ancestry*.

OntoSoar [15] extracts data using NLP techniques to segment and parse the text, and a cognitive reasoner (Soar [13]) to semantically analyze the parse of each segment and map results of the analysis to an ontology. OntoSoar's segmenter chunks semi-structured text like that in Figure 6.1 into clauses which may or may not be sentential in structure but are nevertheless parsable by its Link Grammar parser. The analyzer in our implementation has 240 Soar production rules. These rules build meaning using ideas inspired by construction grammars, which (1) pair textual forms with meaning; (2) construct knowledge structures with inference rules; and (3) map knowledge structures to ontologies by comparing their common entities and relationships. The mapping provides a conduit for populating the ontological conceptualization in Figure 6.4 with data.

GreenDDA is an experimental tool, with which we are investigating the use of standard machine learning, but requiring only a minimal amount of clean training data. It is "green" in the sense that it takes its clean training data from user-checked and -corrected filled-in forms for a page. Its DDA (Decision Directed Adaptation) [18] component then trains a classifier, applies it to a subsequent page, takes the results and adds them to its set of training data, and then repeats this process on additional pages. If the process converges to a stable state, the trained classifier is then applied as part of the ensemble to unprocessed pages in an attempt to improve the extraction.

6.2.3 Merge Extracted Information

The next step in the Fe6 pipeline is to merge the results obtained from the extraction engines. Merge proceeds by noting the position on the page of extracted text strings. Identical strings appearing at the same location on a page are merged, as are strings with significant overlap. For example, if one tool extracts "Judge Caleb Halstead Andruss" from the page in Figure 6.1 and another tool omits the title, "Judge", extracting only "Caleb Halstead Andruss", they are nevertheless merged as one. Since persons are instantiated by ontological commitment with names, name merge implies person-object merge as well.

We keep multiple string values for each lexical object. First is the text of the extracted string itself along with its page location. Second is a cleaned string in which we attempt to (1) fix common OCR errors such as the "i" in "i860" in the birth year of Theodore Andruss in Figure 6.1 and (2) resolve end-of-line hyphens so that "McKen-\nzie" in Figure 6.1 becomes "McKenzie". Third is a mapping of the date values into a Julian date string which can easily be converted into an integer for date comparison operations. Thus, for example, the death date of Mary Augusta Andruss in Figure 6.1, which is "Nov. 4, 1898", becomes "1898308".

We next evaluate the merged/cleaned data and fix egregious anomalies. Unlike most databases which require data to be valid with respect to declared constraints, we allow our conceptual models to be populated with invalid data, preferring to specify ontologically correct constraints and let violations stand until they can be resolved. For example, the model instance in Figure 6.4 declares that a *Person* has exactly one *BirthDate* as specified by the functional arrow and the absence of an "o" (an "o"ptional indicator) on its tail connection. But the extraction engines may find zero or several birth dates for a person. Min-violations of a cardinality constraint [14] merely mean that information is unknown, but max-violations are egregious and should be fixed. Consider the participation constraint *2* in Figure 6.4 declaring that a *Child* has exactly two parents. This is a commonly encountered violation because of the difficulty of specifying how far ahead to look for a child list for a couple. In Figure 6.1, the amount of text to skip between Mary Augusta Andruss and her first child, Charles Halstead, is greater than the amount of text to skip between Joel M. Gloyd, who has no children, and the next couple's first child, Mary

Ely. To not miss parent-child associations, the extraction engines need rules with both short and long skip-lengths. The result in this example is that Mary Ely has four parents, Mary Eliza Warner, Joel M. Gloyd, Abigail Huntington Lathrop, and Donald McKenzie. This egregious anomaly can be reliably and automatically fixed by discarding *Child–is_child_of–Person* relationships for all but the closest couple.

6.2.4 Check Quality

Figure 6.5 shows the user interface for COMET, our **C**lick-**O**nly, or at least **M**ostly, **E**xtraction **T**ool, which allows users to fill in forms on the left from a document on the right. Users click on text tokens in the document to fill in a field of focus in a form. The document is an image of a scanned page superimposed over hidden OCRed text. Users may edit field values, for example, to correct OCR errors. They may also move to previous or subsequent pages to enable annotating records that cross page boundaries such a list of children that continues onto a subsequent page. As Figure 6.5 shows, hovering over a filled-in record highlights the fields of the record and the corresponding extracted text in the document.

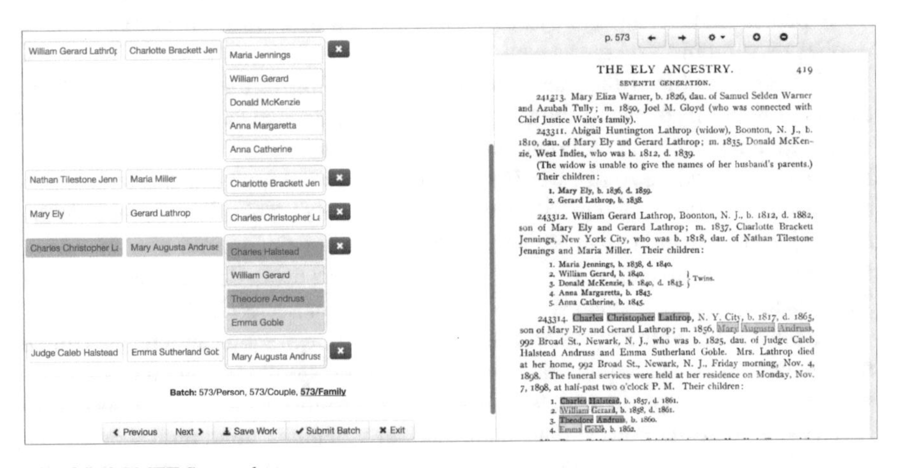

Fig. 6.5 COMET Screenshot.

Form-records in COMET correspond precisely with ontological conceptualizations [23]. Thus, when a user fills in a *Family* form record in Figure 6.5, the underlying system populates the *Family* view in Figure 6.4 with the data. Conversely, when the extraction engines populate the target extraction ontology in Figure 6.4, the form records for any of the various views are filled in so that a user only has to check the work of the ensemble of extraction engines and make corrections—e.g. delete erroneous records with the red-x button in Figure 6.4, add a missing record, or click on a filled-in field to edit or replace the field value.

Users work on a batch of pages at a time as controlled by the buttons in the lower left of the interface. After clicking on *Submit Batch*, the system invokes a semantic check of the data to find violations of ontologically declared constraints and missing person or place names in authority lists. Declared constraints consist not only of the conceptual model's cardinality constraints but also of Datalog-like general constraints declared over the model's object and relationship sets [26]. Authority lists comprise tens of thousands of person and place names known to FamilySearch. When irregularities are found, icons are added to fields in question and the batch is returned to the user for further review.

Users can click on the icons to obtain explanations. For example, clicking on the question-mark icon for the child Francis Argyle in Figure 6.6 yields the pop-up, which explains that Elizabeth Eudora McElroy cannot be her mother since Elizabeth died before Francis was born. After resolving raised issues, users again click on the *Submit Batch* button, and the system accepts the results. If accepted person or place names are missing in the authority lists, the system adds these missing names to local, book-specific authority lists, which are checked along with global, FamilySearch-provided authority lists so that when checking subsequent pages, the system will not mark these names as possible errors.

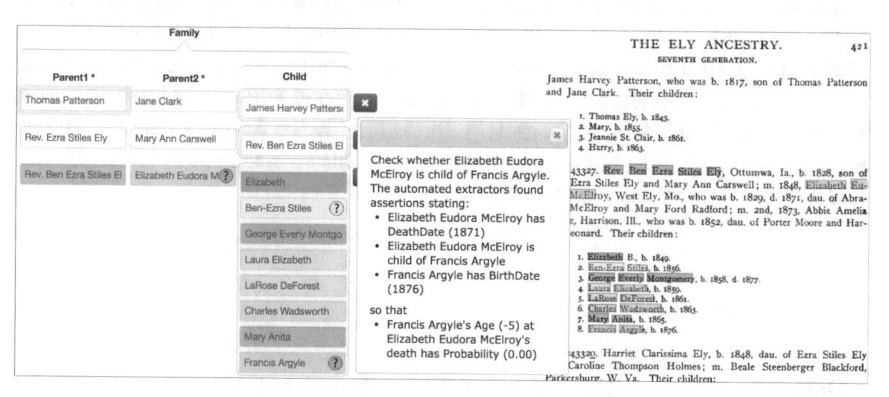

Fig. 6.6 Screenshot of Constraint Violation: Child Born After Mother's Death.

6.2.5 Enhance Data

At this point in the Fe6 pipeline, the data is assumed to have been correctly extracted. The data, however, is not necessarily in a preferred form and desired data that is not directly extractable but is strongly inferred is not present.

We standardize dates and person and place names. For example, Mary Augusta Andruss's death date in Figure 6.1 is extracted as "Nov. 4, 1898" and standardized as "4 November 1898". We standardize a name by ordering its components with title(s) first, followed by given names, surnames, and suffixes, and we use standard upper- and lower-case nomenclature. Place names are taken from FamilySearch's place-name authority when a match can be found, and, in any case, are ordered by administrative levels, local to global.

Gender is almost never directly extractable in family history books because authors do not normally use the words "male" or "female". Instead they expect readers to infer gender by context. We can reliably do the same inference automatically. We do directly extract "gender designators" such as "he", "she", "Mrs.", etc., and we use them as reliable indicators of gender. A married person in a historical document whose gender is unknown but whose spouse's gender is known can also be reliably inferred. Lastly, first given names are good indicators of gender and can be used as a last resort. Drawing from the billion-plus persons in *Family Tree*, FamilySearch has a 92-megabyte file of names paired with their probability of being male. Using a threshold of above 0.95 for males and below 0.05 for females, we can be quite sure of the gender. If there is insufficient information, we leave gender unknown.

Inferring birth and married names is tricky because we do not know which name form has been extracted. In Figure 6.1, the listed child names consist only of given names (no birth surnames); parent names are birth names that may or may not have a title like "Judge"; one of the names, namely "Mrs. Lathrop", has no birth-name components at all; another, namely "Miss Emma Goble Lathrop", includes the full birth name and adds a title. In other documents names like "Mr. and Mrs. Charles Christopher Lathrop" appear in which no part of the birth name of the female spouse is included, and married female names appear with and without maiden surnames, e.g. either of "Mary Augusta Andruss Lathrop" or "Mary Augusta Lathrop". However, given enough information about father and male spouse names, birth and married names can reliably be sorted out.

6.2.6 Update Tree

At this point in the Fe6 pipeline, we will have the conceptual model in Figure 6.3 populated with information—one instance for each page that contains genealogical information in a given family history book. The information collected will have been automatically extracted by the ensemble of extraction tools, checked and edited as needed by a human to ensure accuracy, and automatically enhanced by inferring critical information that is not directly extractable. Further, all of the extracted and inferred lexical data will have been converted to a standard form acceptable for input into *Family Tree*.

In preparation for ingesting this generated information into *Family Tree*, we next transform the data from the pipeline's conceptual model to GEDCOM X [9]—a standard conceptual model for exchanging genealogical information. Each GEDCOM X document contains the information for one page and may include some information from prior and subsequent pages when the focus page has cross-page annotations. We also gather into each GEDCOM X document citation information for the book and bounding-box coordinates for each extracted data instance on the focus page and on any surrounding pages.

For ingest into *Family Tree*, we generate a person information record (see Figure 6.2) for each person listed in a GEDCOM X document. Taking a person's record document as input, we programmatically fill in a form with the information and invoke a search for the person in *Family Tree*. The search form has fields for title, first names, last names, suffix, gender, living or deceased status, date of birth, birth place, date of death, death place, father first names, father last name, mother first names, mother last name, spouse first names, and spouse last name. From the record in Figure 6.2, we can fill in 13 of these 16 fields. When executed, possible matches are returned, ordered best first according to FamilySearch's matching algorithm. We programmatically scrape information from the top three possible matches and compare it with the person's information record. Each field that matches for a given search result increases the score. For Mary Andruss, first names, last names, gender, deceased status, father first names, father last name, mother first names, mother last name, spouse first names, and spouse last name all match individually, and our match algorithm declares that the Mary Augusta Andruss whose extracted information is in Figure 6.2 matches Mary Augusta Andruss whose ID in *Family Tree* is K4B6-VCT.

Having found Mary Andruss in *Family Tree*, we can now automatically add any missing information, add any alternative conflicting information, and add a source document to validate these updates. Our proposal for automating actual updates to *Family Tree* while also satisfying FamilySearch's human oversight requirements is in Section 6.3.1. Here, we note that by hand, we added Mary's death date, burial date, and married name, which were all missing, and we changed Mary's birth date from "about 1831" to "1825". To document these tree updates, we also added the image in Figure 6.1 as a source document.

6.3 Project Status

6.3.1 Human Oversight of Automated Updates

The oversight for ensuring that the information is correct with respect to the source document is centered in COMET along with the pipeline's interactive quality checking procedures. Thus, so long as the downstream inference and standardization algorithms function properly, the information presented for ingest should be considered as having had sufficient human oversight.

The automated search for matches in *Family Tree* can have several outcomes: (1) insufficient evidence to be confident of any match, (2) sufficient evidence to be confident of (2a) zero matches, (2b) one match, or (2c) several matches. For (2b), which is like the Mary Andruss example above, automatic ingest removes the tedium of adding facts and source documentation by hand. When merging conflicting information, a new fact should replace an existing fact only if the new fact properly subsumes the existing fact or if the existing fact is specifically marked as being questionable (e.g. "about 1831"). For (1) and (2a), automatic ingest is straightforward, but the decision to create a new person depends on policy. An alternative would be to create a new node in a tree for the book outside of *Family Tree*. Then, upon completion of the book, node clusters with links to *Family Tree* nodes can be automatically ingested as can node clusters deemed by policy to be large enough to add to *Family Tree*. For (2c) a human must be in the decision-making ingest loop. Interestingly, as we explain next, a conceptual-modeling view of the results of running the pipeline can aid the decision-making process.

Figure 6.7 shows a conceptual-modeling view laid out as proposed in D-Dupe [11], a visualization tool aimed at helping users integrate new information into a database and deduplicating information already in the database. Each named rectangle is an object set derivable as a role-specialization of the *Person* object set in the conceptual model in Figure 6.3. *Father*, for example, is a male person who has a child. The relevant objects for the question at hand appear inside the object sets. Objects are denoted by their internal ID's and, since they are all persons established by ontological commitment, their names also appear to make the view human readable. Lines denote relationships and together with the objects form a subgraph of the larger underlying graphs of both the pipeline's conceptual model and *Family Tree*'s conceptualization. Attribute values for persons in the two *Person* object sets provide additional information for determining duplicates.

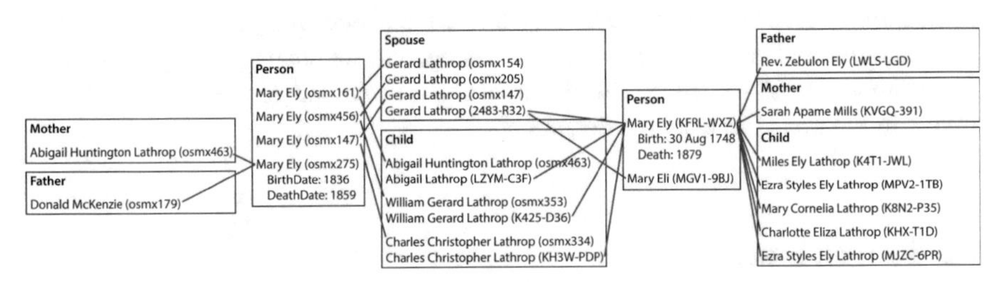

Fig. 6.7 Integration and Deduplication of Mary Ely.

A D-Dupe view for integration and deduplication can be generated whenever the automated search returns several matches—Case (2c) above. For example, "Mary Ely (osmx161)", the first Mary Ely in the page in Figure 6.1, matches two persons[1] in *Family Tree*, Mary Ely (KFRL-WXZ) and Mary Eli (MGV1-9BJ). The D-Dupe view in Figure 6.7 has the two *Family Tree* Mary Ely instances in the *Person* object set on the right and the extracted Mary Ely instance in the *Person* object set on the left. Also in the *Person* object set on the left are other Mary Ely instances judged by FROntIER-like inference [21] as potential duplicates. As Figure 6.7 shows, all one-hop person-person relationships also appear. The object sets *Spouse* and *Child*

[1] Two person instances of the ever evolving *Family Tree* instance on June 5th, 2017.

between the two *Person* object sets hold groups of objects judged by our match algorithm to be the same.

To make merge decisions, a user has, in addition to a D-Dupe view like the one in Figure 6.7, access to all the information about persons in *Family Tree* by clicking on a person's FamilySearch ID, and access to source document information including the page of interest and the entire book by clicking on a person's extraction-assigned ID. Once a decision is made, a user can alter the contents of the *Person* object sets and then click on a "go" button to request the ingest. In our example, a user would remove "Mary Ely (osmx275)" from the left *Person* object set and then request the ingest. The system would react by automatically directing the user to FamilySearch's merge page where "Mary Ely" and "Mary Eli" would be merged using FamilySearch's merge procedure and would then automatically ingest each of the three remaining extracted "Mary Ely"s.

6.3.2 Pipeline Implementation

The pipeline is coded in Java up to the point of information ingest, which is coded in Python using Selenium [22] to automate interaction with the FamilySearch web site and update *Family Tree*. The pipeline runs from beginning to end, and the code is being improved as we gain experience and encounter new edge cases. The given-name/male-probability list and the name-authority list have been curated and are used in the pipeline, but the place-authority list has not yet been created. The D-Dupe-like integration and deduplication tool is only in the proposal stage.

The ensemble of extraction engines, COMET, and the user interface for the pipeline management system are coded using Java, PHP, JavaScript, jQuery, CSS, and HTML5 and make use of a variety of off-the-shelf tools, including Soar, the LG Parser, and Stanford Core NLP packages. The extraction engines are all in their individual academic prototype stage. They all run, but considerable work will be required to tech-transfer them into tools usable by anyone besides ourselves. COMET has been used by subjects in some experimental evaluations; they generally find it usable after a few minutes of training. We have only begun to build a management system that will control the processing of books through the pipeline.

6.3.3 Initial Field Tests

Ely [25]. To compare the effort between manually and automatically ingesting information, we updated *Family Tree* by hand according to the information in Figure 6.1. We filled in search forms with the genealogical data from the generated person information records (e.g. see Figure 6.2), identified matching *Family Tree* records, merged duplicates (if any), checked the matching records, and added to them source documentation and missing information. Of the 31 unique person information records, 28 matched exactly one *Family Tree* person record. The record for Mary Ely married to Gerard Lathrop matched two, as Figure 6.7 shows, and we merged them. Donald McKenzie's and Abigail Huntington Lathrop's person information records each matched three records that were themselves duplicates, and in both cases we merged the three records. We added highlighted source documents like the one in Figure 6.1 for all 31 matched tree records. Overall, we (1) replaced two primary names with more complete names (e.g. "Emma Sutherland Goble" in place of "Emma S. Goble"); (2) replaced six uncertain BMD (Birth/Marriage/Death) facts (e.g. "about 1831" or merely "deceased") with certain facts; (3) added two missing BMD facts, and (4) added eight supplementary facts such as married names or alternate spellings of names. All of this work, which could have been done fully automatically within seconds of compute time, took more than five hours of tedious typing, checking, clicking, and waiting for responses from the FamilySearch web site.

Kilbarchan [10]. In a fully automatic extraction run over the 143 pages of the Kilbarchan, Scotland, parish record, the ensemble created person information records like the one in Figure 6.2 for 8,539 individuals. The automatic extraction's F-score was judged to be near 95%. Our matching algorithm found that 38% of these individuals were already in *Family Tree*. In a sample of 150 person information records, we checked our match-scoring algorithm, and for those that matched correctly, we determined how much and what kind of information could be immediately added to the tree. For match scores of 8 or more, meaning roughly that the person in the Kilbarchan data and the person in *Family Tree* matched on eight separate items of information, our match algorithm correctly matched 100% of the time and correctly matched 64% of those with match scores between 5 and 7. Of those correctly matched, 20% had information in the Kilbarchan data that could be immediately added to the tree to improve the data, including adding or fixing first and last names, birth and marriage dates, and parent-child relationships.

Miller [16]. Similar to our Kilbarchan field test, in a fully automatic extraction run over the 396-page Miller Funeral Home Records from Greenville, Ohio, we extracted information for 12,226 individuals. The match rate of individuals already in *Family Tree* for the Miller records was lower than for the Kilbarchan book—just over 10% compared to 38% for Kilbarchan. Of the 1,280 individuals our matching algorithm found, the Miller records provided information that could be automatically added to 57% of them—a complete name, full birth date, full death date, or names of an individual's spouse, parents, or children.

6.4 Conclusions

The Fe6 ingest pipeline is fundamentally grounded in conceptual modeling: The principles of ontological modeling and ontological commitment facilitate the identification and extraction of individuals and their genealogical information from semi-structured text. The strong correspondence between forms and conceptual models provides coherent user views that ease the human check-and-correct of results produced by the ensemble of extraction engines. Inference rules written with respect to conceptual object and relationship predicates drive the semantic sanity checks and the inference of critical data that cannot be directly extracted. And human oversight of entity resolution via deduplication and record integration is likely best achieved by viewing a relevant graph of the entities and their relationships embedded in conceptually derived object sets.

The Fe6 pipeline can accelerate ingest into *Family Tree* while simultaneously maintaining FamilySearch-required oversight. With COMET we can guarantee human-level accuracy of extracted information. Depending on the outcome of automatically matching extracted data with the tree, information can either be automatically attached or, when human oversight is required for entity resolution, can be presented in a generated view of the information that facilitates a quick and accurate resolution. As a rough estimation of expected acceleration, it took about 5 hours to ingest the genealogical information from the Ely page in Figure 6.1 manually into *Family Tree*. Using COMET, it took less than 30 minutes to annotate the information from scratch and less than 10 minutes when the form records were prepopulated with data by the ensemble of extraction engines. Except for assessing duplicates, the ingest can be fully automatic. Thus, we can estimate a potential 10-fold speed-up without the involvement of the ensemble of extraction engines and a 30-fold speed-up with them.

References

1. Dori, D.: Model-based Systems Engineering with OPM and SysML. Springer (2015)
2. Embley, D.: Object Database Development: Concepts and Principles. Addison-Wesley, Reading, Massachusetts (1998)
3. Embley, D., Campbell, D., Jiang, Y., Liddle, S., Lonsdale, D., Ng, Y.K., Smith, R.: Conceptual-model-based data extraction from multiple-record web pages. Data & Knowledge Engineering 31(3), 227–251 (1999)
4. Embley, D., Kurtz, B., Woodfield, S.: Object-oriented Systems Analysis: A Model-Driven Approach. Prentice Hall, Englewood Cliffs, New Jersey (1992)
5. Embley, D., Liddle, S., Lonsdale, D.: Conceptual modeling foundations for a web of knowledge. In: Embley, D., Thalheim, B. (eds.) Handbook of Conceptual Modeling: Theory, Practice, and Research Challenges, chap. 15, pp. 477–516. Springer, Heidelberg, Germany (2011)
6. Embley, D., Thalheim, B. (eds.): Handbook of Conceptual Modeling: Theory, Practice, and Research Challenges. Springer, Heidelberg, Germany (2011)
7. ER web site. `http://conceptualmodeling.org/`
8. FamilySearch. `http://familysearch.org/`
9. GEDCOM X. `http://www.gedcomx.org/`
10. Grant, F. (ed.): Index to The Register of Marriages and Baptisms in the PARISH OF KILBARCHAN, 1649–1772. J. Skinner & Company, LTD, Edinburgh, Scotland (1912)
11. Kang, H., Getoor, L., Shneiderman, B., Bilgic, M., Licamele, L.: Interactive entity resolution in relational data: A visual analytic tool and its evaluation. IEEE Transactions on Visualization and Computer Graphics 14(5) (September/October 2008)
12. Kim, T.: A Green Form-Based Information Extraction System for Historical Documents. Master's thesis, Brigham Young University, Provo, Utah (2017)

13. Laird, J.: The Soar Cognitive Architecture. The MIT Press, Cambridge, Massachusetts (2012)
14. Liddle, S., Embley, D., Woodfield, S.: Cardinality constraints in semantic data models. Data & Knowledge Engineering 11(3), 235–270 (1993)
15. Lindes, P.: OntoSoar: Using Language to Find Genealogy Facts. Master's thesis, Brigham Young University, Provo, Utah (2014)
16. Miller Funeral Home Records, 1917 – 1950, Greenville, Ohio (1990)
17. Nagy, G.: Estimation, learning, and adaptation: Systems that improve with use. In: Proceedings of the Joint IAPR International Workshop on Structural, Syntactic, and Statistical Pattern Recognition. Hiroshima, Japan (November 2012)
18. G. Nagy, DDA: Decision Directed Adaptation. personal communication
19. Olivé, A.: Conceptual Modeling of Information Systems. Springer, Berlin, Germany (2007)
20. Packer, T.: Scalable Detection and Extraction of Data in Lists in OCRed Text for Ontology Population Using Semi-Supervised and Unsupervised Active Wrapper Induction. Ph.D. thesis, Brigham Young University (2014)
21. Park, J.: FROntIER: A Framework for Extracting and Organizing Biographical Facts in Historical Documents. Master's thesis, Brigham Young University, Provo, Utah (2015)
22. SeleniumHQ: Browser automation. `http://www.seleniumhq.org/`
23. Tao, C., Embley, D., Liddle, S.: FOCIH: Form-based ontology creation and information harvesting. In: Proceedings of the 28th International Conference on Conceptual Modeling (ER2009). pp. 346–359. Gramado, Brazil (November 2009)
24. Thalheim, B.: Entity-Relationship Modeling: Foundations of Database Technology. Springer, Berlin, Germany (2000)
25. Vanderpoel, G. (ed.): The Ely Ancestry: Lineage of RICHARD ELY of Plymouth, England, who came to Boston, Mass., about 1655 & settled at Lyme, Conn., in 1660. The Calumet Press, New York, New York (1902)
26. Woodfield, S., Lonsdale, D., Liddle, S., Kim, T., Embley, D., Almquist, C.: Pragmatic quality assessment for automatically extracted data. In: Proceedings of ER 2016. vol. LNCS 9974, pp. 212–220. Gifu, Japan (November 2016)

Chapter 7
Model Centered Architecture

Heinrich C. Mayr, Judith Michael, Suneth Ranasinghe, Vladimir A. Shekhovtsov and Claudia Steinberger

Abstract This paper advocates a rigorous model focused paradigm of information system development and use. We introduce the concept of "Model Centered Architecture" that sees an information system to be a compound of various networked models, each of which is formed with the means of a Domain Specific Modeling Language. This languages are tailored to the particular circumstances of the respective system aspect. I.e., from a MOF perspective, MCA focuses on the MOF levels M_2 (definitions of the DSMLs to be used for the specification of the system and it's contexts), M_1 (Specification of all System and Data Components using the DSMLs) and M_0 (the instances, i.e. models of concrete objects, functions and processes). The transformation of M_0 citizens to the respective implementation concepts (Structure $\rightarrow$ Data, Function $\rightarrow$ Program, Process $\rightarrow$ Workflow) is delegated to mapping functions defined on M_2, restricted on M_1 to the particular schemata (in the sense of mappings between the respective sets of schema instances), and instantiated on M_0 for the concrete instances. The paper shows how such model centered approach may be applied in practice using two real development projects as running examples.

Heinrich C. Mayr
Alpen-Adria-Universität Klagenfurt, Universitätsstraße 65-67, 9020 Klagenfurt am Wörthersee, Austria, e-mail: heinrich.mayr@aau.at

Judith Michael
Alpen-Adria-Universität Klagenfurt, Universitätsstraße 65-67, 9020 Klagenfurt am Wörthersee, Austria, e-mail: judith.michael@aau.at

Suneth Ranasinghe
Alpen-Adria-Universität Klagenfurt, Universitätsstraße 65-67, 9020 Klagenfurt am Wörthersee, Austria, e-mail: suneth.ranasinghe@aau.at

Vladimir A. Shekhovtsov
Alpen-Adria-Universität Klagenfurt, Universitätsstraße 65-67, 9020 Klagenfurt am Wörthersee, Austria, e-mail: volodymyr.shekhovtsov@aau.at

Claudia Steinberger
Alpen-Adria-Universität Klagenfurt, Universitätsstraße 65-67, 9020 Klagenfurt am Wörthersee, Austria, e-mail: claudia.steinberger@aau.at

© Springer International Publishing AG 2017

J. Cabot et al. (eds.), *Conceptual Modeling Perspectives*,
https://doi.org/10.1007/978-3-319-67271-7_7

Key words: Conceptual Modeling, Model Centered Architecture, Meta Object Framework, Model Mapping, Model Transformation

7.1 Introduction

7.1.1 Motivation

Models are the fundamental human instruments for managing complexity and understanding. As such they play a key role in any scientific and engineering discipline as well as in everyday life. Many modeling paradigms evolved over time in the various disciplines leading to a huge variety of modeling languages, methods and tools that came and went. This in particular is true for Informatics, which is a modeling discipline per se, and since long tries to systematize the realm of modeling by (1) clarifying the hierarchy of model layers like e.g. in MOF (meta object framework) [26], (2) introducing ontological commitments into model hierarchies for a better semantical grounding, (3) harmonizing various modeling approaches to unified/universal ones, and (4) providing a framework for a systematic domain specific modeling method (DSMM) ([9, 23]) design where universal approaches fail.

Since the seventies of the last century, related research and practice focuses on Conceptual Modeling. This approach basically uses a formal language the terms of which have an associated semantic interpretation (e.g. by grounding in an ontology) and a more or less transparent graphical or textual representation (supporting an efficient linguistic perception [8]). Usually, such language is embedded in a Model-/Meta-model-Hierarchy. The dimensions of conceptual modeling languages are structure, dynamics (behavior) and functionality; for instance, the Entity Relationship Model family focuses on structure, the Business Process Modeling Notation (BPMN) on dynamics and the Unified Modeling Language (UML) on all three dimensions.

A vast wealth of research has been published about conceptual modeling languages, tools and methodologies, many of them having fallen into oblivion again. Antoni Olive's fundamental contributions, however, are still present. We dedicate this paper to Antoni in deep gratitude for his inspiring work.

7.1.2 Related Work

We start from the observation that despite of all efforts there is still no comprehensive and consistent use of conceptual modeling in practice. Often, conceptual models are used merely as prescriptive documents, which – e.g. in the realm of software development or business process management – seldom are synchronized with the developed artefact so that reality and model are stepwise diverging.

There is a huge body of knowledge regarding Conceptual Modeling in general, and modeling paradigms and methods used for system development in particular. Thus it is not possible to give a comprehensive overview here. Also we will not discuss our own related previous research.

Model Driven Architecture (MDA) [16] and Model Driven Software Development (MDSD) [6, 19] try to master this challenge by backing model transformation [Li11] from the (conceptual) requirements model, which is defined by means of a meta-model, down to the implemented code (which clearly again is a kind of model), see also [7]. MDA can be viewed as an instance of Model Driven Development (MDD) by using the Object Management Group (OMG) standards as the core standards; i.e. Unified Modeling Language (UML), Meta Object Facility (MOF), XML Metadata Interchange (XMI), and the Common Warehouse Meta-model (CWM).

However, just as UML is not the only object-oriented modeling language, so also MDA is not the only model driven approach. There are numerous non-MDA initiatives that continue to advance the state of the art in MDD, e.g. metaprogramming [32], domain specific modeling [14], generative programming [5]. However, as there are still obstacles to overcome, e.g. regarding a bidirectional model transformation (in particular, bottom up, which would enhance synchronization), model completeness on all levels, and easy model checking, also these approaches did not yet have an unlimited breakthrough into the developer's minds.

Models@runtime [3, 4] aims at using models (in a general sense, not specifically conceptual models) as artifacts at runtime; this is related to the wider promise that the boundary between development time and runtime artifacts should eventually disappear [2]. Run-time models are intended to enable the adaptation of a system and its context at run-time by maintaining semantic relationships between the run-time models and the running systems. This allows for analyzing and planning adaptations on the model-level (see [10] etc).

7.1.3 The Paper's Aim

What we will propose and illustrate within this paper is, in some ways, an add-on to the MDA/MDSD and the models@runtime methodology that is intended to attract more attention to conceptual modeling in information system development processes.

The main idea is to understand such processes as mere modeling processes (diverging from [7]) and thus focusing on models (and their meta-models) in any development step up to the running system. We, therefore, call this paradigm "Model Centered Architecture (MCA)". By MCA we will not introduce a new technology. We just aim at contributing perspectives on the power of conceptual modeling as has been done, e.g., by Antoni Olivé in [27].

The paper uses the results of two medium-term research endeavors, which we ran within the last years, as running examples. It is structured as follows. In section 2, we concentrate on models, their meta-models and Domain Specific Modeling Languages (DSML) as the key building blocks of knowledge intensive systems, around which any application and management software can be built. To make these building blocks comprehensive, the complete ecosystem context of a planned information system has to be covered. This is illustrated in section 3. In addition to that, sections 4 deals with all interfaces of such systems from a modeling perspective: the interfaces to the various user groups, to systems to be coupled, to data and knowledge sources etc. In section 5 we then present a first set of patterns for a Model Centered Architecture. The paper closes with some conclusions and an outlook on future research to be done.

7.2 The Model Centered Perspective

MCA is based on models, their related universal or domain specific meta-models (MMs together with the modeling languages defined in connection with these MMs, as well as on mechanisms for the transformation of models into other representations.

7.2.1 Background: Models and Metamodels

[11] define several features of models: (1) Mapping: A model stands for something else (its original), (2) Reduction: models map only those aspects of the original - and these possibly in a changed form - which are relevant for the given modeling purpose, (3) Pragmatics: reflects the intended use of a model, i.e. prescription in the sense of a specification, description for explanations, simulation or formal evaluation for analysis purposes etc.

Usually, modeling is done in a way that is commonly perceived as “top-down”. For example, when designing a traditional relational database application, we start with the Relational Model as a meta-model. Using the associated Data Definition Language we define a model, the “database schema” which describes all possible states (sets of concrete tables) of the intended database. I.e., a particular database state is an extension of such schema, and again is a model: namely a model of those aspects of the original that where intended to be described by that database.

However, modeling can also be done “bottom-up”. For example, given several concrete states of relational database the schema of which is not explicitly available. So we could mine from that database an Entity-Relationship Model and represent this graphically. In this case, the data in the database are the originals.

The same data can be extensions of different models, and the same model may have different representations. As an example for the latter, suppose we are dealing with the data in a specific application, that are extensions of a, e.g., UML class diagram. This data can be represented in both, an ontological form (e.g. as OWL individuals) and using a graphical notation. These representations can replace each other depending on the current aim: being a representation for easier end user validation or a representation for enhanced reasoning. As they serve for different purposes, they have different properties as the way of representation.

It is thus clear that the hierarchy of model layers, which first was introduced in the context of Information Resource Dictionary Systems [18] and now is propagated as Metaobject Framework by [26], is helpful for understanding and managing the relations between these layers.

Meta-modeling frameworks like ADOxx[1] support the definition of Domain Specific Modeling Languages (DSMLs) and the creation of related modeling tools. Given these supporting facilities and the work of the Open Models Initiative[2], DSMLs and DSML development gain increasing attention [14]. The creation of a DSML as part of a comprehensive Domain Specific Modeling Method (DSMM) has been discussed in, e.g., [9] and [23]. [13] and, years ago, [15] argued modeling methods to consist of several components, that should be taken under consideration in design processes: (1) the modeling language the a syntax of which is described by means of a meta-model, the semantics by explanation or more formal descriptions, and the notation by a set of graphical elements; (2) the modeling procedure that describes how to apply the modeling language to create resulting models as well as (3) mechanisms and algorithms that work with and on these models.

Model transformation is a key technique used in MDA, where one or multiple target models are automatically generated from one or more source models according to a transformation definition [21]. Model merging, where several models are integrated into one resulting model, is included in this definition.

7.2.2 MCA: The Concept

The core concept of MCA is to take models not only as representatives of underlying originals but to use them as *the core of a system* for both the addressed application functionality and the flexible definition of the system's *interfaces* as is illustrated in Fig.7.1 based on the MOF hierarchy.

On the M2 (meta-model) level the concepts of the DSMLs for the application domain, the user and device interfaces, and the data exchance interfaces are defined. This is done using a meta-modeling language provided on level M3 (meta-meta-model, not shown on the picture), and by specifying the symbols for language representation. The DSMLs thus are extensions of M3 and models (intensions) for M1. M2 interfaces allow for handling meta-models as MCA artifacts (*meta model management*, e.g. using authoring environments) and for integrating external meta-models (*meta-model exchange*).

On the M1 (model) level the various M2 meta-models are instantiated for a concrete application situation; the extension links are shown as dashed arrows. This

[1] `http://www.adoxx.org`

[2] `http://openmodels.at`

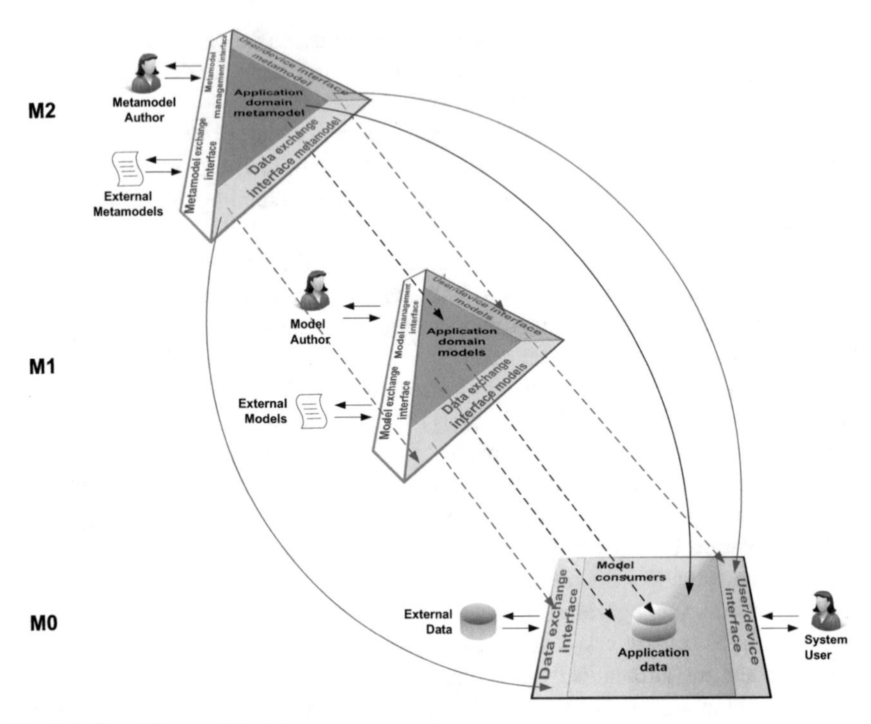

Fig. 7.1 Model Centered Architecture: an overview

leads to a (domain specific) *application model, user and device interface models* as well as a *data exchange model*. Again, for handling models as MCA artifacts, management (including modeling) and exchange interfaces are defined for this level, as they are typically provided by a meta-modeling framework.

On the M0 (instance) level, the application itself results from creating extensions of the M1 application model elements (visualized in Fig.7.1 again by dashed arrows).

If a comprehensive DSML is defined on M2 (i.e., providing concepts for structure, dynamics and function) and used on M1, then the M0 extension form the models@runtime which are handled by an interpreter that is orchestrated by M2. The solid lines in Fig.7.1 visualize that correlation. Thus, the system components are implemented as model consumers and handlers which directly use and manipulate application domain and interface models to provide the necessary functionality.

MCA based approaches may work with different kinds of conceptual models as well as MMs for defining DSMLs and DSMMs. By defining them for each relevant interface and data core, it is possible to create powerful domain-specific systems. Also, model transformation is a key mechanism for MCA based approaches, since different representations, excerpts and aggregations as well as different purposes exist for models.

7.2.3 Running examples

To become more concrete, this paper introduces the MCA concept based on our experiences made in the HBMS[3] and QuASE[4] projects.

The *QuASE* project [30] aimed at providing an information system offering flexible means of harmonizing the stakeholders' views on communicated information (e.g. stored in industrial project repositories such as Issue Management Systems[5] (IMS) databases) in software development projects. These means are based on terminology adaptation and the support for communication-related decisions. The core of the QuASE system is a conceptual model of the communicated information and the communication environment.

The *HBMS* project [20] aims at deriving support services from integrated models of abilities, current context and episodic knowledge that an individual had or has, but has temporarily forgotten. The core of the HBMS system is the *Human Cognitive Model (HCM)*. It preserves the episodic memory of a person in the form of conceptual models of behavior linked to context information related to these activities. The interfaces to activity recognition systems as well as multimodal user interfaces are again defined via domain specific modeling languages.

7.3 Models in QuASE and HBMS

7.3.1 Models in QuASE

Implementing QuASE as a model centered solution was motivated by the following considerations: (1) the knowledge about quality-related communications varies from company to company so that it should be separately configurable for a particular deployment site; (2) the communicated information typically is stored in project repositories (e.g. Jira databases); its conversion into knowledge (for being exploited by reasoning mechanisms approach) preferably should be integrated into the site-specific configuration.

As a consequence, a meta-model together with a visual domain-specific modeling language, the *QuASE site DSL* [29, 30], has been developed which serves for defining the *QuASE site model* as the kernel of a deployment. This model also specifies the mapping between the project repository and the modeling concepts thus allowing for an automatic generation of the knowledge base instances from the repository data (see Section 4). The DSL includes the following basic concepts: (1) *site:* owner of the given QuASE installation, e.g. a software provider; (2) *context:* units possessing certain views on communicated information e.g. projects, organiza-

[3] Funded by the Klaus Tschira Stiftung gGmbH, Germany

[4] Funded by FFG (Die Österreichische Forschungsförderungsgesellschaft), Austria

[5] E.g. Atlassian Jira

tions, involved stakeholders; (3) *content:* units shaping communicated information e.g. issues/tickets; (4) *knowledge:* units encapsulating communicated knowledge.

A QuASE knowledge unit is composed of: (1) *ontological foundation*: a reference to the conceptualization of the particular piece of knowledge through ontological means; (2) *representation:* the representation of the knowledge unit in a format that could be perceived by the communicating parties (e.g. plain text); representation units are also contained in content units; (3) *resolution means:* the means of resolving understandability conflicts related to the given knowledge unit (e.g. textual explanations).

Context units possess *capabilities* to deal with knowledge units. The capabilities e.g. refer to the ability of understanding a given knowledge unit or explaining it with resolution means.

The elements of the MOF levels M0-M2 are outlined in Fig.7.2. Note that M3 has been omitted since a standard subset of UML-like class diagram concepts is used here which should be intuitively understandable.

The functionality of the QuASE Tool (the end user component) consists of exploiting the knowledge base by means of queries against the meta-model of the DSL, i.e. these queries refer only to M2-level concepts. This way, the resulting solution is truly model centered as it is completely customizable by defining new site models.

7.3.2 Models in HBMS

The HBMS MCA is backed by four meta-models: (1) The HBMS Context meta-model covering all aspects to be taken into account when it is about supporting a person, (2) the Operating Instruction meta-model that, in connection with the context meta-model, allows for specifying the functionality of context elements, (3) the Activity Recognition meta-model which serves for a flexible specification of the interfaces to arbitrary activity recognition systems [28], and (4) the Multimodal Support meta-model that serves for specifying the user/device interfaces for various device types. Regarding MCA as depicted in Fig.1, the Context and Operating Instruction meta-models correspond to the Application Domain meta-model, the Activity Recognition meta-model to the data-exchange meta-model, and the Multimodal Support meta-model to the user/device meta-model.

Fig.7.3 visualizes the HBMS MOF hierarchy, the unreadable components will be subsequently zoomed and explained. Again M3 has been omitted in the figure.

HBMS Context Model. The processing of context information gives humans the ability to adopt their behavior to the world around them [12]. As HBMS aims to actively assist individuals in activities of daily living and other situations using their own episodic knowledge, the relevant aspects of the user's context have to be known [25]. The corresponding context meta-model is structured into four clusters as shown (without details) in Fig.7.4:

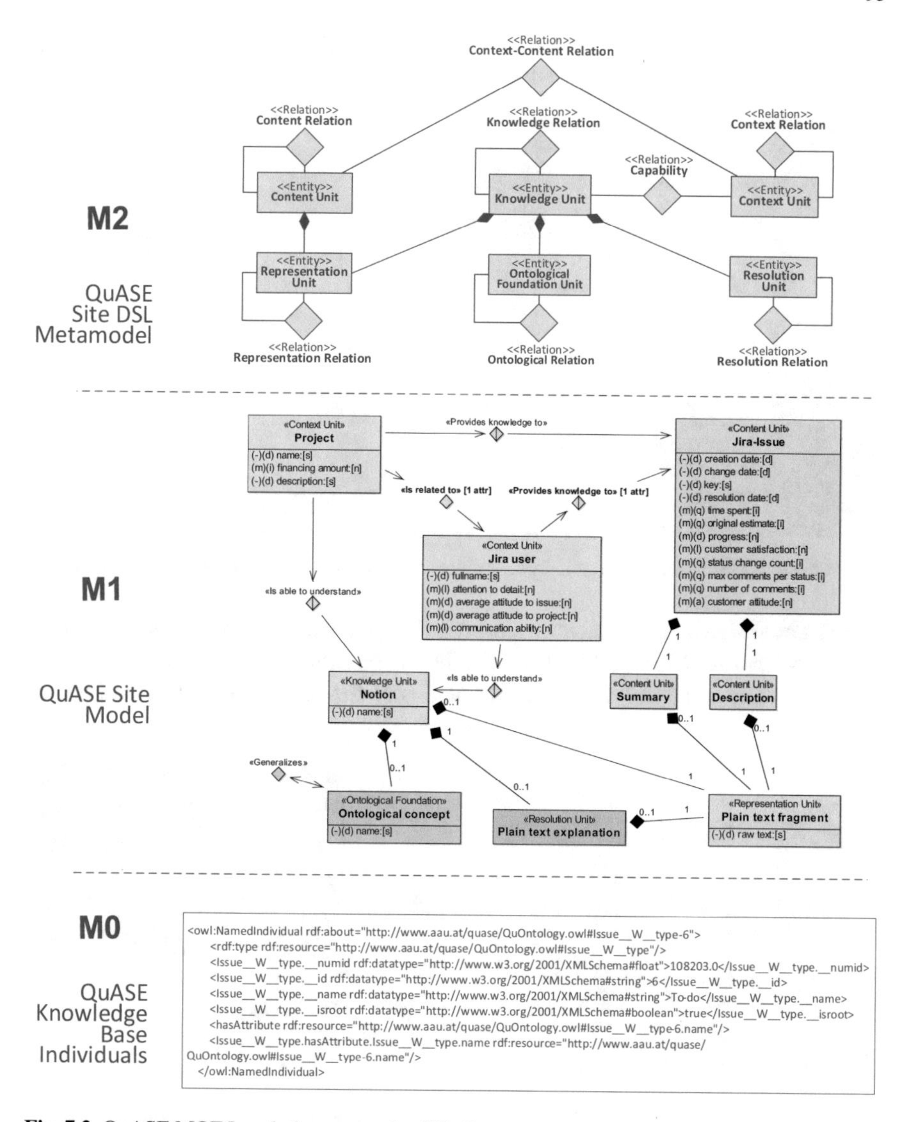

Fig. 7.2 QuASE MOF Levels (excerpts, simplified)

(1) The *Environmental Context* of a user: covers the resources that are utilized in operations of the assisted user or are placed as equipment in the spatial context of the user and participate in operations;

(2) The *Personal and Social Context* of a user: covers the abilities that a user holds together with the level of ability fulfilment as well as the social surrounding;

(3) The *Spatial Context* of a user: covers the location in which the user should be actively assisted;

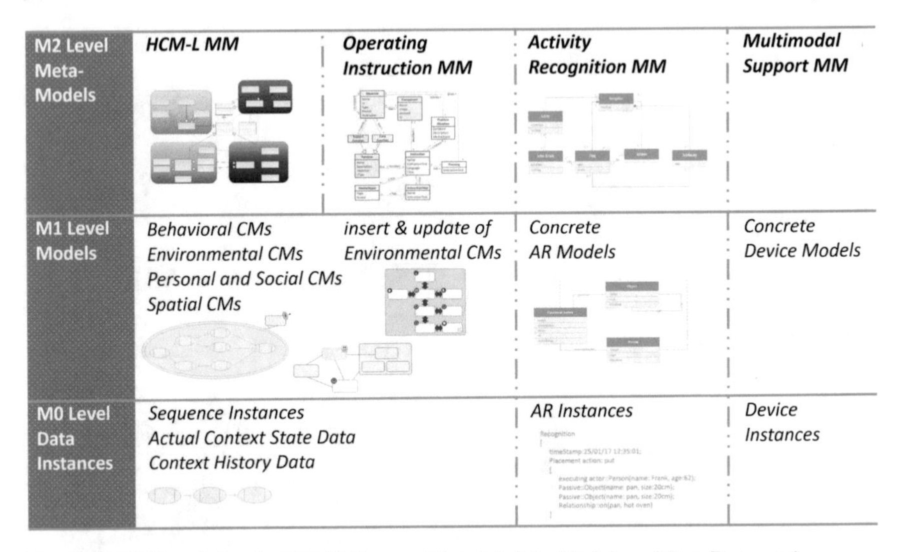

Fig. 7.3 MOF Levels for the HBMS-System (Meta-Models, Models and Data/Instances)

(4) The *Behavioral Context* of a user: covers the user's relevant behavior in so-called *Behavioral Units (BUs)* that describe the possible sequences of actions (*Operations* connected by *Flows*), their *Pre-* and *Post-Conditions* as well as their *Goals*.

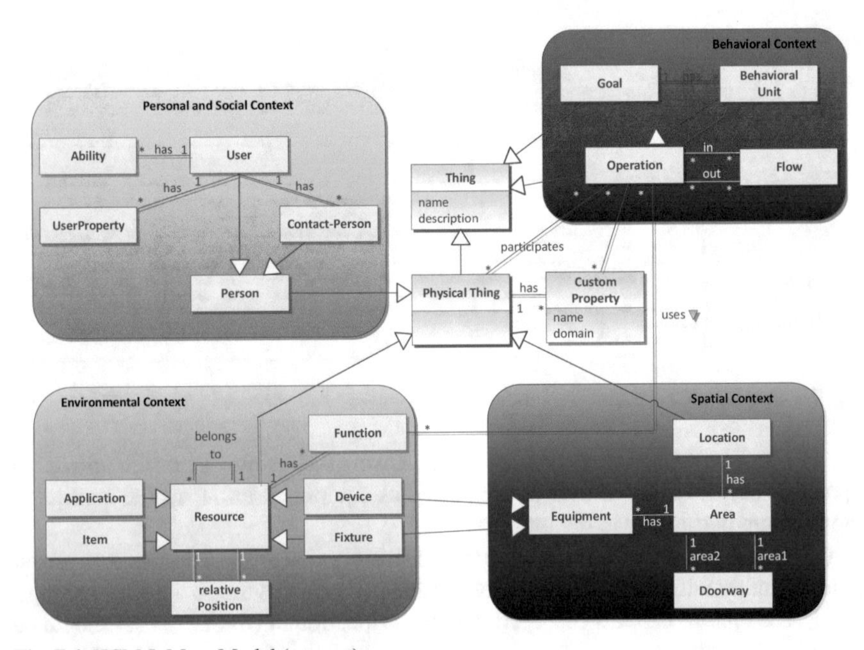

Fig. 7.4 HCM-L Meta-Model (excerpt)

In sum, the user's episodic knowledge and the related context is represented and preserved at level M1 which forms the *Human Cognitive Model (HCM).*

The HBMS context meta-model is the backbone of the lean domain specific modeling language HCM-L (Human Cognitive Modeling Language [22]). This language was designed to be as intuitively understood as possible by the relevant stakeholders in the active assistance domain [24]. It is supported by the HCM-L Modeler [1] which allows to work on the HCM.

The use of HCM is twofold: it serves (1) as a conceptual model for communication and validation purposes between stakeholders and system engineers, and (2) as a machine readable context representation allowing for retrieval, reasoning, interoperability and reuse.

7.4 Model Centered Interfacing

We now proceed to illustrate the concept of model-based interface design as mentioned in section 2. The targeted domains are activity recognition, multimodal support and operating instruction integration.

7.4.1 Model Centered Interfacing in QuASE

QuASE obtains the data from the project repositories (such as Jira databases) and converts it into knowledge stored in its knowledge base. To implement this conversion, it includes the *knowledge base builder component* which implements a *model centered interface to project repositories.*

To support such interface, every conceptual element of a QuASE site model includes a *repository mapping specification.* This specification contains a repository query and a description of the mapping between the attributes to be returned by the query and the custom attributes of the conceptual element. It is used by the knowledge base builder as follows: during the synchronization of the knowledge base, the queries specified for the current site model are executed against the repository, the relational data returned by these queries is converted into the knowledge base individuals based on the ontological knowledge derived from the model structure, and the repository mapping specification.

The flexibility of this mapping allows large amounts of existing data to be integrated automatically. The QuASE system "can be seen as a bridge which connects end users, the data in project repositories and the (extendable) set of machine learning and natural language processing techniques" [30, p. 10] which are applicable to the data after the communication environment is described as a QuASE site model.

7.4.2 Model Centered Activity Recognition Interface

The implementation of an Activity Recognition interface was motivated by the fact that behavior support systems require complete knowledge about the current user behavior to provide context-aware support to its target users (e.g. elderly or disabled people in the AAL case). Moreover, in the case of HBMS we aim at supporting a person on the basis of her/his previous episodic knowledge which is to be learned via sensor based observation. Because of the limitations of current Human Activity Recognition (HAR) systems, such complete knowledge can only be established by using several HAR's and integrating their outputs. This led us to provide, for HBMS, a model centered HAR interface that is capable of transforming heterogeneous AR data into a common representation understandable to the target system.

Fig.7.5 shows the main concepts of the corresponding meta-model (MOF level M2) which defines the domain specific modeling language AREM-L (Activity Recognition Environment Modeling Language):

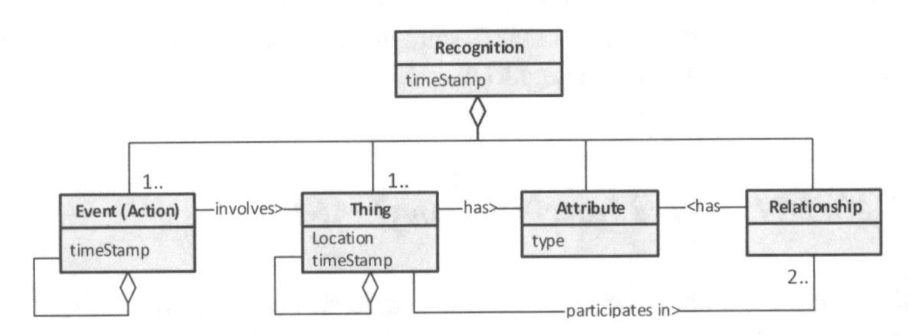

Fig. 7.5 Model centered HAR interface meta-model

Recognition, the top-level concept, comprises (1) a recognized *Event/Action* conceptualizing recognized simple or complex activities, (2) observed *Things,* i.e., persons or contextual objects that are connected to each other by *Relationships* and are involved in Actions, e.g., as passive elements or executing actors. For a concrete HAR to be connected, these concepts are to be instantiated appropriately on level M1. Note that then several "kinds" of events (instances of the M2 concept event), several kinds of things and relationships etc. may be defined to meet the particular HAR interface specification. The same is true for the cardinalities of the (meta-)relationships which are, for a maximum flexibility, reduced to a minimum on level M2. As an example, recognition kinds might be specified that have no event part (this is possible as there is no cardinality constraint from Recognition to Event), e.g. for covering temperature measurements of an object. On the other hand, if an event kind is specified on Level M1, it must belong to at least one Recognition kind.

At run-time, the specified interface models are used to drive the data transformation in the behavior support system.

7.4.3 Operating Instruction Integration

Operating instructions typically describe the core functions of a resource and give instructions for its handling. Moreover, warnings as well as typical problem situations are included. While human readers can sift through complex operating instruction and are mostly able to understand particular support information at a glance, search engines, Active Assistance Systems and other digital services need extra information to be able to use such information. Therefore, the intersection of semantic technologies and operating instructions seem to be a promising approach [31].

Fig.7.6 shows the refinement of the Environmental Context, describing resources and their components, functions and operating instructions relevant for HBMS-System.

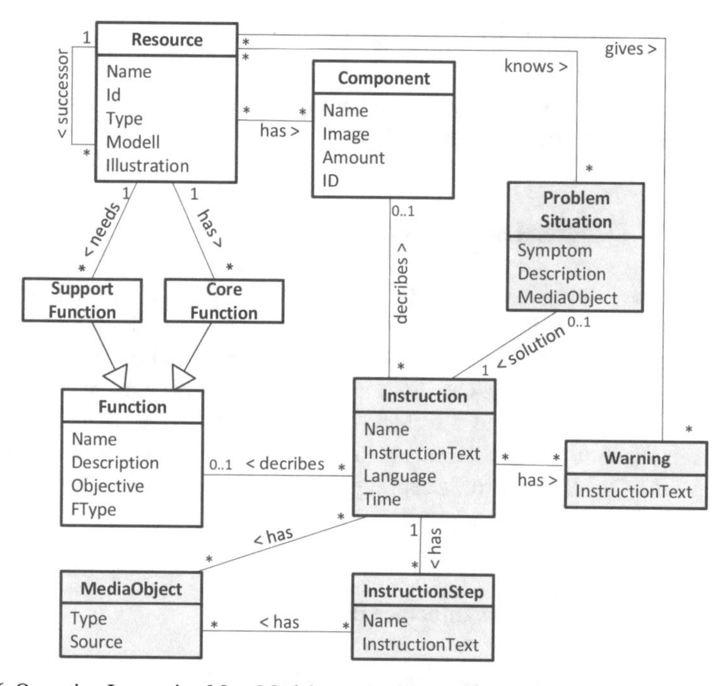

Fig. 7.6 Operating Instruction Meta Model as part of the Environmental Context

Components are parts or accessories, which are necessary to prepare or to assemble the resource or which are required for special resource functions. Functions are specialized into core functions and support functions for maintenance and setup. Instructions describe how to handle functions and how to interact with the resource from the user perspective. Every instruction consists of a name and mostly an instruction text written in a certain language. Instructions that are more complex can consist of several instruction-steps, which the user is suggested to follow.

Media-Objects like assembly sketches, images, audios or videos can be associated to instructions as well as to instruction steps. Warnings are operating instruction elements that are related either to an instruction directly or to the resource in general. In addition, typical problem situations can be found in an operating instruction with references to instructions to handle them.

If an operating instruction is provided online by a manufacturer in the form of structured data (e.g. using schema.org [31]), this data can be collected from the web, transformed and automatically integrated into the Environmental Context Model of HBMS-System using the Environmental Context meta-model for interfacing. The HCM-L Modeler then can be used for visualizing or manipulating the integrated data.

7.4.4 Model Centered User Interface

The user interface of a system again can be implemented based on model centered principles (as a *model centered user interface*).

7.4.4.1 Model Centered User Interface in QuASE.

The QuASE system provides a model centered integration of user interface fragments into the user interface of industry issue management systems (IMS) such as Jira thus enabling Jira users to access QuASE support scenarios. This support includes (1) the concepts of the QuASE site DSL for describing the subset of model elements to be integrated into the IMS; (2) an IMS extension (e.g. Jira plug-in) which forms the control requests and transfers these to the QuASE tool; (3) the functionality of the QuASE tool for accepting IMS requests and rendering the QuASE UI fragment according to the request.

7.4.4.2 Multimodal Support Interface in HBMS.

The HBMS Support Engine provides assistance to a person based on matching the person's observed actions with the current knowledge base HCM. For transmitting assistive information to this person and for interaction purposes, a multimodal user interface is provided that works with different media types (audio, handheld, beamer, Laserpointer, light sources, etc.). Again, this interface is intended to be defined according to the MCA paradigm by introducing a domain specific modeling language; such language is currently under development in the context of a PhD work.

7.5 MCA: Patterns and Implementation Examples

7.5.1 Architectural Patterns for MCA solutions

Based on the concepts defined in the previous sections, we identify a set of architectural patterns to be implemented by the components of a MCA-based system (Fig.7.7).

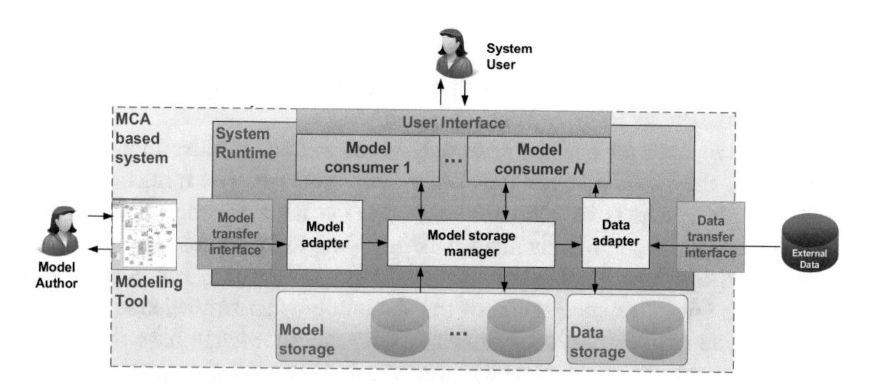

Fig. 7.7 Architectural patterns for MCA-based systems

1. The *modeling tool* pattern describes the means used by the model authors to create and manipulate models according to the given DSML; such tools are driven by given DSML's meta-model describing; they can be either custom built or generated using an existing meta-modeling framework.
2. The *model transfer interface* pattern describes components responsible for transferring models to runtime components.
3. The *model adapter* pattern describes components transforming the transferred models into the format understood by the rest of the system.
4. Both *model storage* and *model storage manager* patterns describe components enabling model persistence; the former describes the storage itself, the latter describes the runtime component responsible for accessing this storage.
5. The *data adapter* pattern describes those components that use models to drive the conversion of external data into the internal (system standard) representation.
6. The *model consumer* pattern describes the components which use the adapted models to provide the functionality of the MCA-based solution.

7.5.2 *Concrete MCA: Pattern Usage in Development Processes*

7.5.2.1 QuASE Architecture.

The result of the implementation activities of the QuASE project was a software solution which utilizes MCA paradigm to provide for flexibility in dealing with the variable structure of communication environments in IT companies. Its architecture is shown on Fig.7.8. It implements MCA patterns as follows:

1. The *site modeler tool* implements the *modeling tool* pattern. It supports the site modeling language (*QuASE-SML*) for describing site-specific communication environments. It communicates with runtime by means of an interface that implements the *model transfer interface* pattern.
2. The *ontology builder* and the *knowledge base builder* utilities implement, respectively, the *model adapter* and *data adapter* patterns. The former transforms QuASE-SML models into the *site ontology*, the latter converts the data from project repositories into individuals corresponding to that ontology.
3. The *knowledge base* implements the *model storage* pattern. It is a triple store containing OWL2 representation of the site ontology and knowledge base individuals. The *QuASE tool* communicates with the knowledge base through the *storage management module* which implements the *model storage manager* pattern.
4. The components of the interactive web-based QuASE tool implement the *model consumer* pattern. They access the knowledge base to implement the end-user support scenarios aimed at harmonizing stakeholders' views.

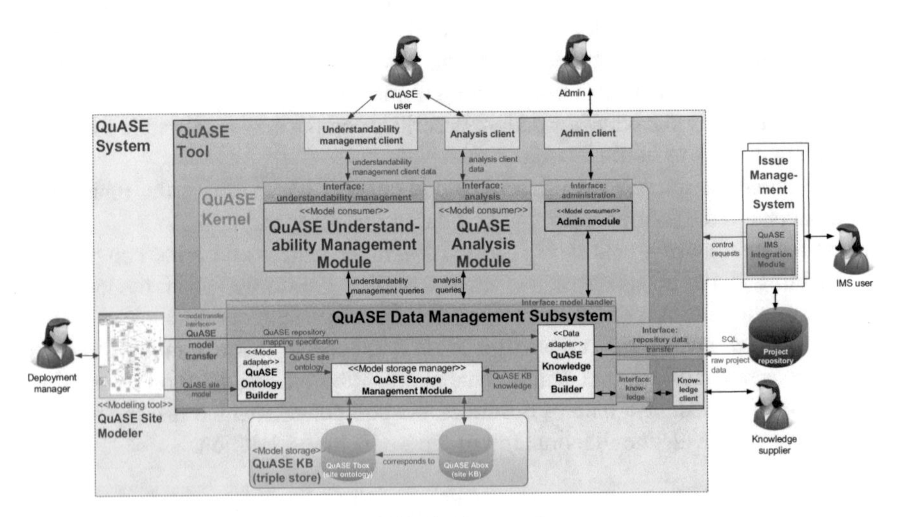

Fig. 7.8 QuASE system architecture as MCA implementation

7.5.2.2 HBMS Architecture.

Within the realm of the HBMS project a flexible MCA based Ambient Assisted Living (AAL) system has been developed which is capable of learning a person's behavioral knowledge for later use when that person needs support. The HBMS system implements the MCA patterns as follows (see Fig.7.9):

1. The *modeling tool* implements the *modeling tool* pattern. It is used for creating and maintaining HCM-L and AREM-L models, and communicates with the HBMS kernel by means of the *model transfer interface* implementing the related pattern.
2. The *HCM-L-OWL converter* implements the *model adapter* pattern. It transforms HCM-L models into OWL2 representation used by the HBMS kernel.
3. The *knowledge base* implements the *model storage* pattern being a triple store holding HCM and behavioral data. The kernel communicates with it through the *Data Management Subsystem* that implements the *model storage manager* pattern.
4. The *activity recognition system (ARS) adapter* is a middleware listening to the data coming from an ARS and making it HBMS-compliant. It implements the *data adapter* pattern being driven by the AREM-L description of the particular ARS interface;
5. The *HBMS kernel* contains the following components implementing the *model consumer* pattern: (1) *Observation Engine:* responsible for communicating to ARS through the ARS adapter; (2) *Behavior Engine*: responsible for handling the behavior data arriving from the Observation Engine in context of the current HCM; (3) *Support Engine:* responsible for controlling the behavior of the assisted users through the multimodal user interface.

7.5.2.3 MCA support infrastructure.

Within the context of the HBMS and QuASE projects we established a flexible software development infrastructure to back MCA-based applications. This infrastructure is subdivided into:

1. *modeling tool infrastructure:* the infrastructural elements assisting the developers of meta-models to be used for defining MCA models such as the means for selecting the subset of the models to be transferred to the runtime components;
2. *model transfer interface infrastructure*: the elements assisting the developers of the model transfer interface such as (1) the *transfer script* callable from the modeling tool (it converts the selected models into the transfer format and uploads them to the system runtime), (2) the Java implementation of the *model listener*: a component of the kernel which listens to the communication port used for uploading the models, captures the uploaded models, and makes them available to the rest of the kernel;

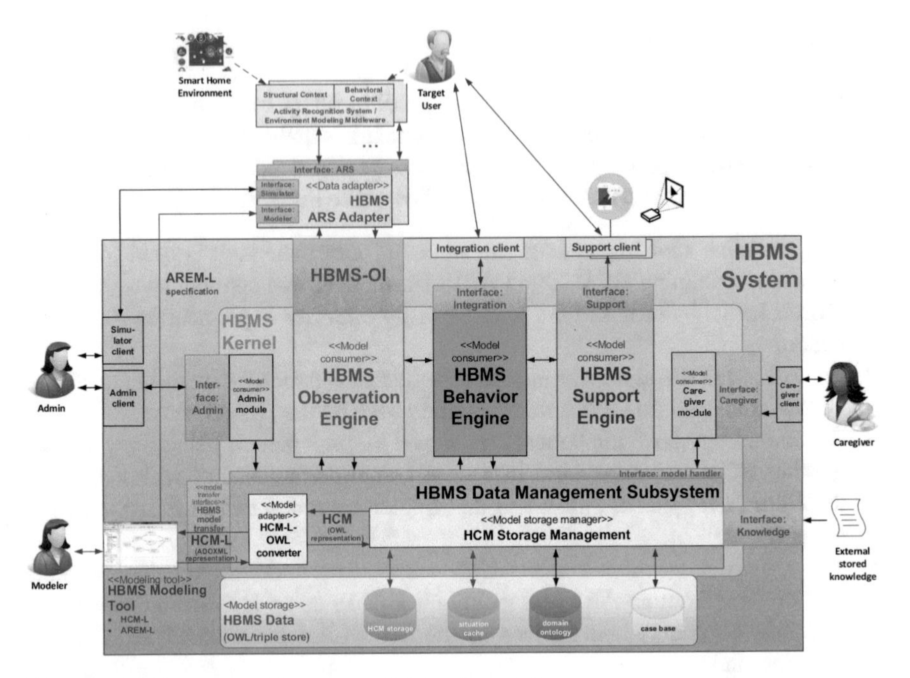

Fig. 7.9 HBMS system architecture as MCA implementation

3. *kernel infrastructure*: the elements assisting the developers of the kernel components such as the implementation of (1) the *model mapper* transforming models into a set of internal objects to be used by the rest of the kernel, and (2) the *model serializer* transforming OWL2 model representations into a triple store.

Applied in the development process, this infrastructure decreases the development effort by taking the responsibility for the technical issues related to the implementation of MCA-based solutions: from defining the models to utilizing the models at runtime.

7.6 Conclusions and Future Work

With the MCA paradigm we want to contribute to a more comprehensive use of conceptual modeling in practice. The paradigm provides transparent means of synchronizing models and developed artifacts on all software development stages, and also in the running system. By applying this paradigm, the conceptual models are not restricted to being the prescriptive documents which eventually diverge from what is used by the running system, instead, they are considered as crucial system artifacts directly influencing the functioning of the system interfaces and components at runtime. In fact, they become "first-class citizens" of the running system.

The MCA paradigm allows for increasing the adaptability of software solutions by providing DSMLs as application specific and flexible means of (1) specifying the application context and the relevant interfaces comprehensively, and (2) driving the runtime behavior of the system.

The MCA paradigm could be extended in future along the following directions:

- To investigate in more detail the ingredients of interface modeling languages; possible research topics here could be the formalization of such languages, related quality characteristics etc.
- To review the traditional notions of quality for conceptual models w.r.t. their validity in the MCA realm.
- To investigate the adaptability of the MCA paradigm in agile software development.

References

1. Al Machot, F., Mayr, H.C., Michael, J.: Behavior Modeling and Reasoning for Ambient Support: HCM-L Modeler. In: Proc. of the International Conference on Industrial, Engineering and Other Applications of Applied Intelligent Systems, IEA-AIE (2014)
2. Baresi, L., Ghezzi, C.: The Disappearing Boundary Between Development-Time and Run-Time. In: Proceedings of the FSE/SDP workshop on Future of software engineering research, pp. 17-22. ACM (2010)
3. Bencomo, N., France, R.B., Cheng, B.H., Aßmann, U.: Models@ run. time: Foundations, Applications, and Roadmaps, LNCS, Vol. 8378. Springer (2014)
4. Blair, G., Bencomo, N., France, R.: Models@ run. time. Computer 10, 22-27 (2009)
5. Czarnecki, K., Eisenecker, U.: Generative Programming: Methods, Tools,and Applications. Addison-Wesley Professional, Boston, Massachussets, USA (2000)
6. Embley, D.W., Kurtz, B.D., Woodfield, S.N.: Object-oriented Systems Analysis: A Model-Driven Approach. Prentice-Hall, Englewood Cliffs, New Jersey (1992)
7. Embley, D.W., Liddle, S.W., Pastor, O.: Conceptual-Model Programming: a Manifesto. In: Handbook of Conceptual Modeling, pp. 3-16. Springer (2011)
8. von Foerster, H.: Perception of the Future and the Future of Perception. Instructional Science 1, 31-43 (1972)
9. Frank, U.: Domain-Specific Modeling Languages: Requirements Analysis and Design Guidelines. In: Reinhartz-Berger, I. et al. (eds.): Domain Engineering. pp. 133-157, Springer (2013)
10. Heinrich, R. et al.: Runtime Architecture Models for Dynamic Adaptation and Evolution of Cloud Applications. Universität Kiel (2015)
11. Hesse, W., Mayr, H.C.: Modellierung in der Softwaretechnik. eine Bestandsaufnahme. Informatik-Spektrum, 31, 377-393 (2008)
12. Hoareau, C., Satoh, I.: Modeling and Processing Information for Context-Aware Computing. A Survey. New Gener. Comput. 27(3), pp. 177-196 (2009)
13. Karagiannis, D., Kühn. H.: Metamodelling Platforms. In E-Commerce and Web Technologies, K. Bauknecht, A. M. Tjoa and G. Quirchmayr, Eds. LNCS. Springer, Berlin, Heidelberg, p. 182 (2002)
14. Karagiannis, D., Mayr, H.C., Mylopoulos, J. (eds.): Domain-Specific Conceptual Modeling: Concepts, Methods and Tools. Springer (2016)
15. Kaschek, R., Mayr, H.C.: A Characterization of OOA Tools. Assessment of Software Tools, 1996., Proceedings of the Fourth International Symposium on, pp. 59-67. IEEE (1996)
16. Kleppe, A.G., Warmer, J.B., Bast, W.: MDA Explained: The Model Driven Architecture: Practice and Promise. Addison-Wesley Longman Publishing Co., Inc. (2003)

17. Lewis, P.R. et al.: Architectural Aspects of Self-Aware and Self-Expressive Computing Systems: From psychology to engineering. Computer 48, 62-70 (2015)
18. Leymann, F., Altenhuber, W.: Managing Business Processes as an Information Resource. IBM systems journal 33, 326-348 (1994)
19. Liddle, S.W.: Model-Driven Software Development. In Handbook of Conceptual Modeling, pp. 17-54. Springer Berlin Heidelberg (2011)
20. Mayr, H. C. et al.: HCM-L: Domain-Specific Modeling for Active and Assisted Living. In: Karagiannis, D.; Mayr, H. C.; Mylopoulos, J. (eds.): Domain-specific conceptual modeling. Concepts, methods and tools. pp. 527-552, Springer (2016)
21. Mens, T.; Czarnecki, K.; van Gorp, P.: A Taxonomy of Model Transformation. Proc. Dagstuhl Seminar on Language Engineering for Model-Driven Software Development. Internationales Begegnungs- und Forschungszentrum (IBFI), Schloss Dagstuhl (2005)
22. Michael, J., Mayr, H.C.: Conceptual Modeling for Ambient Assistance. In: Ng, W., Storey, V.C., Trujillo, J. (eds.): Conceptual Modeling - ER 2013, pp. 403-413. Springer (2013)
23. Michael, J., Mayr, H.C.: Creating a Domain Specific Modeling Method for Ambient Assistance. In: International Conference on Advances in ICT for Emerging Regions (ICTer2015). IEEE (2015)
24. Michael, J., Mayr, H.C.: Intuitive Understanding of a Modeling Language. In: Proc. of the Australasian Computer Science Week Multi-conference (ACSW'17), Asia Pacific Conference on Conceptual Modeling (APCCM), pp. 1-10. ACM (2017)
25. Michael, J., Steinberger, C.: Context Modeling for Active Assistance, submitted for publication
26. Object Management Group OMG: Meta Object Facility (MOF) Core, URL: http://www.omg.org/spec/MOF/, last accessed 09.08.2016
27. Olivé, A., Cabot, J.: A Research Agenda for Conceptual Schema-Centric Development. In: Conceptual Modelling in Information Systems Engineering, pp. 319-334. Springer (2007)
28. Ranasinghe, S., Al Machot, F., Mayr, H.C.: A Review on Applications of Activity Recognition Systems with Regard to Performance and Evaluation. International Journal of Distributed Sensor Networks 12, (2016)
29. Shekhovtsov, V.A., Mayr, H.C., Kop C.: Facilitating Effective Stakeholder Communication in Software Development Processes. In: Nurcan, S., Pimenidis, E. (eds.): Information Systems Engineering in Complex Environments, LNBIP, Vol. 204, pp. 116-132. Springer (2015)
30. Shekhovtsov, V.A., Mayr, H.C.: View Harmonization in Software Processes: from the Idea to QuASE. In: Mayr, H.C., Pinzger, M. (Hrsg.). INFORMATIK 2016, 26.âĂŞ30. September 2016. Proceedings, pp. 111-123, LNI, Vol. P-259, GI, (2016)
31. Steinberger, C., Michael, J.: Semantic Mark-Up of Operating Instructions for Active Assistance, submitted for publication
32. Štuikys, V., Damaševičius, R.: Meta-Programming and Model-Driven Meta-Program Development: Principles, Processes and Techniques, Springer (2012)

Chapter 8
Design-time Models for Resiliency

Andrea Marrella, Massimo Mecella, Barbara Pernici and Pierluigi Plebani

Abstract Resiliency in process-aware information systems is based on the availability of recovery flows and alternative data for coping with missing data. In this paper, we discuss an approach to process and information modeling to support the specification of recovery flows and alternative data. In particular, we focus on processes using sensor data from different sources. The proposed model can be adopted to specify resiliency levels of information systems, based on event-based and temporal constraints.

8.1 Introduction

As information systems (ISs) are becoming more and more complex and interconnected, the information provided by the system and by other networked businesses and components can be of varying quality depending on the functioning of the modules of the IS itself, both at the hardware and the software level.

According to the *error-chain* paradigm described in [5], an erroneous situation in a system is not always evident, and becomes apparent when a *failure* occurs; such a failure may originate from different *error states*, which in turn are possibly originated by different *faults* in system components. Faults may be transient or

Andrea Marrella
Sapienza Università di Roma, Italy, e-mail: marella@dis.uniroma1.it

Massimo Mecella
Sapienza Università di Roma, Italy

Barbara Pernici
Politecnico di Milano, Italy

Pierluigi Plebani
Politecnico di Milano, Italy

© Springer International Publishing AG 2017

J. Cabot et al. (eds.), *Conceptual Modeling Perspectives*,
https://doi.org/10.1007/978-3-319-67271-7_8

permanent and they may be difficult to diagnose, in particular in the case of intermittent faults. Therefore, different ways of managing possible failures have to be considered, depending on the state of the system and on the possibly originating fault, and the different effects of the faults must be taken into account, with the goal of resuming normal functioning, or at least guaranteeing some limited functionality.

In this paper, we focus on designing ISs to make them resilient by design, i.e., considering the improvement of their reliability in case of expected and unexpected faults. In [26], we analyzed the characteristics needed for designing a *resilient information system* using a process-based representation of the IS. As in most process-based approaches to IS modeling, the data model is considered only marginally and often detached from the process model. However, in the design of a resilient IS, one important aspect are data and their temporal characteristics. As in the case of faults, also data faults may be transient or permanent, and different design approaches have to be considered depending on the type of fault and on the desired resiliency level.

Temporal aspects in conceptual modeling have been studied extensively in the literature (e.g., [18, 7, 24, 25]), and in particular in connection with the representation of events. In this work, inspired by the classification of temporal features of entity types and relationships proposed by Olivé et al. in [7], we discuss its application in the different phases of designing resilient information systems.

The goal of this paper is to discuss the temporal characteristics of information in resilient ISs and to propose a model to support resilient IS design.

The rest of the paper is organized as follows. In Section 8.2, we introduce the motivations and our approach to IS resiliency, presenting their characteristics in Section 8.3. In Section 8.4, we introduce the proposed process and data models, discussing their application for designing systems of different resiliency levels in Section 8.5. Finally, in Section 8.6 we relate our work to the state of the art.

8.2 The Approach

The approach underlying this work consists of the following building blocks:

- A designer provides a specification of the process s/he is dealing with in some process specification language, e.g., BPMN - Business Process Model and Notation, CMMN - Case Management Model and Notation, etc.
- In addition to such process specification, the designer provides an information model, detailing the data used in the process, both for routing the control flow (process data) and needed during tasks' execution.
- Such process model and information model are the main artifacts over which a *design-time resilience analysis* should be conducted, in order to identify possible breaches, propose alternative specifications, etc.

From an abstract point of view, our approach is a method that, given a process and an information model specifications, returns a quantification of how much such specifications allow the deployment of a resilient process, and possible guidelines for improving such specifications are offered. The availability of such a conceptual tool is quite important: organizations operate in ecosystems, in which each actor is a potential source of failures, and therefore the *awareness on resilience* is a critical element during the design of an IS and its applications.

Some previous work has attempted to analyze the issues of resilience, but generally satisfying resilience requirements is considered mainly as a run-time issue, as it is related to the ability to cope with unplanned situations: several approaches [27] have been proposed to keep business processes running even when some unplanned exceptions occur, by enacting countermeasures. Clearly, if we focus on what to do in case of a failure, this approach seems to be the only possibility. However, if we focus on what is affected when a failure occurs, some improvements can be done also at design-time. In [26] we proposed an approach for assessing the resilience of business processes modeled with CMMN, and assigning to the specification a value in the range [0..3] in order to measure how much the specification has been designed with resilience in mind. In this work, we focus on providing more specific details on the conceptual modeling languages to be used during the specification, focusing in particular on representing temporal aspects which play an important role for resilience, as it will be shown in the following examples.

8.3 Resiliency Scenarios

In this section, we describe some characteristics of IS resilience discussing some example scenarios (shown in Table 8.1), covering a broad variety of typologies of information systems with resiliency requirements. We take into consideration the information sources needed by the scenarios and their characteristics and possible actions to improve resilience. In the following of the paper we will discuss how to model and evaluate impacts of possible failures, focusing on resilient IS design.

In the first type of scenario, *periodic reporting* based on sensor data is considered. In this case, e.g., considered in [26], the input source is a stream of collected sensor data, and the system is based on the data collection interval and it can be influenced also by its frequency. Where data sources are considered unreliable, there is the need of investigating if other sources of information (current or historical) are available. In general, this is done at run time, to recover from failures on an ad-hoc basis, while anticipating failures at design time designing alternatives could make the recovery phase more rapid and systematic.

In the second scenario, inspired from the work presented in [13], *self-healing processes* with mechanisms for recovering from failures through partial rework are discussed. The approach, which uses planning techniques to derive repair plans, is based on modeling dependencies among data being used in business processes. In this case, the impact of erroneous data is evaluated, and pre-designed compensation and recovery tasks are used to dynamically generate recovery plans.

In *alerting systems*, such as for monitoring production in factories or in smart buildings (e.g., [37]), the focus is on monitoring the current situation to detect anomalies. As in the first case, alternative sources of information should be planned, and the timeliness of data is important.

Finally, a *data movement* scenario is considered, where moving large quantities of data takes time, and resilience could be weakened due to late/missing data. In this case, preparation strategies to anticipate possible failures can be envisioned, such as transferring data in advance, pre-selecting data, changing data location and redundancy policies [10].

Type of scenario	**Description**	**Critical input sources**	**Characteristics of sources**	**Compensation**
Periodic reporting	Analysis of sensor data	Sensors data collection	Interval of collection, frequency	Alternative source, using data from previous periods
Self-healing processes	Tasks exchanging info / Results of previous tasks	External sources	Any type	Reworking tasks
Alerting system	E.g., factory monitoring (device)	Sensors data collection	Interval of collection, frequency	Alternative source
Data movement	Transferring large documents	Documents available from different locations	Documents do not vary in time	Alternative location

Table 8.1 Scenarios characteristics.

At design time "what if" analyses of possible failures in data availability can support the design of more resilient systems. Other data quality properties could also be considered (data which are not accurate, that cannot be trusted, incomplete, and so on), however in the present paper we focus on their time-dependent characteristics and we attempt to derive a meta-model to support resilient IS design and to study the properties of the system being designed.

8.4 Modeling Processes and Data for Resiliency

8.4.1 Modeling Processes

Process modeling usually relies on imperative/procedural notations where the control flow represents the element around which the activities and the data are organized. In the recent period, BPMN[1] has emerged as the standard de facto notation used to model processes according to this activity-centric approach. As also mentioned in [11], activity-centric modeling notations, although intuitive and close to the way of thinking of the process modelers, suffers from some drawbacks especially when resilience needs to be captured. In fact, activity-centric modeling makes

[1] cf. `http://www.bpmn.org/`

a clear distinction between the normal execution and the exceptional executions. In some way, the modeler is forced to identify which is the right way to enact the business process and to decorate this process with additional activities that might be enacted only if some particular situations occur. In case of resilient processes, the normal execution could be more complex and depends on several variables that could also be unknown at design time. For this reason, we suggest to revert to artifact-centric notations as they provide the required flexibility with the main limitation that the modeling could become cumbersome.

Among the several alternatives, like GSM, Declare, and many others [21], in this paper we adopt CMMN[2] as artifact-centric modeling language. With a lot of synergies with BPMN (they are both proposed by OMG), CMMN provides a set of constructs that help the modeler to design a business process in terms of states in which the activities can be (or cannot be) performed. Instead of imposing a specific control flow and of considering such flow as the ideal one, the modeler can define conditions under which the state of system can be considered acceptable and to enable, or disable, activities.

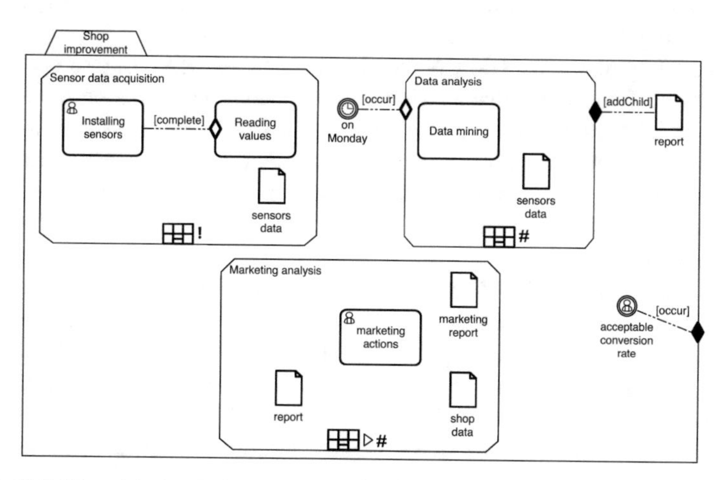

Fig. 8.1 CMMN model of an IoT-based case study [26].

In the next few paragraphs, the basic elements of CMMN useful to understand the content of this paper are introduced. To this aim, we refer to the example shown in Fig. 8.1 representing a real case study [26] concerning a process in charge of collecting data coming from a set of sensors. These sensors monitor the behavior of the customers inside a shop. Every week, these data are analyzed to create a report that constitutes the basis for creating marketing reports useful to identify marketing strategies (e.g., how to better distribute the items in the shelves, to identify the best products, and so on).

[2] cf. `http://www.omg.org/spec/CMMN/1.0`

The main concept of CMMN is the *case* that is defined by the *case file* (data managed in a case), the *case plan* (how the case evolves), and the *case roles* (the stakeholders). Focusing on the first two aspects, CMMN does not focus on the order in which the activities are performed, but only on the dependencies between the different states of execution of the process based on information stored in the case file.

In more detail, a case plan (represented as a manilla folder and which must be unique for a given model) is a composition of stages (represented by a rectangle shape with angled corners). The stages represent the episodes of a case which, in turn, could contain other stages or tasks, i.e., atomic units of work. Stages and tasks can be defined as mandatory (with a solid border) or discretionary (with a dashed border) to identify which are the elements of the case that actors must or could execute. Tasks and stages can be further characterized by the entry and exit criteria represented by, namely, white and black diamonds. These criteria define when a task or a stage opens and when they can be considered as closed. Finally, listeners (represented by circles) represent events that might occur during the execution of the case plan and that could determine the start or the end of a task or stage.

Concerning the information model, although this is a crucial element of artifact-based modeling notations, CMMN simply includes the possibility to specify data objects (typical document shape) without any specific restriction on the format or the content. If, from the one side, this leaves the freedom to consider any type of data, on the other side the model cannot express any type of data semantics. For this reason, as also proposed in [26], an extension of the information model where also discretionary data and a more rich set of association types between stage/task and objects are proposed.

Having quickly introduced the main elements of CMMN, and moving back to the case study in Fig. 8.1, here the case plan is composed by three main stages (i.e., sensor data acquisition, data analysis, and marketing analysis). While the data analysis starts every Monday and closes when a report is produced, the other two stages always run as neither entry nor exit criteria are defined. The entire case closes when the conversion rate (the ratio between people entering into the shop w.r.t. the people that buy some goods) becomes acceptable for the shop owner. Finally, as defined in the sensor data acquisition stage, it is possible to express some dependencies between the tasks. In fact, the sensor reading tasks start only when the sensors have been completely installed.

As previously mentioned, the information model provided by CMMN is not so rich. For this reason, we can simply add data objects to the stages to clarify which are the data that are considered (without any possibility to specify the nature of the operations on them) when a stage is running.

8.4.2 Modeling Time Varying Information

As discussed above, CMMN provides a high level view on the data objects needed in the different stages. For supporting resiliency at design time, it is clear that more information is needed on the data being used in the process. We adopt a notation based on UML class diagrams to represent data objects, their components, and their relationships.

However, as discussed by Olivè et al. [7], the notation of UML class diagrams assumes that "the information base contains the current instances of entity and relationship types". On the other hand, temporal information about the available data for the process is essential in processes such as the one shown in Fig. 8.1. In fact, for instance, the report is produced periodically from sensor data that must be available for the period considered in the report. Sensor data also need to be defined, as they are acquired from sensors within the considered period, and therefore they are a time series taken as an input for a given stage. It has also to be noted that the process is continuing, producing reports periodically, until its exit goal is reached. Therefore, in general, several reports will be produced periodically, starting from different sensor data.

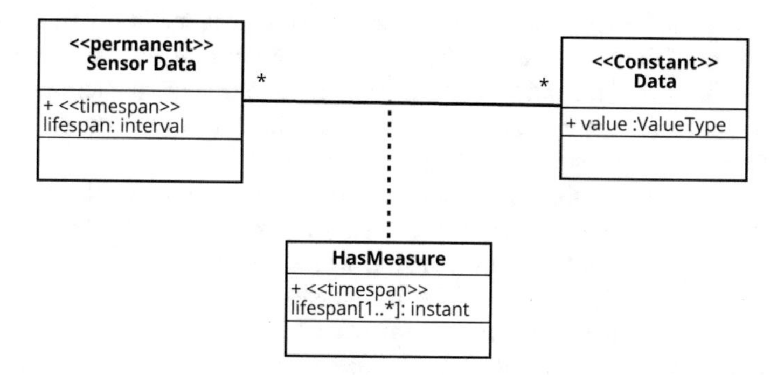

Fig. 8.2 Time series representation for sensor data.

In Olivè et al. [24], two dimensions are considered: durability and frequency. The *durability* feature is used to describe if an entity type is instantaneous or durable. The *frequency* feature is defined so that "entity type *E* is single if all its entities can only be instance of *E* during one classification interval. Otherwise, *E* is intermittent."

Starting from the dimensions described above, six ways for classifying an entity or a relationship type wrt. its temporal features are proposed in [7]:

- *Instantaneous, single*, if two entity types can be related only once, at a given time.
- *Instantaneous, intermittent*. If two entity types can be related several times, at different time instants.
- *Durable, single*. Two entity types can be related for a period of time, only once.

- *Durable, intermittent.* Two entity types can be related for a period of time, several times.
- *Permanent.* A relationship once established does not change.
- *Constant.* For unchanging entities.

The representation of input sources for data in our case study of Fig. 8.1 can be represented using the notation proposed in [7], to be able to represent the temporal characteristics of entities used in the model. In Fig. 8.2, we show how the Sensor data source is formed: as it is a stream of data, it is considered a durable intermittent entity type in our case study, where the intervals indicate the periods in which data are gathered. Its lifespan is indicated as a set of intervals. Note that if the stream is always correctly working, it will contain a single interval from the beginning of the measurement to the current date. If an interruption in the stream occurs, a new lifespan interval is created instead. So the intervals indicate all periods in which Sensor data measurements are actually collected.

8.5 Analyzing Resiliency Data Properties

During a generic process enactment, unplanned situations might occur. Depending on the nature of the raised issues, the magnitude of their impact varies and one or more activities may be involved. At the same time, different countermeasures can be taken to mitigate these negative effects. As an example, in a cyber-physical process for many reasons the sensors might not be able to send data, and an alternative source of information might be considered, to be able to equally infer relevant behaviors to be monitored, or at least in a slightly degraded form. Another example is about frequencies (temporal constraints): a sensor might not be able to send information very frequently, still alternative techniques can be adopted to infer missing data or to calculate aggregated measurements. Similarly to what is usually done in emergency management [32, 20], where a *preparedness phase* aims to improve the systems by learning from the previous emergencies, in [26] we propose an approach which helps the process designers in improving their process models by considering the previous experiences in failures generated by data unavailability. For this, the ability to model the process and the information model and possible temporal constraints for the purpose of resilience awareness is crucial.

Having clearly modeled the process and the information model, allows the development of an approach to categorize resilience characteristics, then to define resiliency levels, and to model the resilience improvement aspects from a modeling perspective. With the modeling approach previously introduced, it is possible to analyze a (possibly multi-party) business process resilience from a *data perspective*: data dependencies among the involved parties and relationships between process activities and data are taken into account to identify the *sources of possible failures*, and how the process can be better modeled to make it resilient with respect to these failures. We are able to consider *Parties*, i.e., actors involved in the process. Then we deal with *Tasks*, i.e., units of work performed by parties, which consume data as input and produce data as output. The data produced by a task must be required by at least another party, and *Data*, i.e., units of storage used by the data producer to store/write data and by the data consumer to read such data. Producers and consumers are parties performing tasks. Data can also be used to verify the entry and exit conditions, thus to realize when a stage or task starts or terminates. As previously introduced, the temporal constraints over read/write of data are crucial in modeling resilient processes.

Resilience of processes depends on both the reliability of the tasks and the lack of data availability. The *reliability of the task* concerns the possibility that one or more tasks cannot be executed: i.e., the required infrastructure to perform the job is not available, also including the human resources for which the unavailability of data can block the execution of manual tasks. On the other side, *lack of data availability* (including a wrong frequency of the data) is a situation in which the data consumed by a task are not available. This situation can occur for different reasons. Firstly, it may be directly connected to the task reliability, as all the tasks by definition produce data and these data are relevant for at least one of the participating parties, and problems on tasks may have also the side effect to make data unavailable. Moreover, there are situations in which tasks are properly working, but the returned data, although available, do not have a sufficient quality level to enable processing, thus they can be considered unavailable. Completeness, timeliness, and accuracy are some of quality parameters through which we can define the acceptable level of data quality for considering the data available [6]. For this reason, the definition of the data could be coupled with the definition of quality levels that are considered acceptable for a task that is using such data.

Having modeled the process and the information model, it is then possible to define levels of resilience on the basis of the ability of the process to adjust the possible unexpected failures. We aim to classify the way resilience can be considered and obtained, in terms of preparedness to unexpected events which might be caused or have impact on data availability. In particular, the following four levels of designed resilience have been identified:

- **Level 0 – None.** At this level business processes are designed without taking into account the data unavailability that might cause failures during the execution. As a consequence, also countermeasures to be adopted in case of critical situations are not defined. The designed process only reflects the wishful scenario where it is assumed that all the parties correctly execute their tasks and all the data are transferred among them as expected. Although a process design of this type can be useful to define the agreement between the parties, no support is given to the resilience.

- **Level 1 - Failure-awareness.** A first step for improving the process design is to make the process aware that there are possible sources of failure, so there will be the need to make it resilient. In this work, we consider failures caused by data unavailability, which might impact on one or more tasks of the same party that is producing such data, or tasks performed by other parties. For this reason, failure-aware business processes are designed to have a clear map of which are the relevant data subject to failures, as well as the impact of these failures. The analysis of potential failures depends on several factors: amount of data, how the data are collected, how the data are stored. As an example, data stored on a local server have a probability of failure that is lower than data stored on a smart device connected to a wireless network. Similarly, if data created by one party and used by several parties becomes unavailable, the impact of this failure will be greater than the one produced by data created and consumed by the same party.

- **Level 2 – Identifying alternatives for data and goals.** For processes classified in this level, the model of the process makes an initial attempt to overcome possible failures, whose nature and impact have been defined with the previous level. In more detail, there are two aspects to be taken into account:
  - *Alternative Data*: based on the information about the source of failures and the potential impact of these failures, the designer can decide to include in the process model the alternative data. In this way, starting from the data having more probability of failures and greater impact, the designer has to specify if there are alternative data sources and how to reach them. A more precise model requires an analysis of the gap between the quality of the data in the original data source with respect to the quality of the data in the alternative data source. The issue of quality of data has been extensively addressed in traditional information systems, e.g., [6], but the quality of big data (which includes sensor-generated data) is still to be precisely defined [12].
  - *Alternative Goal*: as the process resilience implies to mitigate the effect of a failure, a possible mitigation includes revising the initial expectations of the process to achieve a given goal. The designer defines, for each party, a new goal that represents a status that can terminate the execution of the process in an acceptable way. If the initial goal corresponds to the optimal goal, the alternative goal could be considered as a best-effort goal.

  It is worth noting that the business process models at this level do not prescribe any specific actions to cope with the failures at run-time. For this reason, a model at this level only supports who is in charge of executing the process, to select, in case of failures, new data sources as well as to decide to consider satisfactory the result of the execution even if the initial goal is not possible to be fulfilled, accepting a weaker goal.
  In [26], we propose an extension to CMMN to represent *alternative data*, represented with document shaped icons with dashed borders as shown in Fig. 8.3.
  Using the data model introduced in Section 8.4.2, we can represent also the relationships between entities in the process. As shown in Fig. 8.4, the Report to be produced for a given interval is based on the Sensor Data for a period, but can also use as an alternative Public data available for the period of interest of the report. The source of data that will be actually selected (either Sensor Data or the alternative Public Data) will become permanently liked to a given report using it.

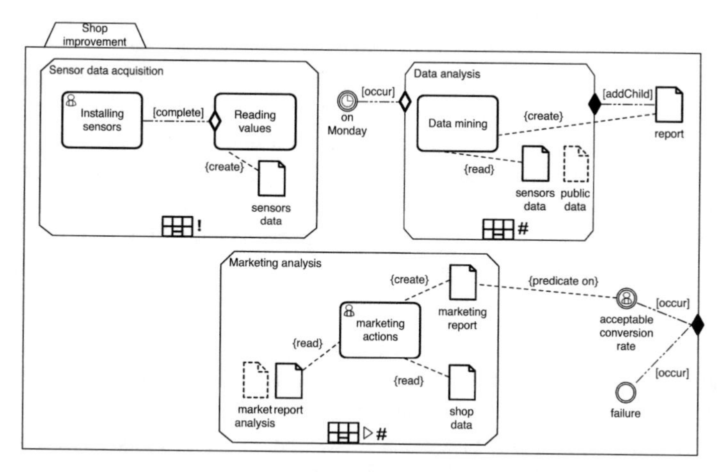

Fig. 8.3 CMMN model extended with alternative data [26].

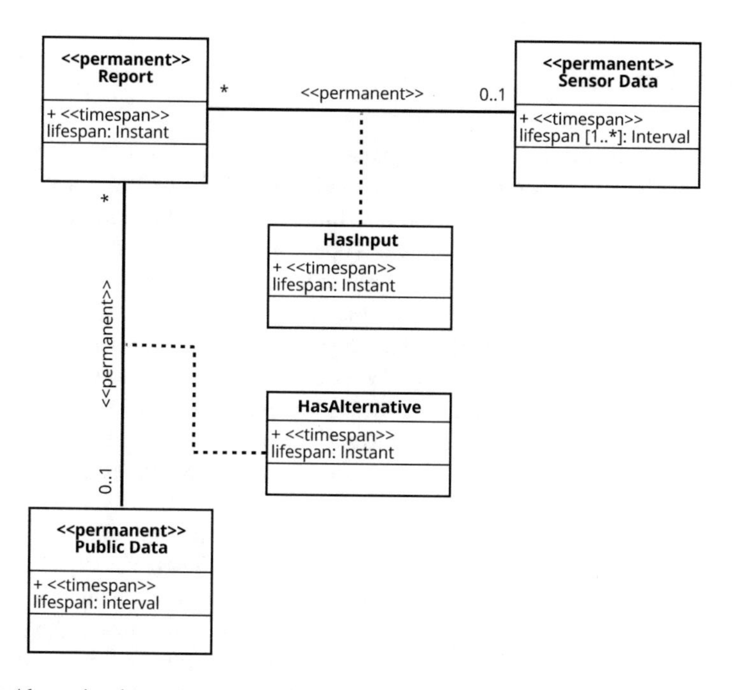

Fig. 8.4 Alternative data sources representation.

- **Level 3 – Defining alternative actions.** At this level, processes have been designed by considering also actions to be taken in case of failures. Design-time mechanisms are conceived to be able to (semi)-automatically move the process to an acceptable state when unexpected or unplanned failures occur. Based on the information about the alternatives (both data and goal), the designer can embed in the business process how these alternatives could be effectively managed. New tasks can be added to the process to express the activities to be performed in order to improve the quality of the data alternatives to a quality level equivalent to the original service.

With these levels of resilience, we aim at supporting the process designer in understanding if the resilience is modeled, and if there is room to improve the process model by specifying possible alternative solutions. As an example, once the designer understands that the modeled processes are at level 0, the first step should be to start considering the evolution of the data in the process.

8.6 Related Work

Research on *resilient systems* encompasses several disciplines, such as psychology [34], ecology [14], sociology [3] and engineering [17]. In information systems, *resilience engineering* has its roots in the study of safety-critical systems [17], i.e., systems aimed to ensure that organizations operating in turbulent and interconnected settings achieve high levels of safety despite a multitude of emerging risks, complex tasks, and constantly increasing pressures. A system is considered as resilient if its capabilities can be adapted to new organizational requirements and changes that have not been explicitly incorporated into the existing system's design [23]. In the BPM field, cf. [23] and [28], this means that respective business processes are able to automatically adapt themselves to such changes. Over the last years, change management in BPM has been mainly tackled through the notions of *process flexibility* [27] and *risk-aware BPM* [31, 30].

On the one hand, research on process flexibility has focused on four major flexibility needs, namely *(i) variability* [15, 16, 27], *(ii) looseness* [2, 19], *(iii) adaptation* [29, 22], and *(iv) evolution* [8, 9]. The ability to deal with changes makes process flexibility approaches a required but not sufficient mean for building resilient BPM systems. In fact, there exists a (seemingly insignificant but) relevant gap between the concepts of flexibility and resilience: (i) process flexibility is aimed at producing "reactive" approaches that reduce failures from the outset or deal with them at run-time if any "known" disturbance arises; (ii) process resilience requires "proactive" techniques accepting and managing change "on-the-fly" rather than anticipating it, in order to allow a system to address new emerging and unforeseeable changes with the potential to cascade. On the other hand, while relatively close to the concept of risk-aware BPM, which evaluates operational risks on the basis of historical threat probabilities (with a focus on the "cause" of disturbances and events), resilient BPM shifts attention on the "realized risks" and their consequences, to improve risk prevention and mitigation, and therefore aim at complementing conventional risk-aware approaches.

Surprisingly, the fact is that there exists only a limited number of research works investigating resilience of BPM systems [4, 36, 35], and they are all at conceptual level. For example, the work of Antunes and MourËIJao [4] derives a set of fundamental requirements aimed at supporting resilient BPM. The approach of Zahoransky et al. [36] investigates the use of process mining [1] to create probability distributions on time behavior of business processes. Such distributions can be used as indicators to monitor the level of resilience at run-time and indicate possible countermeasures if the level drops. Finally, the work [35] provides a support framework and a set of measures based on the analysis of previous process executions to realize and evaluate resilience in the BPM context.

In our previous work [26], we started to approach IS resiliency in a systematic way, with the goal of defining possible levels of resiliency, and of investigating which models, or variants of models, can support the design of resilient IS.

Considering conceptual models, there is a specific need for conceptualizing the evolution of the information. To this purpose, we considered previous work on the representation of time and events at conceptual level. The fundamental concepts for representing temporal data have been discussed and presented in [18]. In the direction of conceptual modeling, the information systems group lead by Antoni Olivé has given an important contribution, studying possible extensions for modeling temporal aspects of information and events in IS design (see e.g., [7, 25, 24]. Part of the work presented in this paper has been based on the classification and notations proposed by Olivé et al. for extending UML with temporal features.

If compared with the aforementioned works, our research aims to provide guidelines to model resilient-by-design business processes by focusing on the data exchanged between the activities composing the process, an aspect neglected in the existing approaches to process resilience. In this work, we have tackled the issue of modeling the temporal dimension of the data, in order to have a coherent approach both in the process and in the information model.

8.7 Conclusions and Future Work

Adopting design-time models to represent resilience aspects allows the IS designer to take a "preparedness" approach, to anticipate what should be done in case of possible occurring or anticipated failures, to guarantee a certain level of resilience. Following a continuous improvement approach, we propose to analyze temporal features of data over time evaluating past failures of the system. Further work is needed in this direction, with the goal of improving resilience. A focus on a preparedness phase can help improving the models by learning from previous failures. Further modeling and analysis techniques are also needed to represent possible interferences among processes, as unexpected consequences may arise over time from apparently unrelated processes [33].

Acknowledgements This work is partly supported by the H2020 European project no. 731945 DITAS - "Data-intensive applications Improvement by moving daTA and computation in mixed cloud/fog environmentS"[3] and by the Sapienza project "Data-aware Adaptation of Knowledge-intensive Processes in Cyber-Physical Domains through Action-based Languages".

References

1. van der Aalst, W.M.P.: Process Mining: Data Science in Action. Springer (2016)
2. van der Aalst, W.M.P., Pesic, M., Schonenberg, H.: Declarative workflows: Balancing between flexibility and support. Computer Science - R&D 23(2) (2009)
3. Adger, W.N.: Social and ecological resilience: are they related? Progress in human geography 24(3), 347–364 (2000)
4. Antunes, P., Mourão, H.: Resilient Business Process Management: Framework and services. Expert Systems with Applications 38(2), 1241 – 1254 (2011)
5. Avizienis, A., Laprie, J., Randell, B., Landwehr, C.E.: Basic concepts and taxonomy of dependable and secure computing. IEEE Trans. Dependable Sec. Comput. 1(1), 11–33 (2004)
6. Batini, C., Scannapieco, M.: Data and Information Quality - Dimensions, Principles and Techniques. Springer (2016)
7. Cabot, J., Olivé, A., Teniente, E.: Representing temporal information in UML. In: UML 2003 - The Unified Modeling Language, Proc. 6th Intl. Conference on Modeling Languages and Applications, San Francisco, CA, USA. pp. 44–59 (2003)
8. Casati, F., Ceri, S., Pernici, B., Pozzi, G.: Workflow evolution. Data & Knowledge Engineering 24(3), 211–238 (1998)
9. Dadam, P., Rinderle, S.: Workflow evolution. In: Encyclopedia of Database Systems, pp. 3540–3544. Springer (2009)
10. D'Andria, F., Field, D., Kopaneli, A., Kousiouris, G., García-Pérez, D., Pernici, B., Plebani, P.: Data movement in the internet of things domain. In: Service Oriented and Cloud Computing - 4th European Conference, ESOCC 2015, Taormina, Italy, September 15-17, 2015. Proceedings. pp. 243–252 (2015)
11. Fahland, D., Lübke, D., Mendling, J., Reijers, H.A., Weber, B., Weidlich, M., Zugal, S.: Declarative versus Imperative Process Modeling Languages: The Issue of Understandability. In: 10th Int. Workshop on Business Process Modeling, Development, and Support (BPMDS). pp. 353–366 (2009)
12. Firmani, D., Mecella, M., Scannapieco, M., Batini, C.: On the Meaningfulness of "Big Data Quality". Data Science and Engineering 1(1), 6–20 (2016)
13. Friedrich, G., Fugini, M., Mussi, E., Pernici, B., Tagni, G.: Exception handling for repair in service-based processes. IEEE Trans. Software Eng. 36(2), 198–215 (2010)
14. Gunderson, L.H.: Ecological Resilience–in Theory and Application. Annual review of ecology and systematics pp. 425–439 (2000)
15. Hallerbach, A., Bauer, T., Reichert, M.: Capturing variability in business process models: the Provop approach. Journal of Software Maintenance and Evolution: Research and Practice 22(6-7) (2009)
16. Hallerbach, A., Bauer, T., Reichert, M.: Configuration and Management of Process Variants. In: Handbook on Business Process Management vol.1. International Handbooks on Information Systems, Springer Berlin Heidelberg (2010)
17. Hollnagel, E., Woods, D.D., Leveson, N.: Resilience Engineering: Concepts and Precepts. Ashgate Publishing, Ltd. (2007)
18. Jensen, C.S., Dyreson, C.E., Böhlen, M.H., Clifford, J., Elmasri, R., Gadia, S.K., Grandi, F., Hayes, P.J., Jajodia, S., Käfer, W., Kline, N., Lorentzos, N.A., Mitsopoulos, Y.G., Montanari,

[3] `http://www.ditas-project.eu`

A., Nonen, D.A., Peressi, E., Pernici, B., Roddick, J.F., Sarda, N.L., Scalas, M.R., Segev, A., Snodgrass, R.T., Soo, M.D., Tansel, A.U., Tiberio, P., Wiederhold, G.: The consensus glossary of temporal database concepts - february 1998 version. In: Temporal Databases, Dagstuhl. pp. 367–405 (1997)
19. Marrella, A., Lespérance, Y.: Synthesizing a Library of Process Templates through Partial-Order Planning Algorithms. In: 14th Int. Conf. on Business Process Modeling, Development, and Support (BPMDS). pp. 277–291 (2013)
20. Marrella, A., Mecella, M., Russo, A.: Collaboration On-the-field : Suggestions and Beyond. In: 8th Int. Conf. on Information Systems for Crisis Response and Management (ISCRAM) (2011)
21. Marrella, A., Mecella, M., Russo, A., Steinau, S., Andrews, K., Reichert, M.: Data in business process models, A preliminary empirical study. In: 8th IEEE SOCA 2015, Rome, Italy, October 19-21, 2015. pp. 116–122 (2015)
22. Marrella, A., Mecella, M., Sardiña, S.: Intelligent Process Adaptation in the SmartPM System. ACM TIST 8(2) (2017)
23. Müller, G., Koslowski, T.G., Accorsi, R.: Resilience - A New Research Field in Business Information Systems? In: 16th Int. Conf. on Business Information Systems (BIS). pp. 3–14. Springer (2013)
24. Olivé, A.: Relationship reification: A temporal view. In: Advanced Information Systems Engineering, 11th International Conference CAiSE'99, Heidelberg, Germany, June 1999, Proceedings. pp. 396–410 (1999)
25. Olivé, A.: Definition of events and their effects in object-oriented conceptual modeling languages. In: Atzeni, P., Chu, W.W., Lu, H., Zhou, S., Ling, T.W. (eds.) Conceptual Modeling - ER 2004, 23rd International Conference on Conceptual Modeling, Shanghai, China, November 2004, Proceedings. Lecture Notes in Computer Science, vol. 3288, pp. 136–149. Springer (2004)
26. Plebani, P., Marrella, A., Mecella, M., Mizmizi, M., Pernici, B.: Multi-party business process resilience by-design: A data-centric perspective. In: Proc. Conference on Advanced Systems Engineering, CAiSE'17. Springer (June 2017)
27. Reichert, M., Weber, B.: Enabling Flexibility in Process-Aware Information Systems - Challenges, Methods, Technologies. Springer (2012)
28. Rosemann, M., Recker, J.: Context-aware Process Design Exploring the Extrinsic Drivers for Process Flexibility. In: 7th Int. Workshop on Business Process Modeling, Development, and Support (BPMDS) (2006)
29. Sadiq, S., Orlowska, M.: On Capturing Exceptions in Workflow Process Models. In: 3rd Int. Conf. on Business Information Systems (BIS), pp. 3–19. Springer (2000)
30. Suriadi, S., Weiß, B., Winkelmann, A., et al.: Current Research in Risk-aware Business Process Management: Overview, Comparison, and Gap Analysis. Communications of the Association for Information Systems 34(1), 933–984 (2014)
31. Tjoa, S., Jakoubi, S., Goluch, G., Kitzler, G., Goluch, S., Quirchmayr, G.: A Formal Approach Enabling Risk-Aware Business Process Modeling and Simulation. IEEE Transactions on Services Computing 4(2), 153–166 (2011)
32. Van De Walle, B., Turoff, M., Hiltz, S.R.: Information Systems for Emergency Management. M.E.Sharpe (2009)
33. Vitali, M., Pernici, B.: Interconnecting processes through IoT in a health-care scenario. In: IEEE International Smart Cities Conference, ISC2 2016, Trento, Italy, September 12-15, 2016. pp. 1–6 (2016)
34. Yates, T.M., Masten, A.S.: Fostering the Future: Resilience Theory and the Practice of Positive Psychology. John Wiley & Sons Inc (2004)
35. Zahoransky, R.M., Brenig, C., Koslowski, T.: Towards a Process-Centered Resilience Framework. In: 10th Int. Conf. on Availability, Reliability and Security (ARES). pp. 266–273. IEEE (2015)
36. Zahoransky, R.M., Koslowski, T., Accorsi, R.: Toward Resilience Assessment in Business Process Architectures. In: Computer Safety, Reliability, and Security: SAFECOMP 2014 Workshops. pp. 360–370. Springer (2014)

37. Zhou, S., Lin, K., Na, J., Chuang, C., Shih, C.: Supporting service adaptation in fault tolerant internet of things. In: 8th IEEE International Conference on Service-Oriented Computing and Applications, SOCA 2015, Rome, Italy. pp. 65–72 (2015)

Chapter 9
Web System Development Using Polymorphic Widgets and Generic Schemas

Scott Britell, Lois M. L. Delcambre and Paolo Atzeni

Abstract Current tools allow non-technical users to create systems to store, display, and analyze their data on their own using whatever schema they choose. At the same time, developers of these systems can create generic widgets that may work across any number of domains. Unfortunately, to use a generic widget an end-user (the domain expert) must make their data conform to the schema of the widgets, possibly losing meaningful schema names. This paper presents a solution to this problem in the form of generic widget models (*canonical structures*), local schemas for domain experts, and an intermediate model (*domain structures*) that—through the use of mappings between the different models—allows generic functionality while preserving local schema. We present the three user roles in our system: widget developers, domain experts, and domain developers (people who develop and map domain structures). We introduce the concept of canonical structures and show how they are mapped to domain structures. We introduce a new relational query operator for writing queries against canonical structures and show how those queries are rewritten against the domain structures. We also provide an evaluation of the overhead of our system compared to custom code solutions and a modern web development framework.

Scott Britell
Computer Science Department, Portland State University, PO Box 751, Portland, OR 97207 USA
e-mail: `britell@cs.pdx.edu`

Lois M. L. Delcambre
Computer Science Department, Portland State University, PO Box 751, Portland, OR 97207 USA
e-mail: `lmd@pdx.edu`

Paolo Atzeni
Dipartimento di Ingegneria, Università Roma Tre, Via della Vasca Navale 79, 00146 Roma, Italy
e-mail: `atzeni@dia.uniroma3.it`

© Springer International Publishing AG 2017

J. Cabot et al. (eds.), *Conceptual Modeling Perspectives*,
https://doi.org/10.1007/978-3-319-67271-7_9

9.1 Introduction

Early on, if an end-user created a website using a word-processing tool like Microsoft Word® that website would be little more than just documents on the Internet. To go beyond that, they would have needed to work hand-in-hand with a developer who had the expertise to take the client's conceptual model and realize it in an application.

Today, technologies such as web development frameworks have democratized the creation of complex systems by allowing non-technical (non-developer) users to define their own content types and create complex data models (i.e., conceptual models) while abstracting away the complexities of database and application creation. Thus, end-users who are experts in their own data, can choose schema names that are meaningful. We call end-user-created schemas *local schemas*.

Modern web frameworks also allow developers to create widgets that can be plugged into any site built upon that framework. These widgets use a conceptual model of the developer's choosing and are typically related to the functionality of the widget.

Traditionally, in order for a widget to work there are two choices. Developers may rewrite the same widget multiple times for the different conceptual models of the end systems. For example, in the case of a calendar widget the developer could modify the widget to work with each different event type. Or, the end systems must conform to the model of the widget; in the case of the calendar widget, each end-user would have to use the event type defined by the widget. This is the common case in use today by most web development frameworks.

Here, we present a different way to solve this problem. We begin by introducing intermediary conceptual models (that we call *domain structures*) between the end-user models (*local schemas*) and the widget models (*canonical structures*). We then define mappings (such as that used in traditional information integration and schema mapping) between the different levels (local schema↔domain structures and domain structures↔canonical structures). We allow end-users to create local schemas with meaningful names and allow widget developers to create generic widgets with canonical structures. And, we allow those generic widgets to show the local schema names using what we call *local radiance*.

Our system has three main roles. We call the end-user a *domain expert* since we consider someone creating an application for their data to be an expert in their data. The domain expert is responsible for deciding the local schema and data which will be used in the system. This person will enable instantiated widgets by creating mappings between the local schemas and the domain structures.

We call the developer responsible for creating generic widgets described above the *widget developer*. This person writes widget code that interacts with generic schemas, the canonical structures, that produce information that can be displayed on a webpage or used elsewhere in a web framework.

We add a third role to the two traditional roles: the *domain developer* whose responsibility is to create mappings between the generic schemas of the widgets and the schema of the domain expert. The domain developer usually has some (possibly

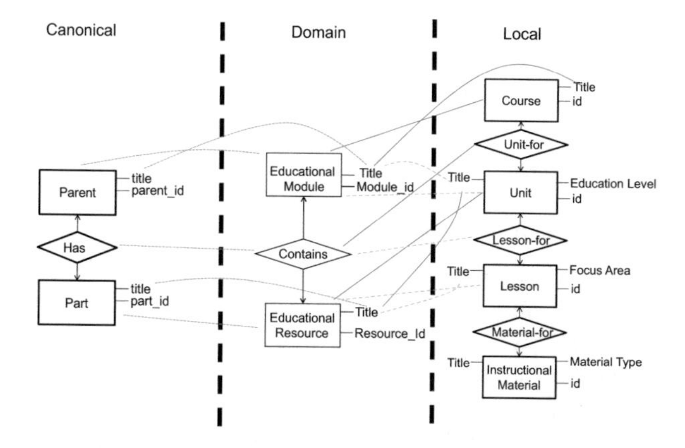

Fig. 9.1 An example use of a generic canonical structure (left), an educational domain structure (middle), a local educational schema (right), and mappings between them.

in-depth) knowledge of the domain but their main responsibility is more likely IT-based (database/web/application development) rather than domain analysis. Domain structures will typically be defined by domain developers. Domain structures are small schemas with names that are understandable to a domain expert. This person may work with the domain expert to create the website or may work with widget developers to allow the generic widgets to be used in specific application areas.

The rest of this paper is structured as follows. Section 9.2 describes the background of our previous work that contributed domain structures, local schemas, the mappings between them, and our query language. In Section 9.3 we explore the widget schemas that we call canonical structures, their mappings to the intermediary model (domain structures), and query rewriting. In Section 9.4 we evaluate the cost of using our system compared to a generic web framework and hard-coded widgets. We present related work in Section 9.5. Section 17.5 concludes the paper.

9.2 Background

In our earlier work we developed a system called information integration with local radiance (IILR) [8] which consists of three main parts: (1) domain structures (schema fragments with domain appropriate names), (2) mappings comprised of simple correspondences from local schemas to domain structures, and (3) a query algebra to allow queries against the domain structures to retrieve data from the local schemas—including the ability to retrieve local schema names. IILR corresponds to the middle and right parts of Figure 9.1.

Figure 9.1 shows the three levels of schema used in our system and mappings between them. In this example we have an hierarchical canonical structure with a domain structure and local schema from an educational domain. These three levels correspond to the three roles described above.

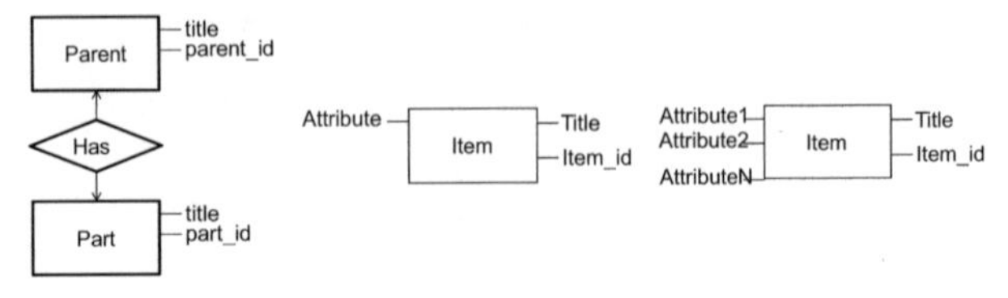

Fig. 9.2 Three examples of canonical structures.

On the left side of the figure, there is a canonical structure for a "Parent" and "Part" related by "Has" that will be used for a hierarchical navigation widget.

A domain developer then may create a domain structure (center of Figure 9.1) to work with the canonical structure of the widget. Note that the domain structure (or a subset of the domain structure) must be isomorphic to the canonical structure. The main difference between the domain structure and the canonical structure is the use of schema names that should be recognizable to a person working in the educational domain, for this example. The domain developer then creates a set of mappings between the canonical structure and the domain structure to instantiate the widget in a domain. In this case, the domain structure represents a hierarchical setting of an "Educational Module" that contains "Educational Resources". This domain structure is identical to the canonical structure albeit for the changing of names.

The domain expert has a local schema (shown on the right of Figure 9.1) and is able to use the instantiated widget in their website by creating mappings from the local schema to the domain structure. Here we see that the local schema is mapped multiple times to the domain structure allowing the widget to show "Units" inside a "Course" (the blue-solid lines between local and domain), and "Lessons" in a "Unit" (the green-dashed lines between local and domain).

A canonical structure is usually rather simple, essentially a "data pattern", on top of which widget code is implemented. A canonical structure often involves a single entity (like those shown in the middle and right in Figure 9.2), to be used by widgets that manage (search, analyze, update, ...) objects of a given data type (phone books, recent messages, calendars, ...).

Figure 9.3 shows a small sample of domain structures across a number of domains. On the left we see two domain structures for an educational domain. We use these structures throughout the rest of this paper. The "Educational Module" structure shown previously is on top and on bottom there is a structure for an educational resource.

In the middle of Figure 9.3 there are two domain structures from a financial domain. The top structure shows "Organizations" and their "Sub-organizations" which may be used for company schemas with departments, divisions, or labs. Below that there is a domain structure for a "Financial Instrument" which can be used for grants, budgets, or other financial entities. Being isomorphic to the educational structures, these structures will work with any widgets that the educational ones do (once mappings are in place between the canonical and domain structure).

On the right of Figure 9.3 there are two domain structures for the sports domain. The top structure represents a "Team" that has people in both coaching and par-

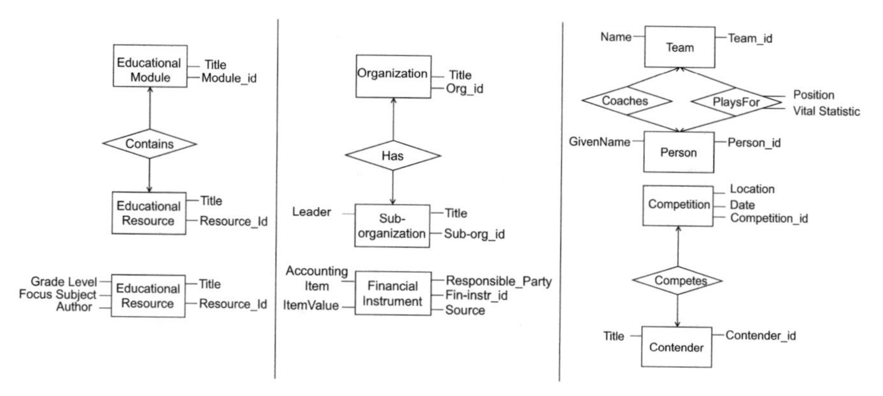

Fig. 9.3 Examples of domain structures from the educational (left), financial (middle), and sports (right) domains.

ticipant roles. The bottom structure represents "Competitions" and "Contenders" which can be used for local schemas ranging from football games to tennis and boxing matches.

Figure 9.4 then shows how the various domain structures from the financial and sports domains can be mapped to the canonical structures. The mappings on the right side of the figure are straightforward. The mapping in the upper left shows how a subset of the domain structure can be isomorphic to a canonical structure. In this case, both the coaches of the teams and the players are mapped to the canonical structure separately so that they can both show up in the hierarchical widget, but only an isomorphic part of the structure is mapped at a single time. The bottom left of the figure shows a more complex mapping where multiple attributes of the domain structure are mapped to a single attribute in the canonical structure. This will perform an operation similar to an unpivot[19] of the local schema (when local types are included in a query result, a feature supported by IILR).

Figure 9.5 shows an example of an educational local schema on the right and a domain structure on the left. There are two mappings between the two schemas. The blue-solid lines show the mapping between the Course/Unit-For/Unit structure in the local schema and the domain structure while the green-dashed lines show the mapping between the Unit/Lesson-For/Lesson structure and the domain structure. In our previous work [9], we performed a user-study that showed that domain experts with and without technical expertise could understand and create these mappings using simple and complex schemas.

We defined a query language at the domain level to enable information integration and querying of multiple local schemas with a single domain query. This enables both integration and data analysis and enables the widgets described later in this paper. Our query language extends the nested relational algebra (σ, π, $\bowtie$, ν, ..., plus γ for grouping [11]) with two operators: apply (α) and type (τ). Our *apply* operator ($\alpha(DS)$) is the basis of every query in our system. The *apply* operator uses correspondences that comprise the mappings between local schemas and a domain structure to perform information extraction/integration/transformation. The result of the *apply* operator is a set of relational tuples which can be passed to other relational

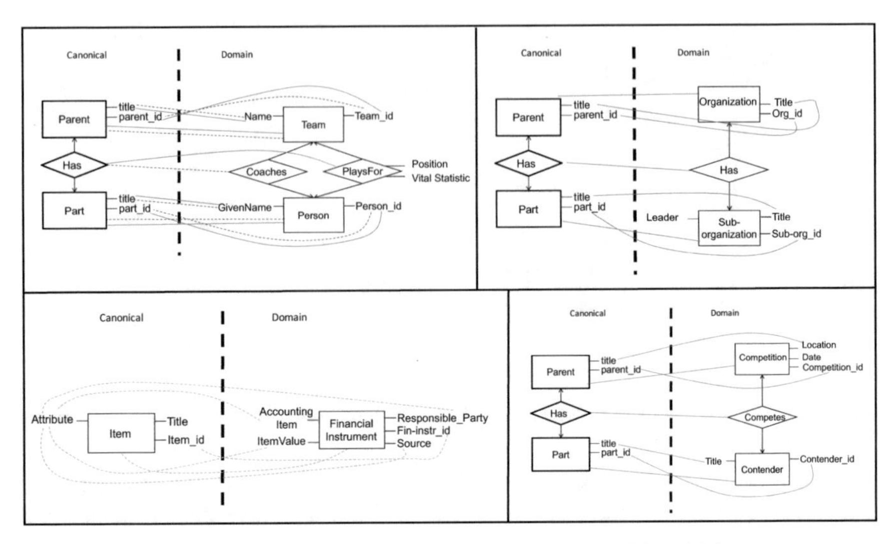

Fig. 9.4 Mappings of all domain and canonical structures in Figures 9.2 and 9.3

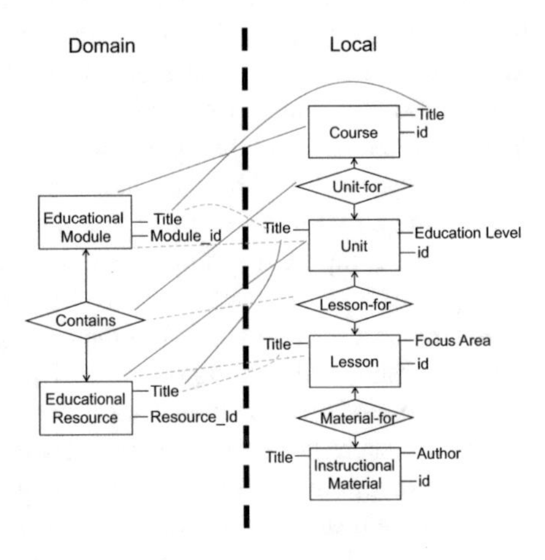

Fig. 9.5 A domain structure (left) and local schema (right) with two mappings between them (the blue-solid mapping and the green-dashed mapping). Each mapping consists of a number of correspondences (single lines).

algebra operators as part of more complex queries. For example, Figure 9.6 shows sample data in the form of the local schema from Figure 9.5. Then the left and middle parts of Figure 9.7 show the use of the apply operator against the "Educational Module" and "Contains" parts of the domain structure from Figure 9.5.

The local *type* operator ($\tau_n(\chi)$) takes a domain structure component (n) and a query (χ) and introduces an attribute into the query result containing the local structure name to which the domain structure component (entity, attribute, or relationship) was mapped. For example, the right part of Figure 9.7 shows the type operator being used after the apply on the "Instructional Resource" part of the domain structure from Figure 9.5. The type operator allows the local names to come to the

Course

Title	Id
Intro to CS	324

Unit-For

Course_id	Unit_id
324	834
324	982

Unit

Title	Id	Education Level
Python	834	12th Grade
Java	982	12th Grade

Lesson-For

Unit_id	Lesson_id
834	835
834	836
982	983

Lesson

Title	Id	Focus Area
Intro to Python	835	CS
Advanced Python	836	CS
Intro to Java	983	CS

Fig. 9.6 Sample local data using the local schema from Figure 9.5.

α(Educational Module)

Title	Module_id
Intro to CS	324
Python	834
Java	982

α(Contains)

Module_id	Resource_id
324	834
324	982
834	835
834	836
982	983

$\tau_{Instructional\ Resource}\ \alpha$(Instructional Resource)

Title	Resource_id	Intructional_ Resource.type
Python	834	Unit
Java	982	Unit
Intro to Python	835	Lesson
Advanced Python	836	Lesson
Intro to Java	983	Lesson

Fig. 9.7 Use of the apply and type operators on the domain structure from Figure 9.5 using the local data from Figure 9.6.

domain level in a generic fashion meaning that generic widgets can display local schema names; in essence the local names radiate to the domain level hence the name information integration with local radiance.

9.3 Canonical Structures

A canonical structure is a generically named schema fragment used by a widget developer. As an example, the left side of Figure 9.1 shows the canonical structure that is used to build the navigation widget described below.

Another basic canonical structure is a single entity with a small set of attributes such as that shown in Figures 9.2 and 9.8. This simple schema allows a variety of different generic widgets to be built. We say that the widget is polymorphic because it can be used with multiple domain structures (and multiple local schemas in turn).

9.3.1 Widgets

We describe three polymorphic widgets that use canonical structures to give the reader some idea of what widgets are and how they can represent different local schemas.

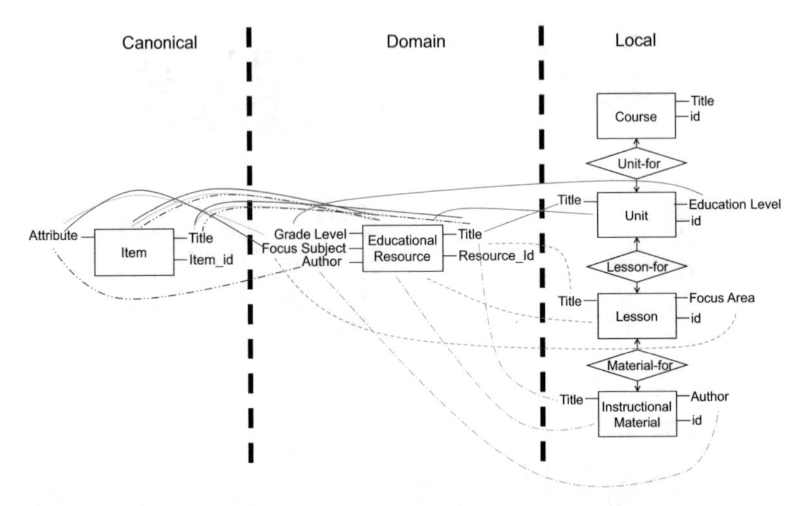

Fig. 9.8 A set of mappings is shown for the data analysis widget. The mappings between local and domain are straightforward. The mappings between the canonical and domain perform an unpivot operation.

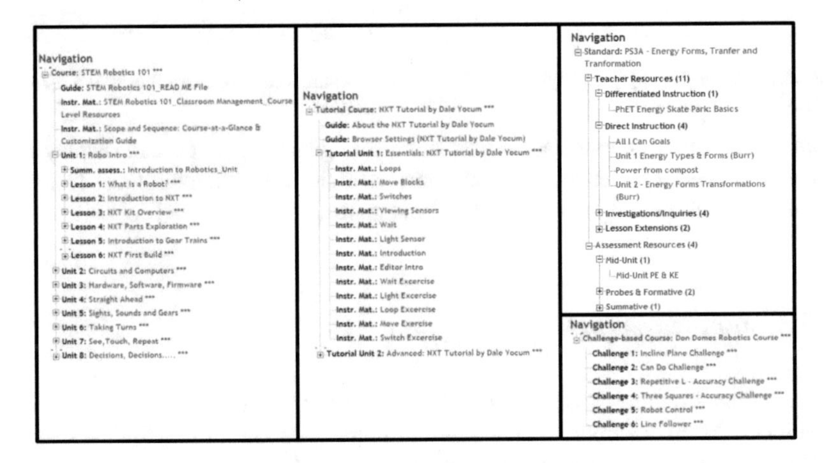

Fig. 9.9 The navigation widget

9.3.1.1 The Navigation Widget

is designed to provided a tree-based navigation browser across a site. As can be seen in Figure 9.9, the widget works across various different schemas like the "Course" on the left and the "Educational Standard" in the upper right. The widget exploits the part-whole relationships in the system.

The widget is written against the "Parent-Part" canonical structure by the widget developer. A domain developer creates a domain structure for "Educational Module-Educational Resource". A domain expert then creates mappings between their local schema and the domain structure.

9.3.1.2 The Data Analysis Widget

shows aggregated information about attributes in a system. For example, the left of Figure 9.10 shows the different focus area of resources within the "Robo Intro" unit while the right side shows aggregated data for the authors of resources within a course.

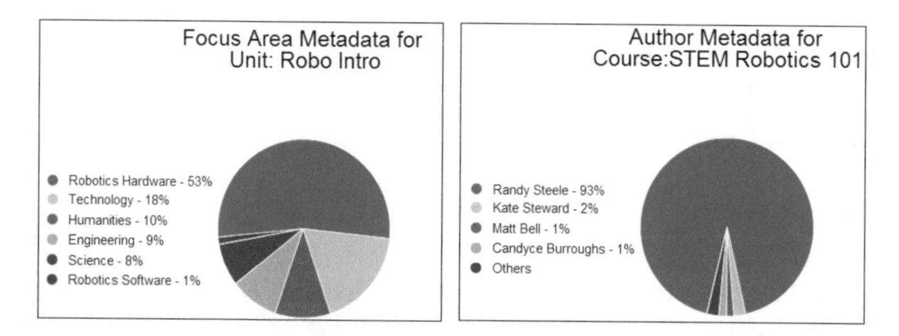

Fig. 9.10 The data analysis widget.

This widget performs an unpivot operation where multiple attributes at the domain level are mapped to a single canonical attribute; this is seen in Figure 9.8 where the different attributes of the domain structure ("Grade Level","Focus Subject", and "Author") all all mapped to the single "Attribute" in the canonical structure. This allows the widget to be written generically for all possible attributes that may appear in the local schemas. The widget builds off the Parent-Part structure used in the navigation widget described above and adds the "Item" canonical structure shown in Figures 9.2 and 9.8 and uses the type operator to bring the local type names into the widget.

9.3.1.3 The Faceted Navigation Widget

uses the canonical structures of the navigation and data analysis widgets together to create an hierarchical tree structure that is able to be restructured by the attribute data used in the analysis widget. Figures 9.11 and 9.12 show the functionality of this widget. The widget starts with a hierarchical view of a collection, in this case, it is for a digital library of computing resources but it could also be a course like those displayed above using the hierarchical widget. The widget allows a user to facet the collection by any of the local schema attributes that have been mapped. Figure 9.12 shows the collection faceted by class week. Each of the subtrees below the values of the class week facet may then be further faceted.

The faceted navigation widget uses the same canonical structures as the data analysis widget but performs a different task. Canonical structures and their mappings to domain structures may be reused multiple times.

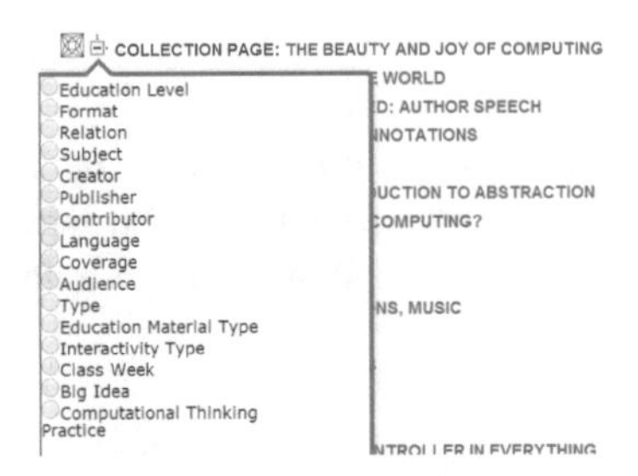

Fig. 9.11 The faceted navigation widget. Attributes that the tree can be faceted by are shown after clicking the diamond symbol next to the tree.

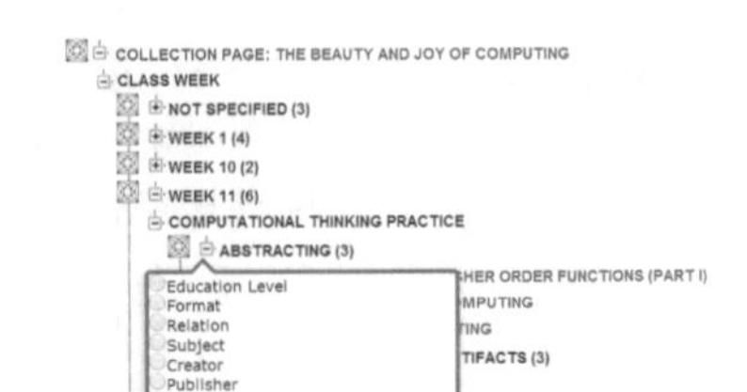

Fig. 9.12 The tree has now been faceted by "Class Week" and "Week 11" has been faceted by "Computational Thinking Practice".

9.3.2 Mappings

In order to instantiate the navigation widget, the domain developer creates a widget specification which includes the mapping (such as those shown between the left and center parts of Figure 9.1) between the canonical structure with which the widget is associated and the domain structure.

A domain expert can then enable a widget for use in their website by creating mappings between a local schema and a domain structure such as those shown between the center and right of Figure 9.1. Here we see one mapping between the "Course-Unit" part of the local schema to the domain structure and a second mapping between the "Unit-Lesson" part of the local schema. Similar mappings are created for the various different local schemas that may exist in the educational domain. For the sake of brevity we do not show those mappings but intuitively it follows that each relationship and its entities in the local schemas can be mapped to the domain structure to enable the different widgets shown in Figure 9.9. As mentioned above, we impose one constraint on the mappings between canonical and domain structures which is that the mapped portion of the domain structure must be isomorphic to the canonical structure.

Since our implemented systems use relational databases, we have built our information integration with local radiance system on top of that and use the nested relational model and algebra to store our mappings and perform our queries. We use a straightforward translation between the Entity-Relationship model shown in the figures in this paper and relational tables in our implemented system. Mappings between canonical structures and domain structures are stored in the nested relation

$$CSDSmap(ID, CR, DR, CScorr(ID, CA, DA))$$

where each mapping has an id, the canonical relation and domain relation in the mapping, and a nested relation of the correspondences between the canonical attributes and the domain attributes. An example tuple for the mapping between the "Has" canonical relationship and the "Contains" domain relationship shown in

Figure 9.1 would be

$$(1,'Has','Contains',((1.1,'Parent\_title','EducationalModule\_Title'),\\ (1.2,'Parent\_parent\_id','EducationalModule\_Module\_id'),\\ \ldots))$$

9.3.3 Query Rewriting

In order for our widgets to work we must perform query rewriting from queries addressing the canonical structure to queries addressing the local schemas at the time of execution. As described above, in our previous work we defined the apply operator to translate queries against domain structures into queries against local schemas. We use our mappings and introduce a new operator perform the next step in rewriting a query against a canonical structure into a domain structure-level query. The rewrite operator (θ) is defined as follows, given a canonical relation cr,

$$\theta(cr) = \bigcup_{\substack{\forall id \in \pi_{CSDSMap.ID}(\\ \sigma_{CSDSmap.CR=cr} CSDSmap))}} \rho_{\substack{CSDSmap.CScorr.DA \rightarrow \\ CSDSmap.CScorr.CA, \\ \tau(CSDSmap.CScorr.DA) \rightarrow \\ CSDSmap.CScorr.CA\_type}} \alpha(CSDSmap.DR)$$

The rewrite operator works by using all the mappings between the given canonical relation and all mapped domain relations. For each mapping it performs the apply operation on the domain relation and then renames the domain attribute names to the canonical attribute names such that they will work in the widget using the canonical names. It also bring the type information from the apply operator so that generic widgets can show local type information as desired.

9.4 Evaluation

In our previous work [9] we have shown that people with and without technical expertise can perform the mappings between domain structures and local schemas required in our system. Here, we evaluate the overhead imposed by our system from our extra layers of modeling and mappings.

We compare our system against a hard-coded custom widget which performs queries directly against its own schema and stores all data in a single table requiring no joins in the resultant query. For the results in Table 9.4, this system is referred to as HC (hard-coded). Since the hard-coded system does not perform any of the overhead associated with our system we consider this to be a good target for fast performance that we would hope to achieve in our best-case. Our best-case scenario (USb) only has simple mappings that require no extra joins to perform.

We also compare ourselves to the default Drupal rendering system (labelled D in Table 9.4). As mentioned above, Drupal stores each attribute of an entity in a separate database table, so in order to render a page it must create a join query joining all the tables of all of the attributes. This is similar to our worst-case (USw) performance because if a user has composed complex mappings that involve the unpivot operation, our system must perform a similar join query. Note also that like Drupal (and most other web systems) these costs are usually one-time costs, since the output of these queries can be cached.

Table 9.4 shows the results of the performance test. Our system is shown in both the best-case (USb) and worst-case (USw) scenarios. All systems were tested with 2, 10, and 20 attributes and on a database with 100, 1000, and 10000 entries. Times are shown in milliseconds and are the average of 10 runs each. All tests were performed on a server with an Intel I7 processor and 8GB of RAM.

Table 9.1 Performance comparison of our system in a best-case scenario (USb) and worst-case scenario (USw) to a hard-coded (HC) single query widget (an optimal but most labor intensive solution) and to the Drupal (D) page rendering system (a generic widget that can render arbitrarily complex types). All three systems tested with 2, 10, and 20 attributes. All times in milliseconds.

Rows	HC2	HC10	HC20	D2	D10	D20	USb2	USb10	USb20	USw2	USw10	USw20
100	6.2	7.2	8	6.6	29.6	47	6.5	9.9	12.6	7.3	33.5	52.6
1000	8.8	16.9	19.9	7.5	40.3	72.9	9.4	27.4	39.5	9.9	53.3	93.7
10000	31.5	79.1	129.6	40	145.7	326.5	46.9	174.5	322.9	67.9	245.3	524.8

From Table 9.4 we see that, in our best-case scenario, we are competitive to a hard-coded solution for a smaller number of rows which is a great result for our naive implementation directly written against the IILR formalism. This naive implementation introduces constants for mapping and type information for every attribute in every row which, unsurprisingly, leads to the slower performance at larger row and attribute sizes. Even with this overhead we are comparable to Drupal in our worst-case scenario and the same or better in our best-case, even at larger row sizes. Our performance can be improved by storing the constant data in the database and optimizing queries using standard relational algebra equivalences. Note that our system is performing local radiance which cannot be done by either the hard-coded or Drupal system.

9.5 Related Work

Generic schemas and functionality have been explored extensively in programming and data management and bring with them many benefits. Generic schemas aid in development by allowing functions, code, and constraints to be defined generically. It also allows reuse and aids in the definition and creation of new (more complex) schemas and systems and allow for a greater reuse of schema [17]. Using generic schemas can provide faster development even with complex models while minimizing development complexity [17]. Generic types in programming language like Java [4] or C# [1] can provide common functionality to many different heterogenous types. We take this approach and add the ease of use of schema mapping systems like CLIO [14] to enable non-technical users to make use of generic functionality.

Web development frameworks [2] also often provide a generic relational mapping to convert complex user defined schemas into generic formats in their database backends. Often an instance of a content type created by a user in the web front-end is stored in the database with a table for each field of the object plus an instantiation of some base class. This is in contrast to Object-Relational Mappers (ORMs) [12] that provide an algorithmic mapping between objects and relational tables that contain attributes for each of the fields in an object. Web development frameworks can provide some basic generic functionality for building pages and websites, but more complex widgets are limited to predefined models.

Work has been done to create reusable semantic web widgets [13, 16]. While these widgets are reusable in a number of sites and can leverage the genericity of self-describing models like big data document stores and triple stores [10] and web models like XML [3] or RDF [6]; they are still limited to predefined models stored in the model or application.

A hybrid approach is often used in electronic medical records (EMR) [15] where there is a predefined schema for many of the entities in the system such as doctors, patients, or vital signs and generic (triple-store-like) tables that allow an EMR to be customized; and, a similar approach in SAP [5] which has transparent, pooled, and clustered tables. While this allows the data storage to be predefined while allowing heterogeneity of end-systems, the conceptual model is usually built into the application logic of the systems.

Our canonical structures are similar to data model patterns [7]. These patterns often are used for common reoccurring schema elements. Our canonical structures are also very similar to generic relationship types in information systems [17, 18]. Generic relationship types like the part-whole relationship or is-a relationship are often instantiated repeatedly in an information system, for example, a book entity has chapters which have sections which have paragraphs. If we know that the relationships between books, chapters, sections, and paragraphs are all instantiations of the part-whole relationship, we can then pre-define constraints and functionality on the part-whole relationship that will apply to all of its instantiations. If IILR was used in a system with such known relationship types we could automatically generate mapping from relevant canonical structures to the local schema.

9.6 Conclusions

We have implemented our system on top of the Drupal framework. As part of our future work, we hope to expand this to other frameworks and potentially create a framework of our own based on these principles.

We have shown how using canonical structures it is possible to write generic widgets that can be used in any number of systems while still maintaining local schema. We believe that the added overhead in terms of runtime costs and personnel is both minimal and justified. Our evaluation shows that in the worst-case scenario we still perform competitively. The notion of having three roles in our system is easily analogous to the different roles in a web framework where there are framework developers (writing completely generic code), community module developers (often writing domain specific widgets), and end-users instantiating frameworks in whatever domain they wish. We believe that this is an important step in allowing end-users to maintain more control over how their data is stored and presented.

We also hope to explore how we could use this paradigm to enable non-technical users to accomplish even more technical tasks, e.g., programming or complex query writing. We believe that by empowering end-users we may encourage them to increase their technical knowledge and possibly help solve the problem of a shortage of developers.

Acknowledgements This work was supported in part by National Science Foundation grants 0840668 and 1250340. Any opinions, findings, and conclusions or recommendations expressed in this material are those of the author(s) and do not necessarily reflect the views of the National Science Foundation.

References

1. C# | Microsoft Docs, `https://docs.microsoft.com/en-us/dotnet/csharp/csharp`
2. Drupal, `http://drupal.org`
3. Extensible Markup Language (XML), `https://www.w3.org/XML/`
4. Java 8, `https://java.com/en/download/faq/java8.xml`
5. Pooled and Cluster Tables
6. RDF - Semantic Web Standards, `https://www.w3.org/RDF/`
7. Blaha, M.: Patterns of Data Modeling. CRC Press, Boca Raton,FL (jun 2010)
8. Britell, S., Delcambre, L.M.L., Atzeni, P.: Flexible Information Integration with Local Dominance. Information Modelling and Knowledge Bases XXVI, 21–40 (2014)
9. Britell, S., Delcambre, L.M.L., Atzeni, P.: Facilitating Data-Metadata Transformation by Domain Specialists in a Web-Based Information System Using Simple Correspondences, pp. 445–459. Springer International Publishing (2016)
10. Cattell, R., Rick: Scalable SQL and NoSQL data stores. ACM SIGMOD Record 39(4), 12 (may 2011)
11. Gupta, A., Harinarayan, V., Quass, D.: Generalized projections: A powerful approach to aggregation. In: Proc. 21st VLDB Conf. pp. 11–15 (1995)
12. Keller, A.M., Jensen, R., Agarwal, S.: Persistence software: bridging object-oriented programming and relational databases. ACM SIGMOD Record 22(2), 523–528 (jun 1993)

13. Mäkelä, E., Viljanen, K., Alm, O., Tuominen, J., Valkeapää, O., Kauppinen, T., Kurki, J., Sinkkilä, R., Kansala, T., Lindroos, R., Others: Enabling the Semantic Web with Ready-to-Use Web Widgets. In: FIRST. pp. 56–69 (2007)
14. Miller, R.J., Hernández, M.A., Haas, L.M., Yan, L., Howard Ho, C.T., Fagin, R., Popa, L.: The Clio project. ACM SIGMOD Record 30(1), 78–83 (mar 2001), `http://dl.acm.org/citation.cfm?id=373626.373713`
15. Nadkarni, P.M., Brandt, C., CS, J., A, S., M, D., WE, H.: Data Extraction and Ad Hoc Query of an Entity–Attribute–Value Database. Journal of the American Medical Informatics Association 5(6), 511–527 (nov 1998)
16. Nowack, B.: Paggr: Linked Data widgets and dashboards. Web Semantics: Science, Services and Agents on the World Wide Web 7(4), 272–277 (dec 2009)
17. OliveÌĄ, A.: Conceptual modeling of information systems. Springer (2007)
18. Olivé, A.: Representation of Generic Relationship Types in Conceptual Modeling, pp. 675–691. Springer Berlin Heidelberg, Berlin, Heidelberg (2002)
19. Wyss, C.M., Robertson, E.L.: A formal characterization of PIVOT/UNPIVOT. In: Proceedings of the 14th ACM international conference on Information and knowledge management - CIKM '05. p. 602. ACM Press, New York, New York, USA (oct 2005)

Chapter 10
Model-Based Engineering for Database System Development

Bernhard Thalheim

Abstract A model functions in a utilisation scenario as an instrument. It is well-formed, adequate and dependable. It represents or deputes origins. This conception of the the model is a very general one. Computer engineering uses models for description of development intentions and for prescription of the system to be build. It typically uses a number of models depending on the layer of abstraction, the scope, the context, the community of practice, and the artefacts to be represented. Model-based development is one of key success factors for development of database systems. This paper thus develops foundations for model-based engineering. Database system development is used as the illustration example for this investigation.

10.1 Models in Computer Science and Computer Engineering

Models are a kernel element of Computer Science and Computer Engineering (CS&CE). They are used sometimes without any definition or with an intuitive understanding. We know, however, a large variety of model notions (e.g. the 46 notions in [46]). A general theory, technology, art, science, and culture of modelling remain to be one of the research lacunas.

10.1.1 The Model

A **model** *is a well-formed, adequate, and dependable instrument that represents origins.* [11, 44, 45]

Bernhard Thalheim
Christian Albrechts University Kiel, Department of Computer Science. Olshausenstr. 40, D-24098 Kiel, Germany. e-mail: thalheim@is.informatik.uni-kiel.de

© Springer International Publishing AG 2017

J. Cabot et al. (eds.), *Conceptual Modeling Perspectives*,
https://doi.org/10.1007/978-3-319-67271-7_10

Its criteria of well-formedness, adequacy, and dependability must be commonly accepted by its community of practice within some context and correspond to the functions that a model fulfills in utilisation scenarios.

The model should be well-formed according to some well-formedness criterion. As an instrument or more specifically an artifact a model comes with its *background*, e.g. paradigms, assumptions, postulates, language, thought community, etc. The background its often given only in an implicit form.

10.1.2 Multi-Model Modelling

Most sciences use coexisting models as a coherent holistic representation of their understanding, their perception, and their theories. For instance, medical research [8] typically considers medical models as experimentum, practicale, ratio, speculativum, and theoreticalis. These models are developed with different scale, precision, variability, vision, veracity, views, viewpoints, volume, and variation.

Each of the models has some functions in utilisation scenarios, for instance, communication, negotiation, construction, and representation and depiction functions. Depending on these functions, the model may be considered to be adequate and dependable. If we use several models then coherence of these models becomes an issue. We may explicitly represent coherence of models through model suites [7, 43]. We may also layer models based on their abstraction and scale, e.g. [17]. UML [32] uses ensembles of models that are loosely coupled.

A *model suite* consists of a set of models, an explicit association or collaboration schema among the models, controllers that maintain consistency or coherence of the model suite, application schemata for explicit maintenance and evolution of the model suite, and tracers for the establishment of the coherence.

A specific model suite is used for co-design of information systems that is based on models for structuring, for functionality, for interactivity, and for distribution [39]. This model suite uses the structure model as the lead model for functionality specification. Views are based on both models. They are one kernel element for interactivity specification. Distribution models are additionally based on collaboration models, e.g. [38].

A specific model suite consists of two models which share most of their background, context, community of practice, their application scenario, and thus also function within these scenarios. These models coexist together, are interdependent, and are correlated to each other. We call such models *co-model*. Co-models form a diptyph[1].

They can be coalesced into one model with two different sub-models or they may depend from each other (see, for instance, the Königsberg bridge models in [28] with the topographical, topological and graph-theoretic models). Origins are often also models and thus form together with their model a co-model. The orgin

[1] A diptych is work made of of two parts. So, we might call co-models also *di-models* or *diptych models*.

M_1 thus conditions its model M_2, i.e. M_2/M_1 is a *conditional*. Modern CS&CE is full of examples of such co-models, e.g. [2, 9, 10, 13, 16, 25, 26, 31, 32, 34, 36, 41]. A model in a co-model also often inherits adequacy and dependability of the other model. Sometimes, they follow however also different backgrounds. For instance, eER-based conceptual modelling uses a global-as-design paradigm. BPMN-based conceptual models are based on a local-as-design approach with an orientation of actors with their roles.

10.1.3 Science and Engineering

Science and engineering are two rather different activities. According to the Encyclopedia Britannica [35], science is (1) the state of knowing, (2a) a department of systematized knowledge as an object of study, (2b) something (as a sport or technique) that may be studied or learned like systematized knowledge, (3a) knowledge or a system of knowledge covering general truths or the operation of general laws especially as obtained and tested through scientific method, (3b) such knowledge or such a system of knowledge concerned with the physical world and its phenomena alike in natural sciences, and (4) a system or method reconciling practical ends with scientific laws.

Engineering is nowadays performed in a systematic and well-understood form [1]. It also well supported in software engineering, e.g. CMM or SPICE [18]. Engineering is the art of building with completely different success criteria (see [37]: "Scientists look at things that are and ask 'why'; engineers dream of things that never were and ask 'why not'." (Theodore von Karman) "Engineers use materials, whose properties they do not properly understand, to form them into shapes, whose geometries they cannot properly analyse, to resist forces they cannot properly assess, in such a way that the public at large has no reason to suspect the extent of their ignorance." (John Ure 1998)).

S. Oudrhiri [33] considers four elements of matured engineering: "(a) the technological know-how, (b) a set of established practices, (c) a scientific approach for defining the underlying principles of these practices, and (d) an economical model to explain the implications of such practices in terms of value delivered (effectiveness) and resources consumed (efficiency)". Engineering is inherently concerned with failures of construction, with incompleteness both in specification and in coverage of the application domain, with compromises for all quality dimensions, and with problems of technologies currently at hand. [48] distinguishes eight stages of engineering: inquire, investigate, vision, analyse, qualify, plan, apply, and report.

10.1.4 Co-Models and Model Suites in CS&CE

CS&CE often uses direct associations of models, i.e. a model is based on another model. Modelling is then concerned with two models at the same time. For instance, completed database structure modelling starts with a situation model that is represented by a perception model. This perception model is the basis for the business model which is again the basis for the conceptual model. The conceptual model is mapped to a logical model according to the platform for realisation of the database system. The logical model is then mapped to the physical model. This pairwise modelling is based on a dichotomy of the models.

This dichotomy is used for closing the gap between the user world (where the information system is a social system) and the IT world (where the information system is a technical system). Figure 10.1 displays the mediating functions of typical information system models. Classical development methodologies are often based

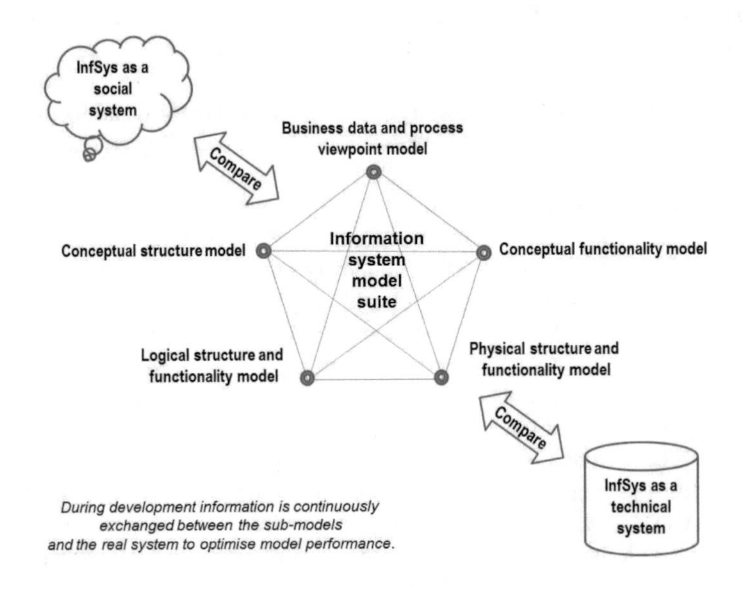

Fig. 10.1 Model suites: The five main models that comprise a complete model of a database system

on consideration of two models. For instance, structure modelling might start with a business data model that is intentionally based on the perception model within the user world. This business data model is refined to a conceptual structure model in a conceptual modelling language such as ER [42]. The conceptual structure model is enhanced, transformed or compiled to a logical data model. If we follow a systematic approach then the logical data model is refined, enhanced and transformed to a physical data model.

10.1.5 Model-Based Engineering as Specific Model-Based Reasoning

Model-based reasoning is reasoning with the aid of models, reasoning about models in their own right, and reasoning that is model-determined [27, 30]. Models have then three different functions depending on these reasoning scenarios [6, 46]: models are instruments for reasoning which implies their prior construction and the reasoning necessary for their construction; models as targets of reasoning; models as a unique subject of reasoning and its preliminary. Abduction has been considered the main vehicle of model-based reasoning. In CS&CE, reasoning is also based on explicit consideration of adequacy and dependability of models within the description/prescription scenario. From one side, models are used as a representation of some thought or better some mental models (e.g. *perception models*) which are representing the (augmented) reality (i.e. the perceived *situation model* and the objectives for system construction). From the other side models are used as blueprints for realisation of intentions by software systems. In the last case, models are also *documentation models* for the software system, at least at the first completion of the system.

Model-based engineering has been considered for a long time as '*greenfield*' development starting from scratch with a new development. Engineering is however nowadays often starting with legacy systems that must be modernised, extended, tuned, improved etc. This kind of '*brownfield*' development may be based on models for the legacy systems and migration strategies [22]. Again, we observe a co-model approach with a legacy model for revision, redevelopment, modernisation and migration and a target model for development of the new modernised and extended system. So, the legacy model (or legacy models) is associated with a sub-model of the target system.

10.1.6 The Objectives of the Paper

Model-based engineering attracts a lot of research, e.g. [3, 21, 23, 40]. Model-driven software development (MDSD) distinguishes enterprise, platform independent, platform specific, and code models. MDSD on the basis of model suites and with a direct consideration of model properties has not yet been investigated. So, we start with a case study in Section 10.2. This case study is used for derivation of principles in Section 10.4. Finally, Section 10.5 discusses the role of conceptual models in model-based engineering of database system development.

Due to space limitations, the paper cannot discuss in detail techniques that are necessary for systematic model-based engineering. Many techniques are already developed for specific modelling languages, for specific application domains, and for specific development approaches. A systematic generalisation and harmonisation of these techniques is still a research task. We illustrate the approach based on entity-relationship modelling (ERM) languages, on data-intensive applications and ERM-based development. The paper aims thus in a methodological background for model-based engineering. We restrict the paper to co-models and their specific style for model-based engineering.

10.2 A Case Study for Structure-Representing Co-Models

Let us consider two cases of co-models. It is often claimed that the ER modelling language can be used at the business and the conceptual layer in a similar form. If we look a bit more into the details then we discover essential differences that must be taken into consideration. For instance, we might have models that cannot be mapped to models at the lower layer or models that cannot be represented at the higher layer. At the same time, we might have many choices for lower layer models (Figure 10.2). Moreover, data models at one layer might not be entirely represented by data models

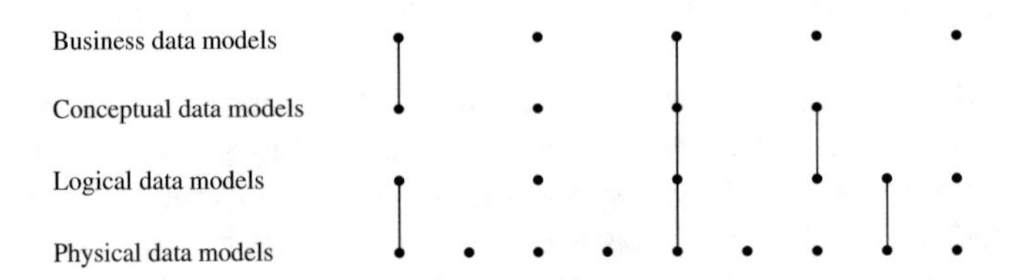

Fig. 10.2 Association of models in multi-layer modelling

at the other layer. For instance, cardinality constraints might not be representable by classical relational constraints. We must either enhance the relational language or represent constraints by procedural features of the relational database platforms.

10.2.1 Co-Models: Business Data Models and Conceptual Models

Business data models reflect the way how business users consider their data. Each business user considers only specific data within a specific viewpoint. A business application provides some kind of collaboration or exchange mechanism for these data.

The origins that are reflected in business data models are the situation model of a given application area and a collection of perception models that reflect specific viewpoints of business users. The understanding of data by business users is based on the way of work at business. So, data models represent their rather specific understanding of the application domain. These data models follow a local-as-design representation style. Conceptual models follow however a global-as-design approach [47], i.e. the model consists (i) of a global schema that harmonises and integrates the variety of viewpoints and (ii) of generalised (external) views that are derivable from the form the global schema and represent the local viewpoints. The two kinds of models - the business data models and the conceptual model - are tightly associated by an explicit infomorphism (i.e. generalised di-homomorphisms, see below). Adequateness and dependability of the conceptual model is derived from this association. Additionally, well-formedness of the conceptual model is based on the language, e.g. an extended entity-relationship (eER) modelling language, e.g. HERM [42].

Business (layer) data models and conceptual (layer) data models are a typical example of a *vertical model suite* since the first one is typically more abstract and the second one can be considered to be a refinement of the first one. The binding among these models is often implicit. We may however enhance the two models by a mapping that maps the first model to the second one. This mapping combines and harmonises the different views that are used at the business user layer.

10.2.2 Co-Models: Conceptual Models and Logical Models

Logical models are based on the same underlying semantics for the modelling language, e.g. set semantics. Physical data models typically use multi-set semantics (also called bag semantics) for (object-)relational database management systems. Logical models may follow object-relational approaches or purely relational approaches. eER conceptual models have an implicit semantics beside the explicit semantics. For instance, relationship types obey an inclusion and an existence constraint that restricts existence of relationship objects by existence of their referred component objects – in most cases entity objects.

Conceptual views are represented by a collection of object-relational views. We have a number of potential associations between conceptual and logical models. Which one is appropriate depends on choices for structuring, for re-organisation or optimisation or normalisation, for treatment of constraints, for handling of missing values, for controlled redundancy, for treatment of hierarchies, for naming, etc. Additionally, specific platform-oriented features are integrated into the logical model. The transformation follows rules and uses specific decisions.

So, the conceptual and the logical models are co-models that follow a refinement approach [49] (1) by injecting specific styles, tactics, embeddings, and language pattern to the logical model [1] and (2) by rules for transformation, extension, enhancement, and specialisation applicable to the logical model [12]. So, a conceptual model is typically associated to many logical models depending on the style of chosen refinement. We may consider an abstract description of the refinement approach as *pragmas* which are already given together with the conceptual model. The refinement may also result in an *information loss*. For instance, the view schemata defined for the conceptual model are mapped to a collection of relational views. The interrelation among the relational views is however not maintained in an explicit form.

Conceptual (layer) data models and logical (layer) data models also an example of a *vertical model suite* with a straightforward mapping from the conceptual layer to the logical layer.

10.2.3 Co-Models: Conceptual Co-Design of Structuring and Functionality

Database design and development typically is based on two models for structuring and functionality. The structure model is the 'lead' model for functionality since it defines the signature of the basic terms. The structure model imposes however also restrictions to the functions due to the integrity constraint enforcement and maintenance. Functionality is specified as a set of create-retrieve-update-delete functions. The data modification functions can be extended for preservation of integrity. The retrieval functions are defined based on a number of retrieval pattern and as algebraic expressions, e.g. HERM+ [42]. So, the lead model is some kind of 'order' model and the functionality model is partially 'enslaved' [15].

Structure models and functionality models form a *horizontal model suite*. Their association is based on an infomaorphism (see the similar vertical case in Section 10.4.1). All elements of the models are associated in a bipartite graph. The edges in the graph may be enhanced by existence dependencies, e.g. an operation or query uses the structural notions which are defined in the structural model. The control of such dependencies may be defined in a form similar to referential integrity.

10.2.4 Lessons Learned for Model-Based Engineering

A modelling language has its own obstinacy. It injects its background, its limitations and its treatment of semiotics into the model. Therefore, model-based engineering must explicitly represent these language specifics. Whenever models are used within a model suite, the association of models is language-biased and language-limited. Next, models are also driven by the directives, i.e. the artifacts to be represented, the profile of the model that is intended, the community of practice that might accept the model, and the context into which the model is set. Furthermore, the capacity and potential of the model itself restricts applicability. From the other side, we may restrict engineering to some kind of 'best' effective and efficient model. Finally, the classical approach to arbitrarily enhance a lower layer model limits the usefulness of the higher-layer model.

We may now consider either co-models at the same layer of abstraction ("*horizontal co-models*") or at different layers of abstraction ("*vertical co-models*"). Database structure development is typically based both on vertical co-models that are on adjoining layers and on horizontal co-models in the co-design case.

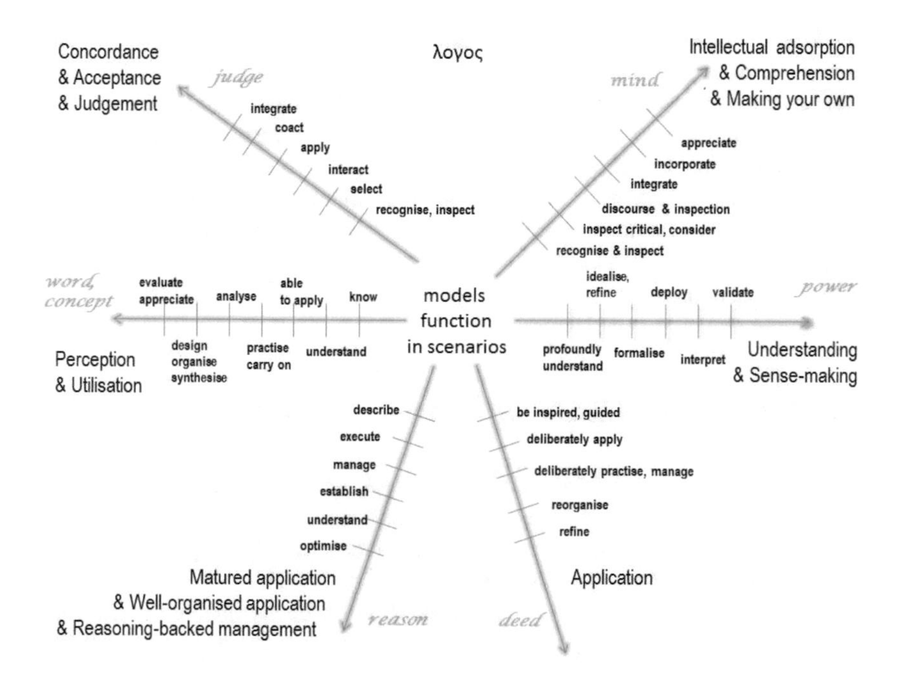

Fig. 10.3 Utilisation scenarios for models and stages of their deployment

10.3 The First Principle of Modelling

10.3.1 Logoi of Modelling

Modelling results in a model as a *surface structure* and is in reality combined with a *deep structure* that is based on the background and the directives of the model. The deep structure of a model is represented by the *modelling logos*[2] [5, 24] that is the rationale or first principle behind modelling.

The model has its *background* $\mathfrak{B}$ consisting of an undisputable grounding from one side (paradigms, postulates, restrictions, theories, culture, foundations, conventions, authorities) and of a disputable and adjustable basis from other side (assumptions, concepts, practices, language as carrier, thought community and thought style, methodology, pattern, routines, commonsense) which represent the nature of things themselves. The background provides the deep structure of the model by explanations, analysis and manifestation. It is governed by its inner directives (origins/artefact to represented $\mathfrak{O}$, profile of the models (goal, purpose, function)) $\mathfrak{P}$ and

[2] In the Faust poem by J.W. Goethe, Faust reasons in the study room scene on the meaning of the word 'logos' λόγος. This word has at least 6 meanings where Faust used only four of them: word, *concept, judgement,* mind, power, deed, and *reason*.

the outer directives (community of practice, and the context) $\mathfrak{D}$. It is based on a language $\mathfrak{L}$ with its general notion, capacity and potential. Model development is based on actions $\mathfrak{A}$ and modelling and utilisation methods with their rational choice, i.e. the rationality expressed in the model as code, in interpretation and in action.

The ***modelling logos***[3] consists of the background, the outer directives, the language, and actions. The modelling logos is expected to understand before model development and utilisation. The logos thus determines the modelling notions of trueness, verifiability, rationality, and correctness. Parameters for models themselves are the inner directives. We claim that models cannot be understood without understanding the modelling logos.

10.3.2 Scenarios and Resulting Functions of Models

These different meanings of the Greek word logos are used in different utilisation scenarios. Concept and conceptions are the basis for the perception and utilisation scenario. A *conceptual model* is a model that incorporates concepts and conceptions. Models might be accepted in a community of practice based on judgements of members of a community of practice [19]. Models may be acceptable for this community and be thus intellectually absorbed. Models then gain an expressive power and make sense within an application. Models can also be used and applied in a development process. This application may also use methods of matured development. The last one is based on model-based reasoning which can be guided by maturity approaches, e.g. CMM and SPICE. So, we observe a number of scenarios which are depicted in Figure 10.3.

Models *function* as ***instruments*** in these scenarios at various stages of maturity. For instance, the application scenario may use models as an inspiration for further development. This stage is often observed for UML-backed programming. Instead, models may be deliberately applied or managed. They may be used as co-models and thus co-evolve together with the realisation, i.e. they become reorganised during utilisation. This reorganisation may also based on systematic approaches and thus be based on a refinement strategy.

10.4 Engineering for Vertical Co-Models

10.4.1 Database Development with Vertical Co-Models

Vertical co-models are widely used in CS&CE. The methodologies developed so far do however not consider the nature of multi-models. The case studies in Sec-

[3] The logos combines specification of the language, the knowledge behind, the reality under consideration, and the actions. [24]

tion 10.2 showed the influence of the *background-ladeness* of models. It is not easy to switch from a local-as-design paradigm to a global-as-design paradigms. Models are also *directives-laden*, especially with the outer directives community-of-practice and context. It is simpler if data are of the same granularity, scale and scope. For this reason conceptual models use an approach to represent data at their lowest scale and smallest granularity. Scientific databases (and also industrial databases, e.g. [20]) often start with raw data and consider them as the basis of all derived, purged, combined, and analysed data. They fail whenever size of databases matters.

The association between co-models can be based on the notion of the *infomorphism*. We extend the notion in [22] for models as follows. Two models M_1, M_2 are E_1, E_2-*infomorph* though two transformations E_1, E_2 with $E_1(M_1) = M_2$ and $E_2(M_2) = M_1$ if any model object o defined on M_i can be mapped via E_i to objects defined on M_j for $i, j \in \{1,2\}, i \neq j$.

We notice that this notion allows to associate models with different granularity, models that incorporate views defined on top of a global schema, model suites within the local-as-design style that have a latent association model underneath, and co-evolution of models within a model suite. It can also be extended to model refinement similarly to [49]. We may use the infomorphism also for justification of one model by another model similar to the associations discussed in Subsections 10.2.1 and 10.2.2.

10.4.2 Model-Based Engineering with Co-Models

Model-based engineering is turning an idea into a reality on the basis of models. Models are used as the tacit knowledge for engineering through conception, feasibility, design, manufacture and construction. They reduce complexity while at the same time providing means for sustainable development and for coping with the interdependencies between systems - technical ones as well as social ones, at different layers at the same time.

Engineering of information systems still needs a lot of research, theories, skills and practices. System development becomes nowadays based on iterative development. The time of one-way models is over. Models are becoming reused, reconfigured, continuously evolving and integrated. So, the five plus two models in Figure 10.1 must co-evolve. Modern CS& CE is not anymore concentrated on a singleton development but has to look outwards, to handle the 'big picture', to think and to reflect during practising, to manage complexity and risks at the same time in an economic form.

The details of sub-systems are beyond common sense. We must rely on instruments as an abstract source of understanding and managing. One central instrument are *models* for the system world, for a system, for sub-systems, for embedded systems, and for collaboration of systems. Models allow us to understand what we want, what we think to know and to manage, how we make achieve what we want, what actually to do, and finally what we think might be the consequences. Since engineering is also a business activity, engineering activities must be affordable and financially predictable. Models provide a practical commonsense view that helps us to manage professionally and at acceptable risks. So, *model-based engineering* is one of the main issues of modern CS&CE. It goes far beyond model-driven development and model-driven architectures.

Therefore, we need *first-class models* and a technology to *handle models in a holistic manner*. One approach to master development is *layering*, i.e. coherently deploying various models of social systems and various models for technical systems. We develop this approach on the basis of business/conceptual and conceptual/logical co-models. In a similar form co-design of structuring and functionality may be managed and mastered.

So far we considered the modelling logo as a description logo. We may also consider the other model suite logos such as *control, application, organisation, economics, and evolution logos* for controllers, application, and tracers within model suites. Let us now sketch the controller and application ingredients for model-based engineering with co-models.

The *model suite association style* is based on general schemata for supporting programs (sub-model pattern for release, sharing, and access including scheduling of access), style of association (peer-to-peer , component, push-event, etc.), and on coordination activities describing the interplay among models. The control might be based on lazy or eager control styles.

The *association pattern* among models can be based on wrapping, componentisation, interception, extension or model models. The application processing can be active, proactive, synchronising or obligation-oriented. Synchronisation may use a variety of pattern. Whether association is based on parallel execution depends on the style of the association.

The *model suite architecture* describes inner association among models or submodels and is given by a general network with pairwise or n-ary bindings among these models.

The *model suite exchange* is based on constraints, their enforcement and the handling mechanisms for associations among models and sub-models. They might include also obligations for maintenance of changes within a model suite.

The main issue behind this approach is to deeply understand how these models can coexist, co-evolve, influence and restrict each other, and support or hinder the other. So, we first develop an insight into the deployment and especially the modelling logo of such model suites for a co-model example.

10.5 Conceptual Models as Mediators Within a Model Suite

The conceptual model is often used as a medium and mediator [29]. "Models function not just as a means but also as a means of representation" [14] with a deep background such as starting points and questions, knowledge, theories, actual hypotheses, tacit knowledge in tools, goals and objectives, tools, data generation, data on hand, data processing, and data interpretation [4]. Mediating models are retrospective and prospective at the same time and ravish. Beside mediation, other and different models can also be developed for documentation, communication, negotiation, orientation, inspiration, etc.

10.5.1 The Dichotomy of Description and Prescription for eER Models

The main function of eER models is its utilisation during database structure construction. The model consists of a schema, a number of views, and the realisation style [39, 47]. It is descriptive and prescriptive. The descriptive part reflects the business user models and thus uses an explicit association by views. The prescriptive part can be based on realisation templates. Adequacy is given due to the association to the business models, due to the objectives of description and prescription, due to the explicit restriction to the model focus, and due to the realisation context. Dependability is based on the association to the business user model, on the objectives of co-design, and on the capacity and potential of logical modelling languages that we intend to use. So, the model reflects two rather different origins, the business model and the logical model.

10.5.2 Some Modelling Logos of ER Modelling

Modelling logos of (extended) entity-relationship modelling languages are hidden within the language and not explicitly discussed in the ER literature. They are partially reflected in literature that introduce other languages. They should however be known whenever ER modelling is performed.

The background is reflected by (for details see [42]): In the *Global-As-Design* approach, the schema reflects all viewpoints. Local viewpoints are derivable and somehow reflectable. *Explicit existence existence* postulates that any object must exist before there can be a reference to it, i.e. rigid separation of creation and use. The model assumes a *closed-world view* and *unique names*. It is based on a well understood *name space* or glossary or ontology. *Salami-slice* representation uses homogenous, decomposed types (potentially with complex attributes) with incremental type construction. *Functionality representation* is deferred without consideration of the performance impact to the schema. *Separation into syntax and semantics* allow to define semantics on top of the syntax. Explicit semantics is based on constraints. *Paradigms, postulates, assumptions* of database technology and database support are assumed due to the three main quality criteria (performance, performance, performance). *Basic data types* are hidden with some mapping facilities to DBMS typing systems. *Visualisation* is represented by one holistic diagram that displays the entire syntax and semantics.

Outer directives are (for details see [42]): The *context* is entirely determined by DBMS technology of the last decades and heavily restricted by the platform and the systems that should be used. Data must become identifiable. The *population* is *finite* what causes problems with cyclic constraints, e.g. locally defined cardinality constraints are then global constraints. The community of practice consists mainly of DBMS professionals, modellers and may be business deciders. The first two groups are used to and biased by the paradigms, postulates, assumptions, etc. of DB technology.

The potential and capacity of the ER modelling language is restricted by the flatness of the schema definition. Schema construction may be guided by style guides and well-formedness characteristics. *Construction* of schemata is entirely *hierarchical* (or incremental or inductive) and follows approaches known for (hierarchical) first-order predicate logics. Construction is restricted to *3 or 4* or more *constructors* (entity, attribute, relationship types; additionally cluster types). Schema semantics is *canonically* defined. *Hidden set semantics* is used with *implicit* pointer semantics for relationship and cluster types. *Generalisation and specialisation* of all kinds are reflected through specific subtype or grouping (clustering) constructs. The manifold of specialisations is separated. Semantics is *static*. All schema elements are *completely defined*. Explicit semantics is defined through constraints which might however require *treatment beyond* (canonical) first order predicate logics. *Viewpoints* are defined through views on top of the schema definition via algebraic expressions. *Derived attributes* are defined via algebraic expressions. *Algebra* is restricted to terms that can be constructed for the algebra operations. Expressions may be generically defined with structures as parameters, e.g. insert(type) as generic operation.

Classical development methods are based on the kind of ER schema and view construction. They include methods for stepwise incremental construction, extension, decomposition, design, validation, and evaluation (see [42]). We may use a number of methodologies, such as top-down, bottom-up, modula, inside-out, and mixed. Classical utilisation actions and resulting methods are mapping and transformation methods (see [42]). Methods for integration, calibration, verification, control, reconfiguration, migration, and evolution are still under investigation.

The profile is restricted to the system construction function for mediating models.

10.6 Conclusions

Model-driven engineering and development has become an area of intensive research. Roles, limitations, background and directives of the model have however not been taken into consideration. In the past, panels often discussed which modelling approach and which modelling language is most appropriate. We realise now the models and also modelling languages have their own obstinacy. So, model-based engineering is background-laden directives-laden.

Model-based engineering is based on the modelling know-how, on modelling practices, on modelling theory, and on modelling economics. We discussed the ingredients for model-based engineering for the case of co-models and of mediating models. This approach can be generalised to full co-design of structuring, functionality, interactivity and distribution. So far, the approach uses model suites. How this approach can be extended to any kind of model collections is an open research problem.

The paper has been restricted to the general programme of model-based engineering. The explicit and detailed description is the topic of two forthcoming papers. Model-based engineering uses a number of practices similar to SPICE or CMM approaches [18].

We may now combine our investigation in Figure 10.4. We distinguish the six dimensions: community of practice, background / knowlegde / context, application scenario and stories of model utilisation, situation / state / data, dynamics / evolution / change / operations, and models as representations and instruments. Models are used in a variety of functions. For instance, models of situations / states / data are often used for structuring, description, prescription, hypothetic investigation, and analysis. Models are used by members of the community of practice for communication, reflection, understanding, and negotiation. So, we observe that the function

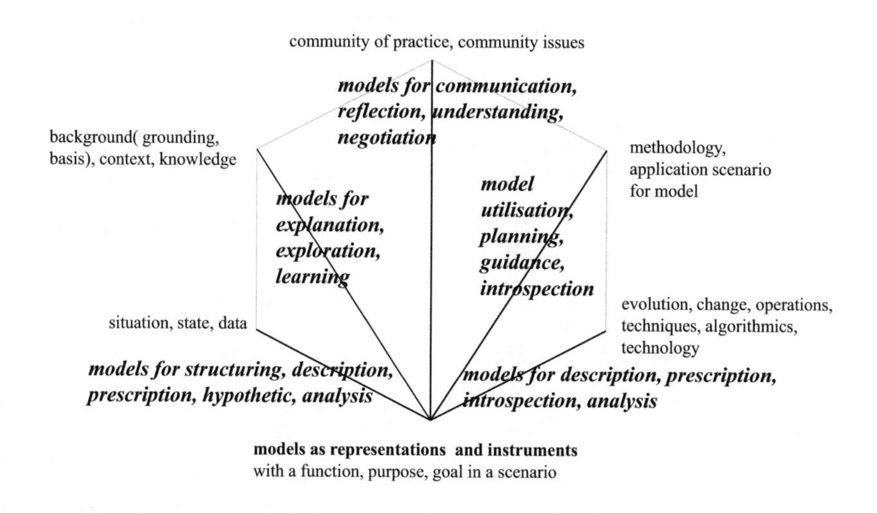

Fig. 10.4 Models and the five concerns in model-based engineering

(or simpler the purpose or the goal) of the model is determined by the concrete way how a model is used. Model-based engineering is thus engineering supported by models that are used according to the function that a model might play in the engineering process.

References

1. B. AlBdaiwi, R. Noack, and B. Thalheim. Pattern-based conceptual data modelling. In *Information Modelling and Knowledge Bases*, volume XXVI of *Frontiers in Artificial Intelligence and Applications, 272*, pages 1–20. IOS Press, 2014.
2. N. Aquino, J. Vanderdonckt, J. I. Panach, and O. Pastor. Conceptual modelling of interaction. In *The Handbook of Conceptual Modeling: Its Usage and Its Challenges*, chapter 10, pages 335–358. Springer, Berlin, 2011.
3. D. Bjørner. *Domain engineering*, volume 4 of *COE Research Monographs*. Japan Advanced Institute of Science and Technolgy Press, Ishikawa, 2009.
4. C. Blättler. *Wissenschaft und Kunst der Modellierung: Modelle, Modellieren, Modellierung*, chapter Das Modell als Medium. Wissenschaftsphilosophische Überlegungen, pages 107–137. De Gruyter, Boston, 2015.
5. E. Brann. *The logos of Heraclitus*. Paul Dry Books, 2011.
6. J.E. Brenner. The logical process of model-based reasoning. In L. Magnani, W. Carnielli, and C. Pizzi, editors, *Model-based reasoning in science and technology*, pages 333–358. Springer, Heidelberg, 2010.
7. A. Dahanayake and B. Thalheim. Co-evolution of (information) system models. In *EMMSAD 2010*, volume 50 of *LNBIP*, pages 314–326. Springer, 2010.
8. W. Doerr and H. Schipperges, editors. *Modelle der Pathologischen Physiology*. Springer, 1987.
9. D. Dori. Object-process methodology for structure-behavior codesign. In *The Handbook of Conceptual Modeling: Its Usage and Its Challenges*, chapter 7, pages 209–258. Springer, Berlin, 2011.
10. A. Düsterhöft and K.-D. Schewe. Conceptual modelling of application stories. In *The Handbook of Conceptual Modeling: Its Usage and Its Challenges*, chapter 11, pages 359–380. Springer, Berlin, 2011.
11. D. Embley and B. Thalheim, editors. *The Handbook of Conceptual Modeling: Its Usage and Its Challenges*. Springer, 2011.
12. D. W. Embley and W.Y. Mok. Mapping conceptual models to database schemas. In *The Handbook of Conceptual Modeling: Its Usage and Its Challenges*, chapter 1, pages 123–164. Springer, Berlin, 2010.
13. E. D. Falkenberg, W. Hesse, and A Olive, editors. *Information system concepts: towards a consolidation of views*. Chapmann & Hall, 1995. Proceedings IFIP WG8.1 Conferences ISCO3.
14. I. Hacking. *Representing and Intervening. Introductory topics in the philosophy of natural science*. Cambrdge Press, 1983.
15. H. Haken, A. Wunderlin, and S. Yigitbasi. An introduction to synergetics. *Open Systems and Information Dynamics*, 3:97–130, 1995.
16. W. Hesse. Modelle - Janusköpfe der Software-Entwicklung - oder: Mit Janus von der A- zur S-Klasse. In *Modellierung 2006*, volume 82 of *LNI*, pages 99–113. GI, 2006.
17. P. J. Hunter, W. W. Li, A. D. McCulloch, and D. Noble. Multiscale modeling: Physiome project standards, tools, and databases. *IEEE Computer*, 39(11):48–54, 2006.
18. ISO/IEC. Information technology - process assessment - part 2: Performing an assessment. IS 15504-2:2003, 2003.
19. R. Kaschek. *Konzeptionelle Modellierung*. PhD thesis, University Klagenfurt, 2003. Habilitationsschrift.
20. Y. Kiyoki and B. Thalheim. Analysis-driven data collection, integration and preparation for visualisation. In *Information Modelling and Knowledge Bases*, volume XXIV, pages 142–160. IOS Press, 2013.
21. A. Kleppe, J. Warmer, and W. Bast. *MDA Explained: The Model Driven Architecture - Practice and Promise*. Addison Wesley, 2006.
22. M. Klettke and B. Thalheim. Evolution and migration of information systems. In *The Handbook of Conceptual Modeling: Its Usage and Its Challenges*, chapter 12, pages 381–420. Springer, Berlin, 2011.

23. J. Krogstie. *Model-based development and evolution of information systems*. Springer, 2012.
24. A.V. Lebedev. *The Logos Heraklits - A recomnstruction of thoughts and words; full commented texts of fragments (in Russian)*. Nauka, 2014.
25. P. C. Lockemann and H. C. Mayr. *Computer-based information systems*. Springer, Berlin, 1978. In German.
26. L. Maciaszek. *Requirements analysis and design*. Addison-Wesley, Harlow, Essex, 2001.
27. L. Magnani, W. Carnielli, and C. Pizzi, editors. *Model-Based Reasoning in Science and Technology: Abduction, Logic, and Computational Discovery*. Springer, 2010.
28. B. Mahr. *Mathesis & Graphé: Leonhard Euler und die Entfaltung der Wissenssysteme*.
29. M.S. Morgan and M. Morrison, editors. *Models as mediators*. Cambridge Press, 1999.
30. N. J. Nersessian. *Creating Scientific Concepts*. MIT Press, 2008.
31. A. Olivé. Conceptual schema-centric development: A grand challenge for information systems research. In *Proc. CAiSE*, pages 1–15, 2005.
32. A. Olivé. *Conceptual modeling of information systems*. Springer, Berlin, 2007.
33. R. Oudrhiri. Software engineering economics: A framework for process improvement. In I. Comyn-Wattiau, C. du Mouza, and N. Prat, editors, *Ingenierie Management des Systemes D'Information*, 2016.
34. K. Pohl. *Process centred requirements engieering*. J. Wiley and Sons Ltd., 1996.
35. J.E. Safra, I. Yeshua, and et. al. *Encyclopædia Britannica*. Merriam-Webster, 2003.
36. I. Ramos Salavert, O. Pastor López, J. Cuevas, and J. Devesa. Objects as observable processes. In A. Olivé, editor, *Proc. 4th Int. Workshop on the Deductive Approach to Information Systems and Databases, DAISD'93*, pages 51–72, Lloret de Mar, 1993.
37. A. Samuel and J. Weir. *Introduction to Engineering: Modelling, Synthesis and Problem Solving Strategies*. Elsevier, Amsterdam, 2000.
38. K.-D. Schewe and B. Thalheim. Development of collaboration frameworks for web information systems. In *IJCAI'07 (20th Int. Joint Conf on Artificial Intelligence, Section EMC'07 (Evolutionary models of collaboration)*, pages 27–32, Hyderabad, 2007.
39. K.-D. Schewe and B. Thalheim. *Correct Software in Web Applications and Web Services*, chapter Co-Design of Web Information Systems, pages 293–332. Texts & Monographs in Symbolic Computation. Springer, Wien, 2015.
40. T. Stahl and M. Völter. *Model-driven software architectures*. dPunkt, Heidelberg, 2005. (in German).
41. W. Steinmüller. *Informationstechnologie und Gesellschaft: Einführung in die Angewandte Informatik*. Wissenschaftliche Buchgesellschaft, Darmstadt, 1993.
42. B. Thalheim. *Entity-relationship modeling – Foundations of database technology*. Springer, Berlin, 2000.
43. B. Thalheim. *The Conceptual Framework to Multi-Layered Database Modelling based on Model Suites*, volume 206 of *Frontiers in Artificial Intelligence and Applications*, pages 116–134. IOS Press, 2010.
44. B. Thalheim. The conceptual model $\equiv$ an adequate and dependable artifact enhanced by concepts. In *Information Modelling and Knowledge Bases*, volume XXV of *Frontiers in Artificial Intelligence and Applications, 260*, pages 241–254. IOS Press, 2014.
45. B. Thalheim. Conceptual modeling foundations: The notion of a model in conceptual modeling. In *Encyclopedia of Database Systems*. 2017.
46. B. Thalheim and I. Nissen, editors. *Wissenschaft und Kunst der Modellierung: Modelle, Modellieren, Modellierung*. De Gruyter, Boston, 2015.
47. B. Thalheim and M. Tropmann-Frick. The conception of the conceptual database model. In *ER 2015*, LNCS 9381, pages 603–611, Berlin, 2015. Springer.
48. M. Tropmann and B. Thalheim. Performance forecasting for performance critical huge databases. In *Information Modelling and Knowledge Bases*, volume XXII, pages 206–225. IOS Press, 2011.
49. Q. Wang and B. Thalheim. Data migration: A theoretical perspective. *DKE*, 87:260–278, 2013.

Chapter 11
Quality Improvement of Conceptual UML and OCL Schemata through Model Validation and Verification

Martin Gogolla and Khanh-Hoang Doan

Abstract Model validation and verification tools should provide good support for generating test cases. We here sketch essential use cases for model validation and verification that help developers to find deficiencies in models on the basis of generated test cases and thus improve model quality. Along with such use cases, we demonstrate how to realize them in the UML and OCL tool USE. We apply the tool for a small case study showing the development of a relational database schema on the basis of a conceptual UML schema in form of a UML class diagram and accompanying OCL constraints.

11.1 Introduction

Model-driven engineering (MDE) is a software development approach that puts emphasis on models and not on code. The main purpose of a model is abstraction. By abstracting system complexity through reduction of information, a model can catch the essentials of a system preserving properties relative to a given set of concerns [14]. MDE techniques are able to disregard details of different implementation dependent platforms, thereby allowing to concentrate on essentials characteristics that are valid for many platforms.

Modeling languages, such as the UML (Unified Modeling Language) which comprises the OCL (Object Constraint Language), have found their way into mainstream software development. Models are the central artifacts in MDE because other software elements like code, documentation or tests can be derived from them using model transformations. Finding correct and expressive models is important. Common model quality improvement techniques are model validation ("Are we build-

Martin Gogolla
Database Systems Group, University of Bremen, e-mail: gogolla@cs.uni-bremen.de

Khanh-Hoang Doan
Database Systems Group, University of Bremen, e-mail: doankh@cs.uni-bremen.de

© Springer International Publishing AG 2017

J. Cabot et al. (eds.), *Conceptual Modeling Perspectives*,
https://doi.org/10.1007/978-3-319-67271-7_11

ing the right product?") and verification ("Are we building the product right?") [2]. Among the different aspects of a system to be caught, structural aspects represented by class and object diagrams are of central concern.

The context of our work is the tool USE (UML-based Specification Environment), see [5] and [6] that supports the development of UML models enhanced by OCL constraints. USE offers class, object, sequence, statechart, and communication diagrams. It facilitates class and state invariants as well as pre- and postconditions for operations and transitions formulated in OCL. It allows the modeler to validate models and to verify properties by building test scenarios. One USE component that is in charge for this task is the so-called model validator that transforms UML and OCL models as well as validation and verification tasks into the relational logic of Kodkod [16], performs checks on the Kodkod level, and transforms the obtained results back in terms of the UML and OCL model. The modeler works on the UML and OCL level only without a need for expressing details on the relational logic level, i.e., on the Kodkod level.

In this paper, we discuss how to apply the tool USE in a larger example and demonstrate the advantages of our approach for relational database design. We start with a conceptual UML model in form of a UML class diagram and transform this conceptual schema into a relational database schema that is again represented as a UML class model. The typical constraints in the relational database model as primary and foreign key constraints are formulated as OCL invariants. We check properties of the resulting model with our tool USE.

The rest of the paper is structured as follows: Section 2 sketches our validation and verification use cases. Section 3 shows how the use cases can be applied in the context of a relational database schema and typical relational database constraints. Related work is discussed in Sect. 4. The paper ends with concluding remarks and future work in Sect. 5.

11.2 Validation and Verification Use Cases

Following [6], Fig. 11.1 gives an overview on the options of our approach in form of a UML use case diagram. The central functionalities are shown as eight main use cases that are pictured in light gray whereas the remaining ones in white are subordinate use cases. All main use cases rely on a class model including accompanying OCL invariants and a configuration that fixes a finite search space for the population of classes, associations, attributes and datatypes. Let us go through the eight main use cases one by one and explain shortly their characteristics.

1. The use case 'model consistency' checks whether the model can be instantiated by at least one object diagram under the stated finite search space from the configuration. If this is possible, the consistency of the model has been shown.
2. The use case 'property satisfiability' tests whether a given additional OCL invariant, which can describe a more particular requirement on the model and which is added, can be satisfied with an object diagram as well.

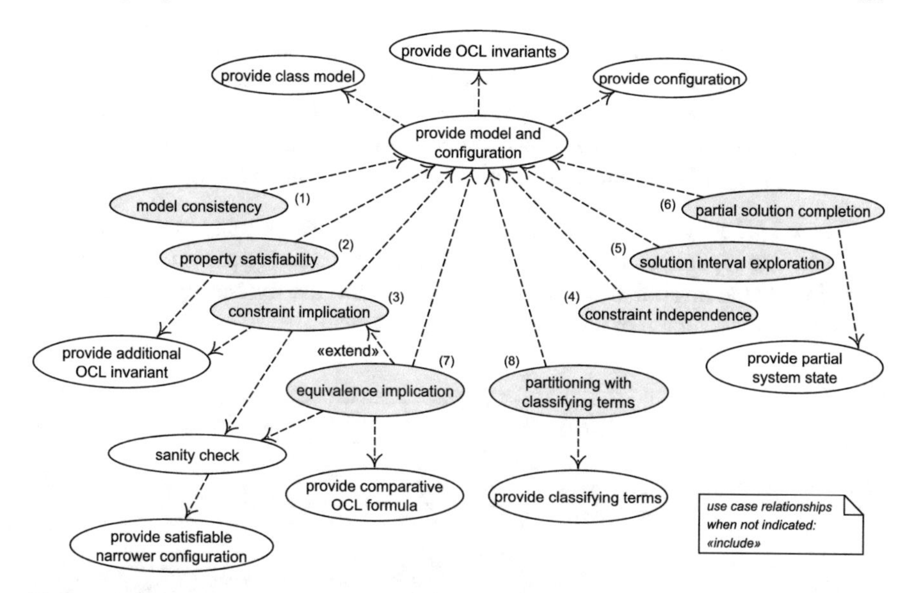

Fig. 11.1 Validation and verification use cases.

3. In a similar way the use case 'constraint implication' is designed for determining whether an additional invariant is a logical consequence of the model. For achieving this, the additional invariant is loaded and then logically negated. If within the finite search space of the configuration an object digram is found, the logical consequence is not valid; if no object diagram is found, the logical consequence is valid in the finite search space.
4. The use case 'constraint independence' tests whether the stated OCL invariants are independent from each other, i.e., it will be checked whether each single invariant is not a logical consequence from the remaining invariants. It is assured that no invariant can be removed without changing the model's induced set of object diagrams.
5. The use case 'solution interval exploration' is intended to be applied in situations where not only one single object diagram of the finite search space is of interest, but all solutions in form of object diagrams should be found. Even for smaller search spaces a comparison of different solutions can give interesting feedback.
6. The use case 'partial solution completion' assumes a partially described object diagram is present that might not yet satisfy model-inherent or explicit constraints; the task is then to find a completion in terms of objects, links and attribute values such that a valid object diagram satisfying all constraints is presented.
7. The use case 'equivalence implication' verifies for two OCL formulas `A` and `B` whether they are equivalent; the use case adds the logically negated invariant `(A implies B) and (B implies A)` and inspects whether that formula holds as a consequence, i.e., it checks that no object diagram exists in the search space and under the negated formula.

8. The last use case 'partitioning with classifying terms' allows to construct object diagram equivalence classes that are characterized by closed OCL query terms; in each equivalence class all OCL query terms evaluate to the same result; for each equivalence class a canonical representative in form of an object diagram is chosen; only a finite number of equivalence classes can be constructed.

Figure 11.2 shows the uses cases from Fig. 11.1 and the primary input and output artifacts. The input is in all use cases the class model, a configuration, (optionally a variation of) the invariants and depending on the use case further input. The output is a single object model or a collection of object models.

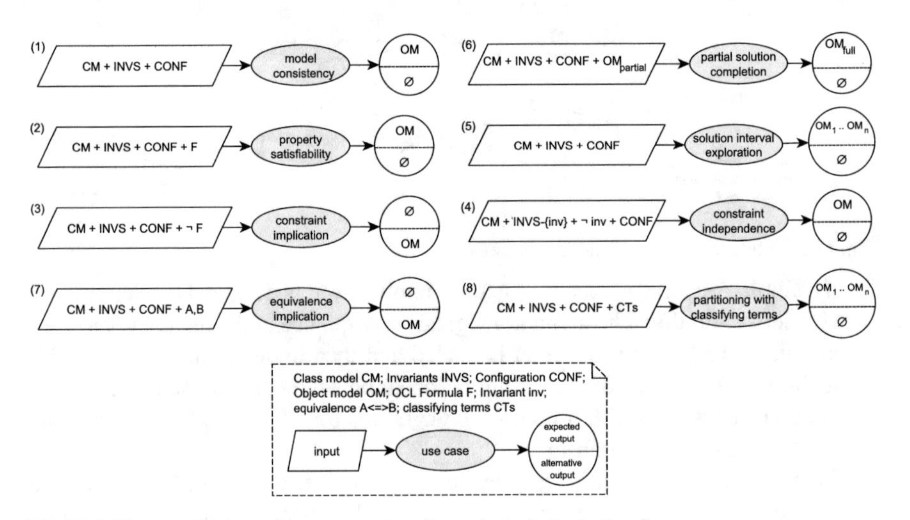

Fig. 11.2 Use case input and use case output for main and alternative flow.

11.3 Use Cases Applied in a Conceptual Modeling Example

This section explores four from the above eight model validation and verification use cases in a conceptual modeling example. The running example in this section discusses a relational database schema where a single table (relation) is modeled as a single UML class, primary and foreign key constraints are described as OCL constraints, and derived associations representing foreign keys from the relational database schema visualize the connection between the referencing tuple and the referenced tuple. Tuples from the relational database are represented as objects from the UML class diagram representing the relational database schema.

The UML class diagram in Fig. 11.3 is an example schema extracted from the book by Antoni Olivé on conceptual modeling [8]. The example is an Order-OrderLine-Product world: an order line belongs to an order and refers to a product;

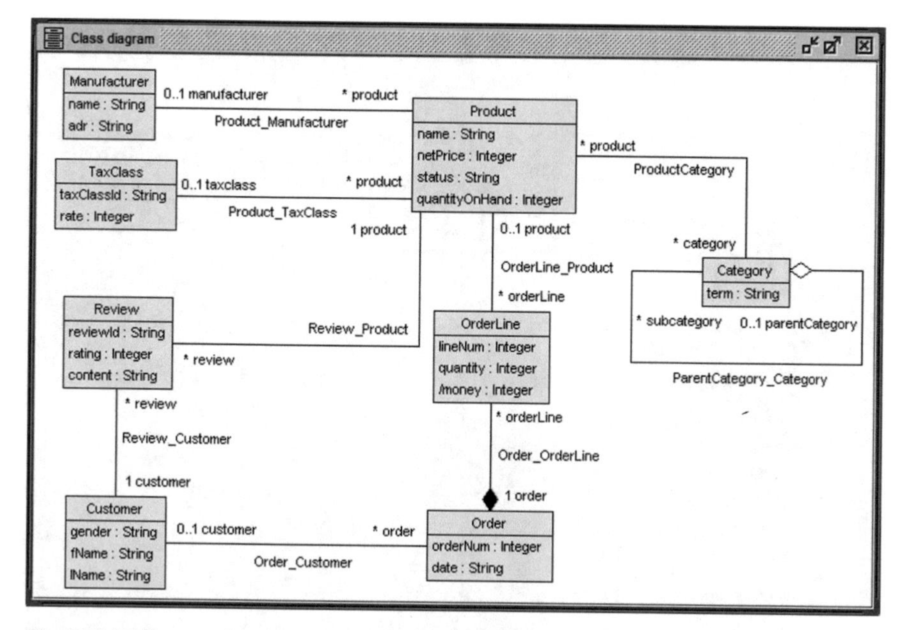

Fig. 11.3 UML example schema from Olive's original work.

products possess manufacturers and tax classes; products can have reviews written by customers who also trigger orders; products are classified by categories on which an ontology with parent categories and subcategories is provided.

The example uses associations of various kinds: many-to-many, functional (partial 0..1 and total 1..1), reflexive (binary association defined on a single class) and part-whole association. We use the term functional association to denote a many-to-one association as a source instance is functionally mapped to at most one or exactly one target instance.

In Fig. 11.4, we see how the UML conceptual schema is represented as a relational database schema in form of another UML class diagram. As a forward reference, one may look at Fig. 11.6 to see a simple object diagram illustrating the representation of a relational database state with tuples. The core of the transformation from the conceptual UML schema to the relational database schema can be characterized as follows: an entity is mapped to a relation that is represented as a class; a functional association is mapped to (a) an attribute (or many attributes) in the relation resp. the class corresponding to the source entity of the functional association and (b) a derived association for the foreign key; a general association (many-to-many) is mapped to (a) one relation represented as a class and (b) derived associations for the foreign keys.

The UML class diagram in Fig. 11.4 shows eight classes originating from entities: Manufacturer, Product, TaxClass, Review, OrderLine, Category, Customer, and Order; and the class diagram displays one class originating from an association: ProductCategory.

Fig. 11.5 shows the OCL constraints: each of the nine classes has a primary key constraint with a name ending in 'PK'. For each functional association (eight associ-

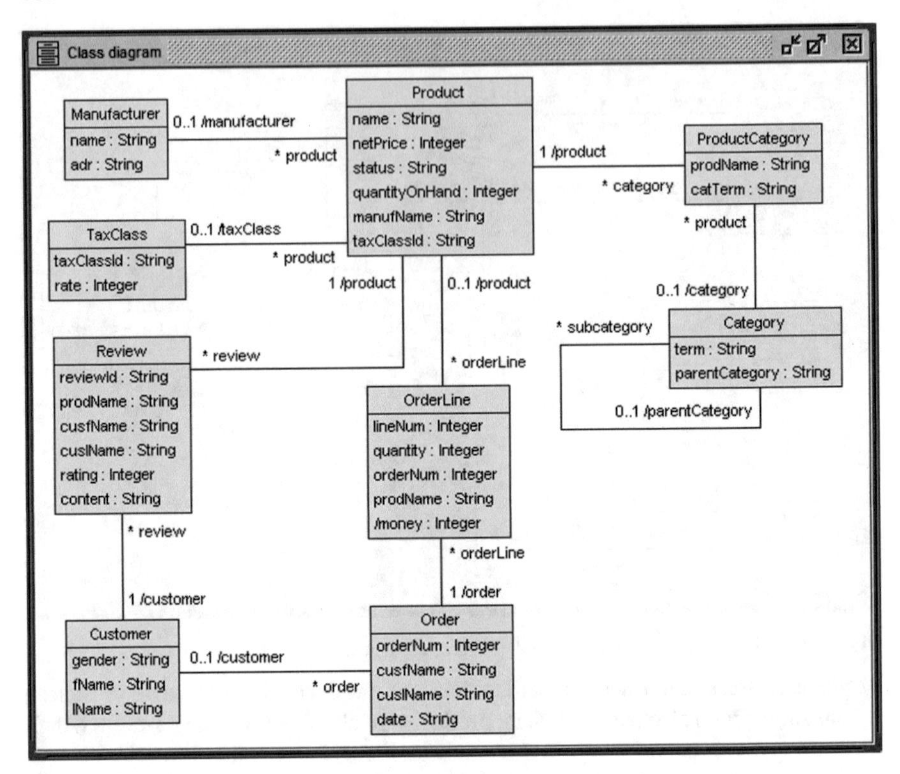

Fig. 11.4 Olive's example as a UML class diagram with classes for relations.

ations) and for each 'arm' of the other association (two 'arms') there is a foreign key constraint with a name containing 'FK' (ten foreign key constraints); the ten derived role names (indicated with the leading dash '/' in the name) are shown in the class diagram; there are nine other constraints, among them 'Category::acyclicSub' which requires the part-whole Category connections to form a directed, acyclic graph. It is a constraint involving the transitive closure. Standard SQL does not support to express this, but OCL due to the presence of the closure operation allows to describe the transitive closure.

A foreign key constraint establishes a connection between two relations. Because a table is represented in our UML model as a class, a corresponding OCL foreign key constraint must connect two classes. If the key of the referenced table consists of one attribute, there is one referencing attribute in the referencing table that points to one tuple in the referenced table. This is formally established with the OCL collection operation one(). We exemplarily show the requirement for the foreign key from OrderLine to Product.

```
context OrderLine inv prodName_FK_Product:
        Product.allInstances()→one(p|p.name=prodName)
```

Taking together the primary and foreign key constraints, all restrictions on the system states for the relational database have been expressed, and all necessary constraints are stated. In particular, the foreign key connection between the referencing

```
Manufacturer::namePK
Product::namePK
ProductCategory::productCategoryPK
TaxClass::taxClassIdPK
Review::reviewIdPK
Category::termPK
OrderLine::lineNumOrderNumPK
Customer::lNameFNamePK
Order::orderNumPK

Product::manufName_FK_Manufacturer
Product::taxClassId_FK_TaxClass
ProductCategory::catTerm_FK_Category
ProductCategory::prodName_FK_Product
Review::cuslName_cusfName_FK_Customer
Review::prodName_FK_Product
Category::parentCategory_FK_Category
OrderLine::orderNum_FK_Order
OrderLine::prodName_FK_Product
Order::cuslName_cusfName_FK_Customer

Product::statusValues
Category::acyclicSub
Category::subcategoryExists
Review::ratingValues
OrderLine::lineNum1exists
OrderLine::lineNumGE1
OrderLine::lineNumNoGaps
OrderLine::lineNumUniqueWithinOrder
Customer::genderValues
```

Fig. 11.5 Constraints defined in Olive's example.

tuple (represented as an object) and the referenced tuple (represented as an object) are manifested through the respective attribute values. Nothing more is needed. Thus only the objects with its values describe a database state. However, as UML and USE support derived associations, we can additionally visualize these connections also in formal terms through derived links. Each derived association is constructed by using a corresponding foreign key derivation term. The following definition shows exemplarily the foreign key derived association between the classes OrderLine and Product. The other derived associations and their roles are formulated analogously.

```
association FK_OrderLine_Product between
  OrderLine [0..*] role orderLine
  Product   [0..1] role product
    derived = Product.allInstances()→any(p|p.name=self.prodName)
end
```

If we compare the original UML schema in Fig. 11.3 and the corresponding relational database schema formulated as a UML class diagram with derived associations in Fig. 11.4, we see that the graph structures of both diagrams are nearly identical. An eye-catching difference is probably that the functional associations are not represented by an independent class, but these associations are integrated into the relation representing the source entity of the functional original association. These associations are present in the UML class diagram for the relational database schema through the referencing foreign key attributes and the derived role names.

The representation of foreign keys as derived associations seems to offer an intuitive way to represent the connections between tuples on the modeling level within a database state.

11.3.1 Model Consistency

As explained in Sec. 11.2, the purpose of the model consistency use case is to ensure that a valid system state (object diagram) can be instantiated, which ideally includes objects from all classes and links from all associations. To achieve this, we use the following configuration. Because we want to keep the generated object diagram in a reasonable size, we here use quite small numbers for the objects in the respective classes. The configuration will also provide finite, concrete sets for attributes values, e.g., `Product` names like `'Apple'` or `'Banana'`.

```
Manufacturer_min = 1         Manufacturer_max = 1
Review_min = 1               Review_max = 1
TaxClass_min = 1             TaxClass_max = 1
Category_min = 2             Category_max = 2
Product_min = 2              Product_max = 2
ProductCategory_min = 1      ProductCategory_max = 1
Order_min = 1                Order_max = 1
OrderLine_min = 4            OrderLine_max = 4
Customer_min = 1             Customer_max = 1
```

Fig. 11.6 shows the generated object diagram when we execute the model validator with the above configuration. As can be seen, the object diagram shows objects being instantiated from all nine classes and links originating from all ten foreign key derived associations. We emphasize the fact that, during the construction process, the model validator must take into account the nine classes and the 28 non-trivial invariants defined in the model.

11.3.2 Property Satisfiability

Basically, checking property satisfiability is finding the answer to the question whether a scenario, which is defined by an additional OCL formula, exists or does not exist. If we provide a sufficient finite search space (via a configuration), the model validator will give the answer (1) as a object diagram, in which the given property is satisfied, or (2) by answering that a valid scenario cannot be constructed within the given finite search space.

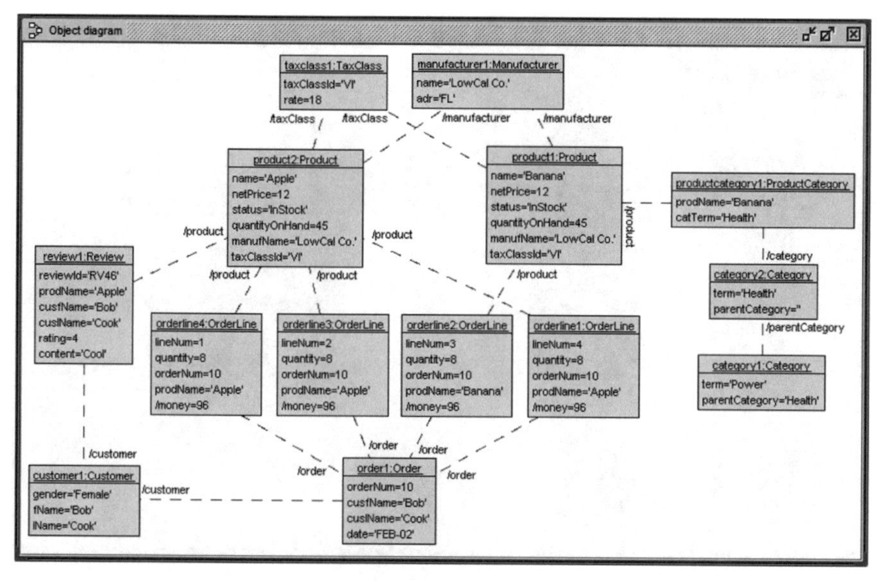

Fig. 11.6 Valid object diagram for model consistency use case.

In this example, we want to check the property 'Is it possible to build a scenario where the Category objects build a tree?'. The property is formulated as the following invariant.

```
context Category inv categroryTree:
  Category.allInstances→one(c | c.parentCategory='') and
  Category.allInstances→exists(c | c.subcategory→size>=2)
```

Executing the model validator after the model has been enriched with the property invariant, we receive a satisfying scenario as shown in Fig. 11.7. We here use a slightly modified configuration as in the model consistency use case.

11.3.3 Constraint Independence

As mentioned before, the constraint independence use case realizes a process that checks whether an invariant is independent from the other invariants. We prototypically select the following invariant that asserts that within an order the order lines are consecutively numbered.

```
context OrderLine inv lineNumNoGaps: lineNum>1 implies
  order.orderLine→exists(ol | ol.lineNum=lineNum-1)
```

In order to check constraint independence, we only do minor changes in the previous configuration. But we have to negate the selected invariant. As shown in Fig. 11.8, the model validator will construct an object diagram where two order lines are present that do not have consecutive numbers. Except of the selected invariant, which is evaluated to false, all other invariants evaluate to true. Thus the selected

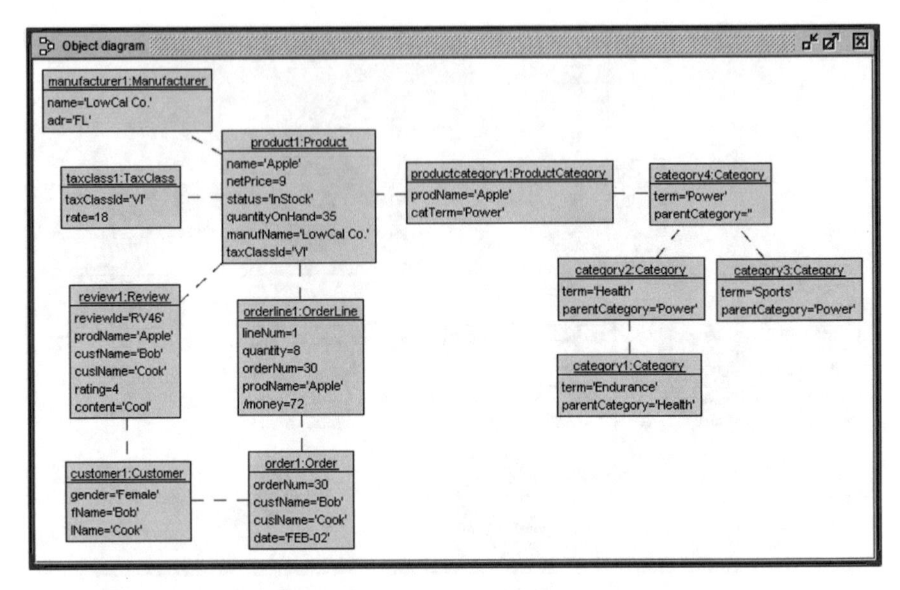

Fig. 11.7 Generated object diagram for property satisfiability use case.

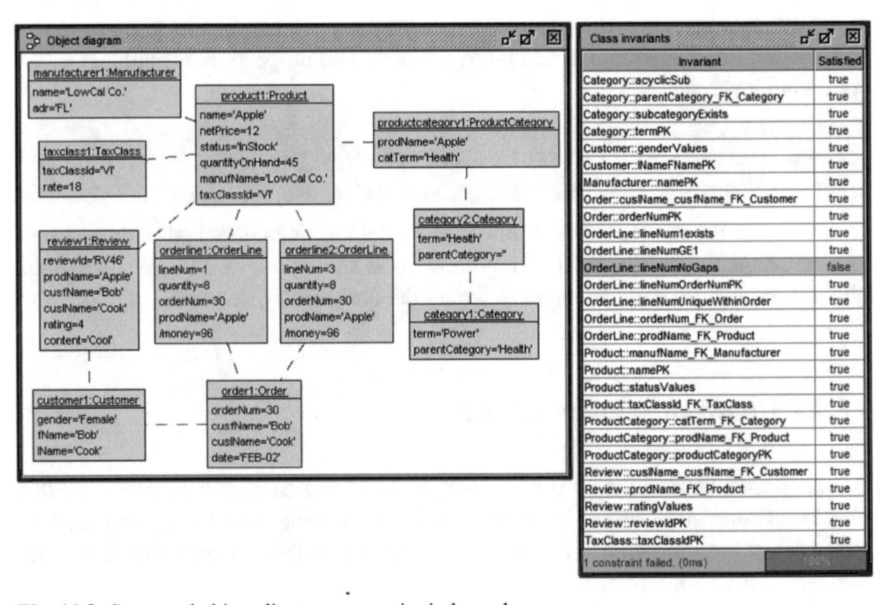

Fig. 11.8 Generated object diagram constraint independence use case.

invariant is indeed independent. It is essentially needed in the model, otherwise unwanted system states like the one in Fig. 11.8 might occur.

11.3.4 Partial Solution Completion

In Fig. 11.9 you see an example for applying the use case 'partial solution completion' in our running relational database schema model.

The upper object diagram and class invariant evaluation picture the starting situation with a partial object diagram and six failing OCL invariants. Among the failing invariants are the Review primary key constraint and the foreign key constraint from Review to Customer. In this use case, the model validator modifies undefined attributes to defined ones, and through this, links for the derived foreign key association between Review and Customer can be established. The lower part of the figure shows the enriched object diagram and the invariant evaluation which proves that after the completion all invariants are valid.

The example nicely demonstrates that proper attribute values have to be available in the configuration. Although the object diagram is quite small, the example illustrates well the use case 'partial solution completion' that is employed here in order to adjust an invalid system state to a correct one.

11.4 Related Work

In recent years, a number of interesting verification and validation approaches of conceptual schemata have been introduced. In [13], [12], [4] a list of major properties, e.g., satisfiability, class liveliness, nonredundancy, consistency, can be verified using different techniques. [12] introduces a fragment of OCL, the so-called OCL-Lite, encoding it in description logic. [4] focusses on the automated reasoning on UML schemata containing arbitrary constraints, derived roles, derived attributes and queries after translating the UML/OCL schema into a first order logic formalisation. The above approaches all translate UML and OCL into logic before reasoning about the conceptual model. The transformation of UML and OCL into formal specifications for validation and verification purposes is a widely considered topic, as it is presented in the following papers. In [15], a translation from UML to UML-B is presented und used for the validation and verification of models, focusing on consistency and checking safety properties. The approach in [1] presents a translation of UML and OCL into first-order predicate logic to reason about models utilizing theorem provers.

Furthermore, incremental checking of OCL constraints is a popular technique for ensuring the quality of a UML schema. A runtime checking approach for the satisfiability of all constraints after changes in the system state is presented in [3]. Similarly, [9] introduces a method to verify OCL constraint violations by checking the emptiness of SQL queries, which are automatically obtained from the OCL constraint.

After checking the problems in a UML schema through verification and validation techniques, automatic fixing and repairing will help to improve the conceptual schema. The approach in [10] can detect non-executable operations in a UML/OCL

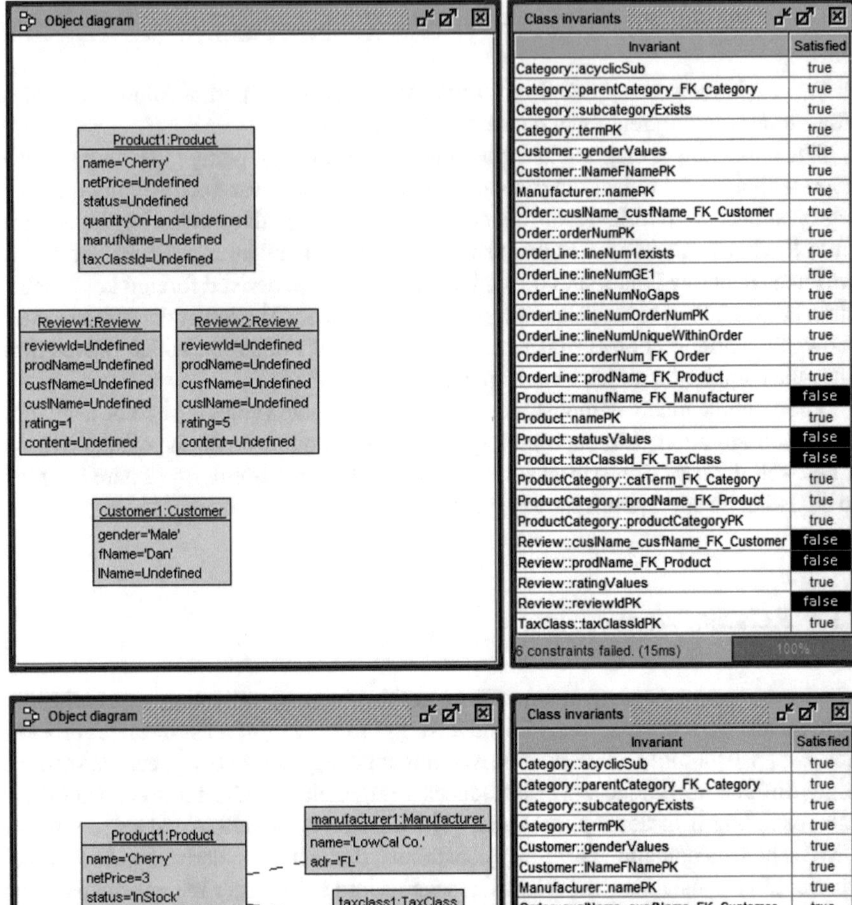

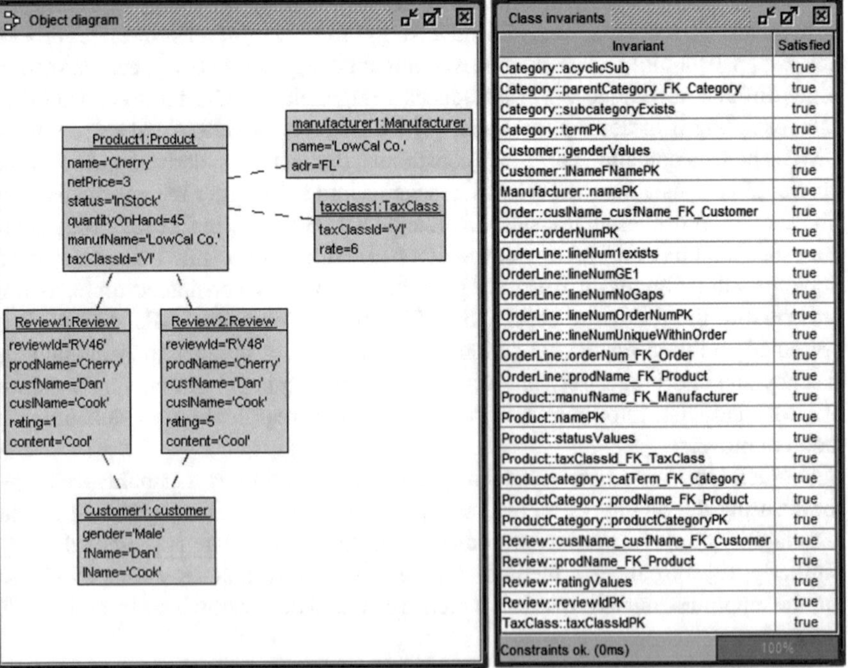

Fig. 11.9 Completion of partial object diagram by the USE model validator.

conceptual schema and automatically correct the missing effects in the postconditions of the operations. Another approach, which is presented in [11], automatically computes the additional changes needed to keep the UML/OCL schema consistent, i.e., all constraints are satisfied, when a set of update events is applied to the system state of the schema.

Testing a conceptual schema is also a research direction for quality improvement. [7] introduces a solution for automatically generating test cases from a UML/OCL model. This approach integrates several existing languages and tools, i.e., the USE tool and the CSTL language. The CSTL language is used as a language for writing automated tests in the approaches presented in [17] and [18].

11.5 Conclusions and Future Work

In this paper, we have presented techniques to utilize an up-to-date modeling tool for a wide range of model validation and verification tasks. Examples are shown with the USE model validator using four use cases: model consistency, property reachability, constraint independence, and partial solution completion.

Future work could concentrate on optimizing the verification tasks by providing help with determining bounds specifically for the presented techniques. Optimizations of the USE model validator itself includes support for more UML features and a more sophisticated handling of strings and large integers. In order to offer support for relational database design, we plan to import SQL database schemata, represent them as UML and OCL models and generate (positive and negative) test database states with the model validator (exported then again as SQL scripts). Finally, larger verification and validation case studies have to further evaluate the individual methods presented.

References

1. Beckert, B., Keller, U., Schmitt, P.: Translating the Object Constraint Language into first-order predicate logic. In: Proc. 2nd Verification WS: VERIFY. vol. 2, pp. 2–7 (2002)
2. Boehm, B.: Software risk management. In: Ghezzi, C., McDermid, J.A. (eds.) Proc. 2nd European Software Engineering Conf. (ESEC 1989). LNCS, vol. 387, pp. 1–19. Springer (1989)
3. Cabot, J., Teniente, E.: Incremental integrity checking of UML/OCL conceptual schemas. Journal of Systems and Software 82(9), 1459–1478 (2009)
4. Farré, C., Queralt, A., Rull, G., Teniente, E., Urpí, T.: Automated reasoning on UML conceptual schemas with derived information and queries. Information & Software Technology 55(9), 1529–1550 (2013)
5. Gogolla, M., Büttner, F., Richters, M.: USE: A UML-based specification environment for validating UML and OCL. Sci. Comput. Program. 69(1-3), 27–34 (2007)
6. Gogolla, M., Hilken, F.: Model Validation and Verification Options in a Contemporary UML and OCL Analysis Tool. In: Oberweis, A., Reussner, R. (eds.) Proc. Modellierung (MODELLIERUNG'2016). pp. 203–218. GI, LNI 254 (2016)

7. Granda, M.F.: Testing-based conceptual schema validation in a model-driven environment. In: Proceedings of the Doctoral Consortium of the 25th International Conference on Advanced Information Systems Engineering (CAiSE 2013), Valencia, Spain, June 21, 2013 (2013), http://ceur-ws.org/Vol-1001/paper6.pdf
8. Olivé, A.: Conceptual modeling of information systems. Springer (2007)
9. Oriol, X., Teniente, E.: Incremental checking of OCL constraints with aggregates through SQL. In: Conceptual Modeling - 34th International Conference, ER 2015, Stockholm, Sweden, October 19-22, 2015, Proceedings. pp. 199–213 (2015)
10. Oriol, X., Teniente, E., Tort, A.: Fixing up non-executable operations in UML/OCL conceptual schemas. In: Conceptual Modeling - 33rd International Conference, ER 2014, Atlanta, GA, USA, October 27-29, 2014. Proceedings. pp. 232–245 (2014)
11. Oriol, X., Teniente, E., Tort, A.: Computing repairs for constraint violations in UML/OCL conceptual schemas. Data Knowl. Eng. 99, 39–58 (2015)
12. Queralt, A., Artale, A., Calvanese, D., Teniente, E.: OCL-Lite: Finite reasoning on UML/OCL conceptual schemas. Data Knowl. Eng. 73, 1–22 (2012)
13. Queralt, A., Teniente, E.: Verification and validation of UML conceptual schemas with OCL constraints. ACM Trans. Softw. Eng. Methodol. 21(2), 13:1–13:41 (2012)
14. Selic, B.: UML2: A Model-Driven Development Tool. IBM Systems Journal 45(3), 607–620 (2006)
15. Snook, C., Savicks, V., Butler, M.: Verification of UML Models by Translation to UML-B. In: Aichernig, B., de Boer, F., Bonsangue, M. (eds.) Formal Methods for Components and Objects, FMCO 2010. LNCS, vol. 6957, pp. 251–266. Springer (2010)
16. Torlak, E., Jackson, D.: Kodkod: A Relational Model Finder. In: Grumberg, O., Huth, M. (eds.) Tools and Algorithms for the Construction and Analysis of Systems, TACAS 2007. LNCS, vol. 4424, pp. 632–647. Springer (2007)
17. Tort, A., Olivé, A.: An approach to testing conceptual schemas. Data Knowl. Eng. 69(6), 598–618 (2010)
18. Tort, A., Olivé, A., Sancho, M.: On checking executable conceptual schema validity by testing. In: Database and Expert Systems Applications - 23rd International Conference, DEXA 2012, Vienna, Austria, September 3-6, 2012. Proceedings, Part I. pp. 249–264 (2012)

Chapter 12
Creating Worlds with Words: Ontology-guided Conceptual Modeling for Institutional Domains

Paul Johannesson, Maria Bergholtz and Owen Eriksson

Abstract Conceptual modeling is often viewed as an activity of representing a pre-existing world that should be faithfully mirrored in an information system. This view is adequate for modeling physical domains but needs to be revised and extended for social and institutional domains, as these are continuously produced and re-produced through communicative processes. Thereby, conceptual modeling moves beyond analysis and representation in order to cater also for design and creation. Following such a view on conceptual modeling, this paper proposes an ontology for modeling institutional domains. The ontology emphasizes the role of institutional entities in regulating and governing these domains through rules and rights that define allowed and required interactions. Furthermore, the ontology shows how these institutional entities are dependent on and grounded in material entities. Conceptual modelers can benefit from the ontology when modeling institutional domains, as it highlights fundamental notions and distinctions in these domains, e.g., the role of rights, the role of processes in creating institutional facts, and the difference between documents and institutional information. The ontology is illustrated using a case on public consultation management.

Paul Johannesson
Department of Computer and Systems Sciences, Stockholm University, Postbox 7003, SE 164 07 Kista, Sweden, e-mail: `pajo@dsv.su.se`

Maria Bergholtz
Department of Computer and Systems Sciences, Stockholm University, Postbox 7003, SE 164 07 Kista, Sweden, e-mail: `maria@dsv.su.se`

Owen Eriksson
Department of Informatics and Media, Uppsala University, Box 513, SE 751 20 Uppsala, Sweden, e-mail: `owen.eriksson@im.uu.se`

© Springer International Publishing AG 2017

J. Cabot et al. (eds.), *Conceptual Modeling Perspectives*,
https://doi.org/10.1007/978-3-319-67271-7_12

12.1 Introduction

Conceptual modeling has been defined as "the activity that elicits and describes the general knowledge a particular information system needs to know", [17, p. xi]. Thus, conceptual modeling is about analyzing and representing some piece of reality, a domain that is to be mirrored in an information system. To support this activity, many researchers have proposed that ontology should be used as a foundation for conceptual modeling, building on the assumption that ontology can help to better understand how reality is constituted, [27, 26, 10]. Physical objects are clearly among the constituents of reality, but there are also realities that are built from other kinds of matter. Sometimes language can hint at the foundations of those non-material realities. Consider the phrases "real property" and "real estate". What is real about them? It is not that they are natural and material objects, because the "real" here is not derived from the Latin "res" meaning "thing", but from the Spanish "real" meaning "royal", or "belonging to the king", [9, p. 86]. They are real because they are recognized and acknowledged by an authority. In other words, they are real because there exists an institution that says they are so.

Developing conceptual models for information systems is very much about investigating social and institutional worlds. These worlds do not exist independently of humans but are created by people that talk them into existence. As pointed out by [17, p. 41], there are not only concepts that can be considered natural, in the sense that their instances are familiar and viewed as natural by everyone, e.g., trees, birds and temperatures. There are also concepts that need to be invented or designed, e.g., leasing contracts, customers and presidents. These concepts are more often than not institutional ones, having the purpose to regulate human interaction by carrying rules and rights that govern how people are allowed and obliged to interact. And the instances of these concepts are not pre-existing but created by people in communicative processes. The need for designed concepts means that conceptual modeling is more than an analysis and representation activity; it also has to include elements of design and creation.

The goal of this paper is to propose an ontology that can support developers in designing conceptual models for institutional domains. The paper extends previous work, [3], [2], primarily by investigating additional kinds of institutional entities, in particular institutional information and institutional rights. The proposed institutional ontology builds on theories for communicative action, as well as existing ontologies for business domains, which are briefly described in Section 2. Institutional entities are created through communicative processes, and Section 2 also offers a brief overview of approaches to business process management. In Section 3, the research method is discussed as well as a case on consultation management, which is used to illustrate and validate the proposed ontology. The ontology itself is presented in Section 4 with examples from the case. Section 5 introduces a conceptual model for the consultation case based on the institutional ontology. Finally, Section 6 summarizes the paper, discusses implications, and suggests directions for future research.

12.2 Related Work

12.2.1 The Construction of Social Reality

Institutions have been defined as "systems of established and prevalent social rules that structure social interactions", [11]. In order to conceptualize the constituents and relationships of institutions, the paper proposes an institutional ontology. It is primarily founded on the work by John Searle, [24], [22], who has investigated how social and institutional reality is constructed by means of language.

Searle acknowledges that there is a material world existing independently of human beings and their beliefs, and he asks "how can we account for social facts within that ontology?" [23, p. 7]. He answers the question by pointing out that humans have a capacity for collective intentionality, through which they are able to assign functions to things. Some of these functions depend solely on the physical properties of the things to which they are assigned, e.g., the ability of a screwdriver to turn screws depends only on its physical structure. Other functions, however, are more abstract and have little to do with the physical properties of the object that provides them. Such functions are called status functions by Searle. The general logical form of the assignments of status functions is "X counts as Y in C", where X is often a thing or a human being that is assigned a status function Y in a context C. For example, John (X) counts as a bank customer (Y) in the context of the statutes of a bank (C). This assignment means that John and the bank are related through a number of mutual obligations and claims, e.g., the bank is allowed to use JohnâĂŹs money but is also obliged to pay a certain interest rate, while John can make deposits and claim interest. Thus, the assignment establishes rules and regulations that structure and govern the interactions between John and the bank.

Through the assignment of status functions, people can recursively build ever more complex and advanced institutional phenomena, e.g. moving from dollar bills to stock options, equity futures, and foreign exchange swaps. These institutional objects require collective intentionality for their creation as well as their continued existence. For example, a piece of metal will be able to function as a medium of value exchange only if people together recognize it as money. And it will become money only through a process in which people declare it to be so. Thus, people use words to create and maintain institutional worlds.

12.2.2 The REA Ontology

The proposed ontology is also informed by work on the REA ontology. REA was originally intended as a basis for accounting information systems, [15], and focused on representing increases and decreases of value in business organizations. In later work, REA has been extended to form a foundation for enterprise information systems architectures, [8], [13], where REA also addresses the policy level in organizations. REA places commitments and contracts into the center of business models, thereby emphasizing their importance for regulating business interactions. While commitments are sufficient for representing most of the rules in business contexts, many institutional settings also require other kinds of rights, such as powers and privileges, see Section 4.1. To address this need, the institutional ontology generalizes REA by allowing for any kinds of rights.

12.2.3 Business Process Management

Business Process Management (BPM) is a discipline that combines knowledge from both information technology and management sciences and applies it to operational business processes, [1]. BPM studies how work is and should be organized with the purpose to produce value for customers. In its early stages, BPM focused on the automation of workflows, but today it also includes process design, process analysis and work organization. BPM can support organizations in becoming more effective, efficient and customer-oriented, as it focuses on value creation in business processes rather than on functionally oriented ways of management.

Much of the work in the BPM field has investigated the activities of business processes, in particular, their ordering and interdependencies, [6]. Thus, the focus has been on the control-flow perspective of processes. But there are also other perspectives on processes. The resource perspective concerns roles, authorizations and organizational structures, while the data perspective addresses data creation and manipulation, forms, and the use of data for process decisions. The time perspective concerns temporal issues including deadlines and durations, and the function perspective addresses applications related to activities.

Processes can be viewed from a system perspective, in which they are enacted to accomplish a goal of a system. In other words, actors carry out processes in order to produce goods or services that are delivered to the environment of the system. Such processes have been named production processes, which are constituted by production acts, [5]. A production act can be material, such as the manufacturing or transportation of goods, or immaterial, such as granting insurance claims or issuing exam certificates. Actors can also perform coordination acts, by which they enter into and comply with agreements about production acts. For example, an actor can order that some goods be transported (a production act) and another actor can accept this order.

Production acts can also constitute new objects in the sense of making them available in a particular institutional context. For example, production acts in car manufacturing are not only about building physical entities but also about making them into institutional ones. This means to declare that some physical entity is to be counted as an institutional entity, in this case a car. Constituting the car in this way is needed for being able to refer to it and identify it in various institutional contexts, e.g. in the relationship with national authorities as discussed in [7]. Summarizing, a key purpose of business processes is to build an institutional world by creating agreements and constituting institutional entities. Therefore, being able to represent and analyze institutional phenomena can help to design and implement business processes.

12.3 Research Setting and the Consultation Case

12.3.1 Research Setting

The ontology presented in the next section has been iteratively developed over a period of five years. Empirically, it is grounded in the study of a number of information systems. The selection of these systems was based on purposeful sampling, [19], where the primary data set consisted of a number of case studies, [2], [3]. Purposeful sampling means that findings are based on the selection of information-rich cases for study in depth, in contrast to probability sampling, which depends on the selection of random and statistically representative samples. In addition to the primary data set, a secondary data set was used, which was also based on purposeful sampling. Design patterns and problems from the mainstream modeling literature, including [26], [14], [7], [25], were selected and used to clarify and investigate modeling problems found in the cases. The primary and secondary data sets were analyzed in several iterations in order to establish and revise the contents of the institutional ontology. This work is on-going and the next sub-section introduces yet another case, which is currently used to validate the ontology.

12.3.2 The Consultation Case

Public consultation is a regulatory process that is often a part of the larger process of developing proposals for laws, policies, and projects in the public sector, [20], [4]. In a public consultation, a public body seeks the opinions of interested and affected groups, typically through organizations that can represent them. The overall goal of a public consultation is to gather comments and criticisms on a proposal. The comments can help to improve the proposal, thereby improving its quality and effectiveness. Furthermore, consultations can strengthen transparency and public involvement in public decision processes. In the following, based on both literature and our own experience of public consultation cases, a typical consultation process is described. The process consists of four phases: preparation, submission, response collection, and response compilation and publication.

12.3.2.1 Preparation

A proposal is prepared before it is sent on consultation. This means that the public body behind the proposal identifies its various parts and classifies them according to their purpose. Some of the parts are suggestions that propose courses of actions, while other parts are assessments that specify how the authors of the proposal evaluate some state of affairs. Furthermore, there are justifications that provide arguments for the suggestions and assessments. The proposal is given a reference number and is recorded in the registry of the public body. Each part, often called a section, is also numbered so that it can be conveniently referenced.

A key activity in the preparation phase is to identify reviewers that will be invited to comment on the proposal. This is done by an administrator proposing a set of reviewers, which is to be confirmed by a manager. Some of the reviewers can be obliged to answer to the consultation, while others may be allowed to disregard it. Furthermore, a reviewer can be requested to comment on specific sections of the proposal, i.e., the reviewer has to provide feedback on those sections but may leave others without commenting on them. The preparation phase also includes deciding on the deadline for reviewers to submit their responses.

A cover letter to send to the reviewers is prepared. This letter informs the reviewers about the submission deadline, whether it is mandatory to answer, the format in which to submit responses (paper and/or electronic), contact persons at the public body, which sections of the proposal to focus on, as well as other instructions and guidelines.

12.3.2.2 Submission

Submitting a public consultation means that the proposal and its cover letter is sent to the reviewers identified in the preparation phase. This is done using both ordinary mail and email.

12.3.2.3 Response Collection

When the reviewers submit their responses, they are archived in the registry of the public body. Each response is archived under the same reference number as the proposal under consultation. Each response consists of a number of comments, one of which concerns the entire proposal, while each of the other comments concern a single section of it.

12.3.2.4 Response Compilation and Publication

The public body compiles the responses and publishes the resulting compilation on its web site. The compilation shows the number of reviewers that have agreed, or not agreed, on the entire proposal, as well as on each of its parts. Furthermore, the compilation includes for each section of the proposal a short text based on the most important responses; these texts are written by an administrator at the public body.

12.4 The Institutional Ontology

The institutional ontology is structured into three levels, as indicated by color coding in Figure 12.1. The bottom level (white in the figure) is the material level that describes material entities, in particular human beings, physical entities, and physical actions. The middle level (yellow in the figure) is the institutional facts level that describes institutional phenomena and their creation. The entities at this level are used to regulate the entities at the material level. Finally, the top level (blue in the figure) is the rule level that includes rules, as well as groupings of rules, that govern how entities are created at the institutional facts level. The ontology is depicted in the form of a UML class diagram (multiplicities are 0..* if not otherwise indicated).

12.4.1 Institutional Rights

The overall purpose of institutions is to regulate, govern and enable human interaction. One way to achieve this structuring of interaction is to create and allocate rights among people, thereby establishing relationships of power and obligations between them. A right is a relational construct that involves at least two agents, e.g., an obligation of one agent to deliver some goods to another agent. In addition, a right can include additional entities that are the objects of the right, such as the goods in the preceding example.

There exist different classifications of rights, but one of the most well-known is the one proposed by [12], who distinguishes between four kinds of rights: claims, privileges, powers and immunities. A *claim* means that one agent is required to act in a certain way for the benefit of another agent, e.g., a person can have a claim on another person to pay an amount of money. An agent has a *privilege* to perform an action if she is free to carry it out without interference from other agents, e.g., privileges of free speech and free movement. A *power* is the ability of an agent to create or modify claims, privileges or powers, e.g., the ability to transfer ownership. Finally, *immunities* are about restricting the power of agents to create formal relationships for other agents. In the institutional ontology, rights are modeled by the classes Right Kind and Institutional Right.

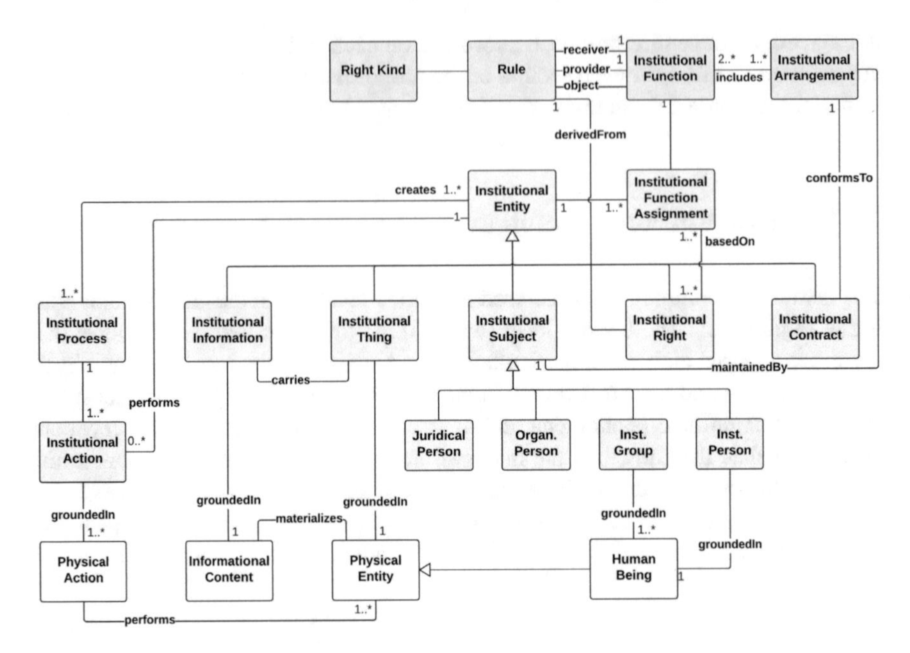

Fig. 12.1 The institutional ontology

12.4.2 Institutional Entities

Institutional entities are entities that have the function of regulating interaction by means of rights. An *institutional entity* is either a right, an entity that can have rights, an entity that is the object of a right, or a grouping of rights. Institutional entities are created through language actions, but their creation often requires that there is some other pre-existing entity on which the new institutional entity is dependent. The institutional entity is said to be grounded in that other entity [14], e.g., a citizen (an institutional entity) can be grounded in a human being (a physical entity). By combining the type of grounding and the way of relating to rights, a number of different kinds of institutional entities can be distinguished.

- Institutional Subject. An *institutional subject* is an institutional entity that can have claims. The ontology recognizes four kinds of institutional subjects. An *institutional person* is an institutional subject grounded in a human being able to possess both legal rights (i.e., rights acknowledged by a state) and non-legal rights. An *institutional group* is an institutional subject grounded in at least one institutional person but only able to possess non-legal rights. A *juridical person* is an institutional subject that is not grounded in any other entity and able to possess both legal and non-legal rights. Finally, an *organizational person* is an institutional subject that is not grounded in any other entity and able to possess only non-legal rights.
- Institutional Thing. An *institutional thing* is an institutional entity that cannot have claims and is grounded in a physical entity or another institutional thing.

- Institutional Information. *Institutional information* is an institutional entity that cannot have claims and is grounded in informational content. Examples of informational content are a text, a picture, and a musical score. While informational content is solely information without any formal status, institutional information is officially acknowledged by an institutional subject as an institutional entity. Thus, it has been created through an institutional process and has received its own identifier. For example, a code such as "ABC123" is just informational content, but it can ground a discount code issued by a company; this discount code is institutional information that is related to one or more rights, in particular it can grant a customer the claim to get a discount on goods she has purchased.
- Institutional Right. An *institutional right* is an institutional entity that represents a relationship of claim, privilege or power between two or more institutional subjects.
- Institutional Contract. An *institutional contract* is an institutional entity that groups together a number of rights, e.g., a purchase contract between two companies.

Informational content can only be materialized through a physical entity, e.g., a musical score can be materialized through a sheet of a paper with musical notation, an electronic document with the same notation, or an audio file. This relationship is captured in the ontology by the association *materializes* between Physical Entity and Informational Content. Analogously, there is an association *carries* between Institutional Thing and Institutional Information. For example, an officially recognized discount coupon can carry a discount code.

12.4.3 Rules and Institutional Functions

When people create and use institutional entities, they do so in a framework of rules that define the functions of the entities as well as the processes for creating them. The institutional entities receive their meaning only by being interpreted in the context of these rules.

Rules are formulated through linguistic expressions, e.g., "the *respondent* has to submit its *overall response* to the *initiator* before the deadline". These expressions include institutional functions that are used for specifying the institutional entities to which the rules should be applied. Institutional functions are similar to roles as they are used for defining bundles of rights that can be bestowed upon institutional entities. Examples of institutional functions are the *respondent* function, the *initiator* function, and the *overall response* function.

Institutional functions never appear in isolation but always in networks, since their meanings are dependent on each other. For example, the meanings of the institutional functions *initiator* and *respondent* depend on each other, in the sense that the one can only be defined by referring to the other. A respondent is someone who is obliged to answer to an invitation from an initiator. A set of interdependent institutional functions is called an *institutional arrangement*. An example is the consultation arrangement consisting of institutional functions involved in consultations, see Section 5.3 for details. Furthermore, an institutional arrangement is maintained by an institutional subject, who defines and monitors all the rules that apply to the institutional functions that make up the institutional arrangement. For example, some public body maintains the consultation arrangement.

Rules do not directly express rights between institutional entities, but instead they refer to institutional functions. However, if all the institutional functions in a rule are assigned to institutional entities, i.e., each institutional function is replaced by an institutional entity, the rule will result in a right between these. Assigning an institutional function to an institutional entity means that the latter gets related to other institutional entities through a number of rights, as given by the rules of the institutional function. For example, the rule above could result in the right "the company Acme has to submit its overall response to the department of justice before the deadline". In this example, the result expresses a right involving an organization and a department, which regulates their interactions. This example illustrates how rules are used in general - through assigning institutional functions to institutional entities, the latter become related and regulated by means of rights. In the ontology, institutional function assignments are used to assign institutional functions to institutional entities.

12.4.4 Institutional Processes

Institutional entities, as well as institutional function assignments, are created by means of language actions. They are, so to say, talked into existence. This is modeled in the ontology by the class Institutional Process that is associated to both Institutional Entity and Institutional Function Assignment. An *institutional process* consists of a sequence of institutional actions. The latter are always grounded in physical actions, i.e., they are performed through physical actions, such as signing paper documents or pressing keys on a keyboard.

12.5 Domain Model for the Consultation Case

The institutional ontology can be used to guide conceptual modelers when they design domain models, i.e., models for specific institutional domains. The main guideline is that every class introduced in a domain model should correspond to one of the classes on the middle level in the ontology, shown by stereotyping. In contrast, classes on the rule level do not correspond to classes in the domain model, but their instances are represented as classes. Institutional arrangements will be represented by classes stereotyped as Institutional Contract, while rules are represented by classes stereotyped as Institutional Right. An example is shown in Figure 12.2, where the rule *Overall assessment*, i.e., that a respondent shall provide a response to a submitted proposal sent from an initiator, is represented by means of a class of its own.

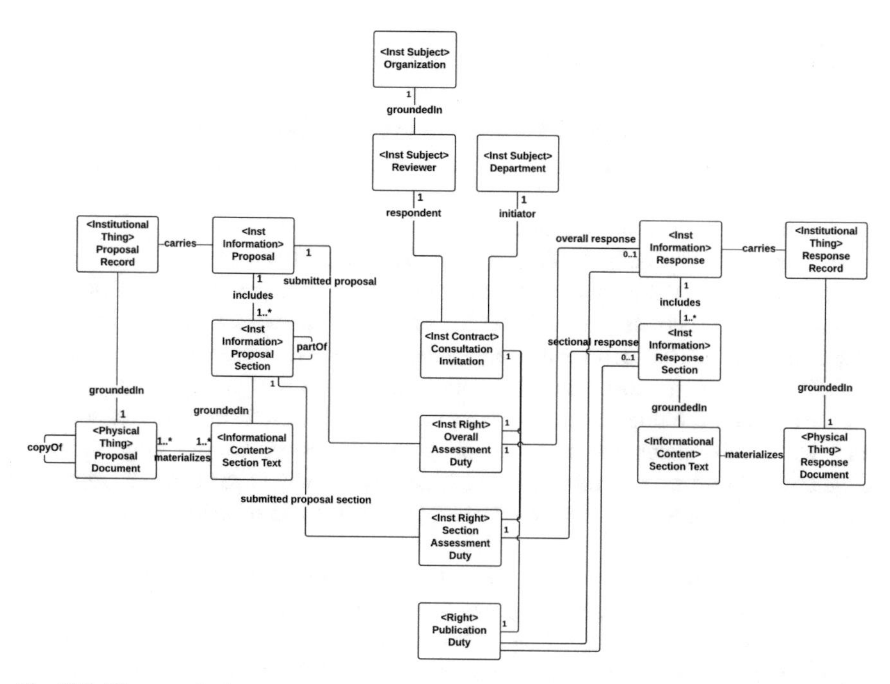

Fig. 12.2 The consultation case

For reasons of simplicity and clarity, not only classes on the rule level are omitted when the institutional ontology is applied, but typically also classes corresponding to institutional function assignments. Instead, they are in most cases represented only as associations between rights, contracts and institutional entities. A domain model of the consultation case is shown in Figure 12.2 in the form of a UML class diagram. The following sub-sections explain how the ontology is applied in the design of the consultation domain model.

12.5.1 Institutional Subjects

The consultation case includes two key kinds of institutional subjects, departments that initiate consultations and reviewers that respond to them. A *department* is a part of the public body that is responsible for issuing proposals and performing consultations. For each consultation, there is a department that initiates it. A *reviewer* is grounded in an *organization*, which is a legal entity, such as a company, an authority, or an NGO.

12.5.2 Institutional Information and Informational Content

Both proposals and responses to them are made by information, and thus many of the classes in the domain model are stereotyped as Institutional Information or Informational Content.

A *proposal* is institutional information that describes new laws, policies, and plans, e.g., bills and budgets. Proposals are intended to be submitted to reviewers for consideration and feedback. A proposal is divided into a number of *proposal sections*. These sections are the basis for structuring answers to a consultation, as described below. The sections are represented by the class Proposal Section in the domain model. A proposal and its sections are grounded in informational content, the *section texts*. While the section texts only consist of information that does not have any formal status, the proposal and proposal sections are officially acknowledged by a department as institutional entities. Thus, they have been created by the department through an institutional process, and each one of them has received its own identifier.

The section texts of a proposal are materialized in physical documents, the *proposal documents*, which can be in paper as well as electronic form. One of the proposal documents is the original one, from which the other documents are made as copies. The proposal documents ground institutional things, the *proposal records*. While a proposal document is just a physical entity, a proposal record is acknowledged by a department. The proposal record that is grounded in the original proposal document is the original proposal record and is given an identifier, the reference number.

A *response* is institutional information that provides feedback on a proposal. Just as for a proposal, a response includes a number of parts, called *response sections*, which are grounded in section texts. And each response section offers comments on exactly one proposal section. Analogously to the proposal documents, there are *response documents* that provide materializations of the section texts, as well as response records grounded in these response documents.

12.5.3 Rules and Institutional Functions

The interaction between the reviewers and the departments are regulated by a number of rules, of which the three most important are:

- Overall assessment: A *respondent* is obliged to provide an *overall response* on a *submitted proposal* to an *initiator*

- Sectional assessment: A *respondent* is obliged to provide a *sectional response* on a *submitted proposal section* to an *initiator*
- Publication: An *initiator* is obliged to publish the *overall response* and the *sectional responses* on a *submitted proposal* from a *respondent*

The rules include a number of institutional functions, which are italicized above. These institutional functions can be viewed as roles that can be played by the institutional subjects and institutional information introduced in the previous sections. A *respondent* is played by a reviewer, an *initiator* by a department, a *submitted proposal* by a proposal, a *submitted proposal section* by a proposal section, an *overall response* by a response, and a *sectional response* by a response section. All of the six institutional functions are mutually interdependent on each other, thereby forming one institutional arrangement, the consultation arrangement.

12.5.4 Institutional Rights and Institutional Contracts

The rules as well as the institutional functions and the institutional arrangement are reflected in the domain model. To each rule corresponds a class that represents rights: Overall Assessment Duty, Section Assessment Duty and Publication Duty. The single institutional arrangement, consultation arrangement, corresponds to the class Consultation Invitation, which represents institutional contracts. Intuitively, a consultation invitation is an agreement between a department and a reviewer about the former providing feedback on a proposal to the latter, who in turn is obliged to publish the comments.

The institutional functions are reflected by associations to the above classes. As respondent and initiator appear in all the rules, these institutional functions can be represented as associations to the class Consultation Invitation. The remaining institutional functions become associations to the classes representing rights. (It would also have been possible to introduce classes corresponding to the Institutional function assignment in the ontology instead of just using associations. This solution would indeed have been closer to the institutional ontology, but as the extra classes have no attributes, the resulting model would have become more complex without providing additional representational capabilities.)

12.5.5 Institutional Processes

The institutional entities represented by the domain model are created by a number of institutional processes, though these for reasons of space are not shown in Figure 12.2. At least five institutional processes are required: one process for creating reviewers; one process for creating departments; one process for creating proposals, their sections, as well as grounding and materializing entities; one process for creating consultation invitations and related rights; and one process for creating responses, their sections, as well as grounding and materializing entities. This case illustrates a general pattern, where there typically needs to exist a process for each class stereotyped as Institutional Subject, Institutional Information, Institutional Thing, and Institutional Contract. Classes stereotyped as Institutional Right do not need additional processes, since they are closely associated to classes stereotyped as Institutional Contract. The same holds for classes that are related to other classes as parts (such as Proposal Section) or classes on the material level.

12.6 Discussion and Conclusions

In this paper, we have proposed an ontology that can support developers in designing conceptual models for institutional domains and have illustrated it through an application on public consultation. In our work with the ontology, we have found that it can support developers in several different ways:

- The ontology helps to distinguish between institutional actions and physical actions, which is particularly useful when different physical actions can be used to ground the same institutional action, e.g., when a contract can be signed both through a paper signature and an electronic signature.
- The ontology helps to distinguish between physical documents and the information they materialize. This distinction is easy to overlook but becomes important when different kinds of documents can materialize the same information, e.g., both a paper document and an electronic one.
- The ontology treats rights as first-class citizens instead of hiding them within other entities. Rights become key entities that are used to regulate the interaction between institutional subjects, and the ontology thereby forces developers to make rights explicit.
- The ontology makes clear that institutional processes do not only relate institutional entities but also create them. The processes bring new entities into existence that together constitute the institutional world.

The institutional ontology can guide conceptual modelers when designing domain models. The paper proposes a set of preliminary guidelines for this task. However, additional guidelines are required in order to utilize the ontology for designing domain models in practice. These include both guidelines for choosing between different modeling constructs if several solutions are possible, as well as guidelines for what processes to include in a domain model to represent the creation of institutional entities.

Another application of the institutional ontology is to use it for analysis of established theoretical and practical problems in conceptual modeling. One example is the disagreements, see for instance [18] and [25], on role modeling where roles are interpreted either as named places in a relationship; a relationship between entities in the form of generalization/specialization; or as separate instances adjoined to the entities playing the roles. The institutional ontology allows for an alternative explanation based on institutional facts. Another theoretical issue is how to analyze rules in rule modeling. Present rule modeling approaches recognize different kinds of rules, e.g., business rules and definitional rules in SBVR [21], and the institutional ontology can provide a theoretical basis for such classifications.

The institutional ontology should also be compared and related to similar approaches in the literature. As already mentioned, it can be viewed as an extension of parts of the REA ontology, [8]. Another relevant work is the commitment-based reference ontology for services proposed in [16].

References

1. van der Aalst, W.M.P.: Business process management: A comprehensive survey. ISRN Software Engineering 2013, 1–37 (2013)
2. Bergholtz, M., Eriksson, O.: Towards a Socio-Institutional ontology for conceptual modelling of information systems. In: Advances in Conceptual Modeling. pp. 225–235. Springer, Cham (19 Oct 2015)
3. Bergholtz, M., Eriksson, O., Johannesson, P.: Towards a sociomaterial ontology. In: Advanced Information Systems Engineering Workshops. pp. 341–348. Springer, Berlin, Heidelberg (17 Jun 2013)
4. Catt, H., Murphy, M.: What voice for the people? categorising methods of public consultation. Aust. J. Polit. Sci. 38(3), 407–421 (1 Nov 2003)
5. Dietz, J.L.G.: Enterprise Ontology: Theory and Methodology. Springer (2006)
6. Dumas, M., La Rosa, M., Mendling, J., Reijers, H.A.: Fundamentals of Business Process Management:. Springer Berlin Heidelberg (2013)
7. Eriksson, O., Henderson-Sellers, B., Ågerfalk, P.J.: Ontological and linguistic metamodelling revisited: A language use approach. Information and Software Technology 55(12), 2099–2124 (Dec 2013)
8. Geerts, G.L., McCarthy, W.E.: Policy-level specifications in REA enterprise information systems. Journal of Information Systems 20(2), 37–63 (2006)
9. Graeber, D.: The utopia of rules: On technology, stupidity, and the secret joys of bureaucracy. Melville House (2015)
10. Gruber, T.R.: Toward principles for the design of ontologies used for knowledge sharing? Int. J. Hum. Comput. Stud. 43(5), 907–928 (1 Nov 1995)
11. Hodgson, G.M.: What are institutions? J. Econ. Issues 40(1), 1–24 (2006)
12. Hohfeld, W.N.: Some fundamental legal conceptions as applied in judicial reasoning. Yale Law J. 23(1), 16–59 (1913)
13. Hruby, P.: Model-Driven Design Using Business Patterns. Springer, Berlin; London, softcover reprint of hardcover 1st ed. 2006 edition edn. (9 Nov 2010)
14. Masolo, C.: Levels for conceptual modeling. In: De Troyer, O., Bauzer Medeiros, C., Billen, R., Hallot, P., Simitsis, A., Van Mingroot, H. (eds.) Advances in Conceptual Modeling. Recent Developments and New Directions, Lecture Notes in Computer Science, vol. 6999, pp. 173–182. Springer Berlin / Heidelberg (2011)
15. McCarthy, W.E.: The REA accounting model: A generalized framework for accounting systems in a shared data environment. The Accounting Review 57(3), 554–578 (1982)
16. Nardi, J.C., Falbo, R.d.A., Almeida, J.P.A., Guizzardi, G., Pires, L.F., van Sinderen, M.J., Guarino, N., Fonseca, C.M.: A commitment-based reference ontology for services. Inf. Syst. 54, 263–288 (Dec 2015)
17. Olivé, A.: Conceptual Modeling of Information Systems. Springer Berlin Heidelberg (2007)
18. Parsons, J., Li, X.: An ontological metamodel of classifiers and its application to conceptual modelling and database design. In: Conceptual Modeling - ER 2007. pp. 214–228. Springer, Berlin, Heidelberg (5 Nov 2007)

19. Patton, M.Q.: Qualitative evaluation and research methods, 2nd ed. Sage Publications, Inc (1990)
20. Rodrigo, D., Amo, P.A.: Background document on public consultations. Tech. rep., OECD (2012)
21. SBVR: SBVR 1.4. `http://www.omg.org/spec/SBVR/1.4/index.htm`, accessed: 2017-5-18
22. Searle, J.: Making the Social World: The Structure of Human Civilization. Oxford University Press, USA, 1 edn. (12 Jan 2010)
23. Searle, J.R.: The Construction of Social Reality. Free Press (1 Jan 1997)
24. Searle, J.R.: Social ontology: Some basic principles. Anthropological Theory 6(1), 12–29 (1 Mar 2006)
25. Steimann, F.: On the representation of roles in object-oriented and conceptual modelling. Data Knowl. Eng. 35(1), 83–106 (Oct 2000)
26. Wand, Y., Storey, V.C., Weber, R.: An ontological analysis of the relationship construct in conceptual modeling. ACM Trans. Database Syst. 24(4), 494–528 (Dec 1999)
27. Wand, Y., Weber, R.: On ontological foundations of conceptual modeling: A response to Wyssusek. Scandinavian Journal of Information Systems 18(1) (2006)

Chapter 13
Quality of Conceptual Models in Model Driven Software Engineering

John Krogstie

Abstract Since the introduction of the ER-language in the late seventies, conceptual modelling has been an important area in information systems development. Conceptual modelling is widely used today, both on an analytical and a design-oriented level, e.g. for model-driven software engineering. The quality of conceptual models have also been investigated and discussed since the mid-nineties. In this paper we present a specialization of a general framework for assessing quality of models for being able to evaluate the quality of conceptual models as used in model-driven software engineering. This has resulted in a useful deepening of the generic framework on this specific kind of models, and in this way improved the practical applicability of the framework when applied to discussing the quality of conceptual models as used in model driven software engineering..

13.1 Introduction

A central area in the work of Antoni Olivé has been conceptual models [20, 28], which have a great potential to be further utilized in systems development [29]. A conceptual model is traditionally defined as a description of the phenomena in a domain at some level of abstraction, which is expressed in a semi-formal or formal visual (diagrammatical) language [13]. As the term is used in somewhat different meanings, we have often delineated this further by the following:

- The languages for conceptual modelling are primarily diagrammatic having a limited vocabulary. The main symbols of the languages represent concepts such as states, processes, entities, and objects. The diagrams typically consist of general (often directed) graphs containing nodes and edges between nodes and edges representing the different phenomena and phenomena classes.

John Krogstie
NTNU, Trondheim, Norway e-mail: John.Krogstie@ntnu.no

© Springer International Publishing AG 2017
J. Cabot et al. (eds.), *Conceptual Modeling Perspectives*,
https://doi.org/10.1007/978-3-319-67271-7_13

- Conceptual models are either used as an intermediate or directly used representation in the process of development and evolution of information systems.
- The traditional conceptual modelling languages were meant to have general applicability, that is, they were not made specifically for the modelling of a limited area. The interest in and application of so-called domain specific languages (DSM [8]) has increased over the last decade, a technique often found useful also in model driven software engineering

According to general model theory [32] there are three common characteristics of models: Representation, Simplification and Pragmatic orientation.

- Representation: Models represents something else than the model itself.
- Simplification: Models possess a reductive trait in that they represent only a subset of attributes of the phenomenon being modelled.
- Pragmatic orientation: Models have a substitutive function in that they substitute a certain phenomenon as being conceptualized by a certain subject in a given temporal space with a certain intention or operation in mind

Thus a model is not just a representation of something else; it is a conscious construction to achieve a certain goal beyond the making of the model itself. Whereas modeling techniques traditionally have been used to create intermediate artifacts in systems analysis and design, modern modeling methodologies support a more active role for the models. For instance in Business Process Management (BPM) [6], Model Driven Architecture (MDA) and Model-driven Software Engineering (MDSE) [3], Domain specific modeling (DSM) [8], Enterprise Architecture (EA) [21], Enterprise modeling (EM) [31], Interactive Models [19] and Active Knowledge Modelling (AKM) [22, 23], the models are used directly as part of the information system of the organization. At the same time, similar modeling techniques are also used for sense-making and communication, model simulation, quality assurance, and requirements specification in connection to more traditional forms of information systems and enterprise development [18].

This chapter will discuss quality of conceptual models, and specializing a generic framework for quality of models in the area of conceptual models for model driven software engineering, in particularly positioning work of Antoni Olive and his colleagues in this landscape. First, we will in the next section present the generic model quality framework SEQUAL.

13.2 Quality of Models – The SEQUAL Framework

Over the years, several frameworks for the quality of models have been developed; see e.g. [2, 25, 26]. We focus her on the SEQUAL framework that has been evolved since the early nineties.

SEQUAL [13] is a framework for assessing and understanding the quality of models and modelling languages. It has earlier been used for evaluation of modelling and modelling languages of a large number of perspectives, including data

[14, 15], ontologies [7], object [11], process [16, 30], enterprise [17], and goal-oriented [9, 12] modelling. It has also been used to look at quality of other representational forms such as maps [27]. The current framework is illustrated in Fig. 13.1. Quality has been defined referring to the correspondence between statements belonging to the following sets (the sets depicted as ellipses):

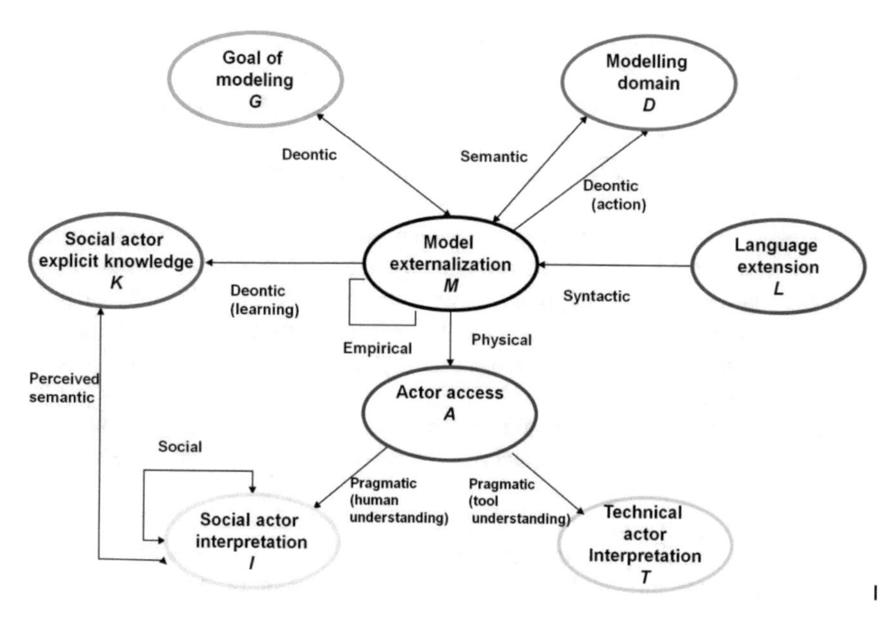

Fig. 13.1 The SEQUAL framework for quality of models.

- ***G***, the set of goals of the modeling task.
- ***L***, the language extension, i.e., the set of all statements that are possible to make according to the syntactic rules of the modeling languages used.
- ***D***, the domain, i.e., the set of all statements that can be stated about the situation.
- ***M***, the externalized model itself.
- ***A***, the part of the model that can be accessed by one or more actor, actors being either persons and tools
- ***K***, the explicit knowledge relevant to the domain of the audience.
- ***I***, the social actor interpretation, i.e., the set of all statements that the audience interprets that an externalized model consists of.
- ***T***, the technical actor interpretation, i.e., the statements in the model as "interpreted" by modeling tools.

The main quality types as illustrated as relationships in Fig. 13.1 are:

1. Physical quality: The basic quality goal is that the externalized model ***M*** is available to the relevant actors ***A***.

2. Empirical quality deals with comprehensibility when a visual model ***M*** is read by different social actors. Before evaluating empirical quality, physical quality should be addressed.
3. Syntactic quality is the correspondence between the model ***M*** and the language extension ***L***. Before evaluating syntactic quality, physical quality should be addressed.
4. Semantic quality is the correspondence between the model ***M*** and the domain ***D***. This includes both validity and completeness. Before evaluating semantic quality, syntactic quality should be addressed.
5. Perceived semantic quality is the similar correspondence between the social actor interpretation ***I*** of a model ***M*** and his or hers current knowledge ***K*** of domain ***D***. Before evaluating perceived semantic quality, pragmatic quality (see below) should be addressed.
6. Pragmatic quality is the correspondence between the available part of the model ***M*** to an actor (i.e. ***A***) and the actor interpretation (***I*** and ***T***) of it. One differentiates between social pragmatic quality (to what extent people understand the model) and technical pragmatic quality (to what extent tools can be made that can interpret the model). Before evaluating pragmatic quality, empirical quality should be addressed.
7. The goal defined for social quality is agreement among social actor's interpretations (***I***). Before evaluating social quality, perceived semantic quality should be addressed.
8. The deontic quality of the model relates to that all statements in the model ***M*** contribute to fulfilling the goals of modeling ***G***, and that all the goals of modeling ***G*** are addressed through the model ***M***. In particular, one often includes under deontic quality participant learning and domain change.

13.3 SEQUAL specialized for conceptual models used for model-driven software development

Model Driven (Software) Development (MDD) and the related area Model-driven Software Engineering (MDSE) are in many areas found useful to handle domain complexity, shorten software development cycle and improve software quality. The successful application of MDSE relies heavily on the Domain Analysis (DA) task as it produces essential domain artifacts for MDSE use, e.g. to make specialized modeling languages (Domain Specific modeling Languages – DSL) fitting both the domain and the implementation environment. Formal DA showed good design result, but the usage of formal DA methods was still limited [4]. This is because such methods are very demanding and often not practical. Rather a more lightweight and flexible DA method is expected, which indicate that you need to be able to evolve the DSLs as you learn more about the domain.

The motivation of MDD is to move the working focus from programming to solution modeling [33]. This is achieved by two important mechanisms: providing abstractions that are close to the problem domain and generating programs from their corresponding models [33]. To play to its strength, MDD should as indicated above be domain specific [8]. This requires Domain Specific Languages (DSLs) to raise the level of abstraction, domain specific code generators to automate code generation, as well as domain specific platforms to reduce the complexity of the code generators.

Initial DSL development usually takes four stages (decision, analysis, design, and implementation) [24]. Domain analysis helps meet two major challenges of DSL: the abstraction challenge (how to provide support for creating and manipulating problem-level abstractions) and the formality challenge (how to formalize the semantics and what aspects of semantics need to be formalized) [5]. Three outputs are usually generated from DA: domain definition, domain specific vocabulary with semantic meanings, and a model describing commonality and variability space. These outputs contribute to not only the construction of DSLs, but also the construction of code generators [24] and platforms. Domain analysis supports decision making up front, and provides concrete inputs for design and implementation afterwards. As a result, the quality of DA is critical for the overall effectiveness and efficiency of MDSE application. When specializing SEQUAL for a specific type of modeling, it is important to first look on the sets. In relation to conceptual modeling in MDSE, we have

- A: Actors that develops or has to relate to (parts of) the model. Can be persons (system developers and user representatives) or tools (technical actors e.g. EMF or ArgoUML).
- L: What can be expressed in the modelling language – Based on UML and specializations/profiles and specifically made DSLs
- M: What is expressed in the model: Here we must both look at the model, the language model of the DSLs, and transformation models between different languages
- D: What can be expressed about the domain (area of interest)
- K: The explicit knowledge of the participating persons
- I: What the persons in the audience interpret the model to express
- T: What relevant tools interpret the model to say e.g. EMF
- G: The goals of the modelling – The primary goal of MDSE is to produce executable systems, but it should also support communication between the actors

In MDSE one can differentiate between both between vertical and horizontal domains. Vertical domain is in MDA-vocabulary differentiated with

- CIM: Computational Independent Model
- PIM: Platform Independent Model
- PSM: Platform Specific Model

In MDSE the main focus is on PIM and PSM, although the different levels of models can be used for a large number of different purposes, as illustrated in Fig. 13.2. Whereas CIM-models are primarily useful for sense-making and communication (between humans), PIM models can be used for quality insurance and guiding traditional manual software development. PSM-models are particularly useful for supporting automatic model deployment e.g. code generation.

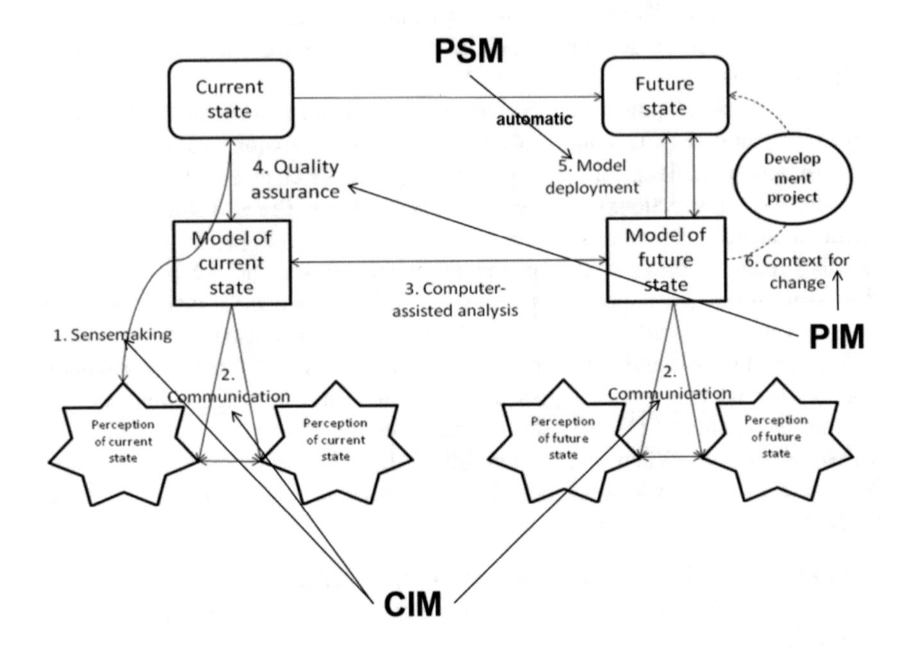

Fig. 13.2 Usage of models on different levels.

13.3.1 Physical Quality

The normal measures of persistence, currency and availability apply as with all other models, although some particular aspects of model management are particularly relevant due to the co-evolution of the language and the models [3].

- Persistence: How persistent is the model, how protected is it against loss or damage. The way of storing the model should be efficient, i.e. not using more space than necessary. Several model-repository solutions exist in the MDSE-area, such as CDO (Connected Data Objects) Model repository, Morsa and MongoEMF
- Currency: How long time ago is it that the model statements were included in the model (assuming the statements were current when entered). De-pending on the type of model, the age of the model statements is of varying importance. When the domain is changing rapidly (has high volatility), currency of the stored model is of more importance for the model to have appropriate timeliness. It is also often important to keep track of several versions of the model. Metrics on currency can

easily be devised and calculated if the model repository support time-stamping of statements. This area will relate to semantic quality (see below), relative not only to the time of entering of a model statement, but also last time the model statement is validated.

- Availability: How available is the model to the audience? Clearly, this is dependent on that the model is externalized and made persistent in the first place. Availability also depends on distributability, especially when members of the audience are geographically dispersed. It may also matter exactly what is distributed, e.g. the model in an editable form or merely in an output format, or a format where you can add annotations, but not change the actual model. The support of collaborative modelling is often important here. Finally one often want to use different tools for different sub-tasks, thus model interchange should be supported.
- Security can be an issue on some models, i.e. that it is only the authorized people that have access to and can change the model.

Many of the modelling techniques and tool functionality in connection with physical quality are based on traditional database-functionality using a model-repository-solution for the internal representation of the model. Some sub-goals for this are

- Support multiple users at multiple locations if necessary
- Have model available over the web (for browsing and annotating)
- Make it possible to print (selected parts of) the models
- Make it possible to work with model fragments (sub-models)
- Support global model management, i.e. the management of all sub-models, transformation models and metamodels the integration between them within an integrated model of model (so-called megamodels).
- Have single sign-on service to the different modeling tools
- Have group definition to control access-rights.
- Have multi-project-support
- Support awareness of users and locking (who is working on what when)
- Versioning of models and model parts. It is typically not sufficient to use a text-versioning system, thus a number of versioning tools and approaches for graphs (models) exist, including EMFStore, AMOR, Epislon Merging Language and the Modeling Team Framework (MTF). These tools only version model information, but typically not it's graphical layout. Since secondary notation is important in a model, layout changes might be significant, but it can be hard to automatically detect if the change of graphical layout is large enough to warrant a separate version.
- Dependency control in order to link or merge models
- Support offline use.
- Provide standard database backup and replication
- Support collaboration. Examples of tools that support collaboration are EMFCollab, Collaboro and Dawn, which is a subproject of CDO. In Collaboro modellers can vote for different proposals for changes, when evolving the model or the metamodel. Discussions are stored, thus one get tracebility to design decissions

Model interchange is also of specific importance warranting functionality such as

- The environment should provide a standard platform for interchange of models. In an MDSE – setting, XMI is such standard, although core XMI do not solve all interoperability problems. OMG has created the Model Interchange Working Group (MIWG) to "enable the public at large to assess model interchange capability of the modeling tools by comparing the vendor XMI exports to the expected reference XMI file for each test case." The current test suite comprises a few dozen UML and/or SysML test models covering all major elements of the specification. This is leading to the definition of a canonical version of XMI (called Canonical XMI) which is a strict subset of XMI. Graphical information is not part of the XMI file. The Diagram Definition (DD) OMG standard tries to facilitate this by providing a mapping between model elements and their graphical information.
- The modelling services should provide a standard API for connecting modelling tools to the repository.
- Should provide interfaces to standard IT systems that will enable that models can support the configuration of software systems.
- To ease the access to repository services for model management one may have to provide services to the external world to simplify modelling and model management. This could mean that part of a model contains data automatically updated from legacy databases or XML or text files

Support for meta-modelling to manage that also the modeling language is evolving

- The meta-model of the language use must be available
- The environment should allow the user to define the attributes required on each object type and each relationship type;
- More general meta-model adaptation should be available, both relative to adapting the concepts and the notation. In MDSE, one would expect meta-models to be MOF-compliant
- Additional meta-modelling capabilities – e.g. for defining templates (diagrams/sub-languages) should be provided – UML profiles is a base mechanism to support this
- Changes has to be tracked to the repository API to be used by other modelling tools
- The ability to add new modelling concepts, to specialize and extend existing concepts, possibly including versioning of class definitions should be available

Changes of a metamodel can be classified in several types

- Non-breaking, where migrations of existing models does not need to be done (e.g. adding an optional attribute, or a new modelling concept.
- Breaking, but resolveable, where migration can be done automatically, e.g. adding a new mandatory property with a default value

- Breaking and unresolveable, e.g. when removing an existing concept that is used in some model

13.3.2 Empirical quality

The conceptual models are visual graph models and traditional guidelines for graph aesthetics such as the following applies:

- Angles between edges going out from the same node should not be too small. An additional aspects that makes this specifically relevant for e.g. a class model is since cardinality constraints are given with annotations.
- Minimize the area occupied by the diagram.
- Balance the diagram with respect to the axis.
- Minimize the number of bends along edges in the diagram.
- Minimize the number of crossings between edges.
- Place nodes with high degree in the center of the model. This is typically central classes, whose positioning in the middle also will help to emphasize these.
- Minimize differences among nodes' dimensions (given nodes of the same type). A challenge here can specifically be in languages where attributes are included within the class symbols as in UML. A positive aspect of this type of languages is that the attributes are not represented by a separate node, thus keeping the number of nodes lower.
- Minimize the global length of edges
- Minimize the length of the longest edge.
- Have symmetry of sons in hierarchies. In particular relevant when you depict generalization-hierarchies.
- Have uniform density of nodes in the model.
- Have verticality of hierarchical structures. This means that in a tree/hierarchy, nodes at the same level in the tree are placed along a horizontal line with a minimum distance between. Also applies in particular to structures such as generalization and aggregation hierarchies.

One can also device guidelines for the naming of concepts, depending on the concrete language.

13.3.3 Syntactic quality

From the generic SEQUAL framework we have one syntactic quality characteristic, syntactical correctness, meaning that all statements in the model are according to the syntax and vocabulary of the language. Syntax errors are of two kinds:

- Syntactic invalidity, in which words or graphemes not part of the language are used.

- Syntactic incompleteness, in which the model lacks constructs or information to obey the language's grammar.

Much work relative to e.g. UML Class diagrams for defining conceptual schemas has been done. Aguilera et al. [1] for instance found more than 100 potential issues only in class diagrams. They can be differentiated according to the following types

- Syntactic: An integrity constraint defined in the UML metamodel.
- Syntactic+: A syntactic integrity constraint applicable when UML is used as a conceptual modeling language (i.e. specialized for particular purpose)
- Best practice: A practice (not including naming guidelines) recommended by some authors in some contexts to improve the quality of conceptual schemas.

Fig. 13.3 illustrates some important guidelines on this level, and how they are supported in a selected number of tools. Note that the naming guidelines are an aspect of empirical quality, whereas the basic properties applies to support the development of models of high semantic quality (See below)

13.3.4 Semantic quality

This relates to validity and completeness of the models. Consistency checking as a way to do model checking is an important mean in this respect, and so is the Basic property (from Fig. 13.3): A fundamental property that conceptual schemas should have to be semantically correct, relevant and complete (e.g. avoid circular generalization hierarchies, is an important mean in this respect. For static models: satisfiability (it is possible to create a valid instantiation of the model) is an im-portant way to do model testing. For dynamic models (e.g. UML Activity Diagram): absence of deadlocks, reachability, and no infinite recursion are important and evaluation of these properties can be done through formal model verification or testing

Tools like USE can create snapshots of a system and evaluate OCL con-straints on them to test the OCL expressions. Especially useful for dynamic models & operations like model transformations E.g. we may want to check a transformation generates a valid output model every time a valid input model is provided

13.3.5 Pragmatic quality

The main quality characteristics of pragmatic quality is comprehension, do the audience understand what the model express? (I-A). This is typically supported by a mix of tool support and method support also found in general modeling tools e.g.

- Model navigation – zoom and pan
- Usage of meaning-reducing and meaning preserving transformations for increased understanding

Syntax+	ArgoUML	SDMetrics	GME	VP
1. Overriding attribute does not redefine the overrides one	○	●	○	○
2. Named element has an illegal name (invalid characters)	●	○	●	○
3. Unnamed class	●	●	○	○
4. Unnamed attribute	●	○	○	○
5. Unnamed datatype	○	●	○	○
6. Property without a type	○	●	○	○
7. Class has specializations and it is marked as a *leaf*	○	●	○	○
8. n-ary association has a navigable member end	○	●	○	○
Basic Properties				
9. Binary association with both member ends as aggregate	●	●	○	○
10. Abstract class is not instantiable	●	●	○	○
11. Cycle of composition relationships	●	○	○	○
12. Abstract class has a parent class that is concrete	○	●	○	○
Naming Guidelines				
13. Class name is not properly capitalized	●	●	○	○
14. Property name is not properly capitalized	●	●	○	○
15. Namespace contains two elements with very similar names	●	○	○	○
Best Practices				
16. Data type as a member end of a binary association	●	○	○	○
17. Class without attributes	●	○	○	○
18. Class with too many associations	●	○	○	○
19. Class with too many attributes	●	○	○	○
20. Class with too many attributes and operations	○	●	○	○
21. Isolated class	●	●	○	●

Fig. 13.3 Some characteristics from [1] and how they are supported in MDSE-tools.

- Filtering(model views)
- Transformation of the model to another visual or textual notation
- Model execution (through code generation or direct model execution)
- Simulation/animation (not so much supported in MDSE)

13.3.6 Social quality

The goal defined for social quality is agreement. Six kinds of agreement can be identified, according to the following dimensions:

- Agreement in knowledge vs. agreement in model interpretation. In the case where two models are made based on the view of two different actors, we can also talk about agreement between models.
- Relative agreement vs. absolute agreement. Relative agreement means that the various sets to be compared are consistent – hence, there may be many statements in the model of one actor that are not present in that of another, as long as they do not contradict each other. Most support of social quality relates to support model comparison (Brambilla et al). Important steps are model matching and comparison:

13.3.6.1 Model matching

- Identify the common elements in the two models
- How do we establish which elements have the same identity?
  - Static identity: explicit id's annotating the elements
  - Signature identity: Identity based on the model element features (i.e. name, contained elements, ...)
- Identity can be a probabilistic function (similarity matching)
- Works better if users redefine the concept of matching for specific DSLs (so that their specific semantic can be taken into account)

13.3.6.2 Model Comparison

- Matched elements are searched for differences
- A difference corresponds to an atomic add / delete / update / move operation executed on one of the elements
- These differences are collected and stored in the difference model

Different model comparison tools exist such as EMF compare that support generic comparison facilities for any kind of EMF model, and differences can be exported as a model patch. SiDiff support mainly similarity-based matching and is adaptable to any graph-like model. Epsilon Comparison Language. This includes a DSL to enable the implementation of specialized higher-level changes. With it, high-level changes such as refactoring may be also detected

13.3.7 Deontic quality

A main goal in MDSE is to generate and evolve running systems. Aspects in connection to this relative to what to model and what to code (partial code-generation) are important aspects for judging e.g., the appropriate language, the completeness of model etc.

13.4 Conclusions

As with the quality of a software requirements specification (SRS) [10] and quality of data model [14] we see some benefit both for SEQUAL and for a frame-work for the quality of a conceptual data models by performing this kind of exer-cise, since we can position different works from different authors including the work of Antoni Olive in its appropriate place in the overall framework

Future work will be to device more concrete guidelines and evaluate the adaptation and use of these empirically in projects including conceptual modelling in MDSE. Some generic method-guidelines exist for the SEQUAL framework, which can be specialized for the quality of conceptual models in MDSE, but also keeping in mind that the particular context for a modelling project might result in that some areas are more important than others due to specific goals of modelling. Analytically it will be interesting to look more on the relationship between the quality of the models at different quality levels, and how to do trade-offs between the different levels, quality across model on the vertical levels (CIM, PIM, PSM) and quality of models vs. quality of modeling languages due to the need to evolve models and modeling languages in parallel.

References

1. Aguilera D., Gómez C., Olivé A. (2013) Enforcement of Conceptual Schema Quality Issues in Current Integrated Development Environments. In: Salinesi C., Norrie M.C., Pastor ó. (eds) Advanced Information Systems Engineering. CAiSE 2013. Lecture Notes in Comput-er Science, vol 7908. Springer, Berlin, Heidelberg
2. Becker, J., Rosemann, M., & Schütte, R. (1995). Guidelines of Modelling (GoM). Wirtschaftsinformatik 37 (5, 435âĂŞ445 (in German)
3. Brambilla, M., Cabot, J., & Wimmer, M. (2017). Model-driven Software Engineering in practice 2nd Edition. Morgan & Claypool publishers
4. Ceh, I., Crepinsek, M., Kosar, T., & Mernik, M. (2011). Ontology driven development of domain-specific languages. Computer Science and Information Systems, 8(2), 317-342.
5. France, R., & Rumpe, B. (2007). Model-driven development of complex software: A research roadmap. Paper presented at the 2007 Future of Software Engineering.
6. Havey, M. (2005). Essential Business Process Modelling, OâĂŹReilly
7. Hella, L., & Krogstie, . (2010). A Structured Evaluation to Assess the Reusability of Models of User Profiles. Proceeding of EMMSAD - Conference on Evaluating Modeling Methods in Systems Analysis and Design, Hammamet, Tunis.
8. Kelly, S., Tolvanen, J-P. (2008). Domain-Specific Modelling: Enabling Full Code Generation, John Wiley & Sons, New Jersey
9. Krogstie, J. (1999). Using Quality Function Deployment in Software Requirements Specification. Paper presented at the Fifth International Workshop on Requirements Engineering: Foundations for Software Quality (REFSQ'99)
10. Krogstie, J. (2001). A Semiotic Approach to Quality in Requirements Specification In Proceedings of IFIP 8.1. Working Conference on Organizational Semiotics, Montreal, Canada, 23-25 July
11. Krogstie, J. (2003). Evaluating UML Using a Generic Quality Framework. In Liliana Favre(Ed.), UML and the Unified Process (pp. 1-22): IRM Press.

12. Krogstie, J. (2008). Integrated Goal, Data and Process modeling: From TEMPORA to Model-Generated Work-Places. In: Johannesson P, Søderstrøm E (eds) Information Systems Engineering From Data Analysis to Process Networks. IGI, pp 43-65
13. Krogstie, J. (2012a). Model-based Development and Evolution of Information Systems: A Quality Approach, Springer
14. Krogstie, J. (2013a). Quality of Conceptual Data Models. Proceedings 14th ICISO, Stockholm Sweden, April
15. Krogstie, J. (2013b). A Semiotic Framework for Data Quality. Proceedings EMMSAD 2013, Valencia, Spain June
16. Krogstie, J. (2016). Quality in Business Process Modeling. Springer
17. Krogstie, J., & Arnesen, S. (2004). Assessing Enterprise Modeling Languages using a Generic Quality Framework. In: Krogstie J, Siau K, Halpin T (eds) Information Modeling Methods and Methodologies. Idea Group Publishing
18. Krogstie, J., Dalberg, V., & Jensen, S. M. (2008). Process modeling value framework. In Y. Manolopoulos, J. Filipe, P. Constantopoulos & J. Cordeiro (Eds.), Selected papers from 8th International Conference, ICEIS 2006 (Vol. LNBIP 3, pp. 309-321). Paphos, Cyprus: Springer
19. Krogstie, J., & Jørgensen, H. D. (2002). Quality of Interactive Models. Proceedings of First International Workshop on Conceptual Modelling Quality (IWCMQ'02).
20. Krogstie, J., Opdahl, A., & Brinkkemper, S. (Eds.). (2007). Conceptual Modelling in Information Systems Engineering: Springer Verlag
21. Lankhorst, M. et al. (2005). Enterprise Architecture at Work - Modelling, Communication and Analysis. Berlin: Springer-Verlag
22. Lillehagen, F., & Krogstie, J. (2002). Active Knowledge Models and Enterprise Knowledge Management. Proceedings of International Conference on Enterprise Integration and Modelling Technology (ICEIMT'02).
23. Lillehagen F, Krogstie J (2008). Active Knowledge Modelling of Enterprises, Springer
24. Mernik, M., Heering, J., & Sloane, A. M. (2005). When and how to develop domain-specific languages. ACM Comput. Surv., 37(4), 316-344. doi:10.1145/1118890.1118892
25. Moody, D. L., & Shanks, G. G. (1994). What Makes a Good Data Model? Evaluating the Quality of Entity Relationship Models. In: Proceedings of the 13th International Confer-ence on the Entity-Relationship Approach (ERâĂŹ94), pages 94-111, Manchester, England
26. Nelson, H.J., Poels, G., Genero M., & Piattini, M. (2011). A conceptual modeling quality framework. Software Quality Journal (2011)
27. Nossum, A., & Krogstie, J. (2009). Integrated Quality of Models and Quality of Maps. Proceedings EMMSAD 2009, Springer
28. Olive, A (2007) Conceptual Modeling of Information Systems, Springer
29. Olive, A., Cabot, J. (2007) A Research Agenda for Conceptual Schema-Centric Development. In Krogstie, J., Opdahl, A. L. and Brinkkemper, S. (Eds) Conceptual Modelling in In-fromation Systems Engineering. Springer
30. Recker, J., Rosemann, M., & Krogstie J. (2007). Ontology- versus pattern-based evaluation of process modeling language: A comparison. Communications of the AIS 20:774-799
31. Sandkuhl, K., Stirna, J., Persson, A., & WiÃ§otzki, M. (2014) Enterprise Modeling: Tackling Business Challenges with the 4EM Method, Springer
32. Stachowiak, H. (1973) Allgemeine Modelltheorie. Springer, Wien
33. Stahl, T., Völter, M., & Czarnecki, K. (2006). Model-driven software development: technology, engineering, management: John Wiley & Sons.

Chapter 14
A Unified Conceptual Framework for Managing Services in the Web Oriented Architecture

Devis Bianchini, Valeria De Antonellis and Michele Melchiori

Abstract In recent years, there has been an increasing adoption of the agile paradigm for developing data-intensive web applications, relying on the selection and reuse of third party components. In parallel, the Web Oriented Architecture (WOA) has emerged, gathering together the notions underneath Service-Oriented Architecture (SOA), REpresentation State Transfer (REST) and web applications. In particular, WOA has promoted the success of: a) RESTful services for access to web data sources, and b) public repositories where these data providing services, in the form of Web APIs, are made available to the community of developers. In this context, it is more and more relevant to support the developers, even operating in community networks, to select from available repositories suitable APIs for their development needs. Nevertheless, recent selection approaches considered different features, complementary and only partially overlapping, among the ones used for service descriptions in the repositories. In this chapter a conceptual framework is defined that considers all the features to enable a flexible selection of data providing services over multiple repositories. To this aim, the framework provides: (i) a multi-perspective model for service description, that also includes a social-based perspective, focused on the community of developers, their mutual relationships and their estimated credibility in web application development; (ii) a collection of search and ranking techniques that rely on the model; (iii) a prototype system that implements the unified conceptual framework on top of service repositories.

Devis Bianchini
Dept. of Information Engineering University of Brescia, Via Branze, 38 - 25123 Brescia (Italy)
e-mail: bianchin@ing.unibs.it

Valeria De Antonellis
Dept. of Information Engineering University of Brescia, Via Branze, 38 - 25123 Brescia (Italy)
e-mail: deantone@ing.unibs.it

Michele Melchiori
Dept. of Information Engineering University of Brescia, Via Branze, 38 - 25123 Brescia (Italy)
e-mail: melchior@ing.unibs.it

© Springer International Publishing AG 2017

J. Cabot et al. (eds.), *Conceptual Modeling Perspectives*,
https://doi.org/10.1007/978-3-319-67271-7_14

Key words: Web Oriented Architecture; RESTful service; developers' social network; collective knowledge; selection; search; ranking; similarity.

14.1 Introduction

In recent years, there has been an increasing adoption of the agile paradigm for developing data-intensive web applications, relying on the selection and reuse of third party components. In parallel, the increasing diffusion of the Web Oriented Architecture (WOA) paradigm has progressively shifted the technologies for web application development, gathering together the notions of Service-Oriented Architecture (SOA), REpresentation State Transfer (REST) and web applications. In particular, WOA has promoted the success of: a) RESTful services for access to web data sources; b) public repositories where these data providing services, in the form of Web APIs, are made available to the community of developers [1]. As a consequence, nowadays, it is more and more relevant to support the developers, even operating in community networks, to select from available repositories suitable data providing services for their needs. Service search and ranking techniques generally exploit different features in service descriptions. Beyond categories, tags and technical features, the following aspects are generally considered: (i) the co-occurrence of APIs in the same applications [2, 3]; (ii) the network traffic, e.g., number of visitors around APIs and applications (also denoted as mashups) [4, 5]; (iii) the ratings assigned by developers [6, 7]. Moreover, social relationships between developers, developers' experience and their credibility are considered relevant features, as already highlighted for traditional database systems [8]. Generally, in the approaches, subsets of features among the ones present in available repositories, such as `ProgrammableWeb` or `Mashape`, are considered. As of May 2017, `ProgrammableWeb` contains over 17,000 Web APIs, that have been used in more than 6,300 mashups (excluding the deprecated ones), while over 100,000 developers are registered in the repository. Web APIs are described through categories, tags and technical features, and the list of mashups that have been developed with the APIs. `Mashape`[1] is a cloud API hub, where each Web API is associated with the list of developers who adopted or declared their interest for it (denoted as *consumers* and *followers*, respectively) and where a developer can follow other developers (leveraging a twitter-like organization). Other public repositories, such as `apigee` or `Anypoint API Portal`[2], focus on a subset of these features.

As it has been proven that conceptual modeling plays a crucial role since the early stages of agile applications development [9, 10], the aim here is to demonstrate its effectiveness in enabling flexible data providing service selection over multiple repositories, by the definition of a unified model apt to consider all relevant features. To this purpose, a conceptual framework is defined to provide a reference model,

[1] `https://www.mashape.com/`

[2] `https://api-portal.anypoint.mulesoft.com`

capturing different service modeling perspectives, and a collection of techniques and methods for service selection in web application development. The conceptual framework is the basis of WISeR (Web apI Search and Ranking) a prototype system that has been developed to implement the service search and ranking facilities. Partial results of our work have been presented in [7, 11, 12], here the final overall framework is presented.

The chapter is organized as follows: in Section 14.2 existing approaches in literature are presented and motivations for a unified conceptual framework are discussed; Section 14.3 describes the multi-perspective conceptual model; Section 14.4 details service search and ranking techniques, that take advantage of the unified model; in Section 14.5 the WISeR system is shortly described; finally, Section 14.6 closes the chapter.

14.2 Related Work

Several approaches in literature based Web API search and ranking strategies on lightweight descriptions. These approaches are referred to as *selection-oriented approaches*. They are conceived to select candidate Web APIs to feed *composition-oriented approaches*, mainly focused on providing support for properly combining available components [13]. Among selection-oriented approaches, there have been research efforts on service selection for mashup development based on API co-occurrence [14, 15], quality of components [16] and collaborative filtering [17].

Table 14.1 State of the art on Web API selection-oriented approaches.

	[18]	[3]	[6]	[4]	[5]	[2]	WISeR
Categories	✗	✗	✓	✗	✗	✗	✓
Tags/keywords	✓	✓	✓	✓	✓	✓	✓
Semantic tagging	✗	✗	✗	✗	✓	✗	✓
Mashup/API tagging	✓	✓	✓	✗	✓	✓	✓
Technical features	✗	✗	✓	✗	✗	✗	✓
Web API co-occurrence	✓	✓	✗	✓	✗	✓	✓
Web API rating	✗	✗	✓	✗	✗	✗	✓
Mashup-contextual rating	✗	✗	✗	✗	✗	✗	✓
Developers' experience	✗	✗	✗	✓	✗	✗	✓
Number of Web API uses	✗	✗	✓	✓	✓	✓	✓
Different search scenarios	✗	✗	✗	✗	✗	✓	✓

The focus here is on approaches that study the effects of taking into account multiple features for Web API selection. For these approaches, a summary of differences against the work described in this chapter is provided in Table 14.1, where all the considered features are reported.

In particular, the approaches in [3, 18] combine descriptive features based on tags with Web API popularity (number of mashups where APIs have been used and users' ratings). The system described in [18] firstly models user's interests as vectors of weighted tags, where tags are extracted by textual descriptions of the mashups the user has interacted with in the past. Similarly, vectors of weighted tags are extracted by textual descriptions of mashups and are used to represent them. Secondly, users' interests are used to recommend mashups based on a composite metrics considering: (i) similarity of vectors describing the user's interests and candidate mashups, (ii) similarity of both APIs and tags contained in the user' request for a mashup and in the candidate mashups. The approach has been extended into the CSCF (Content Similarity and Collaborative Filtering) Web API recommender system [3], where users' ratings have been also considered to refine API ranking. Other selection-oriented approaches include features related to social relationships among developers to discover and propose the best ranked Web APIs to mashup developers [4, 5]. In the SoCo (Social Composer) system [4], based on collaborative filtering, APIs are suggested to the user u considering other users who are similar to u in a social network. Social relationships may be: (a) explicit, that is, u can explicitly declare to share the same interests, in terms of APIs, of other users; (b) implicit, that is, inferred according to the activities of users, e.g., when an user adopts many of the APIs created by other users. A Web API is suggested to u depending on the number of times the API has been used by other users socially related to u and on the social proximity between users. In [5] tags used to annotate both APIs and mashups are classified into topics through a probabilistic distribution. Topics are used to add semantics on top of traditional tagging. In [2] authors distinguish between keywords assigned to mashups and keywords assigned to APIs, and the search takes into account this distinction. Moreover, number of mashups that include a Web API has been used to provide a Web API ranking. The Serviut Rank proposed in [6] has been combined with traditional tag-based or keyword-based search. The rank has been defined taking into account the number of times an API has been used in mashups, but also the popularity of mashups themselves, in terms of users' ratings and Internet traffic.

All the analysed approaches highlight useful features to perform service selection, although different approaches focus on complementary features, as shown in Table 14.1. To improve selection effectiveness and flexibility, we propose here a conceptual framework including a multi-perspective model that relies on all features present in available repositories.

14.3 Multi-Perspective Conceptual Model

14.3.1 Motivations

Different features, based on information available within service repositories, might help developers to select third party components for developing data-intensive applications: (i) the number of service followers and the number of mashups, where services have been used in, might help to identify widespread solutions, used by many developers to design their own applications; (ii) votes/ratings by developers might help to identify services shared by trustworthy providers; moreover, votes assigned to services while used in specific kinds of applications would be properly used to suggest the same service for developing similar applications; (iii) largely used and highly rated data providing services might have at their disposal valuable datasets, as well as functionalities tested by millions of users, so their re-use might offer advantages compared to their development from scratch, saving development costs and testing efforts. The combination of different features might have positive effects on service selection. In fact, service search and ranking focused on a single perspective may bring to misleading results. For example, as underlined in [2], service selection techniques that are based on descriptive features only heavily rely on the quality of information specified by service providers, which in public repositories cannot be always ensured. On the other hand, just considering number of service usages or developers' ratings suffers from the *cold start problem* and *preferential attachment* ("rich gets richer"); this means that the more used is a service, the more likely it will be selected as part of a new application, despite its compliance with requirements, while it is very difficult for new services to enter the market.

These considerations motivate the need of a comprehensive conceptual model that merges together multiple perspectives on service descriptions, in terms of different features.

14.3.2 Representation of data providing services

The unified conceptual model here proposed to describe data providing services brings together multiple features and is divided into three parts for Service Description, Service Annotation and Service Experience, as shown in Figure 14.1.

14.3.2.1 Service Description

Services are represented at two levels of abstraction:

- a *component perspective*, focused on categories, technical features and tags in service descriptions;
- an *application perspective*, focused on service aggregations in mashups.

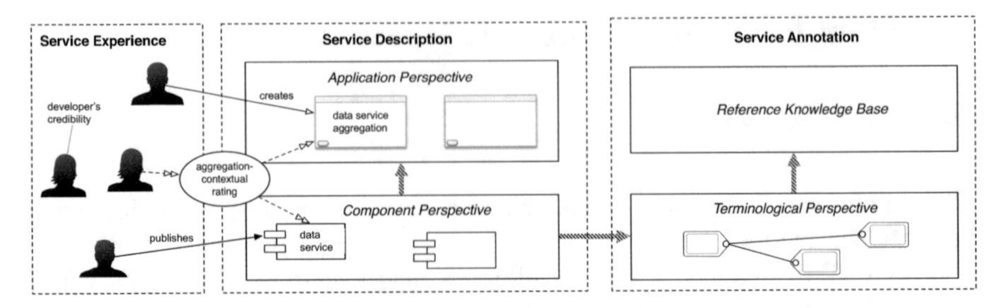

Fig. 14.1 Overview of multi-perspective conceptual model for data providing services.

Definition 14.1. A service s is an operation/method/query to access data of a web source, whose underlying data schema might be unknown to those who use the service. $\mathscr{S}$ denotes the overall set of available services. A service $s \in \mathscr{S}$ is modeled as $\langle n_s, descr_s, URI_s, \mathscr{F}_s, \mathscr{T}_s \rangle$, where:

- n_s is the service name;
- $descr_s$ is a human-readable, textual description of the service;
- URI_s is the unique resource identifier for the service;
- $\mathscr{F}_s$ is an array of elements, where each element $\mathscr{F}_s^X$ represents a technical feature X (e.g., protocols, data formats, authentication mechanisms, to mention features used in `ProgrammableWeb.com`); each technical feature is modeled as a set of allowed values for that feature (e.g., XML or JSON as data formats);
- $\mathscr{T}_s$ is a set of terms used to provide a terminological description of the service (terminological equipment).

The set of terms $\mathscr{T}_s$ is defined for tagging purposes as explained in the following *Service Annotation* description. In Figure 14.2, examples of services taken from `ProgrammableWeb.com` are listed, where URIs and textual descriptions have been omitted.

Application Perspective. Concerning modern application development, to implement a web application starting from available services, developer has to search the set of available services, select the most suitable ones, integrate and compose them, in order to deploy the final application. Within the scope of this chapter, the focus is on the first step, i.e., service selection. Service aggregations are mentioned, instead of web applications, that are the final product of the development process. An aggregation is defined as follows.

Service	Service name	Technical features	Tags
s_1	HotWire	$\mathscr{F}_{s_1}^{DataFormat}$ = {XML,JSON} $\mathscr{F}_{s_1}^{Protocol}$ = {RSS, Atom, REST}	{City, Star, Hotel, Travel}
s_2	EasyToBook	$\mathscr{F}_{s_2}^{DataFormat}$ = {XML} $\mathscr{F}_{s_2}^{Protocol}$ = {SOAP}	{City, Hotel, Travel}
s_3	MyAgentDeals	$\mathscr{F}_{s_4}^{DataFormat}$ = {XML,JSON} $\mathscr{F}_{s_4}^{Protocol}$ = {HTTP}	{City, Star, Near, Hotel, Travel}

Fig. 14.2 Examples of service descriptions.

Definition 14.2. An aggregation represents a set of services that will be mashed-up to deploy a web application. We denote with $\mathscr{G}$ the overall set of aggregations. An aggregation g is modeled as $\langle n_g, descr_g, URI_g, \mathscr{S}_g, d_g\rangle$, where:

- n_g is the aggregation name;
- $descr_g$ is a human-readable, textual description of the aggregation;
- URI_g is the unique resource identifier for the aggregation;
- $\mathscr{S}_g = \{s_g^1, \dots s_g^n | s_g^i \in \mathscr{S}\}$ is the set of services aggregated in g;
- d_g is the developer of the aggregation.

Fictious examples of aggregations are listed in the following, where URIs and textual descriptions have been omitted.

$g_1 \Rightarrow \langle \texttt{TravelPlan}, \mathscr{S}_{g_1} = \{s_1, s_3\}, d_{g_1} \rangle$
$g_2 \Rightarrow \langle \texttt{Stay\&Fun}, \mathscr{S}_{g_2} = \{s_2, s_3\}, d_{g_2} \rangle$

14.3.2.2 Service Annotation

Services are associated with a terminological equipment, composed of terms, that are used for tagging purposes in order to improve search and ranking.

For semantic characterization, a term can be related to an ontological concept or to a WordNet term and a set of other terms (denoted as *bag of words*) can be associated with it. In particular, given a term t^i: (i) if t^i is related to a term in WordNet, its bag of words coincides with the list of synonyms of the term; (ii) if t^i is related to a concept in an ontology, its bag of words is composed of the names of other concepts related to t^i by semantic relationships in the ontology (to this aim, in the current version of the approach presented here, OWL/RDF equivalence relationship is considered); (iii) finally, if t^i is an unrelated term, its bag of words is empty. Starting from the tag specified by the developer, who is performing tagging, a proper wizard is used to support the developer for selecting the intended meaning. The tagging procedure has been extensively described in [7] by using WordNet. When based on ontologies, it is performed in a similar way. The WISeR system is compliant with WordNet and any OWL ontology a developer might choose for semantic disambiguation of terms. The approach here discussed is neutral with respect to the adopted ontologies.

14.3.2.3 Service Experience

The focus is on the set $\mathscr{D}_s$ of developers, who used the service s to develop their own mashups. In particular, a developer $d_i \in \mathscr{D}_s$ can express votes represented by $v(s_j, g_k, d_i) = \mu_{jk} \in [0,1]$ to denote that d_i assigned a quantitative rating μ_{jk} to the service s_j when used within the aggregation g_k (*aggregation-contextual rating*). Votes are assigned according to the NIH 9-point Scoring System[3]. This scoring

[3] `http://enhancing-peer-review.nih.gov/scoring%26reviewchanges.html.`

system has few rating options (only nine) to increase potential reliability and consistency and with enough range and appropriate anchors to encourage developers to use the full scale (from `poor`, to denote completely useless and wrong services, to `exceptional`, to denote services with very good performances and functionalities and easy to use). These options are uniformly distributed over the $[0,1]$ interval so that the highest vote to a service corresponds to 1 and the lowest to 0. The possibility of assigning votes in the context of a specific aggregation is a distinguishing feature of the approach compared to the most popular repositories (and, among them, `ProgrammableWeb`), where votes are assigned to Web APIs regardless the mashups where they have been used. This distinction relies on the fact that a service could be suitable to be used only in specific aggregations.

A social-based perspective focused on the community of developers is also part of the model. In particular, as detailed in the following Section 14.4.3, the service selection phase takes advantage of the aforementioned votes and weights a vote proportionally to the rank of developer who expressed the vote. This rank summarizes the importance of the developer in the social network: high rank indicates high importance in the network, as discussed in the following Section 14.4.2.

Definition 14.3. A social network of developers is a pair $SN = \langle \mathscr{D}, \mathscr{E} \rangle$, where: (a) $\mathscr{D}$ is the set of developers; (b) $\mathscr{E}$ is a set of *follower-of relationships* between developers, defined as $\mathscr{E} = \{d_i \xrightarrow{f} d_j | d_i, d_j \in \mathscr{D}\}$, where $d_i \xrightarrow{f} d_j$ indicates that d_i explicitly declares to be inclined to learn from the choices made in the past by d_j for web application design purposes.

Each developer $d_i \in \mathscr{D}$ is modeled as $\langle \mathscr{G}(d_i), \mathscr{D}^* \rangle$, where $\mathscr{G}(d_i) \subseteq \mathscr{G}$ is the set of aggregations designed by d_i in the past, $\mathscr{D}^* \subseteq \mathscr{D}$ is the set of other developers, whom d_i declares to be inclined to learn from, in order to design web applications, that is, $\mathscr{D}^* = \{d_k | d_i \xrightarrow{f} d_k \in \mathscr{E}\}$.

The organization of the *follower-of* relationships determines the network structure. The developers' social network can be represented as one or more directed graphs, as shown in Figure 14.3, where a graph can assume different topologies. It can be restricted to a hierarchy or can be a peer-based network where developers can mutually follow each other in collaborative and open contexts. An example is the network in Figure 14.3(a). A third kind of topology, see Figure 14.3(b), represents a hybrid case, where a developer is or has been involved in different web application design projects and, maybe depending on the particular application domain, can follow different reference developers (consider, as an example, `dev3`, who declares to follow both `dev4` and `dev8`).

14.4 Model-based service search and ranking

According to application development needs, developers can look for single services or for more services apt to complete existing aggregations. Two search modalities

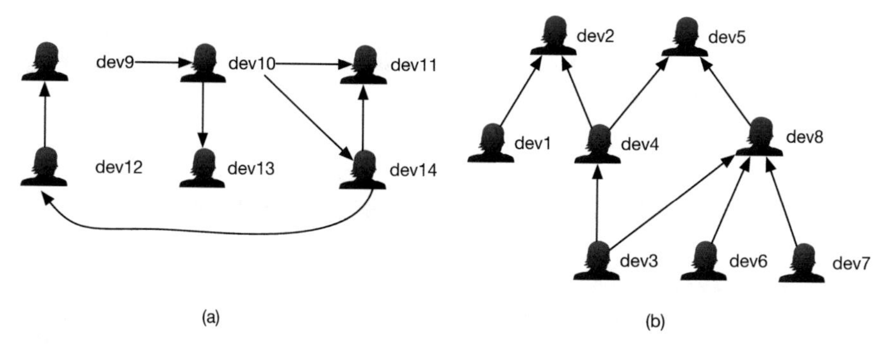

Fig. 14.3 Sample social networks of developers, which present peer-based (a) and hybrid (b) topologies.

can be defined: (i) simple search, and (ii) proactive search. In the *simple search*, the developer receives suggestions about relevant services after explicitly specifying the requested features (e.g., tags, required values for each kind of technical features, and so on). In particular, answering a single request in the context of the simple search modality is based on the component perspective and on the terminological one (see Figure 14.1). In the *proactive search*, the developer does not specify features for the services of interest, because he/she has just a partial idea of what he/she is looking for, and the framework proactively suggests candidate services according to the aggregation that is being developed. Answering to requests according to this modality, in order to complete an existing aggregation, requires using the whole type of knowledge depicted in Figure 14.1, as discussed in the following.

14.4.1 Service request

A service request is formulated according to the following definition.

Definition 14.4. A service request s^r is formally represented as $\langle \mathscr{T}_r, \mathscr{F}_r, g_r \rangle$, where:

- $\mathscr{T}_r$ is a set of terms used to specify what the requester is looking for;
- $\mathscr{F}_r$ is the set of required technical features, that the developer who issues the request can specify for further refining the search constraints; as for the specification of technical features within service description, according to Definition (14.1), $\mathscr{F}_r$ is defined as an array of elements, where each element $\mathscr{F}_r^X$ contains required values for a technical feature X;
- g_r is a set of services, representing the current composition of the aggregation that is being designed; the g_r element is optional.

The presence of the g_r in the request s^r depends on the search target. In particular, in case of searching for a single service (e.g., to search for the first service to be included in a new web application that is being designed) the service request is expressed as $s^r = \langle \mathscr{T}_r, \mathscr{F}_r, g_r \rangle$, where $g_r = \emptyset$.

Answering a service request s^r is based on the following phases: (i) developers' credibility evaluation and ranking; (ii) service search and ranking. In the following, these phases are detailed

14.4.2 Developers' credibility evaluation and ranking

To model the service experience perspective as described in Section 14.3.2, it becomes relevant to estimate the credibility of a developer, who expresses votes. To this purpose, credibility can be assessed based on a majority-based criteria. The basic idea is that, if a given vote on a service does not agree with the majority opinion on that service, the developer's credibility score is decreased, otherwise it is increased. The details of the credibility assessment are given in previous work [12].

Both the credibility scores and the way the social network of developers is organized are used to determine the developer's rank. This type of rank is considered to answer a request, as described in the next Section 14.4.3, in particular to assign a weight to the developer's votes.

Let's suppose d^r be a developer who has submitted a request.The overall rank of a developer $d_i \in \mathscr{D}$, denoted with $dr(d_i)$, is computed as the product of two different ranks, according to the following formula:

$$dr(d_i) = \rho_{rel}^{d^r}(d_i) \cdot \rho_{abs}(d_i) \in [0,1] \quad (14.1)$$

where: (a) a *relative rank* $\rho_{rel}^{d^r}(d_i) \in [0,1]$ ranks developer d_i based on the *follower-of* relationships between d_i and d^r (this rank is introduced to take into account the viewpoint of d^r, who explicitly declared to learn from other developers to select services); (b) an *absolute rank* $\rho_{abs}(d_i)$ is based on the overall network of developers and it takes into account the authority degree of d_i in the network independently of the developer d^r, who issued the request. In particular, the authority degree of d_i can be computed by adapting the PageRank metrics (that calculates the authority degree for Web pages based on the incoming links) to the context considered here.

Relative rank.

The relative rank $\rho_{rel}^{d^r}(d_i)$ is inversely proportional to the distance $\ell(d^r,d_i)$ between d^r and d_i, in terms of *follower-of* relationships, that is:

$$\rho_{rel}^{d^r}(d_i) = \frac{1}{\ell(d^r,d_i)} \in [0,1] \quad (14.2)$$

If there is no path from d^r to d_i, $\ell(d^r,d_i)$ is set to the length of the longest path of *follower-of* relationships that relate d^r to the other developers, incremented by 1, to denote that d_i is far from d^r more than all the developers within the d^r sub-network. Consider for example the network shown in Figure 14.3, where the developer `dev3` is the requester and has to choose among services that have been used in the past by the developers `dev4`, `dev5`, `dev6`, `dev8` and `dev11`, whose *follower-of* relationships are depicted in the figure. In the example, ℓ(dev3,dev4)=ℓ(dev3,dev8)=1, ℓ(dev3,dev5)=2, and ℓ(dev3,dev6)=ℓ(dev3, dev11)=4 + 1=5.

Absolute rank.

The absolute rank $\rho_{abs}(d_i) \in [0,1]$ is evaluated independently of the requester d^r. This rank is composed of two different parts. The first one depends on the number of aggregations designed by d_i, the second one depends on the topology of the network of other developers who declared their interest for past experiences of d_i, that is:

$$\rho_{abs}(d_i) = \frac{1-\alpha}{|\mathscr{D}|} \cdot |\mathscr{G}(d_i)| + \alpha \cdot \sum_{j=1}^{n} \frac{c(d_j) \cdot \rho_{abs}(d_j)}{F(d_j)} \tag{14.3}$$

This expression is an adaptation of the PageRank metrics to the context considered in this chapter. The value $\rho_{abs}(d_i)$ represents the probability that a developer will consider the example given by d_i in using a service for designing a web application. Therefore, $\sum_i \rho_{abs}(d_i) = 1$. Initially, all developers are assigned with the same probability, that is, $\rho_{abs}(d_i) = 1/|\mathscr{D}|$. Furthermore, at each iteration of the computation, the absolute rank of a developer d_j, such that $d_j \xrightarrow{f} d_i$, is "transferred" to d_i according to the following criteria: (i) if d_j follows more developers, his/her rank is distributed over all these developers, properly weighted considering the credibility $c(d_j)$ of d_j(see the second term in Equation (14.3), where $F(d_j)$ is the number of developers followed by d_j); (ii) a contribution to $\rho_{abs}(d_i)$ is given by the experience of d_i and is therefore proportional to the number $|\mathscr{G}(d_i)|$ of aggregations designed by d_i(see the first term in Equation (14.3)). A damping factor $\alpha \in [0,1]$ is used to balance the two contributions. At each step, a normalization procedure is applied in order to ensure that $\sum_i \rho_{abs}(d_i) = 1$.

The algorithm actually used to compute recursively Equation (14.3) is similar to the one applied for PageRank. In particular, denoting with $\rho_{abs}(d_i, \tau_N)$ the N-th iteration in computing $\rho_{abs}(d_i)$ and with $\mathbf{DR}(\tau_N)$ the column vector whose elements are $\rho_{abs}(d_i, \tau_N)$, it follows that:

$$\mathbf{DR}(\tau_{N+1}) = \frac{1-\alpha}{|\mathscr{D}|} \cdot \begin{bmatrix} |\mathscr{G}(d_1)| \\ |\mathscr{G}(d_2)| \\ \vdots \\ |\mathscr{G}(d_n)| \end{bmatrix} + \alpha \cdot \mathbf{M} \cdot \mathbf{DR}(\tau_N) \tag{14.4}$$

where $\mathbf{M}$ denotes the adjacency matrix properly modified to consider credibility, that is, $M_{ij} = \frac{c(d_j)}{F(d_j)}$ if $d_j \xrightarrow{f} d_i$, zero otherwise. As demonstrated in PageRank, computation formulated in Equation (14.4) reaches a high degree of accuracy within only a few iterations.

Developer (d_i)	$\lvert\mathcal{G}(d_i)\rvert$	*Credibility* $c(d_i)$
dev1	5	1.0
dev2	3	0.7
dev3	2	1.0
dev4	4	0.1
dev5	3	0.7
dev6	2	0.2
dev7	2	1.0
dev8	2	0.2
dev9	2	0.7
dev10	3	0.6
dev11	3	0.7
dev12	2	0.9
dev13	1	0.5
dev14	2	0.7

Table 14.2 Example of values for developers' features, i.e., number of developed aggregations $|\mathcal{G}(d_i)|$ and credibility $c(d_i)$.

Let's consider Table 14.2, that lists an example with values for developers' features (i.e., number of developed aggregations, credibility). In particular, $\alpha = 0.6$. At time τ_0 $\rho_{abs}(d_i) = 1/|\mathcal{D}| = 0.0714$ for all d_i. During the next iteration:

$$\rho_{abs}(\texttt{dev4}, \tau_1) = [\frac{1-0.6}{14} \cdot 4 + 0.6 \cdot \frac{1.0 \cdot 0.0714}{2}] = 0.1357$$

Similarly, $\rho_{abs}(\texttt{dev8}, \tau_1) = 0.1299$. After each iteration, normalization is applied to have $\sum_i \rho_{abs}(d_i) = 1$. In the example, after 5 iterations, the error measured as Euclidean norm of the vector $\mathbf{DR}(\tau_5) - \mathbf{DR}(\tau_4)$ is less than 0.001. At the end, $\rho_{abs}(\texttt{dev4}) = 0.0997$ and $\rho_{abs}(\texttt{dev8}) = 0.0801$.

14.4.3 Service selection and ranking

Service selection is performed by exploiting: (a) tags, used for service semantic characterisation, based on the terminological perspective; (b) past use of services matching the request, based on the aggregation perspective, and (c) technical features, based on the component perspective. All the defined perspectives contribute to quantify the matching between a service $s \in \mathcal{S}$ and a request s^r. In particular, in order to answer service requests, similarity metrics, based on the multi-perspective model, have been defined to quantify service-request matching:

- the **tag similarity**, to evaluate the similarity between the request and each service based on tags, either semantically disambiguated or not; tag similarity is denoted as $TagAff(\{t_{s_i}\}, \{t_{s_j}\}) \in [0,1]$, where $\{t_{s_i}\}$ and $\{t_{s_j}\}$ are compared sets of tags;
- the **aggregation similarity**, to evaluate the similarity between the request and each service based on average similarity between the aggregation that is being developed and aggregations where the service s has been used in the past, re-

spectively; this similarity is denoted as $AggSim(g_o, g_p) \in [0,1]$, where g_o and g_p are compared aggregations; the rationale here is that the more similar the services used in the two compared aggregations according to their similarity, the more similar the two aggregations;

- the **technical feature similarity**, to evaluate the similarity between the request and each service based on technical features; similarity for a technical feature X is denoted as $TechSim^X(\{f_{s_i}\},\{f_{s_j}\}) \in [0,1]$, where $\{f_{s_i}\}$ and $\{f_{s_j}\}$ are compared sets of values allowed for feature X.

The overall similarity between two services, computed as a linear combination of the above three similarities, is denoted as $Sim(s_i, s_j) \in [0,1]$. Overall testing and setup of weights, to proper balance tag, technical feature and aggregation similarity, have been discussed in [7].

The aim is to combine this overall similarity value with a ranking function $\rho_{serv} : \mathscr{S} \mapsto [0,1]$, that is based on: (i) the ranking of developers who used $s \in \mathscr{S}$; (ii) the votes $v(s, g_i, d_k)$ assigned to s by each developer d_k who used s in an aggregation g_i. In particular, the better the ranking of developers who used the service s and the higher the votes assigned to s, the closer the value $\rho_{serv}(s)$ to 1.0 (maximum value). The value $\rho_{serv}(s)$ is therefore computed as follows:

$$\rho_{serv}(s) = \frac{\sum_{k=1}^{n} \sum_{i=1}^{m_k} dr(d_k) \cdot v(s, g_i, d_k)}{N} \in [0,1] \quad (14.5)$$

where $d_k \in \mathscr{D}$, for each k, are the developers who used the service s in their own m_k web application design projects, the vote $v(s, g_i, d_k)$ is weighted by $dr(d_k)$ that is the overall rank of developer d_k with respect to the request s^r, as discussed in the previous section. Moreover, N is the number of times the service s has been selected (under the hypothesis that a developer might use a data service s in $m \geq 1$ projects, then $dr(d_k)$ is considered m times), thus $N = \sum_{k=1}^{n} m_k$. The overall service similarity $Sim(s^r, s)$ and $\rho_{serv}(s)$ elements are finally combined in the following harmonic mean in order to rank service s:

$$rank(s) = \frac{2 \cdot \rho_{serv}(s) \cdot Sim(s^r, s)}{\rho_{serv}(s) + Sim(s^r, s)} \in [0,1] \quad (14.6)$$

14.5 The WISeR system for service selection

The WISeR system (Web apI Search and Ranking) has been developed as web application and it implements the framework and the multi-perspective model described in the previous sections. The system functional architecture is shown in Figure 14.4. The WISeR core module is the *Matching and Ranking Engine*, that embeds the similarity metrics presented in previous section and is invoked through the *Search GUI*. Given a service published within a repository, proper wrappers (implemented within the *Web API Features Extractor*) are used to extract service features and

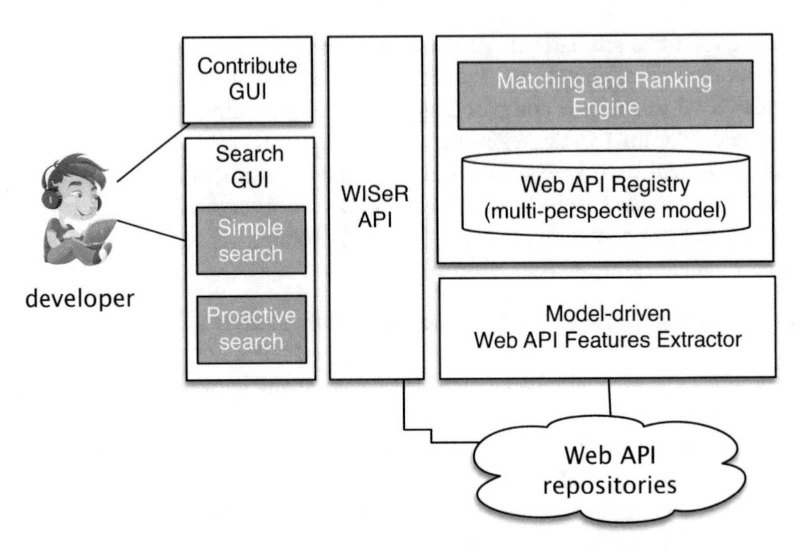

Fig. 14.4 WISeR functional architecture.

store them within the internal *Web API Registry*. The current implementation of WISeR is built upon the `ProgrammableWeb` and `Mashape` repositories. The *Web API Registry* stores categories, technical features, terminological equipment, used for service search and ranking. Note that in WISeR, by means of a specific interface, *Contribute GUI*, developers can add features that are not present in the original repositories, but are exploited by the system matching and ranking techniques. It is the case, for example, of aggregation-contextual votes. To add information related to service experience, developers registration is required. The search interface, *Search GUI*, permits to use both the WISeR service selection modalities and the original keyword-based search mechanisms available in the repositories. The *Search GUI* also embeds a ranking function based on the service publication date: all services are listed starting from the most recently published one.

The WISeR system has been used for experiments aimed to evaluate the effectiveness in service selection and developer's ranking [12]. In particular, these experiments have confirmed the positive contribution and importance of using the multi-perspective model to improve the selection precision.

14.6 Conclusions and Future Work

The diffusion of Web Oriented Architecture and data intensive web application development, relying on the selection and reuse of third party components, called for new data providing service search and ranking approaches. A conceptual framework that merges different Web data service features becomes crucial to build applications starting from ready-to-use components. Beyond descriptive features like categories, tags and technical features, the choice among different alternatives might be inspired by the experiences of other developers in using them, such as developers' ratings and similar applications where services have been included. In this chapter, a conceptual framework is described to provide: (i) a multi-perspective model for service description, that also includes a social-based perspective, focused on the community of developers, their mutual relationships and their estimated credibility in web application development; (ii) a collection of search and ranking techniques that rely on the model; (iii) a prototype system that implements the unified conceptual framework on top of service repositories. Future work will focus on advanced service search and ranking techniques to enable dynamic exploration and access on data of interest, also considering application domains where Internet of Things (IoT) and Internet of Services (IoS) technologies enable sharing and integration of huge quantity of heterogeneous data.

References

1. W. Tan, Y. Fan, A. Ghoneim, M. Hossain, S. Dustdar, From the Service-Oriented Architecture to the Web API Economy, IEEE Internet Computing 20 (4) (2016) 64–68.
2. B. Tapia, R. Torres, H. Astudillo, Simplifying mashup component selection with a combined similarity- and social-based technique, in: Proceedings of the 5th International Workshop on Web APIs and Service Mashups, 2011, pp. 1–8.
3. B. Cao, M. Tang, X. Huang, Cscf: A mashup service recommendation approach based on content similarity and collaborative filtering, International Journal of Grid and Distributed Computing 7 (2) (2014) 163–172.
4. A. Maaradji, H. Hacid, R. Skraba, A. Lateef, J. Daigremont, N. Crespi, Social-based Web Services Discovery and Composition for Step-by-Step Mashup Completion, in: Proc. of Int. Conference on Web Services (ICWS), 2011.
5. C. Li, R. Z. Z. Huai, H. Sun, A novel approach for api recommendation in mashup development, in: Proc. of Int. Conference on Web Services (ICWS), 2014, pp. 289–296.
6. K. Gomadam, A. Ranabahu, M. Nagarajan, A. Sheth, K. Verma, A Faceted Classification Based Approach to Search and Rank Web APIs, in: Proc. of International Conference on Web Services (ICWS), 2008, pp. 177–184.
7. D. Bianchini, V. De Antonellis, M. Melchiori, A Multi-perspective Framework for Web API Search in Enterprise Mashup Design (Best Paper), in: Proc. of 25th Int. Conference on Advanced Information Systems Engineering (CAiSE), Vol. LNCS 7908, 2013, pp. 353–368.
8. D. Archer, L. Delcambre, D. Maier, User Trust and Judgments in a Curated Database with Explicit Provenance, Search of Elegance in the Theory and Practice of Computation (2013) 89–111.
9. A. Olivé, Conceptual Modeling in Agile Information Systems Development, in: Proc. of the 16th International Conference on Enterprise Information Systems (ICEIS14), 2014.
10. M. González, L. Cernuzzi, N. Aquino, O. Pastor, Developing web applications for different architectures: The MoWebA approach, in: Proc. of IEEE International Conference on Research Challenges in Information Science (RCIS2016), 2016, pp. 1–11.
11. D. Bianchini, V. D. Antonellis, M. Melchiori, WISeR: A Multi-dimensional Framework for Searching and Ranking Web APIs, ACM Transactions on the Web, (in press).
12. D. Bianchini, V. D. Antonellis, M. Melchiori, The role of developers' social relationships in improving service selection, International Journal of Web Information Systems 12 (4) (2016) 477–503.
13. O. Díaz, I. Aldalur, C. Arellano, H. Medina, S. Firmenich, Web Mashups with WebMakeup, in: Proc. of ICWE Rapid Mashup Challenge workshop (RMC2015), 2015, pp. 82–97.

14. A. Riabov, E. Boillet, M. Feblowitz, Z. Liu, A. Ranganathan, Wishful search: interactive composition of data mashups, in: Proc. of the 19th Int. World Wide Web Conference (WWW'08), Beijin, China, 2008, pp. 775–784.
15. O. Greenshpan, T. Milo, N. Polyzotis, Autocompletion for Mashups, in: Proc. of the 35th Int. Conference on Very Large DataBases (VLDB), Lyon, France, 2009, pp. 538–549.
16. M. Picozzi, M. Rodolfi, C. Cappiello, M. Matera, Quality-based recommendations for mashup composition, in: Proceedings of the 10th international conference on Current trends in web engineering (ICWE), 2010, pp. 360–371.
17. M. Kayaalp, T. Ozyer, S. T. Ozyer, A mash-up application utilizing hybridized filtering techniques for recommending events at a social networking site, Social Network Analysis and Mining 1 (3) (2011) 231–239.
18. B. Cao, J. Liu, M. Tang, Z. Zheng, G. Wang, Mashup Service Recommendation based on User Interest and Social Network, in: Proc. of Int. Conference on Web Services (ICWS), 2013.

Chapter 15
Handling the Evolution of Information Systems: An Overview of Challenges and Prospective Solutions

Michel Léonard and Jolita Ralyté

Abstract Evolution is characteristic to all enterprise information systems (IS) because of continuing changes in its environment. It is also a necessary condition for guaranteeing IS fitness to the organizational needs and requirements. Nonetheless, each IS evolution presents several risks towards their sustainability and requires an accountable steering. In this chapter we consider two major challenges related to the IS evolution: the way to design and implement legacy IS evolution and the why to govern it. We look for responses to those challenges in existing literature and we review our previous and on-going work. In particular, we promote the use of service-oriented paradigm to deal with the complexity, interoperability and evo-lution of legacy IS, and we propose the concepts of information service and in-formation services system (ISS) as well as different ways to design an ISS. Con-cerning the second challenge, we propose a framework for IS evolution steering that aims to guide the actors responsible for this complex task by providing the in-formation necessary to realise IS evolution activities and to simulate their impact.

15.1 Introduction

Business and information technology innovation are two important evolution drivers in today's organizations. They lead them to take new forms, to reengineer their business processes and update technologies, and they also imply the creation of new types of inter-organizational and networked information systems (IS) and to offer online services. These changes are necessary and permanent at all enterprise lev-

Michel Léonard
University of Geneva, Institute of Information Service Science, Switzerland,
e-mail: michel.leonard@unige.ch

Jolita Ralyté
University of Geneva, Institute of Information Service Science, Switzerland,
e-mail: jolita.ralyte@unige.ch

© Springer International Publishing AG 2017

J. Cabot et al. (eds.), *Conceptual Modeling Perspectives*,
https://doi.org/10.1007/978-3-319-67271-7_15

els: strategic development, business management and operation, and information systems.

In this paper we consider enterprise IS sustainability as one of the major issues in enterprise evolution. It is clear that it is not possible to replace existing IS by new ones for each enterprise business and/or organizational change – legacy IS have to evolve together with enterprise changes. IS evolution can take different forms: the integration of new components from the market or custom-made, the development of services on top of the existing IS, the establishment of interoperability between two or more IS, etc. An inappropriate way to do that would lead to the IS fragmentation, and therefore to the redundancy between different IS parts. IS redundancy entails a need for permanent validation of the consistency of data, processes and rules.

In this context, service-oriented approaches emerge as prospective ones to deal with IS fragmentation, interoperability and evolution situations [6, 15, 32], and as a support for inter-organizational IS development [24, 25, 31]. However, the shift from a conventional IS architecture to a service-oriented one is not an easy task despite of the various service design approaches proposed in the literature. In section 2 of this chapter we discuss the notion of information service as a fundamental concept for designing service-oriented IS that we call Information Services Systems (ISS). Then, we review three different approaches to design an ISS from scratch or by reuse of legacy IS.

IS evolution is a necessary condition for guaranteeing IS fitness to the enter-prise business needs and requirements. However, each IS evolution presents several risks towards its sustainability and further changes. Therefore, another im-portant issue in IS evolution is the impact and the responsibility of its steering.

Every change in enterprise organization, business activity, or regulation inevitably entails a chain of evolutions of its IS and information services. Actors, responsible for IS evolution steering, have to take important decisions those impact on the enterprise business and legacy IS can be devastating. To be able to make these decisions, they must have a thorough knowledge of the situation. In our work, we claim that this information can be extracted from enterprise IS. In section 3 we discuss different issues related to the IS evolution steering and overview some related works. Then, in section 4 we outline our work in this domain and, in particular, we describe our proposal for a framework supporting IS evolution steering.

15.2 A Service-Oriented Perspective to IS

Today, service orientation is considered as a new design paradigm for increasingly complex IS engineering which promises to improve their flexibility and changeability. The literature review demonstrates the advent of proposals to redesign conventional IS architectures into the service-oriented ones [6, 15, 24, 31]. Recently we have introduced the notions of information service [9, 10] and information services system [33] and proposed several approaches applying the service paradigm to support IS evolution [10, 33].

In order to fit the IS context, an information service has to support inter-organizational and/or intra-organizational business activities through a collaborative creation, transformation and transmission of information. An ISS, on its turn, aims to ensure the consistency of enterprise information by supporting its creation, management and sharing through the use of information services. At the same time, it improves the modularity, agility and interoperability of IS architecture. Below, we summarize these two notions and overview three approaches to design ISS.

15.2.1 Information Service

The notion of information service [9, 10] is built upon the concept of IS component [42], and is defined as "a component of an information system representing a well defined business unit that offers capabilities to realize business activities and owns resources (data, rules, roles) to realize these capabilities". In other words, it is de-fined over classes, methods, integrity rules, processes, roles and events that constitute a semantic unit where several actors aim to achieve a common goal. Consequently, an information system can be seen as built of a collection of interoperable information services.

The particularity of the information service definition (in comparison to the web-service definition) consists in requirement for the service to be transparent. In the IS context it is not sufficient to consider services as black boxes with only inter-face part available for their selection and composition purposes. It is essential to make explicit the information concerning service structure, processes, rules and roles, and to be able to identify what is shared with other services. Fig. 15.1 shows the simplified metamodel of the information service where only the main concepts are represented (see [9] for the detailed version). As shown in this figure, the information service definition is composed of four interrelated information spaces: static, dynamic, rules and roles.

The *static space* of the service defines its data structure in terms of classes, relationships between classes and attributes. The notion of *hyperclass* (introduced in [41] to specify IS components) is used to represent complex domain concepts by putting together the corresponding set of classes. Classes are linked only via existential dependencies and specialization relationships. An existential dependency is materialized via an attribute with mandatory and permanent constraints.

The *dynamic space* defines service capabilities in terms of actions and their effects on service classes. An action is triggered by an event that occurs in the service information space and is described by a process to be executed by one or several actors having the responsibility on this action. An action produces one or more effects on the static space trough primitive methods (e.g. create an object of a class, modify an attribute). The notion of effect is used to characterize the result of the action and allows to evaluate the impact of the action on the static space.

The *rule space* deals with service regulation policies that are formalized as integrity rules validating service data, and pre-, post-conditions controlling service actions (not shown in Fig. 15.1). An integrity rule is associated to a context and to a set of risks that represent all the methods of different service actions that could transgress the rule.

Finally, the *role space* describes the roles the actors have on service actions, depending on the responsibilities they assume in the organization. Altogether, the four spaces compose a consistent and complete view of an in-formation service and establish a foundation for different information service and information services systems engineering approaches.

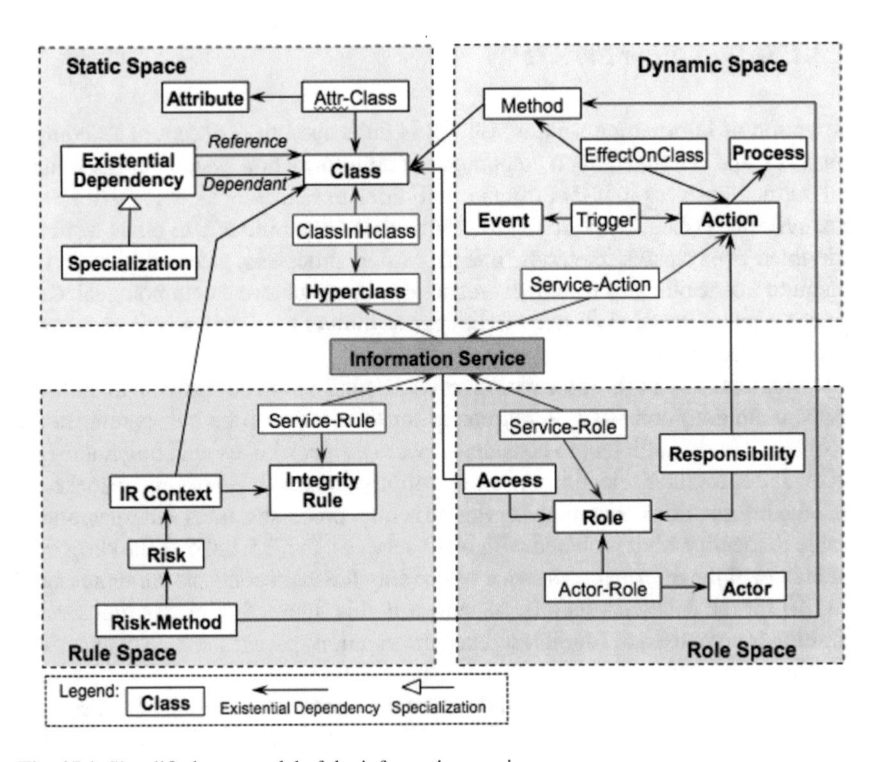

Fig. 15.1 Simplified metamodel of the information service

15.2.2 Information Services System

We define an Information Services System (ISS) [33] as a collection of interoperable information services as presented above. This definition takes inspiration from works by Spohrer et al. [38, 39] in the domain of Service Science. They define a service system as "a value-coproduction configuration of people, technology, other internal and external service systems, and shared information (such as language, processes, metrics, prices, policies, and laws)" with the aim to create a mutual value.

The notion of value coproduction is also key in the domain of information services systems. An ISS aims to provide services that allow actors to co-execute business activities by means of service actions and to coproduce shared information. The scope of actors' behavior inside an ISS depends on the responsibilities assigned to them. It is explicitly described by means of roles that allow to en-act service actions in compliance with the rules embedded in the corresponding services. The main challenge of ISS consists in transforming an integrated and rather rigid IS architecture into a more flexible, modular and sustainable one providing facilities to easily modify existing services and/or integrate the new ones.

15.2.3 Designing Information Services Systems

Shifting from conventional IS to the service-oriented ISS is not an obvious task, especially then various legacy IS are at stake. Such transition needs to be carefully designed and governed. It has to take into consideration not only technical implementation but also conceptual design and business strategic issues.

The review of related literature reveals that the number of approaches for service-oriented IS engineering is growing, however many of them consider only technical integration or migration of legacy IS to the service-oriented technology [6, 17, 21, 44], and propose to reuse legacy code to provide web services [27, 37]. Nevertheless, at design level, a few conceptual frameworks have been proposed including the framework for designing service-oriented inter-organizational IS [24] and the one for service modeling in a network of service systems [25]. A model-driven approach for service oriented IS development introduced in [19] mainly focuses on mapping rules from BPMN models to SOAML diagrams. The goal modeling technique i*, adapted to the service-oriented business modeling, is underpinning in the reference catalogue approach to design an SOA system [28]; it guides the selection of reference business models from the catalogue and their adaptation to the particular case. Finally, at business strategic level, the adoption of service-oriented paradigm also turns to be a real challenge. A few publications discuss how to assess legacy IS for the evolution towards service-oriented architectures [35, 36] and analyze the impact of SOA on enterprise systems [13]. In order to determine whether the introduction of SOA justifies the effort, [40] propose a value-driven approach to design service-oriented IS based on business process modeling and cost/benefit analysis. Other research works define critical success factors of service orientation in IS engineering [5], discuss strategies for service-oriented IS design [4] and how service-oriented design should be applied in an organization in order to adopt SOA for IS engineering [15].

In our research group, we have explored three generic approaches guiding the design of information services systems while taking into consideration the evolution of enterprise legacy IS [33]. Each approach deals with a particular organizational context and ISS design situation, as well as legacy IS reuse. We summarize them below.

15.2.3.1 Services upon Legacy IS

This approach, originally introduced in [23], guides the definition of new information services upon various existing legacy IS by reusing their data, processes, rules, and roles. It aims to bring some flexibility and modularity to the rather monolithic and fragmented legacy enterprise IS without inflicting to them any major transformation. The approach consists in identifying for each new service the existing resources that are potentially scattered in different IS and to guarantee that the execution of the service will keep these legacy IS in a consistent state, i.e. will ensure data consistency and will not violate their rules and responsibilities. The key step of this approach (sketched in Fig. 15.2) consists in defining a common base on top of a set of existing IS. The role of this common base consists in (1) specifying the overlapping information available in different IS, (2) offering each service the access to the precise and consistent information distributed in those IS, and (3) guaranteeing service compliance with a particular organizational context and with the enterprise legal frame, which is a composition of laws and regulation policies that govern enterprise activities.

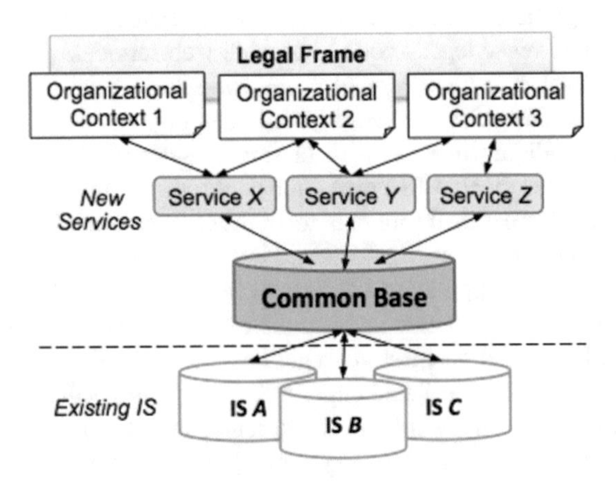

Fig. 15.2 An overview of the approach "Service upon Legacy IS"

15.2.3.2 Fully Service-Oriented ISS

This approach, developed in [10, 32], in the contrary, considers an information system as a composition of information services, where each service provides a sup-port for a particular business or administration activity. Therefore, it requires a preliminary ?decomposition? (at least at conceptual level) of the existing IS into a collection of information services, and defining the overlap (common data, activities, roles, rules) between them. Information overlap management represents the biggest challenge when including new services into an existing ISS. In fact, the overlap between information services can exist in the four information spaces (static, dynamic, rule and role), and the integration of each new service creates new overlap situations (see the idea in Fig. 15.3). Therefore, this approach is based on the analysis and resolution of overlap inconsistencies between legacy and new services.

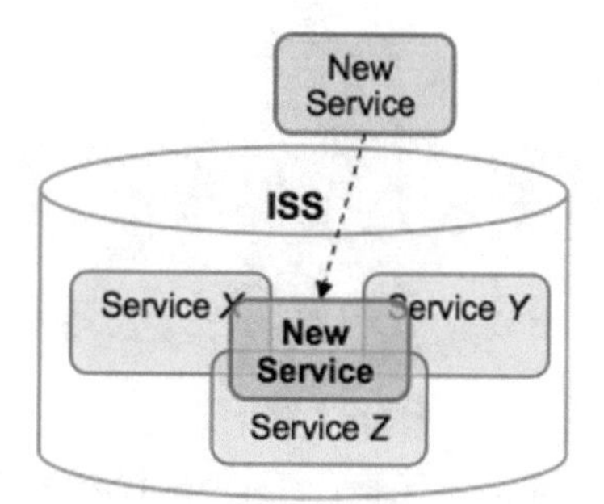

Fig. 15.3 An overview of the approach "Fully Service-Oriented ISS"

15.2.3.3 Information Kernel-Based ISS

This approach proposes an architecture based on a core IS and information services as its extensions. The core IS captures the kernel information – the most stable data, processes and rules – while information services offer capabilities for business activities that are subject to change. In this type of architecture the main challenges consist in (1) defining the information kernel, which is formalized as a collection of kernel services, and (2) preserving this kernel when adding new services to the ISS.

The approach argues that the information kernel can be obtained from the enterprise legal frame that includes laws and other regulation policies governing enterprise activities. Such documents generally define concepts, rules and constraints related to the institutional activities, and represent a rich source of knowledge for the ontological information extraction and the information kernel conceptualization. Therefore, this approach consists in constructing the ontological level model based on the analysis of different legal sources, and then, mapping this model into the conceptual model representing the kernel ISS (see the overview in Fig. 15.4). The extension of the kernel ISS with new services can then follow the Fully Service-Oriented ISS engineering approach. More details about this approach can be found in [33], while some examples of the ontological model construction from the legal frame are given in [22].

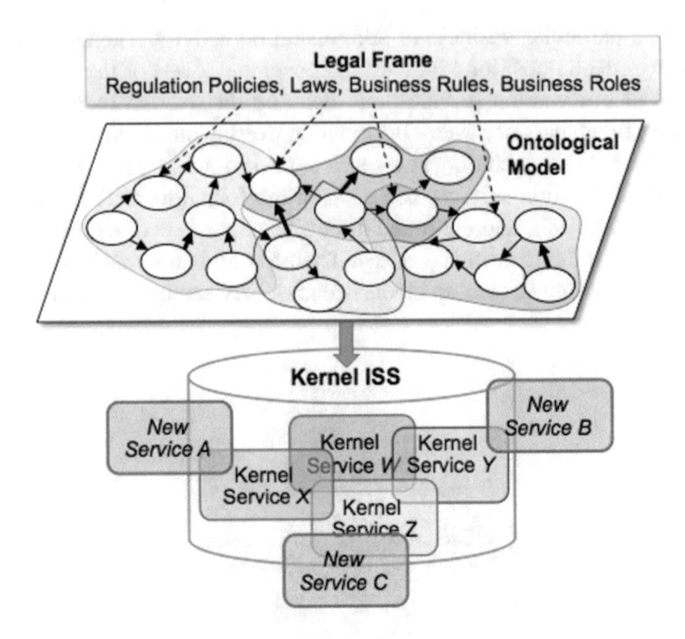

Fig. 15.4 An overview of the approach "Information Kernel-Based ISS"

15.3 IS Evolution Steering

As said in the introduction, evolution is inherent to every IS. Even more, evolving is its permanent condition because of its ever-changing environment where contingencies may arise from various dimensions such as: enterprise structure (e.g. reorganization of business units, merger or buyout of companies) business activity (e.g. establishment of new business processes), technology (e.g. introduction of new hard or soft technology), or regulation (e.g. law abrogation, modification or creation, adoption of new industrial standards). In order to ensure IS sustainability, its evolution must be understood and supported, i.e. steered.

The main challenge of the IS evolution steering is to cope with the proliferation and complexity of enterprise IS as well as with the uncertainty of the impact of their changes on the organization itself. The proliferation and overlap of IS are generally due to the inconsistent management of their evolution. IS complexity, in the contrary, is a characteristic by definition caused by the entanglement of multiple dimensions such as regulation (laws and rules governing enterprise activities), responsibility (organizational units and roles), information (its structure and provisioning), activity (business processes and collaborations), and the underpinning technology. While IS evolution is necessary, it also presents several risks related to the enterprise business. For example, if not all significant information is available during a particular IS change, the evolution can fail to fit business activities or to comply with the enterprise regulatory framework.

In our research, we assume that in every organization several IS are potentially at stake during IS evolution steering. Either wholly (or partly) dependent or independent from each other, they support activities of the organization at different organizational levels (i.e. strategic, tactic, operational). Some of them have been developed and evolved in silos, and therefore testify to the consequences of the organizational restructuring, changes of the organization activities, or the involvement of the organization into new collaborations. This situation causes important issues regarding IS interoperability at the information, technical and organizational levels, and is particularly critical when the organization aims to adopt a service-oriented paradigm.

The responsibility of the IS steering officer is to ensure IS sustainability at each step of its evolution which can be more or less complex. This challenging task needs a methodological and tool support providing the necessary and precise in-formation and the means to simulate IS change and to evaluate its impact before its actual realization. In our work we consider that such information is available in the enterprise IS, and we define a framework for IS evolution steering that allows to obtain this information from enterprise IS and to handle the IS evolution. Concerning the state of the art in the domain, there is no consensus on the definition, goals, models and methods of IS evolution steering. This domain is at the crossroads of several IS research areas such as: Enterprise Architecture (EA) and Enterprise Modeling, Business/IT alignment, IS Governance and Risk Management.

Today, the domain of Enterprise Architecture is rich in EA frameworks (e.g. TOGAF [2], GERAM [12], etc.) and dedicated modeling languages (e.g. DEMO [18], ArchiMate [1], MEMO [20]). Most of those frameworks acknowledge the need for multiple views (e.g. business, function, information, infrastructure) in or-der to manage enterprise complexity, to separate concerns and to address different life spans of EA elements [8]. These frameworks expose best practices and generic principles, and propose modeling notations, but fail to offer a formal steering method. Quite abundant literature is available in the domain of Business/IT alignment proposing various approaches to measure the fitness between enterprise business and its supporting IT, their respective strategies, infrastructures and processes. A systematic review of Business/IT alignment is presented in [43].

Finally, in the domains of IS Governance and Risk Management, risks are generally considered from the perspective of IS security (e.g. [36]) or from the perspective of software development and software project management (e.g. [11]). A literature review and comparison of risk management approaches is proposed in [7]. There is also a large amount of literature dealing with software change impact analysis (see a review in [26]) but rather from software maintenance point of view – the impact of IS change on the organization and its business is not considered. For several authors (e.g. [7, 11, 16]) risk is related to uncertainty. In our on-going work [30], we attempt to provide a holistic approach for IS evolution steering that would allow not only to deal with IS changes but also to measure the impact of the-se changes on the enterprise ant its business. The main objective of this framework is to reduce the uncertainty that IS evolution steering actors are facing at each step of IS change. We present this work in the next section.

15.4 A Framework for IS Evolution Steering

In IS and software engineering the evolution techniques are mostly based on models (e.g. [14, 3]). These works mainly address the problem of structural evolution (e.g. changing a class hierarchy, adding a new class). Their intention is to support the change propagation in order to allow the automation of data migration, to evaluate the impact of metamodel changes on models, to support forward-, reverse-, and re-engineering techniques or to record the model history. However, these models are not designed for IS evolution steering purposes and are not considered as means to support decision making in IS evolution, which is the purpose of our framework for IS evolution steering [30]. The construction of this frame-work is based on the following assumptions:

- the IS evolution steering requires understanding the underpinning IS domain, and vice versa, enterprise IS contain an accurate information about enterprise structure, activities, information and regulation,
- the impact of IS evolution is difficult to predict, so the simulation could help to take evolution-related decisions, and
- the guidance for IS evolution steering is almost non-existent, and therefore needs to be developed.

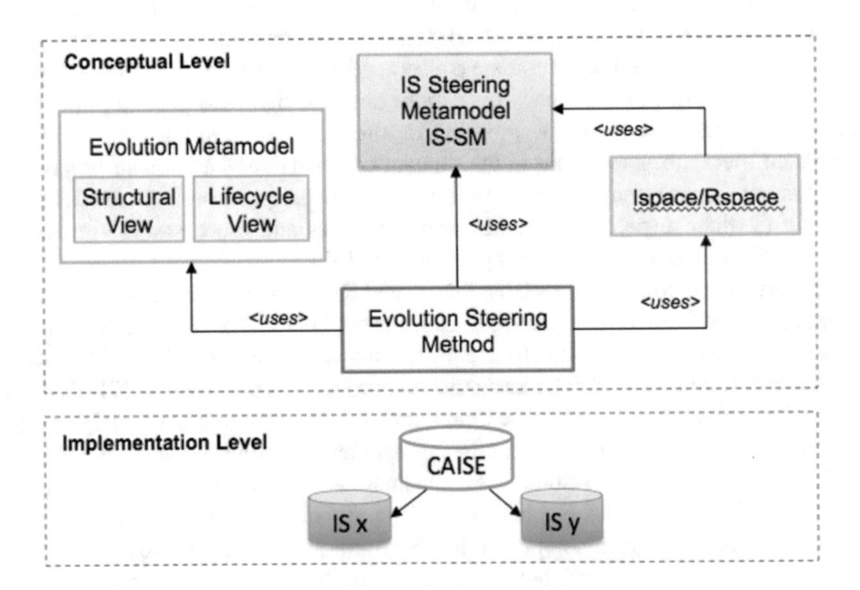

Fig. 15.5 An overview of the framework for IS evolution steering

Therefore, we propose a framework for IS evolution steering based on several models as shown in Fig. 15.5. The aim of this framework is to provide the foundation for the development of a Computer-Aided Information Steering Environment

(CAISE). This decision supporting tool uses existing enterprise information systems as source of information and guides the IS evolution steering actors in the IS change process by providing evolution simulation and impact identification facilities. At the conceptual level, the main element of the framework is the metamodel for IS evolution steering (IS-SM) which homogeneously integrates enterprise activity, regulation and information dimensions. It is complemented with the evolution models and the evolution steering method that provides guidelines for extracting the necessary information and simulating the evolution.

15.4.1 IS-SM

The *IS Steering Metamdel* (IS-SM) represents an information kernel, generic to any organization, and supporting the evolution steering of several IS in the organization. As show in Fig. 15.6, it consists of three models: activity, regulation and information. The *Activity Model* reflects enterprise business structure: *business units*, *positions*, *activities*, *rules*, *roles* and *responsibilities* that different persons hold when are assigned to a particular position. The *Regulatory Model* reflects how the enterprise complies with different laws, policies and other regulations by modeling their structure and relationship with different elements form activity and information models. Finally, the *Information Model* is composed of three sub-models: the *Generic IS Model*, *IS Model* and *Service Model* each of them representing the corresponding information level. The Generic IS Model represents an integrated view of the IS level which can consist of several IS. It allows inter-relating the Information model with the Activity and Regulatory models and defines the generic concepts such as *class*, *role*, *operation*, and *integrity rule*. The IS Model defines the information elements relating to the composition of the enterprise IS – which IS supports which activity in the organization. Finally, the Service Model defines how information services are implemented through the existing IS, knowing that a service can be based on one or several IS.

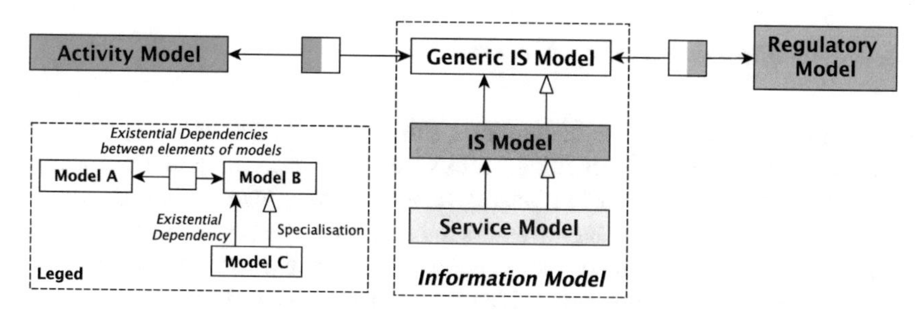

Fig. 15.6 A general structure of IS-SM

15.4.2 Evolution Metamodel

The *Evolution Metamodel* has two views, named structural and lifecycle, that are designed to support respectively the decomposition of a complex IS evolution and to guide the evolution process. In particular, the *Structural View* allows to capture the complexity of an evolution – to define the schema of an evolution that can be composed of several parts each of them being an evolution too. The *Lifecycle View* represents different possible states of an evolution (e.g.: ready, triggered, succeeded, failed) together with the conditions (transactions) allowing the evolution to pass from one state to another. In case of a failure, it allows to identify its cause.

15.4.3 Ispace/Rspace

Each IS evolution has an impact on the IS actors, more exactly on their information space (*Ispace*) and their regulatory space (*Rspace*), that can be extended or reduced. The Ispace and Rspace are based on the notion of responsibility that is a key concept for the impact analysis of an evolution. The responsibility is defined here as a set of information entities that represent the accountabilities and the capabilities of an actor (or group of actors) to perform a task. Therefore, the Ispace of an IS actor represents her responsibility over information elements, i.e. objects, operations, and integrity rules implemented in the IS that she can read/create/modify/delete. The Rspace represents her responsibility over regulatory elements, i.e. laws and regulation policies governing her activities in the organization supported by the IS. The Ispace and Rspace are defined as parts of IS-SM (see [34] for details). They allow to obtain sub-sets of information that inform the IS steering actor about the changes caused by an evolution affecting the responsibility of IS users. Together they allow to simulate the impact of IS evolutions on different IS actors responsibility and to identify potential risks.

15.4.4 Evolution Steering Method

Any change in the enterprise IS implies a shift from a known to an expected, but at the same time unknown, situation. Actors, responsible for IS evolution steering, are accountable for the decision making under a certain level of uncertainty, because the information, necessary to assess the evolution situation, can be incomplete or, in the contrary, overloaded. Consequently, IS steering actors need guidance for obtaining all relevant information, identifying risks, taking decisions about their handling and finally handling them.

Any IS evolution may fail due to its complexity. Guidance for IS evolution steering is essential for understanding and taking into account the various and interrelated components that constitute the complexity of the evolution situations. Therefore, the last, but not least, component of the framework is the Evolution Steering Method that aims to provide guidelines on how to use the aforementioned models in an efficient way and to support the mission of the actors in charge of IS evolution steering.

15.5 Conclusions

In this chapter we consider IS evolution as an ordinary situation in every modern organization. Furthermore, any change in the enterprise IS has impact not only on their own sustainability but also on the enterprise business activity and governance. In this context, we identify risks and challenges related to the enterprise IS evolution and we overview our and related work on this topic.

First, we discuss the adoption of service-oriented paradigm in IS engineering and demonstrate how IS-specific service-oriented architectures can be elaborated to deal with legacy IS evolution towards service-oriented IS that we call ISS. The notion of information service is defined as underpinning building block in the ISS construction. In particular, we briefly overview three ISS construction approaches, namely Services upon Legacy IS, Fully Service-Oriented ISS and Information Kernel-Based ISS. Each of them is dedicated to cope with a particular situation of ISS construction and can be combined with the other two approaches.

In the second part of the paper, we discuss the challenges related to the IS evolution steering and we introduce a framework dedicated to help the actors responsible for IS evolution steering to take critical decisions. The framework aims to ad-dress IS sustainability issues and to reduce the uncertainty by proving clear and complete information allowing to simulate IS changes and to assess their impact. The framework is composed of several models each of them representing a particular IS evolution perspective such as: the related information structure, the evolution lifecycle, the impact on the organization and its IS, and the responsibility. Besides, it provides guidance to use these models. In our future work we aim to ex-tend this framework with the technology dimension and with the support to the potential security risk analysis caused by an evolution.

Finally, it is important to note that all these works, like many others, relating to important subjects in the development of information systems and now services, are based on conceptual models. They were discovered, and established by the work of a few pioneers who established such solid and durable bedrock. Antoni Olivé is one of these pioneers as evidenced by his masterful article [29].

References

1. ArchiMate, http://www.opengroup.org/subjectareas/enterprise/archimate
2. TOGAF version 9.1, http://pubs.opengroup.org/architecture/togaf9-doc/arch/

3. Aboulsamh, M.A., Davies, J.: Towards a model-driven approach to information system evolution. In: ISD 2009. pp. 269–280. Springer (2009)
4. Aier, S.: Strategies for establishing service oriented design in organizations. In: ICIS 2012. Association for Information Systems (2012)
5. Aier, S., Bucher, T., Winter, R.: Critical success factors of service orientation in information systems engineering – derivation and empirical evaluation of a causal model. Business & Information Systems Engineering 3(2), 77–88 (2011)
6. Almonaies, A.A., Cordy, J.R., Dean, T.R.: Legacy system evolution towards service-oriented architecture. In: International Workshop SOAME 2010. pp. 53–62 (2010)
7. Alter, S., Sherer, S.A.: A general, but readily adaptable model of information system risk. CAIS 14, 1 (2004)
8. Armour, F.J., Kaisler, S.H., Liu, S.Y.: A big-picture look at enterprise architectures. IT Professional 1(1), 35–42 (1999)
9. Arni-Bloch, N., Ralyté, J.: MISS: A metamodel of information system service. In: Papadopoulos, G.A., Wojtkowski, W., Wojtkowski, G., Wrycza, S., Zupancic, J. (eds.) Information Systems Development: Towards a Service Provision Society. pp. 177–186. Springer US (2009)
10. Arni-Bloch, N., Ralyté, J., Léonard, M.: Service-driven information systems evolution: Handling integrity constraints consistency. In: PoEM 2009. LNBIP, vol. 39, pp. 191–206. Springer (2009)
11. Barki, H., Rivard, S., Talbot, J.: An integrative contingency model of software project risk management. J. of Management Information Systems 17(4), 37–70 (2001)
12. Bernus, P., Nemes, L.: A framework to define a generic enterprise reference architecture and methodology. Computer Integrated Manufacturing Systems 9(3), 179 – 191 (1996)
13. Bieberstein, N., Bose, S., Walker, L., Lynch, A.: Impact of service-oriented architecture on enterprise systems, organizational structures, and individuals. IBM Systems Journal 44(4), 691–708 (2005)
14. Burger, E., Gruschko, B.: A change metamodel for the evolution of mof-based metamodels. In: Modellierung. LNI, vol. 161, pp. 285–300. GI (2010)
15. Chua, F.: Adoption of service-oriented architecture by information systems. IJAACS 2(4), 317–330 (2009)
16. Copas, J.: Statistical modelling for risk assessment. Risk Management 1(1), 35–49 (1999)
17. Cuadrado, F., García, B., Dueñas, J.C., Parada, H.A.: A case study on software evolution towards service-oriented architecture. In: AINA Workshops at AINAW 2008. pp. 1399–1404. IEEE (2008)
18. Dietz, J.L.: Demo: Towards a discipline of organisation engineering. European Journal of Operational Research 128(2), 351 – 363 (2001)
19. Fazziki, A.E., Lakhrissi, H., Yétongnon, K., Sadgal, M.: A service oriented information system: A model driven approach. In: SITIS 2012. pp. 466–473. IEEE (2012)
20. Frank, U.: Multi-perspective enterprise modeling (memo): Conceptual framework and modeling languages. In: HICSS 2002. pp. 1258–1267 (2002)
21. Khadka, R., Reijnders, G., Saeidi, A., Jansen, S., Hage, J.: A method engineering based legacy to SOA migration method. In: ICSM 2011. pp. 163–172. IEEE (2011)
22. Khadraoui, A., Léonard, M., Thi, T.T.P., Helfert, M.: A framework for compliance of legacy information systems with legal aspect. AIS Transactions on Enterprise Systems 1, 15–26 (2009)
23. Khadraoui, A., Opprecht, W., Léonard, M., Aïdonidis, C.: Service specification upon multiple existing information systems. In: RCIS 2011. pp. 1–11. IEEE (2011)
24. Le Dinh, T., Nguyen-Ngoc, A.V.: A conceptual framework for designing service-oriented inter-organizational information systems. In: SoICT 2010. ACM International Conference Proceeding Series, vol. 449, pp. 147–154. ACM (2010)
25. Le Dinh, T., Pham Thi, T.T.: A conceptual framework for service modelling in a network of service systems. In: IESS 2010. LNBIP, vol. 53, pp. 192–206. Springer (2010)
26. Lehnert, S.: A review of software change impact analysis. Technische Universitat Ilmenau (2011)

27. Liu, Y., Wang, Q., Zhuang, M., Zhu, Y.: Reengineering legacy systems with restful web service. In: COMPSAC 2008. pp. 785–790. IEEE (2008)
28. Lo, A., Yu, E.S.K.: From business models to service-oriented design: A reference catalog approach. In: Conceptual Modeling - ER 2007. LNCS, vol. 4801, pp. 87–101 (2007)
29. Olivé, A.: Conceptual schema-centric development: A grand challenge for information systems research. In: CAiSE 2005. LNCS, vol. 3520, pp. 1–15. Springer (2005)
30. Opprecht, W., Ralyté, J., Léonard, M.: Towards a framework for enterprise information system evolution steering. In: PoEM 2014. LNBIP, vol. 197, pp. 118–132. Springer (2014)
31. Ralyté, J.: Applying transdisciplinarity principles in the information services co-creation process. In: RCIS 2012. pp. 1–11. IEEE (2012)
32. Ralyté, J., Arni-Bloch, N., Léonard, M.: Information systems evolution: A process model for integrating new services. In: AMCIS 2010. p. 431. Association for Information Systems (2010)
33. Ralyté, J., Khadraoui, A., Léonard, M.: Designing the shift from information systems to information services systems. Business & Information Systems Engineering 57(1), 37–49 (2015)
34. Ralyté, J., Opprecht, W., Léonard, M.: Defining the responsibility space for the information systems evolution steering. In: PoEM 2016. LNBIP, vol. 267, pp. 179–193. Springer (2016)
35. Ransom, J., Sommerville, I., Warren, I.: A method for assessing legacy systems for evolution. In: CSMR 1998. pp. 128–134. IEEE (1998)
36. Reddy, V.K., Dubey, A., Lakshmanan, S., Sukumaran, S., Sisodia, R.: Evaluating legacy assets in the context of migration to soa. Software Quality Journal 17(1), 51–63 (2009)
37. Sneed, H.M.: Integrating legacy software into a service oriented architecture. In: CSMR 2006. pp. 3–14. IEEE (2006)
38. Spohrer, J., Maglio, P.P., Bailey, J., Gruhl, D.: Steps toward a science of service systems. Computer 40(1), 71–77 (2007)
39. Spohrer, J., Vargo, S.L., Caswell, N., Maglio, P.P.: The service system is the basic abstraction of service science. In: HICSS 2008. p. 104. IEEE Computer Society (2008)
40. Thomas, O., vom Brocke, J.: A value-driven approach to the design of service-oriented information systems – making use of conceptual models. Information Systems and e-Business Management 8(1), 67–97 (2010)
41. Turki, S., Léonard, M.: Hyperclasses: Towards a new kind of independence of the methods from the schema. In: ICEIS 2002. pp. 788–794 (2002)
42. Turki, S., Léonard, M.: IS components with hyperclasses. In: OOIS Workshops 2002. LNCS, vol. 2426, pp. 132–141. Springer (2002)
43. Ullah, A., Lai, R.: A systematic review of business and information technology alignment. ACM Trans. Manage. Inf. Syst. 4(1), 1–30 (2013)
44. Umar, A., Zordan, A.: Reengineering for service oriented architectures: A strategic decision model for integration versus migration. Journal of Systems and Software 82(3), 448–462 (2009)

Chapter 16
On Warehouses, Lakes, and Spaces: The Changing Role of Conceptual Modeling for Data Integration

Matthias Jarke and Christoph Quix

Abstract The role of conceptual models, their formalization and implementation as knowledge bases, and the related metadata and metamodel management, has continuously evolved since their inception in the late 1970s. In this paper, we trace this evolution from traditional database design, to data warehouse integration, to the recent data lake architectures. Concerning future developments, we argue that much of the research has perhaps focused too much on the design perspective of individual companies or strongly managed centralistic company networks, culminating in today's huge oligopolistic web players, and propose a vision of interacting data spaces which seems to offer more sovereignty of small and medium enterprises over their own data.

16.1 Introduction

Conceptual modeling and meta modeling have been key ingredients for data management tasks such as database design, information systems engineering, data integration, and data analytics since the mid-1970's. However, as data management transcended more and more aspects of our lives and businesses, the roles and thus also the kinds of models, supporting formalisms, and tools had to be continuously adapted to these changing needs.

Matthias Jarke
Database and Information Systems, RWTH Aachen University, Germany,
e-mail: jarke@dbis.rwth-aachen.de
Fraunhofer Institute for Applied Information Technology FIT, Germany

Christoph Quix
Database and Information Systems, RWTH Aachen University, Germany,
e-mail: quix@dbis.rwth-aachen.de
Fraunhofer Institute for Applied Information Technology FIT, Germany

© Springer International Publishing AG 2017

J. Cabot et al. (eds.), *Conceptual Modeling Perspectives*,
https://doi.org/10.1007/978-3-319-67271-7_16

The 1980's saw the emergence of semantic data models, and their interpretation as evolving knowledge bases from which databases and data-intensive transactional applications could be derived in a quality-controlled and semi-automatic manner; Antoni Olivé was one of the major contributors to this perspective with his research on consistent knowledge-base, view updates, and consistent derivation of logical data schemas from conceptual models [43, 57, 2].

The following decades can, in short, be characterized by the contrasting buzzwords of data warehouses and data lakes, perhaps juxtaposed with the relatively new concept of data spaces for information sovereignty.

In the 1990's, it was noticed that transactional data could not just be used for administering day-to-day business but had in fact built up a collective treasure of historical information which could be exploited for data analytics. To enable analytics without concurrency control problems, *data warehouses* were set up separately from transactional databases (now called data sources). This raised additional concerns in the semantically correct integration of independently developed databases, e.g., concerning temporal and spatial validity [37]. Meta languages such as the Meta Object Facility (MOF [53]), Telos [40, 27], or even description logics [28], Lenzerini helped formalize the relationships among source schema and warehouse schema for homogeneous and increasingly heterogeneous data sources (e.g., including the XML/JSON family).

Shortly after the turn of the century, the Big Data movement - originally proposed by Jim Gray for crowd-analytics of astronomy data - began to take off. Multimedia data and mobile data management added to volume and variety of data, but also enriched the context information needed for the characterization of data sources. Additionally, the requirements for near real-time analytics grew rapidly, and various kinds of NoSQL databases were introduced to deal with some of these new challenges, adding to the complexity of data systems integration. Since about 2010, *data lake* architectures have been proposed for the provisioning of data for such richer data analytics tasks, and some huge data lakes have been built up by the leading search engine, eCommerce, and social network vendors.

In this chapter, we review some of the research we and others have done to accompany this evolution, almost exactly in parallel and often interacting with, the impressive research career of Antoni Olivé over the past thirty years. Starting with the logic-based meta data management system *ConceptBase* and its use in the European DWQ project on foundations of data warehouse quality, we arrive via our Generic Role-Based Metamodeling Suite *GeRoMeSuite* to our present work on the *Constance* data lake system and its applications. However, these organizationally rather centralistic viewpoints have recently raised some concerns not just about personal privacy of users, but also about risks for the security of confidential company knowhow, especially for small and medium enterprises which feel threatened by the huge data lakes both of private market leaders and state organizations. The paper ends with a brief overview of the Fraunhofer-led Industrial Data Space initiative in which a large worldwide association from industry and science is investigating innovative solutions for this problem.

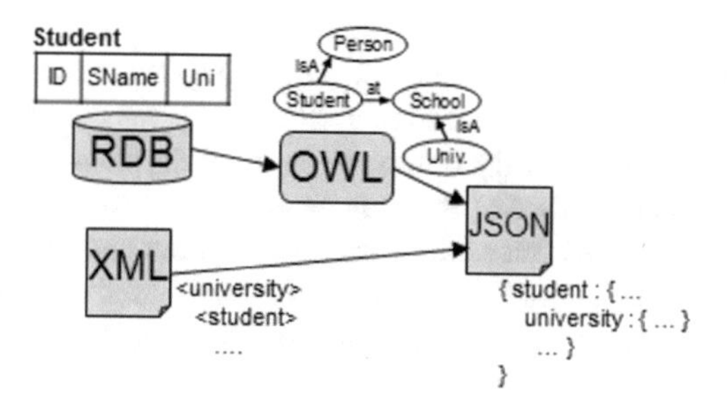

Fig. 16.1 Motivating scenario for heterogeneous data integration

16.2 Conceptual Model Formalization and Model Management for Data Warehouse Integration

Consider the scenario for heterogeneous data integration illustrated in Figure 16.1. There are two data sources (relational and XML) with information about students, their universities, and courses. The relational source is in addition annotated with an ontology which has a mapping to desired target data structure in JSON. The XML source has a direct mapping to the target model.

Within this scenario, several integration challenges have to be addressed:

Schema Matching: The definition of mappings between schemas is often a manual task as the complete semantics of a schema can only be understood by a human. Schema matching methods [51, 54] can support this process by identifying correspondences between schemas.

Schema Mapping: While schema matching produces correspondences that state only a similarity between schema elements, a schema mapping is a formal expression that can be interpreted as a constraint over the sources or as a rule to transform the source data into the target database [34, 10, 33]. Various mapping languages with different expressive powers and complexities have been proposed, which are usually a variant of tuple-generating dependencies [7, 15].

Schema Integration: If the target schema is not given, how can we create a common schema that covers the source schemas and can be used to query both sources in an integrated way [5, 49, 36, 35].

Data & Schema Quality: Data quality problems occur frequently in integration scenarios as the data is used for another application than initially intended. Data quality is not defined only defined by the data itself, but also by the schema describing the data and systems used for processing the data [27, 6, 2].

In the following, we give a short overview on how the techniques to address these challenges have evolved over the last decades. We focus especially on the conceptual modeling aspects in this context.

In parallel to the initial IRDS standardization, a logic-based approach to dealing with an unbounded number of meta levels was investigated in the Telos project jointly conducted between the University of Toronto and several European projects in the late 1980s [40]. An important feature of Telos is the strong and highly efficient formalization in Datalog with stratified negation [29]. Based on this formalization, our deductive metadatabase system ConceptBase [26] was the first metadata repository to also offer effective query optimization, integrity constraint evaluation, and incremental view maintenance at the data level [56], as well as viewpoint resolution [42] and requirements traceability [52] at the meta level simultaneously, thus providing an early example of fully automated model-based code generation.

With the confluence of structured data, text and multimedia capabilities, the World Wide Web, and mobile communications, the range of data models has grown well beyond what could be covered by these early approaches. In [23], an overview of metadata interoperability in heterogeneous media repositories is given which also addresses interoperability between "structural" modeling languages, such as UML, XML Schema, and OWL. The authors classify approaches according to the MOF hierarchy and argue that effective interoperability between systems can only be achieved if data transformations at the instance level are also addressed. Furthermore, they distinguish between standardization and mapping approaches. The former propose metadata standards to enable interoperability, whereas the latter build relationships between different metamodels. Mapping approaches are more complex, but are advantageous in open environments such as the Web, as in these cases, no central authority can enforce a standard [23].

The increasing complexity of information systems [11] requires techniques for automating the tasks of creating models and mappings. The original vision of model management aimed at providing algebraic operations for these tasks [9], because complete automation was expected to be hard to achieve. The creation of models and mappings was considered a design activity which requires a deep understanding of the semantics of the modeled systems. Another important motivation for the definition of a model management algebra was the observation that many applications that deal with models require a significant amount of code for loading and navigating models in graph-like structures.

First model management systems such as Rondo [39, 38] and COMA [14] applied simple, abstract model representations in which a model is represented as a directed, labeled graph. Other approaches focused on schemas, e.g., there is a huge research area on schema matching [51, 55]. Although a graph representation is often sufficient for basic schema matching tasks, semantic details such as constraints cannot be easily represented. Mappings are often just represented as a set of pairwise correspondences between nodes in the graphs. Even though in MISM (Model-Independent Schema Management) [3], schemas are described in a generic way using a multi-level dictionary, the system uses a set-theoretic approach for some model management operators (e.g., Merge), i.e. again only correspondences ('equivalence views'), as the mapping formalism.

In the original vision of model management [9], mappings had a weak representation and were seen as a special type of a model which might include expressions to describe the semantics of a mapping in more detail (e.g., by using a SQL query). In order to automate operations on models and mappings, mappings have to be represented in a separate formalism which is more expressive than just simple correspondences.

There have been several attempts aiming at combining a rich modeling language with powerful mapping languages. For example, in the European DWQ project (Foundations of Data Warehouse Quality [28]), a semantically rich metamodel [27] was combined with an information integration approach based on description logics [12]. Similarly, the Italian MOMIS system used an object-oriented modeling language to support the integrated querying of heterogeneous information sources [8].

Clio [24, 21, 16] introduced a more active mapping language based on tuple-generating dependencies (tgds) [7, 1]. The well-defined, formal basis and the ability to easily translate the mappings into executable code (e.g., queries in SQL or XQuery) proved a significant advantage and caused a re-thinking of the whole definition of model management, dubbed Model Management 2.0 [10]. Here, mappings are involved in all model management operations, at the core of any integration approach. Furthermore, model management remained no longer only a design time issue, because mappings have to be executed eventually to perform data transformation tasks. Thus, model management systems must be able to understand the semantics of a mapping in order to enable mapping operations (e.g., composition, inversion) and produce mappings as output (e.g., in match and merge operations). While Clio explored this issue in the context of (nested) relational data models, we have investigated the extension to the management of heterogeneous data models.

16.3 Generic Modeling Languages for Heterogeneous Sources

The heterogeneity of data management systems and modeling languages used in the web, but also in enterprise information systems, can be addressed by a generic modeling approach which is able to cope with the different modeling formalisms in a single uniform framework. Moreover, this has to be done at simultaneously at the model level and at the data level.

16.3.1 Role-Based Generic Metamodeling

Our generic metamodel *GeRoMe* [31] is a rich modeling language to represent detailed features of various concrete languages such as OWL, XML Schema, UML, or the Relational Data Model (RDM). In *GeRoMe*, a mapping states how the data of one model is related to the data of another model, i.e. mappings relate data and not only models. Because of this, mappings need to be very expressive to be able to represent rich data transformations. Executability of a mapping language means that it must be possible to apply a mapping such that it enables automatic code generation that executes the data transformations specified in the mapping [33].

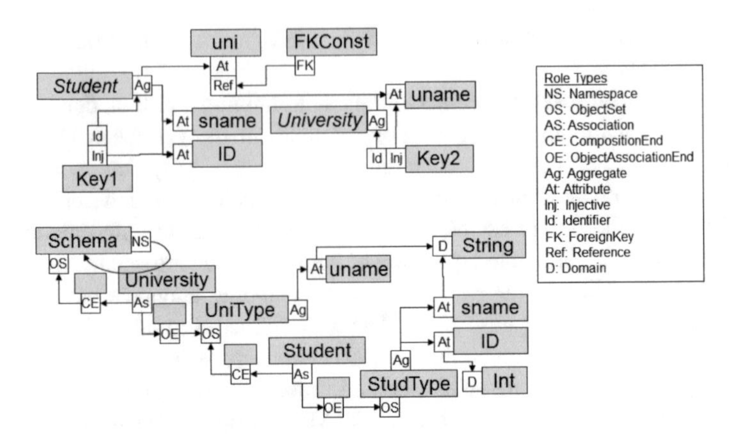

Fig. 16.2 GeRoMe representations of a relational and an XML schema

Figure 16.2 illustrates the generic *GeRoMe* models for our scenario from Figure 16.1. The upper part represents the relational schema with two relations Student and University. These elements are described by the role Aggregate (Ag), which is an element that can have (among other features) attributes. The attributes uname and uni are connected by a foreign key constraint (FKConst). The lower part of the figure shows the *GeRoMe* representation of the XML schema, where University is a root element having the complex type UniType. Student is a nested element with the complex type StudType. As complex types and attributes in XML have the same semantics as relations and columns in the relational schema, the corresponding elements play the same roles (e.g., Aggregate (Ag) and Attribute (At)).

As shown in the example, the generic metamodel unifies different representations and therefore simplifies the implementation of model management operations. For example, a schema matching or integration approach needs to be implemented only once for the generic representation, and does not have to be repeated for all different modeling languages. On the other hand, the examples also show the differences of the original modeling languages. A nesting in XML is a different modeling construct than a foreign key constraint in RDM, although both can be used to model the same semantics (a relationship between two entity types). If the goal is to translate models from one modeling language into another, then model transformation has to be applied in which such modeling constructs are translated [4]. We developed a rule-based model transformation for *GeRoMe* [30] with which we could show that a more detailed fine-granular representation of models is especially beneficial for model management operations that need an exact representation of the semantics of modeling constructs. More abstract representations such as graphs are useful for schema matching [51] in which a less accurate representation of the schema semantics is sufficient, but are usually not appropriate for model transformation or schema integration.

$$\begin{aligned}&\exists F,G \quad \forall u,s,i\\&\texttt{University}(u)\wedge\texttt{Student}(s,i)\wedge\texttt{Studies}(u,s)\rightarrow\\&\quad inst(F(i),\texttt{Student})\wedge inst(G(i,u),\texttt{University})\wedge\\&\quad F(s,i,G(i,u))\wedge G(u)\end{aligned}$$

Fig. 16.3 Mapping from a relational schema to an XML schema

16.3.2 Generic Mappings

The ultimate goal of our *GeRoMe*-based mapping language is to realize data integration and transform data between different, possibly heterogeneous data sources [33]. The mappings are expressed as second-order tuple-generating dependencies [18].

Second-order dependencies are required for mapping heterogeneous models, because nested structures (or models with different structures) need to be mapped. This is in contrast to mappings between relational models, where usually a tuple on the target side is created for each tuple that satisfies the conditions on the source side of the mapping. In nested data structures, multiple elements on the target side might have to be created, e.g., an outer object and multiple nested objects. As models can be very diverse in structure, the full power of second-order tuple-generating dependencies is required to map between these models.

Figure 16.3 shows a mapping between a 'flat' relational model and the nested XML model from our scenario. The relational model from the running example has been slightly modified to handle also students that study at multiple universities (i.e., the relation Studies represents the many-to-many relationship between students and universities. In the XML schema, the structure has been reversed, i.e., students are now at the top level, and their universities are represented as nested elements. The conditional part of the mapping selects all students from the relational source. On the target side, we create two objects: one for the main element Student and one for the nested element University. Those elements are identified by the Skolem terms $F(i)$ and $G(i,u)$. The *inst*-predicate indicate, that the objects represented by the Skolem terms are instances of Student and University, respectively. We use the symbols F and G as function symbols, but also as relation names. Note that the notation presented here is an abbreviated form (inspired by notation of nested mappings in Clio [19, 17]) of our original, more verbose notation presented in [33].

We also developed a mapping composition and optimization algorithm for this kind of generic mappings. The optimization exploits key and foreign-key constraints of the schema. Furthermore, the mappings could be also translated to executable code, e.g., SQL queries to retrieve data from a relational data source, or update operations on an XML document.

In our model management system *GeRoMeSuite* [32], we implemented several model management operators, for example, for schema matching, schema integration, schema mapping, model transformation, and mapping composition. We could show that the detailed representation of models is useful for semantically complex operations, but could also bring a benefit for simpler operations (e.g., schema matching [50]). Despite all these advantages, however, a rich metamodel like *GeRoMe* rather complicates the mapping procedure. Not all detailed constraints of a data model have to be understood when data has to be transformed from one source to another.

16.3.3 Conceptual Modeling and Integration for Data Lakes

This is especially true in 'data lake' Big Data scenarios where the data sources often do not expose a full-fledged schema definition. In data lakes, in contrast to the classical ETL (Extract-Transform-Load) processes of data warehouse systems, the transformation step is skipped and data is loaded in its original structure to avoid upfront integration effort and to make *all* source data available for later data analysis tasks [13]. Thus, the idea of data lakes as common data repositories with no need to define an integrated schema or ETL processes beforehand are in line with the current trends of Schema-on-Read in Big Data and NoSQL systems. Still, to avoid that a data lake turns into a data swamp without any useful understandable data, metadata management is a key element of a data lake architecture. A conceptual architecture of a data lake [46] which we use as a blue print for our data lake system is illustrated in Figure 16.4.

In this context, the term 'Schema-on-Read' is frequently used to describe the situation that schemas are not created *before* data is stored in a data management system, but a schema might be created when the data is read. As this schema creation is usually done automatically, the schemas contain only the core information of the data, i.e., its structure and basic constraints such as keyss and data types. The 'Schema-on-Read' fashion of data processing is also supported by recent NoSQL database management systems and, in fact, one of the main reasons for their popularity [20] as no schema design is required before using the database. The agile style of software development also contributes to this trend; in the early phase of a software project, it is more important to have a few running software modules than to deal with conceptual modeling and proper database schema design. Thus, conceptual models and database schemas are often not stated explicitly or lack a formal representation, which leads to unverifiability of these important artefacts in information systems design [44].

We are currently working on an incremental, interactive integration process in which metadata, including conceptual models and schemas, play a key role [47]. A starting point for the integration process is the metadata extraction from the sources. While some metadata is given explicitly and can be extracted automatically with standard methods (e.g., schemas of relational databases can be extracted with JDBC), other types of metadata have to be extracted with more advanced methods. For example, in the life science informatics project HUMIT[1] with the National

[1] `http://humit.de`

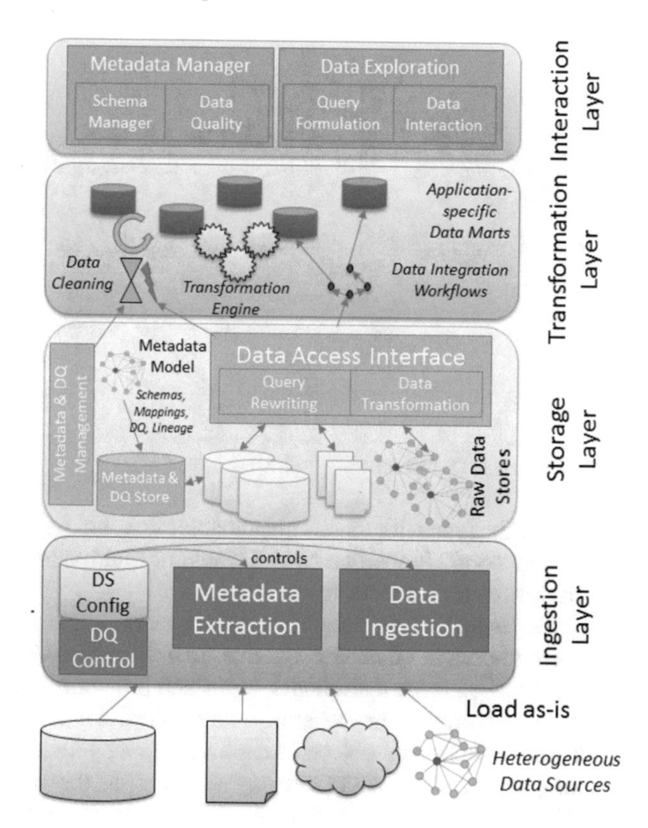

Fig. 16.4 Conceptual architecture of a data lake system

Center for Neuro-Degenerative Diseases, where researchers store most of their data in semi-structured CSV and Excel files, we developed a method to extract metadata descriptions in a semi-automatic way [48]. The extracted metadata include technical metadata (i.e., the structure of the data) as well as descriptive metadata (i.e., information about by whom for which project the data has been created). A user can also incrementally add semantics to the metadata of the data lake, e.g., by annotating the raw metadata with elements of a conceptual model or a standard such as schema.org [58]. The workflow of the HUMIT system is illustrated in Fig. 16.5. The metadata extraction component is part of our data lake system *Constance* [22].

Despite the delaying of transformation steps, modeling and mapping heterogeneous information remain necessary within a data lake system, as data is stored in its original format, e.g., relational, semi-structured, graph-structured, etc. As the rich metamodel of *GeRoMe* does not scale to Big Data problems, *Constance* employs a simple, yet expressive metamodel at its core. It can be seen as a variant of the Entity-Relationship Model, but expressive enough to express all data sets in a data lake. It is also self-describing like JSON and XML. In this model, entities are data objects that can have a type, properties, and relationships to other data objects. The type is just denoted as a string without a particular semantics, but it can be enriched

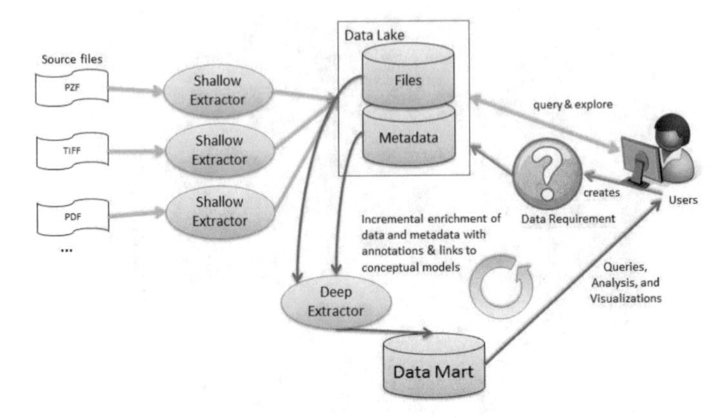

Fig. 16.5 Workflow of the HUMIT System

by a user by annotating the type with more semantical information (e.g., a reference to an element in schema.org). Properties can be single or multi-valued, simple or complex. Relationships are associations to other objects.

This model is independent of a particular storage system, but could be implemented with different underlying database systems. In a document-oriented MongoDB storage with JSON as basic data model, types and properties would be implemented as simple key-value pairs, whereas relationships are implemented as foreign-key references to other data objects. Adapting the mapping language from *GeRoMe* to this simpler metadata model is straightforward, as the *GeRoMe* mappings used also only types, properties, and relationships as the main constructs for any kind of data structure.

16.4 Conclusions: From Data Lakes to Data Spaces

In small and medium enterprises with long-standing market-leading knowhow, the presence of huge data lakes with unclear data ownership and data protection causes great political concern. In Germany and other European states which host a large number of such "hidden champions", a debate on *data sovereignty* has begun, defined as the ability of an organization to decide itself how it wants to use and share its own data. Independent of the fact that data ownership and thus also data sovereignty in themselves extremely controversial terms from legal and social science viewpoints, the Fraunhofer ICT group which I had the honor to chair at the time, decided in 2014 to propose a so-called Industrial Data Space initiative which investigates the related modeling and system requirements of such a concept, along with related questions of regulations, business models, and the like. The idea was quickly taken up by the German government, the European commission, as well as several leading players in the European user industries, and led to funding of an initial design project and the formation of the International Data Space Association which cur-

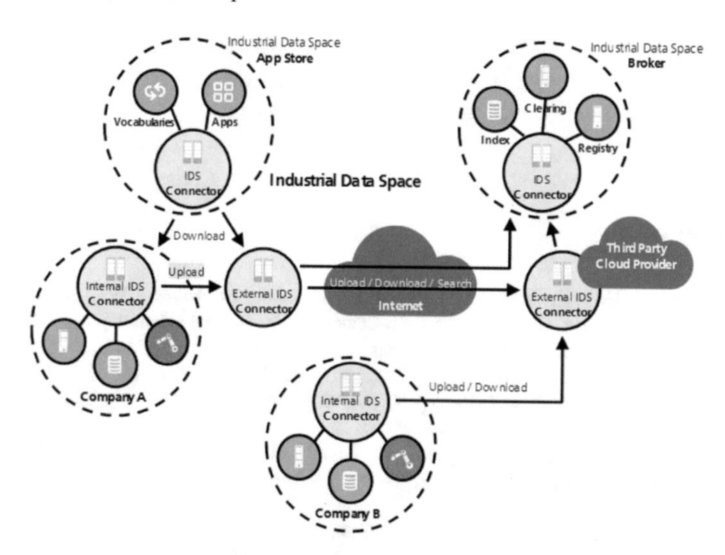

Fig. 16.6 Components of the Industrial Space Reference Architecture

rently already comprises over 80 organizations on four continents. A first version of the Industrial Data Space Reference Architecture [45] was publicly presented at the Hannover Fair 2017, where already 26 research organizations and companies showed initial demonstrators of solutions based on aspects of the Reference Architecture.

Fig. 16.6 gives an overview of the most important player roles and components. Participating companies (here: A and B) use a certified Internal IDS Connector offer or import safely containerized views on their data, with well-defined usage controls. In larger networks, specialized IDS Brokers can offer services for searching, negotiating, and monitoring service and data contracts. Other service providers can bring in data cleaning or analytics services through their App Stores, again connected to the system by IDS Connectors. For confidentiality as well as for performance reasons, service execution should have a choice between policy-based uploading and downloading data, or distribution of the service algorithms themselves which may require additional External IDS Connectors.

The technical elaboration of these and other aspects pf the above-mentioned IDS reference architecture is still in an early stage. From a conceptual modeling perspective, we can see that many of the mapping and integration approaches for heterogeneous data presented in the previous sections can be reused. However, they must be augmented by conceptual models of the players and their desires and permissions, as well as of the physical architecture which explicitly addresses data sharing (or not-sharing) relationships and various optimization strategies around the cloud computing and edge computing literatures; if conceptual modeling is manually done at all in such a setting, it must occur across organizational boundaries and in almost real-time, such that near-realtime collaborative modeling [41] is expected to play a major role in such a setting. Much previous research in conceptual modeling of distributed systems with conflicting goals, e.g. around the i* framework [25], is expected to contribute towards the ambitious goals of Industrial Data Spaces and its variants, e.g., in medical and material sciences, and we look forward to many exciting cooperations in the conceptual modeling community.

References

1. Abiteboul, S., Hull, R., Vianu, V.: Foundations of Databases. Addison-Wesley (1995)
2. Aguilera, D., Gómez, C., Olivé, A.: Enforcement of conceptual schema quality issues in current integrated development environments. In: Salinesi, C., Norrie, M.C., Pastor, O. (eds.) Proc. 25th Intl. Conf. on Advanced Information Systems Engineering (CAiSE). Lecture Notes in Computer Science, vol. 7908, pp. 626–640. Springer, Valencia, Spain (2013), https://doi.org/10.1007/978-3-642-38709-8_40
3. Atzeni, P., Bellomarini, L., Bugiotti, F., Gianforme, G.: Mism: A platform for model-independent solutions to model management problems. Journal of Data Semantics 14, 133–161 (2009)
4. Atzeni, P., Cappellari, P., Torlone, R., Bernstein, P.A., Gianforme, G.: Model-independent schema translation. VLDB Journal 17(6), 1347–1370 (2008)
5. Batini, C., Lenzerini, M., Navathe, S.B.: A comparative analysis of methodologies for database schema integration. ACM Computing Surveys 18(4), 323–364 (1986)
6. Batini, C., Scannapieco, M.: Data Quality: Concepts, Methodologies and Techniques. Data-Centric Systems and Applications, Springer (2006), https://doi.org/10.1007/3-540-33173-5
7. Beeri, C., Vardi, M.Y.: A proof procedure for data dependencies. Journal of the ACM 31(4), 718–741 (1984)
8. Bergamaschi, S., Castano, S., Vincini, M., Beneventano, D.: Semantic integration of heterogeneous information sources. Data & Knowledge Engineering 36(3), 215–249 (2001)
9. Bernstein, P.A., Halevy, A.Y., Pottinger, R.: A vision for management of complex models. SIGMOD Record 29(4), 55–63 (2000)
10. Bernstein, P.A., Melnik, S.: Model management 2.0: Manipulating richer mappings. In: Zhou, L., Ling, T.W., Ooi, B.C. (eds.) Proc. ACM SIGMOD Intl. Conf. on Management of Data. pp. 1–12. ACM Press, Beijing, China (2007)
11. Brodie, M.L.: Data integration at scale: From relational data integration to information ecosystems. In: Proc. 24th IEEE Intl. Conf. on Advanced Information Networking and Applications (AINA). pp. 2–3. IEEE Computer Society, Perth, Australia (2010)
12. Calvanese, D., Giacomo, G.D., Lenzerini, M., Nardi, D., Rosati, R.: Data Integration in Data Warehousing. International Journal of Cooperative Information Systems (IJCIS) 10(3), 237–271 (2001)
13. Dixon, J.: Data lakes revisited. James Dixon's Blog (September 2014), https://jamesdixon.wordpress.com/2014/09/25/data-lakes-revisited/
14. Do, H.H., Rahm, E.: Coma - a system for flexible combination of schema matching approaches. In: Proc. 28th Intl. Conference on Very Large Data Bases (VLDB). pp. 610–621. Morgan Kaufmann, Hong Kong, China (2002)
15. Fagin, R.: Tuple-generating dependencies. In: Liu, L., Özsu, M.T. (eds.) Encyclopedia of Database Systems, pp. 3201–3202. Springer (2009), https://doi.org/10.1007/978-0-387-39940-9_1274
16. Fagin, R., Haas, L.M., Hernández, M.A., Miller, R.J., Popa, L., Velegrakis, Y.: Clio: Schema mapping creation and data exchange. In: Conceptual Modeling: Foundations and Applications. LNCS, vol. 5600, pp. 198–236. Springer (2009)
17. Fagin, R., Haas, L.M., Hernández, M.A., Miller, R.J., Popa, L., Velegrakis, Y.: Clio: Schema mapping creation and data exchange. In: Borgida, A., Chaudhri, V.K., Giorgini, P., Yu, E.S.K. (eds.) Conceptual Modeling: Foundations and Applications. Lecture Notes in Computer Science, vol. 5600, pp. 198–236. Springer (2009)

18. Fagin, R., Kolaitis, P.G., Popa, L., Tan, W.C.: Composing schema mappings: Second-order dependencies to the rescue. ACM Trans. Database Syst. 30(4), 994–1055 (2005)
19. Fuxman, A., Hernández, M.A., Ho, C.T.H., Miller, R.J., Papotti, P., Popa, L.: Nested mappings: Schema mapping reloaded. In: Dayal, U., Whang, K.Y., Lomet, D.B., Alonso, G., Lohman, G.M., Kersten, M.L., Cha, S.K., Kim, Y.K. (eds.) Proc. 32nd Intl. Conference on Very Large Data Bases (VLDB). pp. 67–78. ACM Press (2006)
20. Gessert, F., Ritter, N.: Scalable data management: Nosql data stores in research and practice. In: Proc. 32nd IEEE International Conference on Data Engineering (ICDE). pp. 1420–1423. IEEE Computer Society, Helsinki, Finland (2016), https://doi.org/10.1109/ICDE.2016.7498360
21. Haas, L.M., Hernández, M.A., Ho, H., Popa, L., Roth, M.: Clio grows up: from research prototype to industrial tool. In: Proc. SIGMOD Conf. pp. 805–810. ACM Press (2005)
22. Hai, R., Geisler, S., Quix, C.: Constance: An intelligent data lake system. In: Özcan, F., Koutrika, G., Madden, S. (eds.) Proc. Intl. Conf. on Management of Data (SIGMOD). pp. 2097–2100. ACM, San Francisco, CA, USA (2016), http://doi.acm.org/10.1145/2882903.2899389
23. Haslhofer, B., Klas, W.: A survey of techniques for achieving metadata interoperability. ACM Comput. Surv. 42(2) (2010)
24. Hernández, M.A., Miller, R.J., Haas, L.M.: Clio: A semi-automatic tool for schema mapping. In: Proc. ACM SIGMOD. p. 607 (2001)
25. Horkoff, J., Barone, D., Jiang, L., Yu, E.S.K., Amyot, D., Borgida, A., Mylopoulos, J.: Strategic business modeling: representation and reasoning. Software and System Modeling 13(3), 1015–1041 (2014), https://doi.org/10.1007/s10270-012-0290-8
26. Jarke, M., Gallersdörfer, R., Jeusfeld, M.A., Staudt, M.: ConceptBase - a deductive object base for meta data management. Journal of Intelligent Information Systems 4(2), 167–192 (1995)
27. Jarke, M., Jeusfeld, M.A., Quix, C., Vassiliadis, P.: Architecture and Quality in Data Warehouses: An Extended Repository Approach. Information Systems 24(3), 229–253 (1999)
28. Jarke, M., Lenzerini, M., Vassiliou, Y., Vassiliadis, P. (eds.): Fundamentals of Data Warehouses. Springer-Verlag, 2 edn. (2003)
29. Jeusfeld, M.A.: Änderungskontrolle in Deduktiven Objektbanken. Ph.D. thesis, Universität Passau (1992)
30. Kensche, D., Quix, C.: Transformation of models in(to) a generic metamodel. In: Proc. BTW Workshop on Model and Metadata Management. pp. 4–15 (2007)
31. Kensche, D., Quix, C., Chatti, M.A., Jarke, M.: *GeRoMe*: A generic role based metamodel for model management. Journal on Data Semantics VIII, 82–117 (2007)
32. Kensche, D., Quix, C., Li, X., Li, Y.: *GeRoMeSuite*: A system for holistic generic model management. In: Koch, C., Gehrke, J., Garofalakis, M.N., Srivastava, D., Aberer, K., Deshpande, A., Florescu, D., Chan, C.Y., Ganti, V., Kanne, C.C., Klas, W., Neuhold, E.J. (eds.) Proceedings 33rd Intl. Conf. on Very Large Data Bases (VLDB). pp. 1322–1325. Vienna, Austria (2007)
33. Kensche, D., Quix, C., Li, X., Li, Y., Jarke, M.: Generic schema mappings for composition and query answering. Data Knowl. Eng. 68(7), 599–621 (2009)
34. Lenzerini, M.: Data integration: A theoretical perspective. In: Popa, L. (ed.) Proc. 21st ACM Symposium on Principles of Database Systems (PODS). pp. 233–246. ACM Press, Madison, Wisconsin (2002)
35. Li, X., Quix, C.: Merging relational views: A minimization approach. In: Jeusfeld, M.A., Delcambre, L.M.L., Ling, T.W. (eds.) Proc. 30th Intl. Conference on Conceptual Modeling (ER 2011). Lecture Notes in Computer Science, vol. 6998, pp. 379–392. Springer, Brussels, Belgium (2011)
36. Li, X., Quix, C., Kensche, D., Geisler, S.: Automatic schema merging using mapping constraints among incomplete sources. In: Huang, J., Koudas, N., Jones, G.J.F., Wu, X., Collins-Thompson, K., An, A. (eds.) Proc. 19th ACM Conf. on Information and Knowledge Management (CIKM). pp. 299–308. ACM, Toronto, Ontario, Canada (2010)

37. López, J., Olivé, A.: A framework for the evolution of temporal conceptual schemas of information systems. In: Proc. 12th Intl. Conf. on Advanced Information Systems Engineering (CAiSE). pp. 369–386. Stockholm, Sweden (2000), https://doi.org/10.1007/3-540-45140-4_25
38. Melnik, S., Rahm, E., Bernstein, P.A.: Developing metadata-intensive applications with rondo. Journal of Web Semantics 1(1), 47–74 (2003)
39. Melnik, S., Rahm, E., Bernstein, P.A.: Rondo: A programming platform for generic model management. In: Proc. SIGMOD. pp. 193–204. ACM (2003)
40. Mylopoulos, J., Borgida, A., Jarke, M., Koubarakis, M.: Telos: Representing Knowledge About Information Systems. ACM Transactions on Information Systems 8(4), 325–362 (1990)
41. Nicolaescu, P., Rosenstengel, M., Derntl, M., Klamma, R., Jarke, M.: View-based near real-time collaborative modeling for information systems engineering. In: Proc. 28th Intl. Conf. on Advanced Information Systems Engineering (CAiSE). pp. 3–17. Ljubljana, Slovenia (2016), https://doi.org/10.1007/978-3-319-39696-5_1
42. Nissen, H.W., Jarke, M.: Repository support for multi-perspective requirements engineering. Inf. Syst. 24(2), 131–158 (1999), https://doi.org/10.1016/S0306-4379(99)00009-5
43. Olivé, A.: On the design and implementation of information systems from deductive conceptual models. In: Proc. 15th Intl. Conf. on Very Large Data Bases (VLDB). pp. 3–11. Amsterdam, The Netherlands (1989), http://www.vldb.org/conf/1989/P003.PDF
44. Olivé, A.: Conceptual modeling in agile information systems development. In: Proc. 16th Intl. Conf. on Enterprise Information Systems (ICEIS). pp. IS–11. Lisbon, Portugal (2014)
45. Otto, B., Lohmann, S., Auer, S., Brost, G., Cirullies, J., Eitel, A., Ernst, T., Haas, C., Huber, M., Jung, C., Jürjens, J., Lange, C., Mader, C., Menz, N., Nagel, R., Pettenpohl, H., Pullmann, J., Quix, C., Schon, J., Schulz, D., Schütte, J., Spiekermann, M., Wenzel, S.: Reference architecture model for the Industrial Data Space. Technical report, Fraunhofer-Gesellschaft (2017), http://www.industrialdataspace.de
46. Quix, C.: Data Lakes: A Solution or a new Challenge for Big Data Integration? In: Proc. 5th Intl. Conf. Data Management Technologies and Applications (DATA). p. 7. Lisbon, Portugal (2016), keynote presentation
47. Quix, C., Berlage, T., Jarke, M.: Interactive pay-as-you-go-integration of life science data: The HUMIT approach. ERCIM News 2016(104) (2016), http://ercim-news.ercim.eu/en104/special/interactive-pay-as-you-go-integration-of-life-science-data-the-humit-approach
48. Quix, C., Hai, R., Vatov, I.: Metadata extraction and management in data lakes with GEMMS. Complex Systems Informatics and Modeling Quarterly (CSIMQ) 9, 67–83 (2016), https://doi.org/10.7250/csimq.2016-9.04
49. Quix, C., Kensche, D., Li, X.: Generic schema merging. In: Krogstie, J., Opdahl, A., Sindre, G. (eds.) Proc. 19th Intl. Conf. on Advanced Information Systems Engineering (CAiSE'07). LNCS, vol. 4495, pp. 127–141. Springer-Verlag (2007)
50. Quix, C., Kensche, D., Li, X.: Matching of ontologies with xml schemas using a generic metamodel. In: Meersman, R., Tari, Z. (eds.) Proc. OTM Confederated International Conf. CoopIS/DOA/ODBASE/GADA/IS. Lecture Notes in Computer Science, vol. 4803, pp. 1081–1098. Springer, Vilamoura, Portugal (2007)
51. Rahm, E., Bernstein, P.A.: A survey of approaches to automatic schema matching. VLDB Journal 10(4), 334–350 (2001)
52. Ramesh, B., Jarke, M.: Toward reference models of requirements traceability. IEEE Trans. Software Eng. 27(1), 58–93 (2001), https://doi.org/10.1109/32.895989
53. Raventós, R., Olivé, A.: An object-oriented operation-based approach to translation between MOF metaschemas. Data Knowl. Eng. 67(3), 444–462 (2008), https://doi.org/10.1016/j.datak.2008.07.003
54. Shvaiko, P., Euzenat, J.: Ontology matching: State of the art and future challenges. IEEE Transactions on Knowledge and Data Engineering 25(1), 158–176 (2013)
55. Shvaiko, P., Euzenat, J.: A survey of schema-based matching approaches. Journal on Data Semantics IV, 146–171 (2005), lNCS 3730

56. Staudt, M., Jarke, M.: View management support in advanced knowledge base servers. J. Intell. Inf. Syst. 15(3), 253–285 (2000), https://doi.org/10.1023/A:1008780430577
57. Teniente, E., Olivé, A.: Updating knowledge bases while maintaining their consistency. The VLDB Journal 4(2), 193–241 (1995)
58. Tort, A., Olivé, A.: An approach to website schema.org design. Data Knowl. Eng. 99, 3–16 (2015), https://doi.org/10.1016/j.datak.2015.06.011

Chapter 17
A Method for Emerging Technology Evaluation. Application to Blockchain and Smart Data Discovery

Jacky Akoka and Isabelle Comyn-Wattiau

Abstract Emerging technologies represent a major innovation that offers significant advances to both private and public organizations. Examples of these technologies are the "Blockchain technology" which combines cryptographic mechanisms and peer-to-peer (P2P) architecture and "Smart Data Discovery" combining artificial intelligence and analytics. The importance of these emerging technologies requires the use of evalua-tion methods in order to understand their contribution and the associat-ed risks. The objective of this article is to propose a method supporting the evaluation of emerging technologies. A guidance approach is pro-posed. It is based on the recognition that emerging technologies are complex systems. Our approach combines three conceptual frame-works: the underlying theory of complex information systems, systems theory, and the ISO 25001 standard devoted to software quality. We propose a multi-criteria hierarchy which serves as the basis for the eval-uation. To illustrate this approach, we apply it to the particular cases of "Blockchain" technology and "Smart Data Discovery".

17.1 Introduction

According to [4], emerging technologies (ET) represent an innovation that has the potential to transform an existing industry and / or create new ones. [14] summarize different definitions into five main characteristics: (i) radical innovation, (ii) rapid growth, (iii) coherence, (iv) significant impact, and (v) uncertainty and ambigui-ty. [18] define four stages in the evolution of ET: techno-logical change, implantation of technologies, application of innovation, and innovation through the integration of technologies.

Jacky Akoka
CEDRIC-CNAM & IMT-TEM, e-mail: jacky.akoka@cnam.fr

Isabelle Comyn-Wattiau
ESSEC Business School

© Springer International Publishing AG 2017

J. Cabot et al. (eds.), *Conceptual Modeling Perspectives*,
https://doi.org/10.1007/978-3-319-67271-7_17

There are many examples of ET notably: (i) nanotechnologies that have creative potential in many domains [9]; (ii) fire-fighting information systems including digital maps, dedicated drones, land ro-bots, emergency information systems and intelligent protective clothing [15]; (iii) technologies implemented in the cloud and more particularly Cloud Mobile Learning [1]; (iv) energy storage technologies including "smart grids" [20]. One of the main characteristics of these ET is complexity [8]. Beyond being complex systems, they are more gener-ally complex information systems (IS).

An important issue is the ability of organizations to assess the contribu-tion of these ET and the associated risks. The main objective of this arti-cle is precisely to propose an approach to the evaluation of emerging technologies taking into account the complexity that characterizes them. We illustrate this approach by evaluating the Blockchain and the Smart Data Discovery technologies, which are today among the most important disruptive innovations. We propose a guidance approach to evaluate emerging technologies. This approach is based on a multi-criteria hierar-chy capitalizing on knowledge. The rest of the article is organized as follows. The second paragraph is devoted to a brief state of the art on complexity, complex systems, and methods of evaluating emerging technologies as complex systems. Our approach is presented in Section 3. The following section is devoted to the application of this approach to the emerging technologies of block-chain and smart data discovery. We conclude in the last section and pre-sent some future avenues of research.

17.2 State of the Art

There are several definitions of complexity that reflect the different sys-tems involved and their contexts. [10] presents some thirty definitions of complexity as well as the associated measures. [2] considers that complexity has two dimensions: organizational and technological. [6] characterize complexity by three dimen-sions: trust, fact and interaction. The theory of complex systems consid-ers these systems to be characterized by their degree of self-organization, by their emergence property, their innovative character, and their ability to learn and by their adaptability [17]. Research in this field focuses on notions such as the emergence of collective properties, chaotic behavior, self-organization, redundancy, recursion, etc. [7]. Some authors consider that interde-pendence and size have a significant effect on complexity. Others place greater emphasis on uncertainty [13].

We consider emerging technologies to be complex systems because they have all the characteristics and attributes described above. More generally, we classify them as complex information systems that must respond rapidly to changes in sociotechnical dimensions and to non-functional requirements. They must also take into account changes in user requirements, organizational needs (business processes and man-agement rules), and increased interdependence between individuals, organizations and technologies. They must also incorporate changes in the environment of these systems such as those of markets, regulators, competition, threats and opportunities. Finally, they must be able to cope with the changes generated by proprietary solutions, open source software and the emergence of new applications and protocols. More generally, they must solve the problems arising from rapid changes in information technology, which are an important dimension of complex in-formation systems.

There are several approaches to complexity management, such as the theory of adaptive complex systems [7], reductionist theory [5], and systems theory [16]. We con-sider that systems theory is the most appropriate for facilitating the management of complexity. Indeed, the complexity of the system is linked to its structure, its behavior and its relation to the environment. These three elements are precisely the main characteristics of systems theory [17].

[12] describe many measures of complexity and their limi-tations. The metrics generally used are based on the size of the system considered, its entropy, the information, the hierarchy of costs and the organization. Other metrics are proposed, including those based on Shannon's contributions. Examples of evaluation of complex systems are presented by [12].

There are many methods for evaluating technologies. [19] propose a taxonomy of these methods. Another family of meth-ods falls under the impact assessment (Delphi and SBAM) [3]. Technology-based risk assessment is an approach that attempts to measure "negative synergies" and has resulted in the de-velopment of the ITRACS methodology [21].

Unlike the approaches described above, our approach to evaluating emerging technologies integrates three conceptual frameworks: com-plex information systems, systems theory, and the ISO 25000 (SQuaRE) standard for software quality.

17.3 Our Approach

Our objective is to define a guiding approach for the evaluation of an in-formation system based on emerging technologies. In the first section, we present the multicriteria hierarchy that we have defined to organize the evaluation. In the second part, we describe the proposed approach.

Understanding emerging technology as a complex information system requires analysis of the different characteristics of this system. A system obeys a goal. It has a structure, which can be static or dynamic or which can include a static part and a dynamic part. The system interacts with its environment. it evolves over time. Thus, an emerging technology can be evaluated as a system that has a structure, an environment and an evo-lution. We propose to organize our hierarchy according to these three characteristics.

The theory of complex information systems is based on the socio-technical perspective of information systems, which makes it possible to distinguish social factors from technical factors. The social adjective en-compasses both the organizational dimension and the human dimen-sion, as well as the economic and financial dimension. Similarly, the technical factor covers all aspects of emerging technology, both hard-ware and software, for example. Thus our second level of organization of the hierarchy consists in understanding the system, its environment and its evolution, on the one hand on the social level and on the other hand on the technological level.

The ISO standardization organization has developed a standard called SQuaRE (Software QUAlity Requirements and Evaluation) for software evaluation. This standard is based on an eight-dimensional quality model that is mainly technical (six) and functional (two). Based on the McCall model [11], they represent the three types of factors (opera-tion, scalability, maintainability) recommended by this model. In this way, they are also in alignment with the dimensions previously consid-ered for the description of the complex information system.

Thus, considering successively emerging technology as a system, then as a socio-technical system, then as a software, we obtain a hierarchy in three main levels which can then be refined (Figure 17.1). The eight dimen-sions of the SQuaRE standard (functional relevance, usability, reliability, security, portability, maintainability, performance, compatibility) are then subdivided into about thirty sub-characteristics that have been in-tegrated into the hierarchy.

By a mapping and merging process, for the sake of completeness, the hierarchy was then aligned with those proposed in [8]. Without pretending to completeness, we pre-sent the hierarchy (Figure 17.1).

17.3.1 The Guiding Method

Faced with emerging technology, the decision-maker must find the rele-vant information to understand the issues, the components, the oppor-tunities and the associated risks. It must then organize this information in order to understand and, where appropriate, be assisted by experts for evaluation. He/she can then synthesize this information. The pro-posed process thus comprises five steps described below (Figure 17.2).

17.3.1.1 Hierarchy Feeding

The first step is a parsing process. It consists of gathering documentation on emerging technology, whether it is professional press, white papers, technical or organizational research articles. All data and information col-lected from these sources and deemed relevant are transferred to the nodes of the hierarchy. This process is carried out until saturation i.e. as long as there is any untracked documentation and / or new elements are still discovered. The purpose is to gather and structure decision-making information.

The system	Social	Functional relevance	Functional completeness
			Accuracy
			Functional adequacy
	Technical	Reliability	Maturity
			Availability
			Fault tolerance
			Recoverability
		Security	Confidentiality
			Integrity
			Non-repudiation
			Accountability
			Authenticity
		Performance	Temporal efficiency
			Resource utilization
			Capacity
Its environment	Social	Human Usability	User adequacy
			Recognizability
			Learnability
			Operability
			Error protection
			Interface aesthetics
			Accessibility
		Organizational	Mastery of technical skills
		Economic	Financial risk
			Profitability
			Total cost ownership
			Added value
			Market share
		Societal	Ethical acceptance
			Environmental acceptance
		Regulatory	Privacy
			Intellectual property law
			Conformity with industry regulations
			Compliance with certifications
	Technical Compatibility	Coexistence	
		Interoperability	
Its evolution	Social	Organizational adaptability	
		Functional adaptability	
		Regulatory adaptability	
		Societal adaptability	
	Technical	Portability	Adaptability
			Installability
			Replaceability
		Maintainability	Modularity
			Reusability
			Analyzability
			Modifiability
			Testability
		Scalability	

Fig. 17.1 The evaluation hierarchy.

Fig. 17.2 The evaluation process.

17.3.1.2 Hierarchy-based Evaluation

Depending on its level of expertise, the user can use the hierarchy to evaluate the emerging technology considered. Using the information provided on each aspect the technology, he/she can thus evaluate it. He/she can perform a more detailed analysis enabling the enrichment of the hierarchy for all the aspects considered to be more relevant.

17.3.1.3 Search for Additional Information

In the absence of information, some leaves or even branches of the hierarchy may not be fed, making it difficult to evaluate the technology concerned. These leaves or branches are highlighted for a search for additional information. The expert characterizes the information needed and searches it. This process, for the time being manual, can be automated by using an automatic information search using generalist or specialized search engines. He/she e can then complete the missing elements, performing if necessary experts' inquiries.

17.3.1.4 Editing the Evaluation Report

After the pruning and refinement of the tree structure, a structured re-port can be edited.

17.3.1.5 Knowledge Capitalization

The hierarchy itself can be enriched with the new branches obtained during its use, thus enabling a capitalization of the new evaluation fac-tors proposed by the experts.

The hierarchical model and the guidance method were used to evaluate the blockchain and the smart data discovery technologies, in order to show the feasibility and the usefulness of the approach. For space rea-sons, we describe very briefly each technology and present only a partial result of its application (step 2 of the method). Some conclusions are drawn by comparing the two case studies.

17.4 Application to Blockchain and Smart Data Discovery

17.4.1 The case of Blockchain (BC)

We present below a summary of different sources describing the BC technology.

The concept and the technology of BC is the result of the combination of cryptographic mechanisms and peer-to-peer (P2P) architecture. BC is seen as a disruptive innovation that has the potential to redefine many sectors of the economy. BC functions as a public database or open ledg-er where the details of each bitcoins exchange are recorded. The princi-ple of the BC lies in the fact that each operation is inscribed in thousands of large account books, each subject to the scrutiny of a different ob-server. This system is reliable because it is based on cryptography. It is also resilient thanks to the P2P architecture. The concept of BC is ex-tended to sectors requiring the recording of transactions or contracts. The US Federal Securities and Exchange Commission has approved the use of the BC as a share ownership registry. There are also smart con-tracts applications based on the Internet of objects. The BC generates data using distributed algorithms. It stores these data using encrypted chained blocks. The architecture of the BC model is composed of seven layers (similar to ISO layers). Three major players can be impacted by the BC:

trusted third parties, state institutions and all organizations seeking new forms of financing to manage their capital shares. The main risk is that of security and especially the existence of vulnerabilities that could be exploited by hackers. Another risk is related to the use of different technological approaches. It is the social, legal and financial challenges that this technology will bring to light that could prove to be the most difficult problems to solve.

Applying our guiding method and the multi-criteria hierarchy, we obtain the following results (Figure 17.3). Five types of judgments can be issued: 1) the node does not contain information: this situation may reflect a lack of information on this criterion or the irrelevance of the criterion for this technology, 2) the node contains factual information (gray) with descrip-tive value), 3) the node reflects a positive judgment, an opportunity provided by the technology (green), 4) the node represents an alert (or-ange), informing the decision-maker about an aspect requiring special monitoring, 5) the node represents a risk), which calls for a strength-ened evaluation.

The blockchain technology impacts highly the security of the IS, positive-ly since its mechanism really improves both integrity and non-repudiation levels. However, in terms of confidentiality, there is no basic guarantee. The two main points of vigilance are maturity and compliance with certifications. Many other leaves of the tree could not be feeded, which means that additional information has to be found before con-cluding. For example, there is no information on the performance of the blockchain. Moreover, the adaptability may be questioned.

17.4.2 The case of Smart Data Discovery

Smart Data Discovery (SDD) corresponds to the application of artificial in-telligence to Business Intelligence. Unlike the conventional means used to produce conclusions based on data, SDD provides users with the abil-ity to understand the patterns hidden in the data. It can provide quick insights and advanced data visualization tools offering levels of granulari-ty analysis in a single interface. It enables users to perform self-service analysis including data preparation, native language queries and auto-matic creation of visualizers. It is an encapsulation of predictive analyt-ics, interactive data visualization, pattern matching, and machine learn-ing to assist automated decision support. Using semantic technologies (4), SDD methods improve the effectiveness of BI analytics. Semantic graph databases, which store data as a graph, allow end users to relate to their questions while concentrating on relevance. The architecture of a typical SDD system comprises several modules: data preparation, in-sight generation, data discovery, recommendation engine, and insights delivery. SDD is characterized by an ease of use, a real degree of agility and flexibility, and by an optimal time-to-results. However, it suffers from a limited depth of data exploration and a low complexity of analy-sis. SDD exploits machine learning to automate the analytics workflow. Banks, retailers, and insurance companies are among the main users of SDD. Many tools exist such as DataRPM, run directly on

Social: Blockchain is seen as a disruptive innovation that has the potential to redefine many sectors of the economy, financial markets, public and government activities, as well as high-tech companies. Blockchain functions as a public database or open ledger where the details of each bitcoins exchange	**Functional relevance:** The blockchain records a data set such as a date, and a cryptographic signature associated with the sender. In the case of the bitcoin, it is the number of bitcoins sent, but it could be the digital cryptographic fingerprint, called the hash function, of any electronic document. The blockchain principle lies in the fact that each operation is inscribed in thousands of large account books, each subject to the scrutiny of a different observer. Any blockchain is a register (and therefore a file) existing in a large number of copies. The concept of the blockchain is defined as a system for recording transactions. Beginning in 2014, this concept is extended to sectors requiring the recording of transactions or contracts. For example, the Proof of Existence website allows a user to download any document and record their fingerprint forever in the Bitcoin blockchain. This demonstrates that the person who downloaded the document had this specific document in his or her possession at some point. This can also be used to prove that the document has not been modified since that time.	Functional adequacy
Technical: Created by Satoshi Nakamoto in 2008, blockchain (BC) concept and technology result combine cryptography mechanisms and peer to peer (P2P) architecture	**Reliability :** This system is reliable since it is based on cryptography	Maturity
	Security	Confidentiality
		Integrity: This technology is designed so as to prevent the same bitcoin from being counted in duplicate, without any intermediary, such as a bank. The Stamperya startup has transformed this service into a business enabling other companies to "digitally stamp out" any electronic document or e-mail in order to establish its integrity
		Non-repudiation : It is also resilient thanks to the P2P architecture
		Accountability: The Stamperya startup has transformed this service into a business enterprise that allows other companies to "digitally stamp out" any electronic document or e-mail in order to establish ownership
		Capacity: The two main parameters are the length of the blockchain and the number of copies. For the bitcoin, the length of the blockchain rose from 27 GB in early 2015 to 74 in mid 2016
		Profitability: The attractiveness of this system is that it offers an immediate settlement while traditional stockbrokers offer a 3-day settlement period
	Societal	Ethical acceptance
	Regulatory: The US Federal Securities and Exchange Commission has approved the use of the blockchain as a share ownership registry through the Overstock.com web site. The latter intends to use the alternative trading technology system proposed by To.com to allow individuals to buy and sell shares	Compliance with certifications

Fig. 17.3 Evaluating blockchain through the hierarchy.

Hadoop/Spark as a data source. They offer a natural-language query interface and interac-tive. They also offer visual-based data discovery. Other SDD tools, such as Ayasdi and DataRPM, exploit graph analysis to identify meaningful re-lationships. Finally, the Smart BI software developed by Yseop write in-telligent reports in-stantly and leverage on the company's best practices to explain what actions to take and why.

Application of our guiding method leads to the following result (Figure 17.4).

<table>
<tr><td rowspan="2">Social</td><td rowspan="2">Functional relevance: The latter can provide quick insights. It also provide advanced data visualization tools offering levels of granularity analysis in a single interface. It enables the exploration of data in a less-than-structured way. The smart data discovery process comprises three phases. The first one, related to data preparation, uses algorithms to find schemas and to profile data. It suggests recommendations for data quality improvement and enrichment. It performs data lineage and reuse notably on multi-structured data. The second step is dedicated finding patterns in data. To this end, it uses natural languages query as well as specific algorithms to find all patterns in data. It offers support to users in their context, whether they are business analysts or data scientists. Finally, the last phase aims at sharing and operationalizing the findings obtained in phase two. In general, it uses natural languages to explain the findings to end users. It offers visualization techniques to facilitate the comprehension of the hidden patterns.</td><td>Functional completeness: This is a new trend enabling users to perform self-service analysis including data preparation, native language queries and automatic creation of visualizers. limited depth of data exploration and a low complexity of analysis.</td></tr>
<tr><td>Functional adequacy: The concept of smart technology encompasses all the technologies (physical and logical) that are able to adapt automatically and modify behavior to cope with internal and external changes. It is based on the idea that the smart technology is able to "self-management" and can handle unpredictable events. enhance the contextual offering to the customer.</td></tr>
<tr><td rowspan="7">Technical</td><td rowspan="5">Security</td><td>Confidentiality</td></tr>
<tr><td>Integrity</td></tr>
<tr><td>Non-repudiation</td></tr>
<tr><td>Accountability</td></tr>
<tr><td>Authenticity</td></tr>
<tr><td rowspan="2">Performance</td><td>Temporal efficiency: optimal time-to-results</td></tr>
<tr><td>Resource utilization: optimization</td></tr>
<tr><td rowspan="2">Social</td><td rowspan="2">Human
Usability</td><td>User adequacy: Unlike the conventional means used to produce conclusions based on data, smart data discovery provides users with the ability to understand the patterns hidden in the data. ease of use.</td></tr>
<tr><td>Learnability: It allows users to gain insights using advanced analytics without requiring them to have traditional data scientist expertise</td></tr>
<tr><td>Social</td><td>Functional adaptability: degree of agility and flexibility</td><td></td></tr>
</table>

Fig. 17.4 Evaluation Smart Data Discovery through the hierarchy.

Information on this technology is limited. Is it a niche phenomenon or too emergent technology? Moreover, it appears that no threat or nega-tive impact is mentioned. The assessment comes down to a set of main-ly functional opportunities for easy access to unsophisticated users.

17.4.3 Hierarchies' Comparison

By comparing the two resultant hierarchies, we find that all the dimen-sions are not informed. Moreover, the BC hierarchy is more complete than the SDD one. We argue that the more a hierarchy is complete, the more the underlying technology is disruptive. On the contrary, if the hi-erarchy is incomplete, then the technology can be perceived as a mar-keting phenomenon. In this case, the technology cannot be considered as disruptive. In our case, BC appears to be more disruptive than SDD. in any case, it is important to look for the missing information before de-ciding on the disruptive nature of an emerging technology.

17.5 Conclusions and Future Work

In this chapter, we present an approach to evaluating emerging technol-ogies combining three conceptual frameworks: the theory underlying complex information systems, systems theory and the ISO 25000 stand-ard devoted to software quality. The evaluation process is structured us-ing a multi-criteria hierarchy. We took into account the social and tech-nical dimensions for each component of the system to be assessed, in-cluding the system itself, its environment and its evolution. To illustrate this approach, we have applied it to the cases of âĂIJBlockchainâĂİ and "Smart Data Discovery", which today constitute emerging technologies with many fields of applications. The approach makes it possible to evaluate an emerging technology, to identify the domains where the information is missing and requires complementary expertise, to enrich, and to evolve the hierarchy with each application.

We plan, in terms of future research, to extend the evaluation by asso-ciating metrics to the criteria. It should be noted that the weights of the evaluation dimensions and the criteria are not the same according to the sectors of activity or the fields concerned. Thus, in some cases, spatial adaptability (scalability or scale-up) can be significant. In other cases, regulatory compliance is paramount, while depending on the areas con-cerned. Another line of research concerns an approach that would use the same hierarchical model in reverse engineering, as a framework en-abling organizations to determine the most important factors and best suited to their needs when developing emerging technologies. Finally, another avenue of research is to integrate natural language analysis techniques to automate the analysis phase of the documentation.

Acknowledgements Professor A. Olivé has played an important role in conceptual modeling with a concern to evaluate his contributions. We would like to pay tribute to him for his role as a researcher and educator by proposing a method for evaluating emerging technologies, knowing his interest in these technologies and their evaluation. We are grateful to him for all he has contributed to our conceptual modeling community.

References

1. Al-Arabiat, D., Ahmad, W. F. W., Sarlan, A. (2015). Review on critical factors of adopting cloud mobile learning. In: Technology Management and Emerging Technologies (ISTMET), 2015 International Symposium on (pp. 69-73). IEEE.
2. Baccarini, D. The concept of project complexity–a review, International Journal of Project Management, vol. 14, issue 4, pp. 201-204, 1996.
3. Banuls V.A., Salmeron J.L. A Scenario-Based Assessment Model–SBAM, Technological Forecasting and Social Change, Volume 74, Issue 6, July 2007, Pages 750-762
4. Day, G. S., Schoemaker, P. J., Gunther, R. E. (2004). Wharton on managing emerging technologies. John Wiley & Sons.
5. Emmeche, C., Koppe, S. Stjernfelt (1997) F. Explaining Emergence: Towards an Ontology of Levels. Journal for General Philosophy of Science 28: 83.
6. Geraldi, J., Adlbrecht, G. (2008). On faith, fact, and interaction in projects. IEEE Engineering Management Review, 2(36), 35-49.
7. Holland, J. H. (2006). Studying complex adaptive systems. Journal of Systems Science and Complexity, 19(1), 1-8.
8. Huang L., Yuan Y. (2010). Evaluation on the industrialization potential of emerging technologies based on principal component and cluster analysis. In: Computer Modelling and Simulation (UKSim), 2010 12th International Conference on. IEEE, p. 317-322.
9. Letaba, P. T., Pretorius, M. W., Pretorius, L. (2014, June). The use of bibliometrics in the development of technology roadmaps: Planning for industrial impact of emerging technologies. In: Engineering, Technology and Innovation (ICE), 2014 International ICE Conference on (pp. 1-8). IEEE.
10. Lloyd S. Measures of complexity: a nonexhaustive list. Control Systems Magazine, IEEE, 21:7-8, 2001.
11. McCall, J. A. 2002. Quality Factors. Encyclopedia of Software Engineering.
12. Owen, C. L. (2007). Evaluation of complex systems. Design Studies, 28(1), 73-101.
13. Perminova, O., Gustafsson, M., Wikström, K. (2008). Defining uncertainty in projects–a new perspective. International Journal of Project Management, 26(1), 73-79.
14. Rotolo, D., Hicks, D., Martin, B. R. (2015). What is an emerging technology?. Research Policy, 44(10), 1827-1843.
15. Schlauderer S., Overhage S., Weidinger J. (2016). New Vistas for Firefighter Information Systems? Towards a Systematic Evaluation of Emerging Technologies from a Task-Technology Fit Perspective. In: System Sciences (HICSS), 2016 49th Hawaii International Conference on (pp. 178-187). IEEE.
16. Skyttner, L. General Systems Theory: Problems, Perspectives, Practice. 2nd ed. Singapore: World Scientific, 2005.
17. Sommerville I., Cliff D., Calinescu R., Keen J., Kelly T., Kwiatkowska M., Paige R. (2012). Large-scale complex IT systems. Communications of the ACM, 55(7), 71-77.
18. Song Y., Yin L., Research on species traits of emerging technologies and the path of formation, Management, 2007, 4(2), pp. 211-215.
19. Tran T.A, Daim T. A taxonomic review of methods and tools applied in technology assessment, Technological Forecasting & Social Change 75 (2008) 139-1405

20. Wang K., Yu J., Yu Y.,, Qian Y., Zeng D., Guo S., Xiang Y., Wu J., “A survey on energy internet: Architecture, approach, and emerging technologies," IEEE Systems Journal, no. 99, vol. PP, pp. 1-14, 2017.
21. Wilhite, A., Lord, R. (2006). Estimating the risk of technology develop-ment. Engineering Management Journal, 18(3), 3-10.

Chapter 18
The Early Days of Entity-Relationship Modeling Retrospective on Dataid Project and Beyond

Carlo Batini and Stefano Ceri

Abstract This book, dedicated to Ontoni Olivé, will be presented to him at the 36th International Conference on Conceptual Modeling; this tells us that conceptual modeling established as a research field about 40 years ago, when seminal works on conceptual modeling were published. Our research career started as well about 40 years ago, and modeling has been a constant interest for both of us - not limited to data, but also to process abstractions and to various application domains. In 2013, C.B. was recent recipient of the Peter Chen Award for outstanding contributions to conceptual modeling and S.C. recalls calling for *three important things in databases: modeling, modeling, modeling* when receiving the Edward Codd Award. This paper is a journey over the early years of conceptual modeling, seen from the perspective of two early members of the research community. We will focus on conceptual database design, situated in the more general context of information systems design and of database design.

Key words: Entity-Relationship Modeling, Conceptual Database Design, Data Modeling and Integration

18.1 Conceptual Modeling: An historical Perspective

Data management as a scientific discipline deveoped in the early seventies, with the advent of Ted Codd's relational model [13]. Together with simple and solid modeling principles, based on set theory, the relational revolution brought about declarative query languages and well-understood data semantics. With the rise of

Carlo Batini
Dipartimento di Informatica, Universitá Bicocca, Milano, Italy, e-mail: carlo.batini@unimi.it

Stefano Ceri
Dipartimento di Elettronica, Informazione e Bioingegneria, Politecnico di Milano, 20133, Milano, Italy, e-mail: stefanoCeri@polimil.it

© Springer International Publishing AG 2017

J. Cabot et al. (eds.), *Conceptual Modeling Perspectives*,
https://doi.org/10.1007/978-3-319-67271-7_18

formal methods for querying and managing relations, scientists stated to ask if they could devise other methods for designing good relations, i.e. relations with strong structural properties, and hence less exposed to unexpected behaviors.

As natural complement of query languages, scientists focused on the so called *normalization of relations*, progressively formalizing the definition of functional dependencies, multi-value dependencies, and normal forms [14, 15]. The most advanced relational vendors, including IBM, started to advertise (and sell through professional consultants) the notion of *normalization* as a technique for designing complex relational schemas.

While such theory had certainly an impact on improving the quality of relational databases, it had pitfalls; a complete top-down approach, starting from the *universal relation* consisting of all the domains and then progressively normalizing it, was hardly applicable. Similarly, a complete bottom-up approach, starting from all the functional dependencies and then building relations by structural aggregation, was not applicable. In both cases, although the underlying theory is nice, it was not easy to build the startpoints to which such theory could be applied. The best use of normalization is a local analyis of existing relations, to get rid of anomalous behavior; such local analysis is still in use.

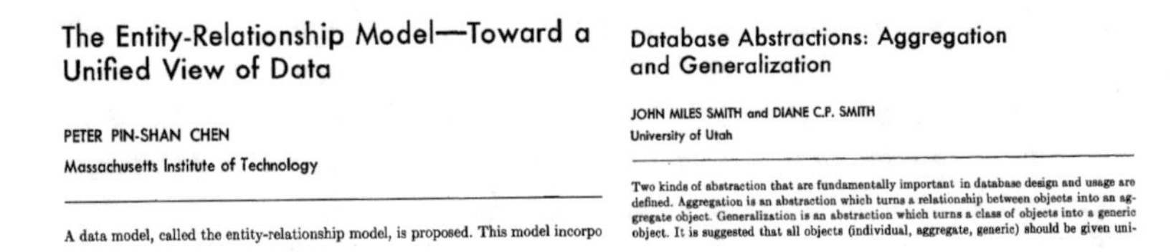
The Entity-Relationship Model—Toward a Unified View of Data

PETER PIN-SHAN CHEN

Massachusetts Institute of Technology

A data model, called the entity-relationship model, is proposed. This model incorpo

Database Abstractions: Aggregation and Generalization

JOHN MILES SMITH and DIANE C.P. SMITH

University of Utah

Two kinds of abstraction that are fundamentally important in database design and usage are defined. Aggregation is an abstraction which turns a relationship between objects into an aggregate object. Generalization is an abstraction which turns a class of objects into a generic object. It is suggested that all objects (individual, aggregate, generic) should be given uni-

Fig. 18.1 Fundamental Works from Late Seventies

A different approach to data design, based on conceptual abstractions, started to be developed in parallel. Early tools for information systems design, developed in Scandinavian countries by Bubenko et al [9] and Solvberg et al. [1], had included abstractions for data modeling. In 1976, the seminal work by Peter Chen defined the Entity-Relational model [12] (see Fig. 18.1); at the same time, John and Diane Smith formalized the fundamental data abstractions of aggregation and generalization [26], and Paolini, Pelagatti and Bracchi proposed the binary data model [8]. The field of conceptual database design was then established in 1978, with two workshops held in New York [28] and New Orleans [16]. At that time, our first publications in the area, both in 1979 (see Fig. 18.2), on *Top-Down Design of Entity-Relationships Concepts* at ER79 [5] and on *View Specification and Verification* at VLDB79 [4].

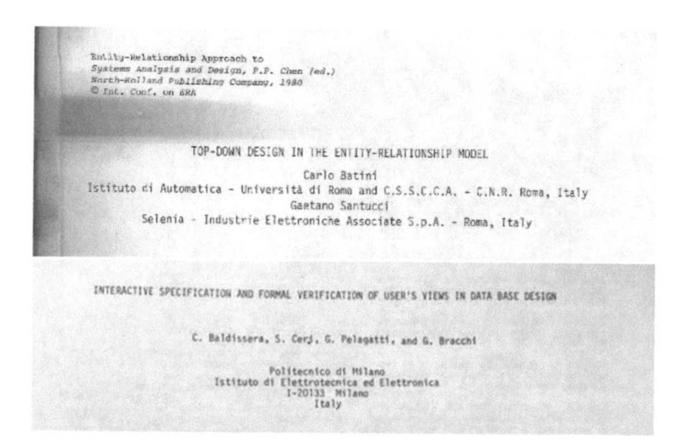

Entity-Relationship Approach to
Systems Analysis and Design, P.P. Chen (ed.)
North-Holland Publishing Company, 1980
© Int. Conf. on ERA

TOP-DOWN DESIGN IN THE ENTITY-RELATIONSHIP MODEL

Carlo Batini
Istituto di Automatica - Università di Roma and C.S.S.C.C.A. - C.N.R. Roma, Italy
Gaetano Santucci
Selenia - Industrie Elettroniche Associate S.p.A. - Roma, Italy

INTERACTIVE SPECIFICATION AND FORMAL VERIFICATION OF USER'S VIEWS IN DATA BASE DESIGN

C. Baldissera, S. Ceri, G. Pelagatti, and G. Bracchi

Politecnico di Milano
Istituto di Elettrotecnica ed Elettronica
I-20133 Milano
Italy

Fig. 18.2 Batini-Ceri Publications in 1979 (ER/VLDB)

18.2 DATAID

In Italy, the National Research Council promoted in 1980 a significant research framework, called *Progetto Finalizzato Informatica* (PFI), perhaps the best and most organized research program for computer science ever organized in the country, striking an effective balance among academic and industrial participation. Within the framework, data management was recognized as crucial for the development of computer science and specifically for the public administration, with a specific Programme (P2). Indeed, the strategic documents leading to the birth of the project included visionary statements: *while until yesterday most people believed that machines were most important and now they think that software and algorithms are most important, data will be the most important in the future: they are the whealth of organizations, behind their sizes and complexity they hide huge power* (P. Bronzoni, 1981). Specifically, the *DATAID* project within Programme P2 was focused on database design.

Thanks to good management and thanks as well to the concurrent blooming of computer science, many young fellows participated to DATAID across the Italian universities (Politecnico in Milano, Sapienza in Roma, Univerity of Milano, Torino and Pisa), CNR research centers and industries; among them, we recall Antonio Albano, Paolo Atzeni, Sandro D'Atri, Valeria De Antonellis, Giulio De Petra, Barbara Demo, Antonio Di Leva, Maurizio Lenzerini, Giacomo Marini, Marina Moscarini, Barbara Pernici, Domenico Saccá, Gaetano Santucci e Paolo Tiberio. The work in DATAID resulted in a very active research community. Early DATAID results are collected in two edited books [10, 3] (see Fig. 18.4).

18.2.1 The Method

During 1981, we defined the so-called *DATAID Methodology*, that has been shared by all the DATAID participants. The method, illustrated in Fig. 18.5, consisted of six

Fig. 18.3 The Dataid Project; Research and Industrial Units

(a) 1983 Book (b) 1985 Book

Fig. 18.4 The Dataid Books

phases, each covered by a book chapter, each written cooperatively by the members of the DATAID project:

1. *Requirement Collection and Analysis*, dealing with the preparation to design by means of glossaries and case descriptions; collected glossary information regarded data, operations and events.
2. *View Conceptual Design*, focused on th design of single views.
3. *View Integration*, dealing with the integration of multiple views to generate a global conceptual schema.
4. *Logical Design*, separatly targeting to relational and to Cosasyl databases.
5. *Physical Database Design for Codasyl Databases*.
6. *Physical Database Design for Relational Databases*.

Some of the aspects of the DATAID methodology have been quite successful, including the clean separation between the conceptual, logical and physical design of databases (where the former is system-independent, the second depends on the type of data model, the third is taylored to a target database management system) and between design and integration steps of conceptual modeling. While the Codasyl databases are no longer in use, the method has been then applied to other targets, such as object-oriented, object-relational and XML databases.

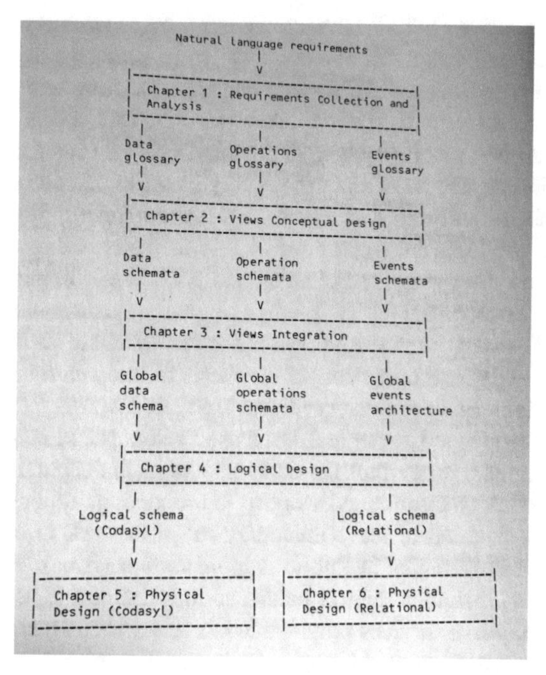

Fig. 18.5 Phases of the DATAID Methodology

Figure 18.6 is an example of ER schema used during conceptual modeling; we shared the conceptual modeling notation, that included cardinality constraints, optional and mandatory participation for both attributes and relationships, internal and external identifiers, repeating and composite attributes, and generaaliztion hierarchies.

During the project, we long debated between two approaches: the Methodology used a rich conceptual model during the early phases of design but then was forced to translating it into much simpler data structures supported by commercial DBMSs. Other research groups (and specifically Antonio Albano from the University of Pisa) were pushing a more revolutionary approach, which aimed at the development of next-generation DBMS directly supporting the conceptual model. Antonio proposed the Galileo language [2], while at the same time other scientists were similarly proposing high-level languages with rich data types - among them, Joachim Schmidt with Pascal-R [27] and John Mylopoulos with Taxis [18]. Follow-ups of this discussion can be traced in the long competition between relational and object-orented databases, where the latter carry more semantics, and, at a broader level, between databases and ontological systems.

18.3 Conceptual Design Book

In 1987, after the end of DATAID, we started our most ambitious project, a book on Conceptual Database Design [6]. The book was contracted by Benjamin/Cummings and co-authored with Sham Navathe, who had been working with C.B. on data integration and with S.C. on distributed databases; Fig. 18.7 shows the book's cover and the three authors, much younger than today, dring an intense day of writing. Although in principle the book's plan was very clear, in practice it took five years to be accomplished - for both of us it was the longest writing project ever. The most critical part was the logical design: none of us was really enthusiast about writing it. In the end, and after some turbolences, the book was completed. The method presented in the book preserves the methodological structure of DATAID and the conceptual models adopted in the two cases are very similar. The book is of course much broader and differs for a stronger emphasis on the *quality* of design results, an argument which then became very relevant to C.B.'s work.

The publication of the Conceptual Database Design book, in 1992, marks also the end of this brief journey into the early phases of conceptual modeling. After completing the book, we continued working on modeling, although with different approaches. C.B. decided to leave university to go to work in a new institution, the Authority for Informatics in Public Administration (Aipa). The main goal of Aipa was to boost in Italian central public administration the use of information technologies to improve services provided to citizens and companies.

The problems C.B. faced in Aipa were immense; fortunately he survived, and as a ïňĄrst activity he was the responsible of a survey focused on the most relevant 400 databases managed in the Ministries. He conceived the repository of conceptual schemas [29], that adopts abstraction-integration primitives; the repository enabled

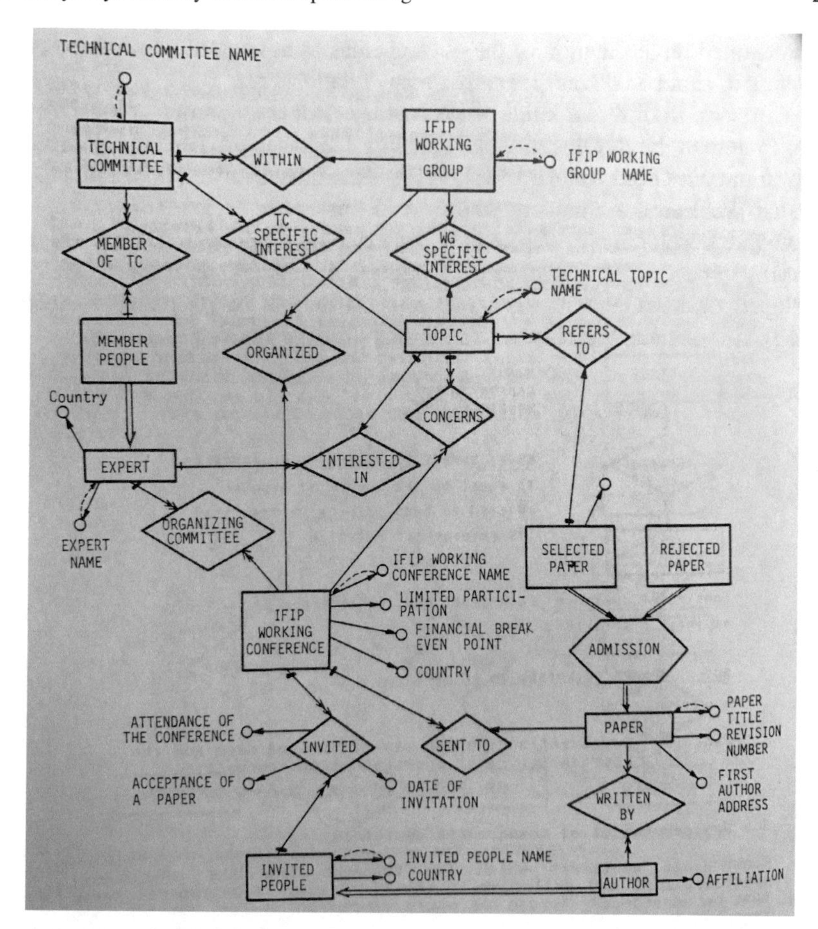

Fig. 18.6 Conceptual Schema in DATAID

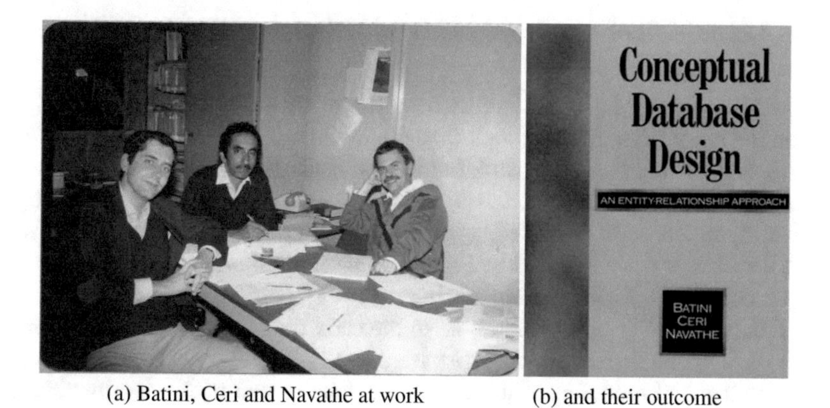

(a) Batini, Ceri and Navathe at work (b) and their outcome

Fig. 18.7 Conceptual Design Book

the integrated representation of the 400 schemas as a pyramid of schemas, corresponding to about 5.000 entities and as many relationships.

S.C. turned to different kinds of conceptual models; in particular together with Piero Fraternali, he developed Web Modeling Language (WebML) [11] - recently evolved into an OMG standard for building data-intensive Web applications - and founded WebRatio, a company whose main mission is a model-driven approach to software development; WebRatio is the name of the commercial tool based on WebML. Recently, S.C. developed an interest in genomic data management and developed GDM (Genomic Data Model) [17] and GCM (Genomic Conceptual Model), two domain-specific models for data-driven genomic computing.

Fig. 18.8 Carlo and Antoni in a recent Ceremony

18.4 Antoni Olivé

This chapter is part of a book dedicated to Antoni Olivé, so we conclude the journey on the early days of conceptual modeling with a brief description of his early contributions. Antoni's earlier work in the field dates 1983 and is entitled *Analysis of Conceptual and Logical Models in Information Systems Design Methodologies* [20]. Bridging conceptual modeling to information system design is also the main purpose of his book, entitled *Conceptual modeling of information systems*, which was published by Springer-Verlag much later, in 2007 [25].

But the main contribution of Antoni to the early developing of conceptual modeling is a focus on deduction. His work is generally inspired by an interest in combining conceptual modeling with deductive databases and with integrity checking or event management. Througout his long academic career, Antoni Olivé has been able to lead a big group of PhD students and researchers, conveying them his love for this specific aspect of conceptual modeling. After his VLDB paper *on the de-*

sign and implementation of information systems from deductive conceptual models [21], he had numerous papers on this general topic with his students: among them, change computation with T. Urpí [22], event method for updating views with Ernest Teniente [23], reasoning about deductive conceptual models with Dolores Costal [24].

Antoni is a friend to both of us. S.C. reminds many trips to Barcelona for attending Schools and Conferences in beautiful places of Costa Brava and for graduating Antoni's students, as external jury member. C.B. reminds that Antoni was present when he received the Peter Chen Award (Fig. 18.8). It was a pleasure to write this chapter and to dedicate it to Antoni Olivé.

References

1. P.S. Aanstrand, G. Skylstad, A. Solvberg: CASCADE - A Computer-Based Docmentation System, in: Bubenko, Langefors and Solvberg (eds): Computer Aided Information System Analysis and Design, 1972.
2. A. Albano, L. Cardelli, R. Orsini: Galileo: A Strongly-Typed, Interactive Conceptual Language. ACM Trans. Database Syst. 10(2): 230-260 (1985).
3. A. Albano, V. De Antonellis, A. Di Leva: Computer-Aided Database Design: the DATAID approach. North-Holland 1985, ISBN 0-444-87735-5.
4. C. Baldissera, S. Ceri, G. Pelagatti, G. Bracchi: Interactive Specification and Formal Verification of User's Views in Data Bases Design. VLDB 1979: 262-272.
5. C. Batini, G. Santucci: Top-Down Design in the Entity-Relationship Model. ER 1979: 323-338.
6. C. Batini, S. Ceri, S. B. Navathe: Conceptual Database Design: An Entity-Relationship Approach. Benjamin/Cummings 1992, ISBN 0-8053-0244-1.
7. C. Batini, M. Lenzerini, S. B. Navathe: A Comparative Analysis of Methodologies for Database Schema Integration. ACM Comput. Surv. 18(4): 323-364 (1986).
8. G. Bracchi, P. Paolini, G. Pelagatti: Binary Logical Associations in Data Modelling. IFIP Working Conference on Modelling in Data Base Management Systems 1976: 12
9. J. A. Bubenko Jr.: IAM: An Inferential Abstract Modeling Approach to Design of Conceptual Schema. SIGMOD Conference 1977: 62-74.
10. S. Ceri: Methodology and Tools for Data Base Design. North-Holland 1983.
11. S. Ceri, P. Fraternali, A. Bongio: Web Modeling Language (WebML): a modeling language for designing Web sites. Computer Networks 33(1-6): 137-157 (2000).
12. P. P. Chen: The Entity-Relationship Model - Toward a Unified View of Data. ACM Trans. Database Syst. 1(1): 9-36 (1976).
13. E. F. Codd: A Relational Model of Data for Large Shared Data Banks. Commun. ACM 13(6): 377-387 (1970).
14. E. F. Codd: Normalized Data Base Structure: A Brief Tutorial. IBM Research Report, San Jose, California RJ935 (1971).
15. E. F. Codd: Further Normalization of the Data Base Relational Model. IBM Research Report, San Jose, California RJ909 (1971).
16. V. Y. Lum et al.: 1978 New Orleans Data Base Design Workshop Report. VLDB 1979: 328-339.
17. M. Masseroli, A. Kaitoua, P. Pinoli, S. Ceri: Modeling and interoperability of heterogeneous genomic big data for integrative processing and querying. Methods, 2016. DOI: 10.1016/j.ymeth.2016.09.002.
18. J. Mylopoulos, P. A. Bernstein, H. K. T. Wong: A Language Facility for Designing Interactive Database-Intensive Applications (Abstract). SIGMOD Conference 1978: 17.

19. S. B. Navathe, M. Schkolnick: View Representation in Logical Database Design. SIGMOD Conference 1978: 144-156.
20. A. Olivé: Analysis of Conceptual and Logical Models in Information Systems Design Methodologies. CRIS 1983: 63-86.
21. A. Olivé: On the design and implementation of information systems from deductive conceptual models. VLDB 1989: 3-11.
22. T. Urpí, A. Olivé: A Method for Change Computation in Deductive Databases. VLDB 1992: 225-237
23. E. Teniente, A. Olivé: The Events Method for View Updating in Deductive Databases. EDBT 1992: 245-260
24. D. Costal, A. Olivé: A Method for Reasoning About Deductive Conceptual Models of Information Systems. CAiSE 1992: 612-631
25. A. Olivé: Conceptual modeling of information systems. Springer 2007, pp. I-XXV, 1-455.
26. J. M. Smith and D.C.P. Smith: Database Abstractions: Aggregation and Generalization, ACM TODS (2), 105-133, 1977.
27. J. W. Schmidt: Some high level language constructs for data of type relation, ACM Transactions on Database Systems (TODS) Volume 2 Issue 3, Sept. 1977.
28. S. B. Yao, S. B. Navathe, J.-L. Weldon: An Integrated Approach to Database Design. Data Base Design Techniques I, New York, 1978: 1-30.
29. C. Batini, G. Di Battista, G. Santucci: Structuring primitives for a dictionary of entity relationship data schemas. IEEE Transactions on Software Engineering, 19(4), 1993: 344-365.

Printed in the United States
By Bookmasters